LES

ŒUVRES

COMPLETES

DE

VOLTAIRE

3C

VOLTAIRE FOUNDATION

OXFORD

2004

ISBN 0 7294 0833 7

Voltaire Foundation Ltd
99 Banbury Road
Oxford OX2 6JX

PRINTED IN ENGLAND
AT THE ALDEN PRESS
OXFORD

Writings of 1723-1728

III

Hérode et Mariamne

Critical edition

by

Michael Freyne

CONTENTS

ILLUSTRATIONS

ACKNOWLEDGEMENTS

I should like to express my gratitude to the institutions and individuals who have helped to make this edition possible. I have benefited from a Fellowship from the Voltaire Foundation, and from several grants of leave and financial support from the University of New South Wales. I am very grateful indeed to the Principal and Fellows of Linacre College, where I have been made welcome on each of my several visits to Oxford, and where I have found a supportive base for work on this edition.

This edition is largely based on material held in the following libraries: the Bibliothèque nationale de France, the Bibliothèque de l'Arsenal and the Bibliothèque de la Comédie-Française in Paris; the Taylor Institution Library in Oxford; the British Library in London; and the Institut et Musée Voltaire in Geneva. I wish to thank the personnel of all these institutions for the willingness with which they have given me access to the riches of their collections, and for their helpfulness in answering my queries. I should like also to acknowledge the valuable assistance which I have received from the National Library of Russia in St Petersburg; the National Library of the Czech Republic in Prague; the University of Toronto Library; and the Australian National Library in Canberra.

I am particularly indebted to Professor William Barber, who first offered me the opportunity to contribute to the edition of the *Complete Works* of Voltaire, and to Mr Giles Barber, a sure guide through the maze of Voltairean bibliography, and whose generous friendship did much else to ease my path. I wish to thank Marie Freyne for her support of my work over many years. For practical support I owe particular debts of gratitude to Lieve Spaas and to Beatrice and Rafid Azzawi. I should also like to thank Dinah Eadie and Afrodity Giannakis, my research assistants at certain points in the preparation of the edition.

ACKNOWLEDGEMENTS

I have deeply appreciated the help and encouragement that many persons associated with the Voltaire Foundation have provided over the years. I thank them all. In particular I am happy to acknowledge my enormous debt to Janet Godden, who through her consummate editorial expertise, and unfailing patience, has made a major contribution to the completion of this edition.

Michael Freyne
November 2003

xiv

KEY TO THE CRITICAL APPARATUS

The critical apparatus, printed at the foot of the page, gives variant readings from the manuscripts and editions discussed in the introductions to the texts.

Each variant consists of some or all of the following elements:

— The number of the text line or lines to which the variant relates.

— The sigla of the sources of the variant as given in the list of editions. Simple numbers, or numbers followed by letters, stand for separate editions of the work; letters followed by numbers are collections: w is reserved for collected editions of Voltaire's works and t for collected editions of his theatre.

— A colon, indicating the start of the variant; any editorial remarks after the colon are enclosed within square brackets.

— The text of the variant itself, preceded and followed by one or more words from the base text, to indicate its position.

Several signs and typographic conventions are employed:

— Angle brackets < > encompass deleted matter.

— Beta β stands for the base text.

— The forward arrow —→ means 'replaced by'.

— Up ↑ and down ↓ arrows precede text added above or below the line.

— A superior + indicates, when necessary, the end of material introduced by one of the above signs.

— A pair of slashes // indicates the end of a paragraph or other section of text.

ABBREVIATIONS

ANL	Australian National Library, Canberra
AUMLA	*Journal of the Australasian Universities Languages and Literature Association*
Bengesco	*Voltaire: bibliographie de ses œuvres* (1882-1890)
BL	British Library, London
BnC	BnF, Catalogue général des livres imprimés, Auteurs, ccxiv
BnF	Bibliothèque nationale de France, Paris
BV	*Bibliothèque de Voltaire: catalogue des livres* (Moscow 1961)
Cioranescu	*Bibliographie de la litterature française du XVIIIe siècle*, 3 vols (Paris 1969)
CL	Grimm, *Correspondance littéraire*, ed. M. Tourneux (1877-1882)
CN	*Corpus des notes marginales de Voltaire* (1979-)
D	Voltaire, *Correspondence and related documents, OC*, vol.85-135 (1968-1977)
ImV	Institut et Musée Voltaire, Geneva
Kehl	*Œuvres complètes de Voltaire* (Kehl 1784-1789)
Moland	*Œuvres complètes de Voltaire*, ed. Louis Moland (1877-1885)
OC	*Œuvres complètes de Voltaire / Complete works of Voltaire*, 1968- [the present edition]
SVEC	*Studies on Voltaire and the eighteenth century*
Trapnell	William H. Trapnell, 'Survey and analysis of Voltaire's collective editions', *SVEC* 77 (1970), p.103-99

INTRODUCTION

'La destinée de cette pièce a été extraordinaire', Voltaire writes in
1725 in the Préface to the first authorised edition of *Hérode et
Mariamne*. A first version of the tragedy (henceforward referred
to as M24) failed sensationally at its première in 1724. It was
withdrawn, and the text was not published. Voltaire suppressed
this version of the play so effectively that only two scenes have
since come to light. A revised version (henceforward M25) opened
the 1725-1726 season at the Comédie-Française, and was highly
successful, being performed many times that year, to great acclaim
not unmixed with criticism. Early in the following year Voltaire
was overtaken by the events which were to lead him to leave
France for England. Although performances of *Mariamne* became
infrequent from then on, revivals in the 1750s with Lekain in the
role of Hérode achieved considerable success. In 1762 Voltaire
reworked the play yet again. The new version (M62), in which the
Roman governor Varus was replaced by the Essenian Sohème,
was performed only twice at the Comédie-Française in 1763 and
was coolly received.

Mariamne is the third of Voltaire's tragedies. After the failure
of *Artémire* and the first *Mariamne*, the great success of the 1725
version confirmed his dominant position in the literary and
theatrical circles of the time, during that early period of heady
celebrity preceding the downfall of 1726 and his departure for
England.

1. *The genesis of 'Mariamne'*

The year 1723 seems to have been particularly busy for Voltaire.
He had returned to France in early November 1722 from the
journey to Holland which he had undertaken with Mme de

Rupelmonde, going first to Bruel, the home of the duc de La Feuillade, and then from early December 1722 to mid-January 1723 he stayed at Ussé with his friend the marquis.[1] His letters show that during this period his principal preoccupation was with *Le Poème de la Ligue*. He now regarded his epic as complete (D144), and in addition to the efforts he was making to arrange publication in Holland, he was also seeking to secure official approval to bring out the work in France (D134). Another dominant preoccupation during this period was the continuing pursuit of Beauregard, the police spy whose denunciations had led to Voltaire's imprisonment in the Bastille in 1717 (D132).

Voltaire returned to Paris in the middle of January 1723. The *Poème de la Ligue* remained at the centre of his concerns during the following months, since he was obliged to change radically his strategy for the publication of the work.[2] He finally lost hope of obtaining a *privilège* that would have allowed him to publish his epic in France, and came to realise that the authorities would not tacitly permit an edition printed in Holland to be put on sale in France. He decided therefore that his poem should appear in a clandestine edition printed secretly in France, and began negotiations with the printer Abraham Viret of Rouen to produce an edition of 4000 copies.

It is in the midst of this grave crisis in the publishing history of Voltaire's epic poem, that the first allusions to *Mariamne* appear in his correspondence. In a letter written from Rouen and dated by Theodore Besterman to 29 March 1723, Voltaire tells Thiriot that he has resolved to return that evening to La Rivière-Bourdet, home of the président and marquise de Bernières, 'pour partager mes soins entre une ânesse et Mariamne'.[3] A little later, in a letter

[1] These dates are established by of Voltaire's correspondence (D136-46).

[2] See O. R. Taylor, introduction to *La Henriade*, *OC*, vol.2 p.46-47; R. Pomeau et al., *Voltaire en son temps*, 2nd edn (Oxford 1995), i.127f. (all references to *Voltaire en son temps* are to the second edition).

[3] D148 (29 [March 1723]). Besterman speculates that Voltaire was dieting on asses' milk.

to Cideville written from La Rivière-Bourdet, and dated tentatively by Besterman to April 1723, Voltaire declares: 'J'ai presque achevé la première ébauche de ma Marianne' (D149). At this early period Voltaire was already demonstrating that capacity to work simultaneously on several fronts which was to characterise his entire literary career.

This same letter to Cideville contains a reference to the tragedy of *Mariamne* by the Englishman Elijah Fenton, which had been staged in London in February 1723 and published in the same year. (Voltaire's attention may have been drawn to it by Cideville in a letter which has not survived.) He does not intend to stop work to wait for it however: '[Je] peux fort bien me passer de [la *Marianne*] de Mr Fenton. [...] Vous devriez bien quelque jour venir à la Rivière Bourdet apporter la Marianne anglaise et voir la française' (D149). A certain ambivalence is thus evident in Voltaire's comment on Fenton's *Mariamne*. His initial assertion implying that this work presents little interest for him sits oddly with the measure of curiosity shown in the last sentence quoted. We shall return later to Fenton when we discuss the sources for *Mariamne*.

During the following months (spring 1723) Voltaire leads a highly mobile existence between Paris, Villars, Maisons, Rouen and La Rivière-Bourdet.[4] In May the company of Lord Bolingbroke, at La Source or elsewhere, seems to have distracted him temporarily from *Mariamne* (D150). He is known to have been present at the première of Houdar de La Motte's tragedy *Inès de Castro* on 6 April 1723,[5] and to have attended other performances as well, one of them on 12 June (D152, D154). In these letters,

---

[4] Pomeau, *Voltaire en son temps*, i.128.

[5] In his journal entry devoted to the performance of *Inès de Castro* on 6 April 1723, Mathieu Marais notes that 'Arouet y était auprès du comte de Verdun', and then recounts an insolent remark addressed by Voltaire to the aged count on that occasion (Mathieu Marais, *Journal et mémoires* [...] *sur la régence et sur le règne de Louis XV, 1715-1737*, ed. M. F. A. de Lescure, Paris 1863-1868, ii.441). For this incident, which Besterman regards as perhaps apocryphal, see D152, n.2. See also Pomeau, *Voltaire en son temps*, i.128.

while admiring the acting of Baron, Voltaire shows scant enthusiasm for the play, even though it was to prove to be one of the great dramatic successes of the eighteenth century. Voltaire recognises that public opinion had been favourable, and we can appreciate that La Motte's play was of the greatest interest to him. Having himself a new tragedy in preparation, he would naturally want to scrutinise the work of a rival writer, and he may have hoped, in the words of R. Pomeau, 'tandis qu'il écrit sa *Mariamne*, de saisir les recettes du succès'.[6]

In the succeeding months (June-September 1723) Voltaire's correspondence shows him mainly preoccupied with his health, financial matters and the continuing saga of the publication of *La Ligue*. At the same time, however, he is taking steps to secure the staging of his new play by the Comédie-Française. By September *Mariamne* is in the hands of Adrienne Lecouvreur (D163). No doubt Voltaire hoped that this celebrated actress, so admired by him and with whom he had enjoyed the closest personal intimacy,[7] and who in February 1720 had played the title role in the ill-fated *Artémire*, would accept the principal role in his new tragedy. Steps were now being taken to organise a reading of *Mariamne* before the actors of the Comédie-Française, although at this stage, Voltaire claims, 'ce n'est qu'une ébauche imparfaite; les vers ne sont point faits' (D163). Voltaire is also busying himself with obtaining official approval for the production of his play, and asks Moncrif to intervene for him with their mutual friend the comte d'Argenson, *lieutenant-général de police* (D164). All his actions regarding the play seem motivated by one overriding concern which finds expression in this letter: 'J'ai extrêmement envie de prendre de justes mesures pour que Marianne soit jouée cet hiver.'

---

[6] Pomeau, *Voltaire en son temps*, i.128-29. Besterman (D153, n.2) discusses the possibility that Voltaire may have been the author of an anonymous criticism of *Inès de Castro*, entitled *Sentiments d'un spectateur français sur la nouvelle tragédie d'Inès de Castro* (Bengesco 2363), though Voltaire strenuously denied the attribution (as in D415).

[7] Pomeau, *Voltaire en son temps*, i.102-103.

According to the *Registres* of the Comédie-Française,[8] the reading of *Mariamne* took place at a special meeting of the company on Tuesday, 28 September 1723, and the eleven members of the troupe present voted unanimously to accept the new tragedy. Voltaire records the favourable decision in a note to Mme de Bernières, with a discrepancy in regard to the date: 'Aujourd'hui lundi [...] j'ai lu à dix heures Mariannes [*sic*] à nos seigneurs les comédiens du roi qui en ont été assez édifiés.'[9]

Although he had now obtained acceptance of his play by the Comédiens, Voltaire continued to refine and develop his text. In early October he writes to Thiriot: 'Je crois que Mariane sera avec un peu de soin digne de l'amitié que vous avez pour l'auteur' (D166). In his next letter (D167) Voltaire tells Thiriot that *Mariamne* will be much changed when he brings it back to Paris. At the same time he lets us glimpse the underlying preoccupation which motivated his continuing revisions (D167): 'Je me suis déterminé à ôter absolument à mon héroïne une passion qui toute excusable qu'elle était ne servait qu'à justifier sa condamnation et par conséquent à diminuer la compassion qu'on doit avoir pour elle. La vertu de Marianne sera désormais sans tache.' Voltaire does not name the character who was the object of Mariamne's 'passion toute excusable' now being written out of the play, but Varus is the most likely candidate. At first, as H. C.

---

[8] *Registres de la Comédie-Française* (henceforward *Registres*), Reg. 361, p.30: 'Aujourd'hui Mardi 28ᵉ septembre 1723 la troupe s'est assemblée extraordinairement dans la salle de son hôtel pour entendre la lecture d'une tragédie [*added in marginal note:* de M. de Voltaire] intitulée Marianne et les présents à lad. assemblée ont signé pr. la recevoir: Baron, Le Grand, De Fontenoy, Quinault de Fresnes, Quinault, Dangeville, Le Couvreur, Duchemin, De La Thorillieres fils, Le Grand fils, Dubreuil.'

[9] D165. Besterman, with hesitation, dates this letter to 8 October 1723, but 8 October 1723 was a Friday. As Voltaire gives no indication of date or month, the firm date given in the *Registres* seems surer than whatever can be surmised for D165. The *Mercure de France* of October 1723 records (p.772-73), without comment, the presentation of Voltaire's *Mariamne* to the Comédiens français as having taken place 'sur la fin de septembre'.

Lancaster suggests, [10] Voltaire must have had Mariamne respond to Varus's passion. This letter makes clear, however, that he had now conceived for his heroine quite a different character from that which he had given to the earlier Artémire, who had considered herself morally compromised by the persistence of her love for the noble Philotas and her inability to love her brutal husband.

Elsewhere in the same letter Voltaire writes: 'Je croi que tous les poètes du monde se sont donnez le mot de faire chacun une Marianne.' It is not clear which poets Voltaire has in mind. He could be referring to his illustrious predecessors, such as Alexandre Hardy and Tristan L'Hermite. But he could also be alluding to his contemporaries, and if so his observation could bear witness to the considerable interest shown at this time by several authors in producing dramatic adaptations of the story of Mariamne. As we have seen, the existence of the English writer Fenton's *Mariamne* was known in France in 1723; furthermore, shortly before accepting Voltaire's new tragedy the Comédie-Française had rejected another *Mariamne* of unknown authorship; [11] moreover the abbé Nadal may have already begun the composition of his *Mariamne*, and if so this may have been well known. [12] Another element in the vogue enjoyed by the story of Hérode and Mariamne at this time is to be seen in the revival of interest in Tristan L'Hermite's tragedy *Mariane* from the previous century: two new editions appeared in 1723-1724, [13] and J.-B. Rousseau was

---

[10] *French tragedy in the time of Louis XV and Voltaire 1715-1774* (Baltimore 1950; New York 1977), p.60.

[11] See *Registres de la Comédie-Française*, Reg. 361, p.24. This *Mariamne* was rejected at a meeting held on 19 August 1723, by seven votes to three, with many members absent.

[12] For Nadal's *Mariamne*, see below, section 3.v.

[13] Troyes, Veuve Oudot, 1723 and Paris, F. Flahaut, 1724. See Amédée Carriat, *Bibliographie des œuvres de Tristan L'Hermite* [Limoges 1955], no.xxi, p and q. See also Tristan, *La Mariane, tragédie*, ed. Jacques Madeleine (Paris 1917), introduction, p.xxxviii-xl. The Flahaut edition was the subject of a notice occupying one full page in the *Mercure de France* of July 1724 (p.1587-88); this no doubt widened further the public whose attention was brought to the story of Mariamne.

soon to be boasting in December 1724 that he had completed a revision of Tristan's tragedy, eliminating turns of phrase and expressions that had become archaic or unacceptable to eighteenth-century ears: he wished to publish this corrected *Mariane* and to have it put on the stage within twelve months.[14]

At this time Voltaire's progress with *Mariamne* was impeded by developments in the Beauregard affair (D168). Writing to Mme de Bernières, he declares that he is eager to join her at La Rivière-Bourdet, and that he will bring *Mariamne* with him: 'Il est juste d'ailleurs que Marianne aille respirer son air natal' (D170). This confirms the evidence provided by earlier letters, notably D148 and D149, that it was at La Rivière-Bourdet that Voltaire composed the first drafts of *Mariamne*.

Voltaire's work on *Mariamne* was interrupted in November 1723 by the smallpox which assailed him while visiting his friend the président de Maisons, who had invited some sixty guests of the highest social rank to attend a brilliant celebration, which was to last three days, and in the course of which Adrienne Lecouvreur was to recite and Voltaire give readings from *Mariamne*.[15] All these festivities were abruptly cancelled, with the guests hastily departing, when Voltaire and his host both fell ill with smallpox on the 4th, Voltaire seriously so. Although he was out of danger by the 15th, and composing verses on the 16th, his illness was severe enough to cause him to fear for his life: 'J'attendis la mort avec assez de tranquillité, non toutefois sans regretter de n'avoir pas mis la dernière main à mon poème [*La Ligue*] et à *Mariamne*, ni sans être un peu fâché de quitter mes amis de si bonne heure' (D173). By mid-December Voltaire was sufficiently recovered to be able to work all day long, as he writes to Mme de Bernières (D175). In his

---

[14] *Œuvres choisies de J.-B. Rousseau* [...] *suivies de sa correspondance avec l'abbé d'Olivet* (Paris, Didot l'Aîné, 1818), ii.263. Rousseau's version of the play was not published until 1731. It was never performed at the Comédie-Française, and we have not discovered that it was ever staged anywhere else.

[15] T. I. Duvernet, *La Vie de Voltaire*, p.50, cited by Pomeau, *Voltaire en son temps*, i.129-30.

Epître à M. de Gervasi médecin, written about this time, he expresses the hope that with *Mariamne* he will be able to revive his friendship with Sully (*OC*, vol. 3A). His fear now is that Adrienne Lecouvreur will be prevented by ill health from acting in *Mariamne* (D175).

This is the first of the surviving autograph letters of Voltaire in which the form 'Mariamne' is found. Hitherto, that is to say, for a period of some nine months since March (D148), he has used the spelling 'Marianne' both for the play and its protagonist. From now on in his letters, except on two occasions (D202, D208), he refers to them as 'Mariamne', and the form 'Marianne' does not recur until 1754 (D5899). This change is perhaps an indication of a realisation by Voltaire that with its acceptance by the Comédie-Française his play was no longer simply a private project. *Mariamne* had entered the domain of the professional theatre, and Voltaire may have felt it incumbent upon him to use the form of the name sanctioned by convention and tradition.[16]

Desmolet's *Nouvelles littéraires curieuses et intéressantes* for 1 December 1723 was the first journal to announce the forthcoming production of Voltaire's play: 'Les Comédiens français se disposent à représenter cet hiver *Mariane tragédie* par M. Aroüet de Voltaire. On ne croit pas devoir prévenir le public; mais le succès d'*Œdipe*, la connaissance que l'auteur a du théâtre, la force de sa versification et son génie vraiment poétique reconnus de tout le monde, répondent, ce semble, assez du succès de cette pièce.'[17]

Letters in verse addressed to Voltaire before the end of 1723 by Cideville and Piron point to a widespread level of expectation

[16] We concur with R. Pomeau's judgement (*Voltaire en son temps*, i.934-35, n.9), that references in D174 to 'votre ouvrage' and 'votre pièce' concern *La Ligue* rather than *Mariamne*.

[17] *Nouvelles littéraires curieuses et intéressantes*, ed. Pierre-Nicolas Desmolets (Paris 1723-1724), 1 December 1723, p.14. The notice continues: 'M. de la Mothe travaille sur le même sujet; et on assure qu'il n'est pas le seul. Le public jugera lequel des trois concurrents aura mérité la palme.' The third contender was perhaps the abbé Nadal. A brief announcement was also included in the *Bibliothèque française* early in 1724 (vol.iii, 2nd part, p.285).

created by the imminence of the production of the new play (D176, D177). Further evidence is found in the journal of Mathieu Marais: 'On nous annonce une comédie de Mariamne, qui va être jouée et qu'Arouet, poète infatigable, nous donne pour ce carême. Il ne peut que bien faire, et toujours de mieux en mieux.'[18]

Early in 1724 Voltaire appears to have sent a manuscript copy of *Mariamne* to Bolingbroke, who comments in a letter to Pope: 'I am read[ing] in a tragedy which he [Voltaire] has just finished and which will be played this Lent. The subject is the death of Mariamne, you will I believe find in it that art which Racine puts into the conduct of his pieces, and that delicacy which appears in his diction, with a spirit of poetry which he never had, and which flags often in the best of Corneille's tragedies.'[19] Bolingbroke adds that Voltaire intended to send *Mariamne* to Pope, but it is not clear that Voltaire did this, or at least whether he did so at this time, although Pope had evidently read the play by December 1725.[20] Although Pope has left us in a letter to Bolingbroke (D187) a lengthy evaluation of *La Ligue*, we have no record of his opinions concerning *Mariamne*.

Tension between Voltaire and the Comédiens arose in the first months of 1724 as preparations were being made for the staging of *Mariamne*. We may surmise from D184 that the actors had become frustrated by his continuing revisions of the play: a definitive text was by now doubtless needed so that roles could be learnt and rehearsals begin in earnest. The arrogance of the attitudes which the Comédiens frequently displayed towards

---

[18] Marais, *Journal et mémoires*, 14 February 1724. After the failed performance of *Mariamne*, Marais returned to this entry and added: 'La tragédie a été jouée et a tombé dès la première représentation. Le poème dramatique est différent de l'épique, et on n'a pas tous les talents'.

[19] Bolingbroke to Pope, 18 February o.s. [1 March n.s.] 1723, quoted from *Correspondence of Alexander Pope*, ed. G. Sherburn (Oxford 1956), ii.221-22, in the commentary to D187, and by Ahmad Gunny, *Voltaire and English literature: a study of English literary influences on Voltaire*, SVEC 177 (1979), p.209.

[20] Sherburn, *Correspondence*, ii.354, quoted at D187 and by Gunny, *Voltaire and English literature*, p.210.

authors is well attested,[21] and it may well be that they did not mince their words in addressing a demand to Voltaire, transmitted to him in a letter from d'Argental which we do not have.

Yet at this late stage Voltaire seems not to have advanced far beyond the end of the first act in the revision and reworking of his text. He is still heavily involved in frantic efforts, obliging him to work day and night, to improve it to a point where he could declare himself satisfied. To the complaints of the actors Voltaire sends in January 1724 (D184) an impatient, sarcastic and (in the final paragraph) contemptuous retort:

Je répondrai à nos seigneurs les comédiens le beau mot que le duc d'Orléans dit aux députés du parlement: allez-vous [...] J'aime mieux Mariamne qu'eux. Je veux qu'elle soit bonne avant que d'être jouée. Je me suis corrigé de mes précipitations, et Inès me fait voir qu'on ne fait rien de bien en peu de temps. Je travaille donc nuit et jour. Je fais peu de vers et j'en efface beaucoup [...] Je ne puis donc répondre précisément à votre lettre. Tout ce que je puis vous dire, c'est que je commence à retravailler le second acte. Soyez, je vous en prie, plus sévère que moi. N'ayez d'indulgence que pour mes défauts; n'en ayez point pour mes vers. En fait d'amitié, votre indulgence me sera utile.

Je pars demain pour votre Ablon avec milord. Je pourrai bien, dimanche, envoyer à ces faquins une mauvaise pièce qui sera encore assez bonne pour eux.[22]

This remarkable document gives a striking picture of the compulsive nature of Voltaire's last-minute revisions and reworkings. But we also see him affirming his sense of the value of his work: nothing must be allowed to prevent him from bringing his creation as close as possible to perfection, even if, as he was to

[21] See for example Voltaire's letter of 7 January 1733 to Père Porée (D392). Looking back to the period when he had submitted Œdipe to the Comédie-Française, he writes: 'Les acteurs [...] étaient dans ce temps-là petits-maîtres et grands seigneurs.' Their attitudes had doubtless little changed a few years later at the time of Mariamne.

[22] This letter does not support the construction which Th. Besterman places upon it when he writes that 'the actors had insisted on putting on the tragedy although Voltaire was not satisfied with it' (Voltaire, Oxford 1976, p.101).

admit a little later in the Préface to *Mariamne*, perfection itself is unattainable: 'Dans tous les arts il y a un terme par delà lequel on ne peut plus avancer. On est reserré dans les bornes de son talent: on voit la perfection au delà de soi, et on fait des efforts impuissants pour y atteindre.'

2. The sources of 'Mariamne'

i. Josephus

The historical writings of the Jewish historian Flavius Josephus are the primary source for Voltaire's *Hérode et Mariamne*, as they are for the more than fifty dramatic works or adaptations of the story of Mariamne which have appeared since the Renaissance. [23] Although Voltaire was an excellent Latinist, it is generally agreed that he did not have a competent grasp of Greek, [24] and it can be assumed that his knowledge of the writings of Josephus was derived essentially from translations. The translation into French which Arnauld d'Andilly had first published in the latter part of the seventeenth century enjoyed enormous prestige for many decades, and was considered authoritative for much of the first half of the following century. [25] This is certain to have been the source which Voltaire consulted for knowledge of the historical events which form the basis of his play. [26]

[23] On these works see Maurice Jacques Valency, *The Tragedies of Herod and Mariamne* (New York 1940).

[24] See Pomeau, *Voltaire en son temps*, i.27.

[25] *Histoire des Juifs écrite par Flavius Joseph sous le titre de Antiquités Judaïques. Traduite sur l'original grec revu sur divers manuscrits par M. Arnauld d'Andilly*, 3 vol. in-folio (Paris 1667); *Histoire de la Guerre des Juifs contre les Romains* [...]. *Traduit du grec par M. Arnauld d'Andilly*, 2 vol. in-folio (Paris 1668). These works were reprinted several times without change (1672, 1676, 1681, 1684, 1701-1703); the most recent edition available when Voltaire began composition of his tragedy had appeared in Paris, 5 vol., in-12°, in 1717-1719.

[26] A.-A. Renouard has identified a context in *Dieu et les hommes* in which it is clear that for information from the writings of Josephus Voltaire, as in this case, consulted the translations of Arnauld d'Andilly; see M.xxviii.193, n.3, quoted also in

Josephus first treated the unhappy union of Herod and Mariamne in his *History of the Jewish War* composed between 75 and 79 AD. Here the events leading to the death of Mariamne occupy no more than a few paragraphs. Josephus returned to the story in his *Jewish Antiquities*, a monumental history of the Jewish nation, completed in 93 AD. Book XV sustains through many chapters a detailed narrative, poignant and rich in colour, of the dramatic series of incidents making up the tragic history of Herod and Mariamne. Josephus explores the personalities of the protagonists, probing their motivations and evaluating their actions.

In the case of Herod, the *Jewish Antiquities* point up the close connection between his private life and his political achievements.[27] They recount how his family, originally Idumean, but converted to Judaism, had come to displace in Judea the ancient royal family of the Asmoneans, descended from the Maccabees. Pompey's capture of Jerusalem in 63 BC had brought Judea under the domination of Rome. In return for support received during the siege of the city, Pompey re-established on the throne of Judea the Asmonean Hyrcanus II, after negotiations in which Hyrcanus was vigorously seconded by his chief minister Antipater, an energetic, forceful and tenacious administrator and general. Antipater went on to achieve great power under the weak Hyrcanus, becoming the effective ruler of Judea; when Antipater was murdered in 43 BC the mantle of his power passed to his sons Herod and Phasaël, who, in spite of the protests of many Jews, were confirmed in their authority by Mark Antony. The position of the Herodians suffered a serious challenge in 40 BC, when the Parthians invaded Judea

---

CN, iv.715, n.490. Voltaire seems to have used the translations of Arnauld d'Andilly throughout his life. Much later in his career his library at Ferney was to include a set of the 1735-1736 reprint of these works. We find him naming Arnauld d'Andilly as the source from which he draws a quotation from Josephus in *La Bible enfin expliquée* (1775): see M.xxx.282.

[27] This link has been clearly described by Alan Howe in his edition of Alexandre Hardy, *Mariamne* (Exeter 1989). The introduction to this edition contains an excellent summary of the Josephan account of Herod and Mariamne.

with a large army and set Antigonus, the nephew of Hyrcanus, on the throne. The invaders captured Jerusalem and took Phasaël and Hyrcanus prisoner, but Herod succeeded in escaping. Josephus evokes in moving terms the pitiable spectacle of his flight and describes his courageous rearguard actions against superior forces of Parthians and Jews. After a difficult journey he reached Rome, where his cause was championed both by his longtime ally Antony and by Octavian, who secured from the Senate a decree declaring him to be king of the Jews. Armed with this endorsement Herod returned to Palestine, and spent the next three years in conquering his kingdom. By 37 BC, with Roman support, he had achieved undisputed mastery over Judea, and Antigonus, the last of the Asmonean kings, had been eliminated. Herod then took steps to consolidate his rule and to gain acceptance for it from the Jews. He entered into alliance with the Asmonean family by marrying Mariamne, the granddaughter of Hyrcanus II and niece of Antigonus. At the same time he sought to eliminate the surviving male members of that ancient and still revered family: in 35 BC he engineered the drowning of Aristobulus III, the younger brother of Mariamne, and had her grandfather Hyrcanus II executed in 30 BC. Josephus vividly evokes the atmosphere of jealousy, suspicion and hatred which characterised the relationships between Asmoneans and Herodians, and in particular between Herod and his sister Salome on the one hand, and Mariamne and her mother Alexandra on the other. It is these hostilities which were to precipitate the events leading to the execution of Mariamne in 29 BC.

Yet Josephus does not portray the death of Mariamne as an exclusively political event. It is also, and perhaps more importantly, presented as a crime of passion, a drama of unrequited and frustrated love. Herod is shown as loving with a consuming ardour exceeding all reasonable bounds a wife who rejected him, and from whom he received only contempt and hatred: 'Il aimait si ardemment Mariamne que l'on ne voit dans aucune histoire que jamais homme ait été plus transporté d'un amour illegitime qu'il l'était de celui de sa femme.' [28] Yet Mariamne had only scorn for him. Herod was the killer of two of her closest relatives, and was in any case a man of low birth unworthy of her. Furthermore Mariamne had been revolted on discovering a decision which Herod had twice taken concerning her. On two separate occasions, when he had gone to appear before the Romans in interviews in which his throne and indeed his life were at stake, [29] he had left secret instructions that, if he were to meet death at their hands, Mariamne too should be done away with so that she would not fall into the hands of another man. 'Il l'aimait', Josephus tells us, 'avec tant de passion qu'il ne pouvait souffrir que même après sa mort elle tombât en la puissance d'un autre.' [30] On each occasion this order was disclosed to Mariamne by the person in whose guard Herod had left her. On his return from Antony she revealed to him her knowledge of the secret order, and Herod concluded that she was aware of it only because she had formed an amorous relation with her guardian, whom, overcome with anger, he at once put to death. Mariamne herself he spared, for (Josephus tells us) his anger was less strong than his passion. On the second occasion, when Herod returned from Rhodes confirmed in his kingship and covered in honours by Octavian, Mariamne, 'outrée de dépit et de colère', [31] did not conceal her aversion for him, refusing all intimacy. The relationship between the spouses degenerated into unremitting hostility, which continued for more than a year after Herod's return. It was at this point that the perfidious Salome

[28] The quotation is from the translation of Arnauld d'Andilly, *Histoire des Juifs*, xv, xi, p.577. An English version of this passage is found in the Loeb Classical Library edition of the *Jewish Antiquities*, xv, para. 218. We refer henceforward to the translations of Arnauld d'Andilly by page number, to the Loeb versions by paragraph number.

[29] In 35 BC, after the death of Aristobulus, Antony had summoned Herod to Laodicea and required him to justify his conduct. And after the battle of Actium in 31 BC, Herod, who had been the ally of the defeated Antony, had gone to Rhodes, fearful of his fate, to give an account of himself before the victorious Octavian.

[30] *Histoire des Juifs*, xv, iv, p.562; *Jewish Antiquities*, xv, para. 66.

[31] *Histoire des Juifs*, xv, xi, p.576; *Jewish Antiquities*, xv, para. 207.

intervened by bribing a cupbearer to make Herod believe that Mariamne had attempted to poison him. While investigating this accusation, Herod learnt of Mariamne's knowledge of his secret order, and at once reached the same conclusion as on the earlier occasion. As then, Mariamne's guardian was immediately executed. Mariamne was put on trial on the false charge of the attempted poisoning before judges anxious to do Herod's bidding, who sentenced her to death. Herod was reluctant to carry out the sentence at once, but his hesitations were overcome by the urgings of his sister Salome. Josephus describes the exemplary dignity with which the innocent Mariamne went to her death, and Herod's terrible remorse which followed. [32]

Josephus does more than provide the outline of a series of tragic events. He also traces with considerable finesse the personalities of the leading characters. It is evident, for example, that he has much instinctive sympathy for Mariamne, whose beauty, dignity and virtue he praises abundantly. Yet these qualities do not blind him to the less estimable features of her character. She is proud to the point of arrogance, she belittles her husband with her scorn, and displays a cruel streak in exploiting the power which his love gives her over him: 'Cette princesse, qui d'ailleurs etait extrêmement sage et très chaste, était de si mauvaise humeur, et abusait de telle sorte de la passion qu'il avait pour elle, qu'elle le traitait quelquefois avec mépris et avec des railleries offensantes, sans considerer le respect qu'elle lui devait.' [33] He adds that 'cette princesse si chaste et si courageuse, mais trop fière et d'un naturel trop aigre' was mistaken in thinking that she had nothing to fear from Herod, and that she had been imprudent in provoking the emnity of Herod's mother and sister. [34]

Josephus's portrait of Herod is similarly perceptive. He does

---

[32] *Histoire des Juifs*, xv, xi, p.578-79; *Jewish Antiquities*, xv, para. 236. See text quoted in note to V.144a.

[33] *Histoire des Juifs*, xv, ii, p.577; *Jewish Antiquities*, xv, para. 219. Cf. *Guerre des Juifs*, I, xvii, p.57; *Jewish War*, I, para. 437.

[34] *Histoire des Juifs*, xv, xi, p.579; *Jewish Antiquities*, xv, para. 237.

nothing to hide the ruthless brutality which marked Herod's career from its beginnings, and enabled him finally to impose himself upon Judea. Yet for Josephus Herod is a great king. He writes with admiration of Herod's political and military skills, and celebrates the courage and determination which he displayed against great odds in adverse circumstances. Herod is seen as a strong king who, in spite of the harshness of his rule, brought a period of peace and prosperity to the Jews. At the same time Josephus gives arresting descriptions of the passion for Mariamne which held Herod in an unrelenting grip, and underlines the contrast between his political and military successes and the failure of his domestic relations: 'Jamais prince n'a eu tant d'afflictions domestiques, ni plus de bonheur dans tout le reste.'[35] One feature of Herod's character which Josephus clearly identifies is the tendency to swing rapidly from one extreme of emotion to its opposite. This is particularly highlighted in the account of events occurring on Herod's return from each of his embassies to the Romans.[36]

These events set out in the histories of Josephus form a subject rich in dramatic potential, mingling political intrigue and private passion. It is not surprising therefore that they have known many adaptations to the stage, both before and after Voltaire.[37]

In treating the material supplied by Josephus, Voltaire took great liberties. He maintains the Josephan account of certain key forces responsible for the tragic death of Mariamne, focusing in particular on the volatility of Herod's emotional states and his extreme susceptibility to jealousy, but he treats in a very cavalier fashion the sequence of events unfolded in Josephus's narrative. In

---

[35] *Guerre des Juifs*, I, xxi, p.88; *Jewish War*, I, para. 665.

[36] *Histoire des Juifs*, xv, iv, p.563-64; *Jewish Antiquities*, xv, para. 81-87 (text summarised in note to IV.98a). *Histoire des Juifs*, xv, xi, p.576f; *Jewish Antiquities*, xv, para. 211 (text quoted in note to IV.82a).

[37] As the abbé Nadal pointed out in the preface to his *Mariamne*, 'la famille d'Hérode, aussi bien que celle d'Œdipe, a fourni des sujets susceptibles de tous les intérêts capables de remuer l'âme du spectateur.'

16

this regard his play forms a sharp contrast with those of his predecessors Alexandre Hardy and Tristan L'Hermite, who, the one in his *Mariamne* (*c.*1610), and the other in *La Mariane* (1636), had by and large respected Josephus's account, even while making their plays conform to the unities of time and place. Voltaire abandons altogether features prominent in the historian's writings, such as the episode of the cupbearer suborned by Salome to accuse Mariamne of attempting to poison Herod; this was a key element in triggering the final crisis both in Josephus and in the earlier plays. At other points he modifies elements of the historical narrative to a point where they become scarcely recognisable. A striking example is the radical transformation of the orders issued by Herod for the death of Mariamne. In Josephus these were conditional orders, to be carried out only should Herod not return from his interviews with the Romans. Voltaire makes the order unconditional. As the play opens we learn that Salome has prevailed upon Hérode to issue an order for the immediate execution of Mariamne, and that Zarès has already arrived in Jerusalem charged with carrying out this order.

Perhaps the greatest violence wrought by Voltaire upon the historical record is the introduction of the Roman praetor Varus as governor of Syria at the time of the death of Mariamne, and the attribution to him of the role of her defender and lover. Publius Quinctilius Varus, who is well known to history,[38] was in fact governor (*legatus*) of Syria, but in the years *c.*6-4 BC, some twenty-five years after the death of Mariamne. An error made by Arnauld d'Andilly in translating Josephus's account of certain events which occured in Damascus shortly after the final crisis in the relationship of Herod and Mariamne may have left Voltaire quite unaware of the anachronism. Josephus relates how the

[38] He was later killed at the battle of the Teutoberg forest in 9 AD, a grave defeat for the Romans involving the loss of several legions which, in addition to grieving the last years of Augustus, probably fixed for ever the limits of the expansion of the Roman Empire into Germanic lands, and so is a highly significant date in European history.

Damascenes, who were subject to constant molestation by brigands from Trachonitis, were granted the protection of the Roman governor of Syria, who was called Varro. Arnauld d'Andilly mistakenly reproduces this name as Varus in his translations of both the *Jewish War* and the *Jewish Antiquities*.[39] In the *Jewish Antiquities* only a few pages separate this incident from the execution of Mariamne. The error cannot have been without influence on Voltaire's choice of Varus for the leading character of the secondary action of the play.

Although he was later to become hostile to the introduction of extraneous romantic interest into tragedy, Voltaire had already written a romantic subplot into *Œdipe*, where a large part of the first three acts is taken up by the reminiscences of Jocaste and Philoctète concerning their youthful love.[40] This he seems to have done partly to conform to the current taste for themes of love and gallantry, partly because it enabled him to expand his subject matter to fill more comfortably the dimensions of length and density required in a five-act tragedy. It is probable that the same considerations were at the forefront of his mind when in the early 1720s he undertook the composition of *Hérode et Mariamne*. He no doubt saw that the theme of the impossible love of the Roman general for the Queen of Judea contained much to attract the

[39] *Guerre des Juifs*, I, xv, p.51; *Jewish War*, I, para. 398-99 (where the error occurs twice); and *Histoire des Juifs*, xv, xiii, p.588; *Jewish Antiquities*, xv, para. 344-45. The error thus appears three times in all, and was not corrected in the successive reprintings of the translations. A Latin translation of the works of Josephus by J. Hudson and others, giving the correct form 'Varro', was published at Amsterdam in 1726. This work was not available at the time of the composition of *Mariamne*, though Voltaire may have known of it later (see *CN*, iv.715, n.490).

[40] Voltaire's attitude to the romantic subplot is discussed by Janet Godden and J. R. Vrooman in their introduction to *Mérope*, *OC*, vol.17, p.115f. Already at the earliest stage of his career as a dramatist Voltaire seems to have had theoretical misgivings about the romantic subplot, and deplored the intrusion of amorous intrigues into French tragedies based on Greek sources. He had criticised Corneille for incorporating a romantic subplot into his reworking of the myth of Œdipus. Yet he himself, with perhaps an instinctive feel for what would bring success, had nevertheless done the very same thing in his own *Œdipe*.

favour of audiences, for both parties could be shown to be conducting themselves according to the highest moral standards, Varus in overcoming his passion, and Mariamne in her dignified refusal of an unacceptable sentiment. Here then was a heroic subject par excellence which would touch the hearts of spectators.

Voltaire also imposes his own interpretation on the portrayal of the characters. He strips Mariamne of the shrewishness and arrogance which figure prominently in Josephus, and gives an idealised portrait of a queen whose virtue is stainless. [41] Voltaire's Hérode develops nuances no more than hinted at in Josephus of a gentler, less violent king. To be sure he is a tyrant, but he is also presented as a confused and unhappy man, burdened with remorse for his past cruelties and anxious to seek reconciliation with Mariamne.

Voltaire therefore exercises a free hand in exploiting his historical sources. His purpose seems to have been to create a dramatic work capable of moving an audience through a range of contrasting and rapidly succeeding emotions, [42] a work which did not depend on fidelity to historical evidence, but one which contained its raison d'être in itself, and generated its own movement and logic. This objective is achieved by the particular structure which Voltaire gave the play, and of which the essential feature is the placing of Mariamne at the centre. The dramatic action develops in a series of stages, each one of which is constructed around her. Thus is true even in act I, in which she does not actually appear. But the opening act has her fate as its central preoccupation, and shows how a danger to her life through Hérode's order for her execution is averted by the intervention of Varus. In act II Mariamne contends with a twofold menace. On the one hand the return of Hérode fills her with fear for her own life

[41] Cf. his letter of October 1723 (D167): 'La vertu de Mariamne sera désormais sans tâche.'

[42] These he enumerates very clearly in the Préface, lines 65-70, 248-61. They include indignation and pity for Hérode, compassion and fear balanced by admiration for Mariamne, horror for Salome.

and those of her children. This physical danger leads to her decision to flee. At the end of the act one can reasonably believe that this plan will be successful, thanks to the help of Varus, and that she will be able therefore to escape from this threat. On the other hand she is at the same time faced with another danger, this one moral, when Varus reveals his love. It is now her virtue rather than her life that is at stake. Her greatness of soul however gives her the victory over this peril, and she thus emerges intact both physically and morally at the end of act II. The movement of act III takes the play in a contrary direction. On his arrival Hérode seems intent on reconciliation. Danger for Mariamne appears therefore to recede momentarily, but revives when Hérode's mood swings abruptly to anger and threats of vengeance in the last scene. Hérode enters act IV profoundly hostile towards Mariamne. But Mariamne's eloquent defence of her honour leads to a change of heart. Hérode begins to entreat her for reconciliation and a fresh start. His pleas bring relief to Mariamne. But fortune turns against her when Hérode, learning that Varus has taken up arms, in a new swing between emotional poles, surrenders once more to anger and the desire to punish. In act V Mariamne, as she awaits death, rejects the means of escape which are offered to her first by Varus and then by Nabal. Her doom is sealed by her resolute refusal of solutions that would compromise her honour. This choice leaves her no further options. All she can do is to display constancy and dignity as she goes to her death.

The fate of Mariamne is thus the centre of dramatic interest in Voltaire's play. The pattern of dangers which form about her and which dissipate only to form anew more seriously give it a sense of movement and progression. At each stage the dangers which gather around Mariamne are dispelled only in part. When they reform, it is with an augmented charge of menace. In this way, at each of the thresholds traversed by the action, Mariamne's situation becomes more and more perilous, until she is carried to destruction in the final explosion of Hérode's anger.

If Voltaire's main intention in this play was to create the internal dynamic which we have described, that would explain why he took great liberties with the historical material at his disposition.

ii. *Other literary sources*

The debts of Voltaire to his seventeenth-century predecessors in France seem non-existent in the case of Hardy and slight in the case of Tristan L'Hermite. It is possible that already in the early 1720s Voltaire had arrived at that contemptuous verdict on the works of Hardy which we find expressed much later in the *Essai sur les mœurs*, where Hardy is described as the author of 'pièces innombrables qui sont autant de monuments de la barbarie'.[43] In any case Hardy follows Josephus faithfully, which makes it difficult to identify specific debts of Voltaire to his French predecessor. It is true that Hardy and Voltaire both present Herod as the murderer of the father, and not the grandfather, of Mariamne. But this error had been introduced by Josephus himself into the *Jewish Antiquities*, and Voltaire no doubt took it from there, in the Arnauld d'Andilly translation.[44]

Voltaire's judgements concerning Tristan's *La Mariane* are likewise far from flattering. Although he recognises that Tristan's tragedy has 'du naturel', he dismisses the play as 'un très mauvais

[43] *Essai sur les mœurs*, 'Chapitre des Arts', ed. R. Pomeau (Paris 1963), ii.850. Elsewhere he asserts that Hardy 'n'écrivi[t] que des platitudes d'un style insupportable, et ces platitudes furent jouées sur des tréteaux au lieu du théâtre' (*Questions sur l'Encyclopédie*, 'Art dramatique', M.xvii.397).

[44] *Histoire des Juifs*, xv, xi, p.577: 'Mariamne [...] lui reprocha la mort de son pere et de son frere' (cf. *Jewish Antiquities*, xv, para. 222). A little later in the same chapter (p.579), a further reference to the father and brother of Mariamne appears to be the translator's rendition of words whose meaning is simply 'relatives' in the Greek. The correct relationship is suggested in the *Guerre des Juifs* (i, xi, p.34) and in the corresponding passage of the *Histoire des Juifs* (xiv, xxv). Voltaire's source was thus somewhat ambiguous on the relationship between Mariamne and Hyrcanus II. If he chose to make them father and daughter, this was no doubt because of the greater potential for compassion for Mariamne afforded by this version. Mariamne's father, Alexander, had been executed by Pompey in 49 BC, in circumstances which did not involve Herod.

ouvrage', even if 'très passable pour le temps où il fut composé'. [45]
Another judgement is harsher: 'Le prodigieux et long succès
qu'eut sa tragédie de *Mariamne* fut le fruit de l'ignorance où l'on
était alors'. [46] This opinion is expressed as early as 1727 in the *Essai
sur le poème épique*, where *La Mariane* is described as 'une très
mauvaise pièce', and included with two other plays as works 'qui
ne devaient leur réputation qu'au mauvais goût du siècle'. [47] It is
more likely than not that Voltaire was already unfavourably
disposed towards Tristan when he began the composition of
Hérode et Mariamne. He probably considered that there was little
in *La Mariane* for him to imitate. Nevertheless, some interesting
similarities are observable between the two plays. The acrimo-
nious conversation between Mariamne and Salome in act II scene ii
of Voltaire's tragedy has its predecessor in the venomous
exchange between the same two characters in act II scene ii of
La Mariane. In both plays the confrontation serves a similar
dramatic function in providing motivation for Salome's hatred of
Mariamne, which in the absence of illustration might otherwise
appear unexplained. Mariamne's soliloquy scene in prison (V.i)
has its counterpart in Tristan (IV.ii), where the sentiments with
which she prepares herself for death are expressed not in
alexandrines but in *stances*. Voltaire too used *stances* for this
scene in the first (1724) version of *Mariamne*. [48] Tristan's list of
characters includes 'Narbal, Gentil-homme, qui raconte la mort de
Mariane'. This could be the source of the name of 'Nabal', who
performs a similar function (and much more besides) in Voltaire's
play. Such similarities do not show that Voltaire borrowed
substantially from Tristan. At most they can be taken to indicate
that he was aware of the way in which his predecessor had treated

[45] *Commentaires sur Corneille*, *OC*, vol.54, p.82.

[46] *Siècle de Louis XIV*, 'Catalogue des Ecrivains'.

[47] *OC*, vol.3B, p.493.

[48] We know this from the 'Extrait' of the play published in the *Mercure de France*
in March 1724 (see below, Appendix B) and from the parody *Le Mauvais Ménage*
(see below, section 4.ii).

the subject. The 'traits prophétiques' which Voltaire was to insert into Hérode's final speech in the revised (1725) version of the play are a slightly different case. As we shall discover, Voltaire was urged by others to follow Tristan's example,[49] and it is not unreasonable to assume that he took his inspiration from that source when writing the additional lines.

As we have seen, Voltaire's letter to Cideville of April 1723 (D149), written at an early date in the history of the genesis of *Hérode et Mariamne*, mentions the *Mariamne* by the English writer Elijah Fenton, which had been staged in London with great success from February 1723. These are the only references in the correspondence of Voltaire, during the early phases of the composition of *Hérode et Mariamne*, which name another author's work on the same theme. Voltaire at first affects indifference towards Fenton, but concludes his letter with a request to Cideville to bring him a copy of the English *Mariamne*. The question therefore arises as to the influence, if any, exercised by Fenton's play in the genesis of Voltaire's play. We do not know whether Cideville complied with Voltaire's request to supply a copy of the play, but even assuming that he did we have to bear in mind that Voltaire's meagre familiarity with the English language at this time would have limited his capacity to have direct access to Fenton's text.[50] We might suppose competence in English in his Rouennais friends Cideville and Thiriot, who could therefore have given him an outline of the play and described its main features. It is even possible that Bolingbroke, still in France, might have discussed the play with him.

Fenton proclaims in his Prologue that his intention is to show 'the tyrant in the lover lost', and this could serve as a useful description of what Voltaire attempts in his portrait of Hérode.

---

[49] See below, section 4.ii.

[50] It is generally agreed that Voltaire did not begin serious study of English before his second emprisonment in the Bastille from mid-April until the beginning of May 1726. See, for example, the conclusions of D. Williams in *OC*, vol.3B, p.141.

Fenton's and Voltaire's plays have a number of common points, but also present significant divergences. Fenton invents a Roman general, Flaminius, who, like Voltaire's Varus, provides a secondary love interest. Flaminius, however, is not in love with Mariamne, but with her chief attendant Arsinoé, and it is she, and not the queen whom he protects, not against Herod, but against his minister Sohemus. Mariamne's death by drinking poison would seem to be another shared feature, though found in Voltaire only in M24. There are differences of presentation: in Fenton Mariamne takes poison off stage and is brought in to die; Voltaire, according to the *Mercure extrait* of M24 and to the testimony of contemporary commentators, has her drink the poisoned cup on stage. Yet the use of poison was a striking innovation: in Josephus and in the earlier plays of Hardy and Tristan Mariamne dies on the scaffold. It has been argued, notably by A. Gunny,[51] that Voltaire may have been indebted to Fenton for this idea, and certainly the possibility cannot be excluded. Wider claims made by other critics for Fenton's influence on Voltaire seem not to be well founded.[52]

The title page of the first edition authorised by Voltaire of *Hérode et Mariamne* (25P), which was reproduced in many subsequent editions, has as its epigraph the same three lines from Virgil, *Aeneid* XII, 666-68, as appear on the title page of Fenton's *Mariamne*. It seems difficult to regard this as a coin-

[51] 'It is possible that under the influence of Fenton Voltaire made Mariamne drink a cup of poison on the stage in the first version of his play' (*Voltaire and English literature*, *SVEC* 177, p.76).

[52] Thus K. H. Hartley, who suggests that if Voltaire 'shows the tyrant alternating with the lover' ('The Sources of Voltaire's *Mariamne*', *AUMLA* 21, 1964, p.12), this is due to the influence of Fenton. But the complexity of Herod's character is already suggested in Josephus. H. Feniger is also a strong advocate of Fenton's influence on Voltaire ('Voltaire et le théâtre anglais', *Orbis Litterarum* 7, Copenhagen 1949), citing as examples the fact that Hérode does not appear until act III, the presence of a secondary love plot, and several other features. It seems to us that in these cases either Voltaire had no need of models, or that, if needed, numerous models were available to him within the familiar French tradition.

cidence, particularly as the word 'Imo' is a variant not found in the standard Virgilian text, which reads 'Uno in corde'.[53] We do not know why Fenton or his publisher gave the quotation in this unusual form, but it may well be that Voltaire, in search of an epigraph that would aptly describe the situation of Herod, simply copied these lines from the title page of the English edition.

iii. *'Artémire'*

Similarities between *Artémire* and *Mariamne* were noted immediately at the single performance of M24, and were seized upon, before even the first staging of M25 the following year, by Piron in the *Prologue des Chimères*, where the new character 'Mariane', on her first entry onto the stage, is mistaken for 'Artémire'. The *Apologie de Monsieur de Voltaire adressée à lui même*, which likewise came into existence before the first performances of M25, links the failure of the two plays and implies that *Mariamne* is simply a copy of *Artémire*. If, as H. C. Lancaster suggests, the character of Artémire's jealous and brutal husband is taken from the story of Herod and Mariamne that Voltaire was soon to dramatise, such similarities are hardly surprising.[54] Condorcet, in his *Vie de Voltaire* (Kehl, xcii.17), considered that *Mariamne* offered 'le sujet d'*Artémire* sous des noms nouveaux, avec une intrigue moins compliquée et moins romanesque'.

In their Avertissement for *Artémire*, the Kehl editors, while considering that 'le fond de l'intérêt' is the same as in *Mariamne* ('C'est également une femme vertueuse persécutée par un mari cruel qu'elle n'aime point'), stress the differences in the ways in which the subject is treated in the two plays: 'La fable de la pièce, le caractère des personnages, le dénouement, tout est différent; et à l'exception d'une scène entre Cassandre et Artémire, qui ressem-

---

[53] The same line ('Uno in corde pudor mixtoque insania luctu') also appears at *Aeneid* x, 871.

[54] Lancaster, *French tragedy*, p.57.

ble à la scène du quatrième acte, entre Hérode et Mariamne, il n'y a rien de commun entre les deux pièces.'[55]

Basing his argument on a passage in the Préface to *Mariamne* in which Voltaire distinguishes between two types of tragedy, those which treat the fate of an entire nation, and those which deal with the private interests of princes, D. Jory has speculated that *Artémire* may have been inspired by an ambition on Voltaire's part, after proving himself the equal of Corneille with his *Œdipe* (which treated a theme belonging to the first category), to show now that he could rival Racine with a play in the second category, in which Racine had produced several masterpieces.[56] The failure of *Artémire* had left this aim unfulfilled. But a new play would give him a further chance to achieve it. In this hypothesis, both *Artémire* and *Mariamne* would proceed from a similar ambition in their author, and in that case once again it would not be surprising to find resemblances.

The presence of similarities should not blind us however to the many significant differences between the two tragedies. The most that we can do is to endorse Lancaster's judgement, that in writing *Mariamne* Voltaire seems to have adopted elements from *Artémire*.[57] But they appear in a highly modified form. It also has to be kept in mind that M25 was not born directly out of *Artémire*: M24, coming as an intermediary stage between these two works, increased the likelihood that source material from *Artémire* would be modified in the transition to M25. We have already seen the decision which Voltaire took, at this early stage of the development of the text, to heighten the image of Mariamne as the

[55] D. Jory has suggested that the Kehl editors expressed themselves so vigorously on this topic only because the similarities between the two plays seemed to them so strong (*OC*, vol.1A, p.397, n.15). H. Lion for his part was convinced that the resemblances outweighed the differences: he saw Mariamne as a 'nouvelle Artémire', and thought that the characters of the two plays could not be distinguished (*Les Tragédies et les théories dramatiques de Voltaire*, Paris 1895, p.31, 33).

[56] *OC*, vol.1A, p.390.

[57] Lancaster, *French tragedy*, p.59.

very embodiment of virtue and fidelity, by excluding from her even the sort of 'passion toute excusable' that Artémire had felt for Philotas. In the case of Hérode it seems more likely that modifications were introduced during the reworking by which Voltaire transformed the failed M24 into the successful M25. It may well be that the Hérode of M24, described by Voltaire himself in the Préface to 25P as 'cruel et politique, tyran de ses sujets, de sa famille, de sa femme', and 'n'étant que criminel', was a direct calque on the jealous and brutal Cassandre from *Artémire*, whose order for the killing of his wife is every bit as arbitrary as Hérode's order for the execution of Mariamne. The Hérode of M25 is a more uncertain and complex figure, divided within himself and burdened with remorse for his past wrongs. In the transition from M24 to M25 Voltaire would seem therefore to have softened the portrayal of Hérode, perhaps taking as his model 'les peintres habiles, qui embellissent en conservant la ressemblance', to whom he refers in the Préface.

Even the scene between Artémire and Cassandre which the Kehl editors regard as an exception to their general judgement that 'il n'y a rien de commun entre les deux pièces' illustrates the differences between the two plays. For on closer examination we find that the movement of this scene is quite unlike that of its counterpart, the act IV scene iv encounter between Hérode and Mariamne. No rapprochement takes place between Cassandre and Artémire when they are at last face to face. An obdurate and vindictive Cassandre remains unmoved by his wife's pleading; her condemnation therefore stands. Nothing has occurred which will bring Artémire and Cassandre closer. In the corresponding scene in *Hérode et Mariamne* Hérode is finally moved by Mariamne's reproaches, admits his wrongs, and begins to beg for the restoration of their love. A prospect of reconciliation dawns briefly; by the final exchanges of this scene the two protagonists have taken steps towards closing the distance separating them. The scene is brought to an abrupt end by the entry of Le Garde, but its dramatic dynamic is quite the opposite of its counterpart in *Artémire*.

27

Although Voltaire, then, took suggestions from *Artémire* in writing *Hérode et Mariamne*, in general it would be imprudent to overstate the resemblances between the two plays. [58]

3. *The Mariamne of 1724*

i. *The first performance*

The première of *Mariamne* at the Comédie-Française took place on 6 March 1724 before a packed house in an atmosphere of great excitement. High expectations surrounded the occasion. The celebrated and long-lived Baron had been cast in the role of Hérode, the enchanting Adrienne Lecouvreur in that of Mariamne, and the other main roles of Salome and Varus were played by Mlle Duclos and Dufrêne. In its *extrait* or review of this first version of the play, the *Mercure de France* tells us that all boxes had been reserved long in advance, and that the climate of eager anticipation had been used to justify a doubling of the admission prices to all parts of the house including the pit. [59] At the first performances of Voltaire's *Artémire* and *Mariamne* the charges were 8 fr. for a seat on the stage or in a lower box, 4 fr. for the second tier of boxes, 3 fr. for the third tier, and 2 fr. for admission to the parterre. [60] Lancaster notes that the doubling of admission prices occurred at no other performance (apart from the closing gala) during the 1723-1724 season. [61] The takings attained the extremely high figure of 5539 *livres* (of which Voltaire received 424 *livres*, less than 8 per cent). Spectators numbered 1257. By way

[58] Some lines from *Artémire* re-appear with little or no change in *Hérode et Mariamne*. These are recorded in the notes to the text.

[59] *Mercure*, March 1724, p.529-39, reproduced below, Appendix B.

[60] See Lancaster, *French tragedy*, p.8.

[61] Lancaster, *The Comédie-Française 1701-1774: plays, actors, spectators, finances*, *Transactions American Philosophical Society* 41 (1951), p.679. At this period it was customary to increase admission prices for the early performances of new plays.

of comparison, Lancaster records that in the same season *Inès de Castro* attracted 1100 spectators at its first performance on 6 April 1723, with receipts of 2496 *livres* 10 *sous* (of which La Motte received 214 *livres* 10 *sous*).[62] *Inès* was the great success of this season: Lancaster's figures show that it was performed more than forty times, and attendances were consistently high. But the first night of Voltaire's new play was an occasion that eclipsed any performance of La Motte's tragedy, including the first performance.

The play failed miserably at its première. The *Mercure* tells us that the public was extremely attentive during the first three acts and part of the fourth,

mais le reste de la pièce ne fut pas exempt de ces tumultes si ordinaires depuis quelques années. Le cinquième acte fut le plus maltraité, quelques mauvais plaisants, ou mal-intentionnés, ayant crié *la reine boit*, dans le temps que Mariamne s'empoisonnait, on ne fut plus en état de rien entendre, et voilà à quoi sont exposés les meilleurs ouvrages.[63]

Voltaire's own formal record of the event is found in the autobiographical *Commentaire historique*, which he composed shortly before his death: 'Mariamne était empoisonnée par Hérode; lorsqu'elle but la coupe, la cabale cria: *La reine boit!* et la pièce tomba' (M.i.74-75). The suggestions we read in these accounts of an organised disruption of the performance find an echo in Piron's satirical *Prologue* to his opéra comique *Les Chimères*.[64] Whether organised in advance or spontaneous, there is no doubt that the play was brought down by hostile interventions from spectators.

The *Nouvelles littéraires* of the abbé Raynal, in a text which is contemporary with the first productions of Voltaire's *Sémiramis*,

---

[62] Lancaster, *The Comédie-Française 1701-1774*. Against the common practice, prices were not increased for the first performance of *Inès de Castro*.

[63] *Mercure*, March 1724, p.529.

[64] In this piece, first performed in February 1725, an aptly named Monsieur de la Cabale claims responsibility for the incident of the cry from the pit.

and so can be dated to 1748, gives a different version of the failure of *Mariamne*: 'On a prétendu que le public se trouvant partagé sur le mérite de cette pièce, le procès fut jugé singulièrement. Il est d'usage qu'après une tragédie, on joue une petite comédie d'un acte. On joua ce jour-là *Le Deuil*. Quelqu'un s'écria: *C'est le deuil de la pièce nouvelle!* Le mot parut plaisant et fit triompher les mécontents.' [65] The comedy which followed *Mariamne* was indeed *Le Deuil* by Hauteroche, [66] but Raynal is a late source, and must be regarded with caution. The second version does not appear in accounts contemporary with the event. The *Anecdotes dramatiques* of Clément and La Porte (1775) combine the *Mercure* and Raynal acounts and produce a more elaborate narrative, in which the failure of *Mariamne* unfolds in two distinct phases. First the cry from the pit (*La Reine boit!*), of which they say that they had been informed by Voltaire himself, [67] and second the story found in Raynal. J.-P.-L. de Luchet presents the two incidents as alternative accounts of the failure of *Mariamne*, and gives his reason for preferring the former: 'Ce qui prouve cependant la vérité de la première version c'est que l'auteur ôta la liqueur fatale.' [68]

The Avertissement of w38 wrongly gives the date of the première of *Mariamne* as 'vers le temps des Rois', perhaps embroidering on the uproar caused by the cry 'La reine boit!'. The Kehl editors (i.200) later comprounded this error, giving the

[65] Raynal, *Nouvelles littéraires*, XXXI, in Grimm, *CL*, i.211.

[66] Lancaster, *The Comédie-Française 1701-1774*, p.679.

[67] J.-M.-B. Clément and Joseph de La Porte, *Anecdotes dramatiques contenant* [...] *toutes les pièces de théâtre* [...] *jusqu'en 1775*, 3 vol. (Paris, Duchesne, 1775), i.522 ('L'auteur lui-même nous apprend que...').

[68] Jean-Pierre-Louis de Luchet, *Histoire littéraire de Monsieur de Voltaire* (Cassel 1780), i.57-58. Luchet continues: 'Les connaisseurs regrettent ce premier dénouement, et croient que si les Comédiens avaient aujourd'hui le courage de présenter cette coupe, le parterre devenu beaucoup meilleur juge, la préférerait au poignard.' In M25 Mariamne's life seems to have been brought to an end by decapitation (see act V, lines 195-99), and the 'fer des bourreaux' is more likely therefore to have been a sword rather than a dagger. Nevertheless Luchet's point is well taken that later in the century the public would have been more willing to accept the notion of a tragic protagonist drinking poison on stage.

date as 'justement la veille de la fête des rois', also found in Duvernet (p.54). The faulty dating, which appears also in certain theatrical almanachs and guides of the latter part of the eighteenth century and in the *Correspondence littéraire* of Grimm,[69] was corrected by Beuchot (M.ii.164).

Only one observation has come down to us concerning the proficiency of the actors at this first production of *Mariamne*, and this is a criticism in the Avertissement of w38 (fourteen years later) of the casting of the elderly Baron in the role of Hérode: 'Il était trop vieux pour soutenir ce caractère violent.'[70]

In the *Nouvelles littéraires* Raynal cites 'l'épitaphe qu'on dressa à cette pièce qui, étant depuis corrigée, a eu un si grand succès:

> Ci-gît qui fut célèbre avant que de paraître;
> Qui paraissant cessa de l'être.
> Un seul jour éclaira sa vie et son trépas;
> Chacun la vit mourir sans regret, non sans trouble:
> Passant, tu n'y perds rien si tu ne la vis pas
> Si tu la vis tu perds le double.'[71]

The reference in the last line is to the increasing of the admission prices for the première of *Mariamne*.

The failure of his play must have been a terrible humiliation for Voltaire. In the words of G. Desnoiresterres, who notes the record box-office takings, 'on ne pouvait tomber devant une chambrée

---

[69] 'Vous savez que cette pièce, dans sa nouveauté fut donnée dans le temps des Rois, et qu'un mauvais plaisant voyant la coupe de Mariamne, cria: "La reine boit! la reine boit!"' (*CL*, 15 August 1754, ed. M. Tourneux, ii.397). J. Taschereau corrected the mistake in his 1829 edition of the *CL*, in a footnote reproduced by Tourneux (*ibid.*). Under the date of 15 September 1763, in discussing the performances of the revised version of *Mariamne*, the *CL* gives a modified account of the events of 1724 which removes the error while preserving the reference to the Fête des Rois: 'A la première représentation, un mauvais plaisant du parterre s'étant mis a crier, "La Reine boit", comme on fait en France, suivant un ancien usage, aux soupers de la fête des Rois, l'Auteur fut obligé [...] de faire périr Mariamne derrière la scène et de mettre son supplice au récit' (*CL*, v.386).

[70] For the Avertissement of w38, see Appendix C.

[71] *CL*, i.213.

plus complète'. [72] The *Mercure* describes Voltaire as 'piqué d'un accueil si peu attendu' (an 'accueil' which, as it adds diplomatically in the same sentence, was also 'peut-être si injuste'). Pique would have been an understandable reaction. Voltaire at once withdrew the play.

There were no further performances of this version of *Mariamne*; publication, however, seems to have been part of Voltaire's intentions even at this stage. The *Registres de la Librairie* in the Bibliothèque nationale list a 'Mariane tragedie' by Voltaire among the manuscripts submitted by their authors for censorship during the period from 28 February to 12 March 1724. [73] No less a figure than Fontenelle was designated as censor. We learn from the text of the *privilège*, which was not granted until 21 July, that Voltaire's application contained a highly novel feature: in addition to the usual requests for permission for himself as author to print and publish the play, and for the prohibition of others from doing so under pain of severe penalty, Voltaire sought the issue of 'défenses à tous acteurs et autres montant sur les théâtres publics, d'y représenter, ni jouer la dite tragédie sans le consentement du dit Sieur de Voltaire, sous les peines portées par le présent privilège, [...] s'il nous plaisait de lui accorder nos lettres de privilège sur ce nécessaires'. This request, recited in the preamble, is ignored in the grant of *privilège* document: Voltaire was given the customary rights on the customary terms for a period of six years in regard to publication alone. The *privilège* which Voltaire had obtained for *Œdipe* in 1719 makes no allusion to a request for rights over performances of that play. His 1724 attempt to secure a monopoly over both publication and performance in regard to *Mariamne* was

[72] G. Desnoiresterres, *Voltaire et la société au XVIIIᵉ siècle. La jeunesse de Voltaire*, 2nd edn (Paris 1871), p.303n.

[73] BnF, mss. fonds fr. 21995, f.24v. The entry in the *Registre* which lists *Mariamne* along with a large number of other works is dated 12 March. It can be assumed that on that day, in accordance with customary practice, an official entered into the register all the works that had been submitted since the last entry had been written up, which had been on 27 February.

therefore an initiative of significant historical interest, even if the authorities did not give him satisfaction. After this rebuff Voltaire seems to have let the matter drop. There is no reference to a request for rights over performances in the *privilèges* for *L'Indiscret* (September 1725), *Brutus* (December 1730) or *Zaïre* (November 1732).[74]

It is impossible to date precisely the moment between 27 February and 12 March when Voltaire initiated the procedures for obtaining a *privilège* for *Mariamne*. The question is of some importance, for it raises the possibility that he may have begun these negotiations before the first performance. Indeed it is more likely that he set the machinery in motion before the disaster of 6 March than during the few days which followed it.

Although Voltaire had submitted *Mariamne* to the censors by 12 March at the latest, the *privilège* bears the date of 21 July 1724. It was to run for a period of six years, and was registered with the Chambre Syndicale des Libraires et des Imprimeurs on 31 July. We do not know what caused the long delay between Voltaire's application and the issue of the *privilège*, but it seems to have been serious enough to make Voltaire give up hope of obtaining a *privilège* and adopt an alternative strategy. The *Registres* show that at a date between 14 and 28 May he resubmitted *Mariamne* to the services of the Librairie. A new censor, Hardion, was appointed, and a *permission simple* valid for three years was granted to Voltaire on 11 June.[75]

Voltaire persisted in his intention to publish *Mariamne* until mid-August 1724. Writing to Thiriot from Paris, in a letter which Besterman dates at 17 August, he declares: 'Je ferai imprimer ici notre Mariamne, ce qui m'y retiendra quelque temps' (D200). Nevertheless, a few days later, he is less sure about publication and

---

[74] The *privilège* for *Mariamne* is discussed also by L. Foulet in *La Correspondance de Voltaire, (1726-1729)* (Paris 1913), appendice VIII, p.281-82. Foulet's otherwise excellent account suggests that Voltaire was granted the rights he sought over performances. This seems to us to be a misreading of the *privilège* document.

[75] BnF, mss. fonds fr. 21995, f.31r.

painfully despondent regarding the interest of his theme and the value of his labours in producing this failed play. In a further letter to Thiriot (of 21 August), we read: 'A l'égard de ma pauvre Mariamne, quelque bien écrite qu'elle soit je ne sais si je la ferai imprimer. Le sujet m'en paraît si peu intéressant que je crains d'avoir fait inutilement de beaux vers. J'ai bien envie d'abandonner tout cela et de songer uniquement à Henri IV' (D202).

Fortunately this lack of confidence only endured for a moment. Voltaire returned rapidly to the challenge of Mariamne, and began what was to prove a highly successful reworking of the text. But in the aftermath of the failure of 6 March 1724 he seems to have been successful in suppressing the text of the play altogether:[76] apart from the sections which Lekain was to bring to light many years later it has disappeared from view.[77]

---

[76] Th. Besterman's claim (*Voltaire*, p.101) that 'we know both versions of the play, that which failed in March 1724 and that which was cheered in May 1725' cannot be taken literally. We have access to the full text of the later play, but for the earlier version our knowledge is fragmentary and comparison of the two plays must be a speculative exercise.

[77] Various attempts have been made to retrieve the full text of M24. One such is documented in a letter from d'Argental to Palissot preserved in the Biblothèque de la Comédie-Française (Dossier 'Mariamne de Voltaire'). The letter is dated: 'A Paris ce 11 7bre', without indication of year, but it clearly belongs to the period following the death of Voltaire. The lines of interest to us are as follows: 'Je n'ai point oublié le conseil, Monsieur, que vous m'avez donné au sujet de l'ancien dénouement de la tragédie de Mariamne, je le crois très juste, je me suis occupé en conséquence des moyens de retrouver le manuscrit conforme à la première représentation, la comédie ne l'a point, M. de Paulmy à qui j'ai eu recours, m'a assuré qu'il n'était point dans sa bibliothèque, je n'ai d'autre ressource que la police. M. le Noir a bien voulu ordonner la recherche des anciens manuscrits, mais comme ce n'est que depuis peu qu'on y a mis quelque ordre, je crains fort que cette recherche ne soit inutile. Dès que vous m'aurez envoyé le mémoire de vos questions, vous ne devez pas douter que je ne sois très empressé d'y répondre, je serai fort aise de contribuer à tout ce qui peut honorer la mémoire de Monsieur de Voltaire, mon nom certainement n'est pas digne d'être à côté du sien, je ne peux servir que d'une très petite épisode dans votre ouvrage, mais je ne saurais qu'être flatté de la mention que vous ferez de la tendre et constante amitié qui a duré sans aucune altération pendant plus de soixante ans entre Monsieur de Voltaire et moi.' This letter is to be

The work of Henri Lagrave provides a context of theatrical misadventure in which to set the failure of Voltaire's *Mariamne*. It happened with a frequency unknown today that the career of a play went no further than a single performance which saw it rejected by the public. Lagrave found that between 1715 and 1750 thirty plays met this fate, representing more than 10 per cent of new plays staged at the Théâtre français, and including seven tragédies. No author was safe from this sort of humiliation: the most recent cases had been the minor writers Jolly (*La Vengeance de l'amour* in December 1721) and Chaligny des Plaines (*Coriolan* in February 1722), but later on plays by prestigious authors such as Marivaux, La Chaussée and Destouches were to meet similar condemnation. The judgement of an implacable public was almost always final: no second chance was given to the unfortunate author. Voltaire's achievement is all the more remarkable, therefore, in transforming the defeat of 1724 into the triumph of 1725.[78]

ii. *Reconstructing the text of 1724*

The material available for the reconstruction of the 1724 *Mariamne* is limited. Only two documents survive: the *extrait* published in the *Mercure* in March 1724, and the text of scenes iii and iv of act III, discovered by Lekain and sent by him for publication in the *Mercure* in 1768.[79] A manuscript copy of these two scenes in the hand of Henri Rieu is preserved in

set beside the following statement by Palissot: 'Nous nous proposions de rétablir dans notre édition l'ancien dénouement, qui eût donné à l'ouvrage même un attrait piquant de nouveauté; mais M. d'Argental et moi nous le cherchâmes vainement, soit dans les dépôts de police, soit dans les archives de la Comédie' (Ch. Palissot, *Le Génie de Voltaire apprécié dans tous ses ouvrages*, 1806, quoted by Moland, ii.160).

[78] Henri Lagrave, *Le Théâtre et le public à Paris de 1715 à 1750* (Paris 1992), p.586-87.

[79] *Mercure*, November 1768, p.55-65. These fragments are reproduced in Appendix A. In February 1775 Lekain wrote to Henri Rieu: 'C'est moi qui déterrai ce fragment et qui le donnai dans le temps à Mr de Fontanelle, l'un des auteurs du Mercure' (D19344).

St Petersburg,[80] and they were later reprinted in Kehl under the title 'Scènes iii et iv du troisieme acte, *telles qu'elles ont été jouées à la première représentation*'.[81] In addition to these fragments the Préface to the 1725 version of the play includes an analysis by Voltaire himself of what he had come to see as the defects of the earlier version. From this it will be possible to draw certain conclusions.

a) The '*extrait* de Mariamne' in the *Mercure de France*

After relating the disastrous première of *Mariamne*, the *extrait* goes on to present a list of the characters and an outline of the plot. A few comments or appreciations are ventured along the way.

The role of Mazaël, the confident of Salome, was evidently very different in 1724 from that in 1725. In the *extrait* he is described as having a character 'assez équivoque': he could be called 'un méchant homme', but he was weak enough to be capable of feeling remorse and pangs of conscience. In 1725 Voltaire introduces Idamas, a character of unimpeachable virtue, and reworks the role of Mazaël so that he lacks any impulses towards the good. Voltaire assigned to the morally ambivalent Mazaël of 1724 the function of discovering the innocence of Mariamne (IV.i) and bringing proof of this to Hérode in the final scene. In fact, the *extrait* tells us it was apparent to all intelligent spectators that Voltaire had created the role specifically for this purpose (see *extrait*, IV.i).

A comparison of the plot outline of M24 contained in the *extrait* with M25 shows that the later version changed numerous points of detail in the unfolding of the drama, without affecting its essential substance, until the entry of Hérode in act III. Some points of difference are interesting. Thus (I.i) the M24 Mazaël, who applauds Salome's revelations, appears a more confident figure

---

[80] See below, description of MS3.

[81] Kehl, i.267-74. The Kehl editors print the fragments in an annex headed 'Variantes des premières éditions de Mariamne'.

than the cautious, even fearful, Mazaël of M25. In II.i the *extrait* suggests that perhaps Mazaël spoke before Salome. The permission to be seated which Mariamne gives to Nabal in II.ii, thus abolishing momentarily the difference of rank between them, does not have an equivalent in M25. Mariamne seems to have responded with anger to Varus's declaration of love (II.3) rather than with disappointment and regret as in M25.

Substantial divergences between M24 and M25 appear from IV.iii onwards. This is the scene of the interview between Hérode and Varus, removed, along with the following scene iv, from M25. The surviving text of these scenes will be studied in the next section. According to the *extrait* Hérode decides in this scene to banish Mazaël and Salome, and his decision is made 'par politique', presumably out of a desire at least to be seen to comply with the wishes of Varus. The surviving text of scene iv, however, which must carry more authority than the *extrait*, shows that Hérode's decision to banish Salome alone (while apparently taking no measures against Mazaël) is motivated rather by remorse for the cruelties which Mariamne has suffered at his hands and by a desire to make amends for his past wrongs. This account of Hérode's motives remains unchanged in M25 (act III, lines 188-95).

The note of triumph sounded according to the *extrait* by Salome at the beginning of act IV of M24 is transferred to Mazaël in M25 and Mazaël's 'espèce de repentir' is absent from M25. In the long confrontation which follows between Hérode and Mariamne (scene iii in M24, scene iv in M25) the first Mariamne shows herself in a completely uncompromising light. She is quite unmoved by Hérode's pleas to forget the past, telling him that she will never love the murderer of her closest relatives. Her obduracy seems to have strengthened Hérode's resolve to put her to death, and it was on this note that the act closed. There is no sign of that movement towards the reconciliation of the estranged spouses apparent in IV.iv in M25, nor, after news is brought that Varus has taken up arms, of Hérode's inability in the last scenes to take a final decision concerning Mariamne's fate. The *extrait* suggests then that both Mariamne and Hérode were more intransigent and more inflexible in their 1724 characterisation. Voltaire himself later admitted as much in the Préface of M25.

The account of M24 in the *extrait* devotes only one short paragraph to the final act which provoked such hostile audience reaction. The first part of the act must have been similar to the revised version found in M25. In both Mariamne is waiting to die. But whereas the *extrait* informs us that 'Mariamne récite des stances qui conviennent à la situation d'une personne qui attend la mort', in M25 she expresses herself in alexandrines. Voltaire's use of *stances* for Mariamne's soliloquy in M24 may have been imitated from the earlier *Mariamne* of Tristan L'Hermite (as suggested above, p.22), or even from Corneille's *Polyeucte*, where in prison and awaiting death Mariamne and Polyeucte adopt this more elegaic, less declamatory form of expression.[82] The concluding scenes of the first version of *Mariamne* were different from the definitive version. Mariamne is condemned to death by Hérode, a cup of poison is brought to her, and she drinks from it. As she is dying, Hérode arrives, aware now of her innocence, and overcome with remorse. M24 concluded with his vain attempts to save her. The death of Mariamne is thus accomplished on stage. This proved to be the last straw for the audience, as we have seen and as Voltaire himself recounts in the Préface of 25P.[83] Reluctantly[84] he yielded to public opinion and in M25 the death of Mariamne takes place away from the audience's gaze.

The *Mercure* provides only a few hints concerning audience reaction to those parts of the play which were able to be performed at this disastrous première. Thus, apart from the judgement already noted of 'tous les spectateurs éclairés' concerning the

[82] Tristan, *La Mariane*, IV.ii, and Corneille, *Polyeucte*, IV.ii. See Lancaster, *French tragedy*, p.64-65. Dominique and Legrand were to seize on this replacement of the *stances* by alexandrines in their parody of *Mariamne*, *Le Mauvais Ménage*.

[83] 'La mort de Mariamne, qui à la première représentation était empoisonnée et mourait sur le théâtre, acheva de révolter les spectateurs' (Préface, lines 90-93).

[84] 'C'est contre mon goût' (Préface, line 97).

role of Mazaël, there was admiration for the scene (II.iii) in which Varus by his silence revealed his love for Mariamne ('Cette déclaration a paru très fine et très neuve', and 'Cette scène est remplie de sentiments très nobles et très délicats de part et d'autre, et tous les connaisseurs en sont convenus'). The interview between Hérode and Mariamne (IV.iii) also found public favour ('Cette scène a paru très belle').[85]

b) The surviving scenes of M24

These two scenes (III.iii-iv, reproduced in Appendix A) form a unity, and constitute an important moment in the development of the play. The quality of the writing is impressive. It is not difficult to see why these scenes should have survived the oblivion into which Voltaire cast the remainder of M24. The interview between Varus and Hérode in scene iii represents the major confrontation between the two most powerful figures in the play, who hold in their hands the destiny of nations. They are both subordinates of Augustus, and in that sense of necessity political allies. Their roles are complementary: each has his part to play in imposing on the nations the world order decided by Augustus. Yet they are uneasy in their alliance, and a deep mutual mistrust is apparent. In the world of private feelings they are irreconcilably opposed to each other through their different relationships with Mariamne, one her husband and oppressor, the other her lover and champion. We sense that Voltaire saw the challenge and the potential of such a confrontation. The lines which he writes, particularly as the scene commences, have a Racinian resonance in the elevation and distinction of their style. Possibly Voltaire had in mind, without exactly taking it as a model, the great scene in *Andromaque* (I.ii)

[85] To these appreciations we may add the later comment of the Kehl editors on the final act (K85, i.288): when the play was interrupted by the cry of 'La reine boit', 'on n'entendit point une scène très pathétique entre Hérode et Mariamne mourante; du moins c'est le jugement que nous en avons entendu porter par ceux qui avaient entendu cette scène avant la représentation'.

where Oreste and Pyrrhus confront each other and feign a common interest in the safeguarding of the cause of the Greeks, yet barely conceal the division in their purposes both public and private. Racine succeeds in maintaining the balance of forces throughout the scene. Voltaire is rather less subtle, for Varus is quick to assert his superior authority. From line 28 he begins to offer unsolicited advice to Hérode, urging him to rule with clemency. He reminds Hérode that henceforth he will be responsible to the Romans, and silences the protestations of Hérode with an unconcealed show of power, which brings the scene to an end.

In scene iv Hérode, left alone with Mazaël, describes the conditions of compromise which enable him to maintain his throne (lines 101-36). The first part of the scene contains an effective defence by Hérode of his position as a client king. Hérode presents a cogent *apologia pro vita sua* which does not have its parallel in M25. Hérode then turns to the one element lacking in his happiness, his troubled relationship with Mariamne. Here we enter ground which M25 also traverses. Yet there is a pleasing sharpness of definition in the surviving passage from M24. Hérode's contradictory feelings in regard to Mariamne are well characterised in lines 145-49. He describes movingly the pain of his rejection, and his regret for the sufferings inflicted on Mariamne. A certain tenderness is evident in his rapid evocation of their early love (lines 189-97), not mentioned at all in M25. The final part of the scene from line 217, in which Hérode resolves to seek reconciliation with Mariamne, reappears in M25, not only in substance, but also in the words used. Until now relatively few lines from M24 are used again in M25. But much of the verse at the end of the scene was retained in M25, as was the abrupt transition, with the arrival of Salome, to the following scene.

The surviving scenes from M24 thus present considerable interest. As we have seen, they are frequently marked by a sharpness of focus and a tightness of expression which make the loss of M24 a matter of great regret. The summing up of La Harpe, formulated much later, remains apt: 'Il n'y a qu'un maître dans l'art d'écrire qui puisse rejeter de pareils morceaux dans les variantes, et il n'y a point d'écrivain qui ne pût s'en faire honneur.'[86]

iii. *A first reaction to M24*

The failure of M24 was a sensation, which no doubt became the talk of Paris during the ensuing weeks. It is not therefore surprising to find that the play received considerable attention in a satirical *opéra comique* which at the close of the 1723-1724 season reviewed and lampooned several of the plays premièred at the Comédie-Française and the Comédie-Italienne in the course of the year.

Les Vacances du théâtre, attributed to Louis Fuzelier,[87] was first performed at the theatre of the Danseurs de Corde at the Foire Saint-Germain on 1 April 1724, only about three weeks after the staging of *Mariamne*, and published soon after.[88] The scene dealing with Voltaire's *Mariamne* is the longest and most developed in the work. Reducing the characters to lowly social status, Fuzelier produced a witty, even biting, mingling of satire and parody, which is focused mainly on weaknesses in the characterisation of Mariamne and Varus. He holds up to ridicule the inconsistency between Mariamne's protestations of unsullied virtue, and the absence of love for her husband, and mocks Varus's proclamation of disinterested love for Mariamne. Two footnotes quote lines from the tragedy which are echoed or parodied in the work. They attest the presence in M24 of one line which is maintained in M25 (I.302: 'Je prétends la venger et non pas la

---

[86] La Harpe, *Cours de littérature ancienne et moderne*, vol.ii (Paris 1840), p.211.

[87] See BnC; Cioranescu.

[88] *Les Vacances du Théâtre, opéra comique représenté à la Foire Saint-Germain...* (Paris, G. Cavelier and N. Pissot, 1724), with an 'approbation' of 17 April 1724. An *extrait* published in the *Mercure de France* in April 1724 (p.736-38) gives us the exact date and place of the first performance.

séduire') and of a second dropped by Voltaire in the revised version (Mariamne to her husband: 'Je ne puis vous aimer, Seigneur, je le confesse').[89]

iv. *Recovery from failure*

A successful reprise of *Œdipe* in June 1724[90] was not sufficient to prevent Voltaire from falling into the mood of discouragement regarding *Mariamne* apparent in his letter to Thiriot of 21 August 1724 (D202). But before the end of September he writes again to Mme de Bernières, and after describing the woeful state to which he has been reduced by 'une galle horrible qui me couvre tout le corps', he informs her that nevertheless she will see 'une nouvelle *Marianne*' when she returns to Paris for the winter.[91] A fortnight later he exhorts Thiriot to come back to Paris as soon as he can, and continues: 'Engagez madame de Bernière à revenir à la St Martin, vous trouverez un nouveau chant de Henri quatre que M. de Maisons trouve le plus beau de tous, une Mariamne toute changée, et quelques autres ouvrages qui vous attendent.'[92] Far from abandoning it, Voltaire had undertaken by the autumn of 1724 a significant reworking of his failed tragedy.

[89] F. Carmody (*Le Répertoire de l'opéra comique en Vaudevilles de 1708 à 1764*, Berkeley 1933, p.390) mentions a lost satirical sketch for marionnettes, *Inès et Mariamne aux Champs Elysées*, which was performed at the Foire Saint-Laurent in March 1724 by the Troupe de marionnettes de Bienfait. On this work see also V. B. Grannis, *Dramatic parody in eighteenth-century France*, New York 1931, p.242, 267, and Lancaster, *French tragedy*, p.65n.

[90] Three performances of *Œdipe* were given at the Comédie-Française on 3, 5 and 8 June 1724, attracting successively 700, 876 and 1110 spectators (Lancaster, *The Comédie-Française*, p.680).

[91] D208 (*c.*20 September 1724). In this letter Voltaire refers to himself as 'un pauvre lépreux', and in a moment of *badinage* offers the following comment on Mariamne: 'je crois que c'est cette misérable qui m'a tuée [*sic*], et que je suis frappé de la lèpre pour avoir trop maltraitté les Juifs'.

[92] D213 [5 October 1724]. St Martin's Day, traditionally the date of the annual 'rentrée des Académies', and hence an important date in the intellectual life of Paris, falls on 11 November.

This is the last reference to *Mariamne* in Voltaire's correspondence until after the first performances of 1725. Other sources, however, enable us to retrace the course of events over the next several months and into the following year. At the point which we have now reached, Voltaire cannot have been indifferent to the fact that the actors of the Comédie-Française had already, on 16 June 1724 – that is to say, several months earlier than the letters just referred to above, and only three months after the failure of his tragedy – unanimously agreed to accept [93] another play on the theme of Mariamne. The enthusiastic acceptance of a new *Mariamne* was also reported in the June issue of the *Mercure*: 'Le seize juin les Comédiens français ont lu et reçu avec de grands éloges une nouvelle tragédie de *Mariamne*, qui sera représentée l'hiver prochain. L'auteur n'est pas encore connu.' [94]

Neither the entry in the *Registres* nor the notice in the *Mercure* indicate the author of the new play, but he was soon revealed to be the abbé Augustin Nadal, [95] who had already composed several tragédies on biblical themes, which had achieved modest, if not durable success at the Comédie-Française. [96] He now returned to the theatre with a new *Mariamne*, perhaps seeking to succeed where Voltaire had failed. [97] At this point the history of Voltaire's

---

[93] Comédie-Française, *Registres* 361, p.71. This entry bears the signatures of fifteen actors, eight of whom had been among the eleven who in 1723 voted, equally unanimously, to accept Voltaire's first *Mariamne*.

[94] *Mercure*, June 1724, p.1187 (Rubrique 'Spectacles').

[95] The December issue of the *Mercure* indexed the notice just quoted under 'Mariamne de Nadal' (p.3178).

[96] From Nadal we have notably *Saül* (1705), *Hérode* (1709) (this play dramatises the events leading to the demise of Alexander, Hérode's son by Mariamne, put to death by his father in 7/6 BC, more than twenty years after the execution of Mariamne herself) and *Antiochus ou les Machabées* (1722).

[97] Lancaster suggests that Nadal may have borrowed from Voltaire the idea of beginning the action of the drama at a moment when Hérode's return to Jerusalem is known to be imminent though not yet accomplished, and also the idea of giving Mariamne a lover who urges her to escape from domestic tyranny (*French tragedy in the time of Louis XV and Voltaire*, p.67).

Mariamne becomes intertwined for a time with that of Nadal's play of the same name.

Voltaire's decision to rework *Mariamne* was not an immediate reaction to the news that another play on the same theme had been accepted by the Comédie-Française for production in the current season. This had been known since June. Yet the previously quoted letter to Thiriot (D202) shows a discouraged Voltaire tempted in August to abandon *Mariamne* altogether. However, it is likely that the emergence of a rival was a factor in his eventual decision. Here was a challenge which the competitive Voltaire would have found extremely difficult to resist. We can also imagine that he would have been reluctant in any case to accept the judgement of the first night audience as the final word on a play to which he had devoted more than a year's serious effort. Out of the debris of *Artémire* he had built the 1724 version of *Mariamne*; so now out of the ruins of M24 he proceeded to construct a revised version of the play. And by his decisive action in suppressing the earlier version after just one performance, he had kept all his options open for the future. [98]

v. *Further reactions to M24*

The failure of the first *Mariamne* remained alive in the public memory well into the season which followed. It featured prominently in two further satirical productions in early 1725. In addition the reception accorded Nadal's *Mariamne* forms part of the history of Voltaire's tragedy.

[98] In 1720 Voltaire had also sought to suppress *Artémire* after the first performance on 15 February had failed to satisfy him. Comparison with what happened at that time shows just how effective Voltaire's suppression of M24 was. In the case of *Artémire*, in spite of his wishes, seven further performances took place between 23 February and 8 March (see *Artémire*, ed. D. Jory, *OC*, vol.1A, p.398). In addition, two fragments totalling about 120 lines were published as early as 1724 in the edition of *La Ligue* published by Desfontaines and disavowed by Voltaire (numbered IV.24[b] by O. R. Taylor, *OC*, vol.2, p.235-36). These limited reverberations of *Artémire* form a striking contrast with the total silence which descended upon M24 after the failed première.

The first of the satirical productions was the *Prologue* to *Les Chimères* by Alexis Piron, first performed at the Foire Saint-Germain on 3 February 1725. [99] This work has as its focus the two highlights of the 1723-1724 season at the Comédie-Française, the triumph of La Motte's *Inès de Castro* and the failure of Voltaire's *Mariamne*. While not sparing *Mariamne*, the satire of the *Prologue* is equally directed at *Inès de Castro*. Piron's concern is with the lack of success of the initial performance of M24, to the almost total exclusion of consideration of the play itself. But he does insinuate in an early scene that *Mariamne* was little more than a revamped *Artémire*. Another passage seems to imply that there may have been calls for further performances of M24: these had been refused, but not without a hint that *Mariamne* would return in a year's time. [100] And another line suggests that the public still expected that M24 would be printed. [101] The essential target of Piron's satire is, however, the sensational failure of M24. Critical analysis of the play is absent, and this is understandable. In February 1725 the play would not have been at the forefront of the minds of Parisian theatre-goers. How could it have been, when there had been only one performance, and that ten months previously? And when in addition the text of the play was not available, because Voltaire had not allowed it to be printed? What would have remained in the collective memory of the theatre-loving world would most certainly have been not the play itself but the drama of its downfall. This was the subject skilfully exploited by Piron in the *Prologue* to *Les Chimères*.

Less than two weeks after the production of *Les Chimères* at the

---

[99] This is the date established by Pascale Verèb, *Alexis Piron, poète (1689-1773) ou la difficile condition d'auteur sous Louis XV*, *SVEC* 349 (1997), p.637. We have consulted the text of the *Prologue* of *Les Chimères* in the *Œuvres complètes d'Alexis Piron, publiées par M. Rigoley de Juvigny* (Paris, Lambert, 1776), iv.149-73.

[100] 'Le Public' related how, after his first disastrous meeting with 'Mariane', he had twice returned to her door, but she had declined to appear, leaving a message that she would not be back for year.

[101] In a heated exchange 'Mariane' retorts to 'Le Public': 'Je vous attends chez l'Imprimeur.'

Foire Saint-Germain, Nadal's *Mariamne* was performed for the first time, on 15 February 1725, by the Comédiens français. It attracted a large audience of 1273 spectators, [102] but several sources establish that the play was not well received. The February 1725 issue of the *Mercure* compared the première unfavourably with a more successful performance which took place the following Saturday, [103] The following month's *Mercure* contained a ten-page *extrait*, in the first paragraph of which we read that the 'nouvelle tragédie de *Mariamne* n'a pas été plus heureuse que celle de l'année dernière'. [104] The *Mercure* thus brackets Voltaire and Nadal together at this point as unsuccessful authors of plays on the subject of Mariamne.

This perception was shared by Mathieu Marais, from whom we receive our most detailed information about the première of Nadal's *Mariamne*. In his letter to the président Bouhier of 17 February 1725 Marais writes: 'L'abbé Nadal s'est avisé de faire une *Mariamne*, qui n'a pas eu plus de succès que celle de Voltaire.' He adds: 'Le parterre a demandé celle du dernier, qui était présent à la représentation, mais on ne croit pas qu'il la donne.' [105]

The failure of Nadal's play at its première is reported with a similar comparison with Voltaire's lack of success in the *Quintessence des nouvelles* of 26 February 1725: 'On vient de représenter la nouvelle tragédie de *Mariamne* de M. l'abbé Nadal. Cette pièce n'a

[102] Lancaster, *The Comédie-Française*, p.682.

[103] *Mercure de France*, February 1725, p.348. Nadal's *Mariamne* received three further performances, on 17, 19 and 21 February. Attendances declined steeply, from 704 to 411 to 306 spectators (Lancaster, *The Comédie-Française*, p.682).

[104] *Mercure de France*, March 1725, p.549. A cast list tells us that Baron played the role of Hérode, as he had for Voltaire. The part of Mariamne was taken by Mlle Duclos, and not by Mlle Lecouvreur, who had been Voltaire's Mariamne. Others in the cast included the Quinault brothers and Mlle Dangeville. The remaining eight pages of the *extrait* are taken up by a synopsis of the plot.

[105] Marais, iii.293-94. Marais was also to note the failure of Nadal's *Mariamne* several months later, in his diary entry of 10 April 1725, where he records the success of Voltaire's revised *Mariamne*: 'L'abbé Nadal a fait une autre *Mariamne* qui a tombé' (iii.174).

pas eu un meilleur sort que celle de M. Voltaire. [...] Ce dernier [...] n'a rien négligé pour la faire tomber: on prétend même qu'il avait gagné les suffrages du parterre avant l'ouverture du théâtre. Le bruit des sifflets et le tintamarre était si grand [*sic*] parmi la faction de ce poète qu'il ne fut pas possible de rien entendre de la pièce, moins encore d'en juger.' [106] That disruptive incidents had marred the first performance is made clear by Nadal himself, who refers, in the Préface to the edition of his play which appeared within a few weeks of the première, [107] to 'le désordre qui en a troublé la première représentation'.

It is impossible to think that the presence of Voltaire as reported by Marais was foreign to the disruption of Nadal's *Mariamne*. It is unimaginable that he attended the première simply as a passive spectator. Even a modest success for Nadal would have been an intolerable humiliation for Voltaire. Nadal himself clearly thought that the disruption of his play was the premeditated work of an organised group. Further on in his Préface, he writes: 'Tout le monde était prévenu, longtemps même avant la représentation de la pièce, sur l'horrible et scandaleuse cabale qui s'est élevée contre moi.' Although Nadal must have known who was the instigator of this affair, he makes a pretence of exempting Voltaire from responsibility, which he attributes to an unnamed but easily identifiable friend of Voltaire. Voltaire's retort to this accusation is contained in a letter to Nadal sent in the name of Thiriot. [108]

The circumstances outlined above seem to exclude the possibility that the call for further performances of Voltaire's *Mariamne* reported by Marais was a spontaneous reaction on the part of an

---

[106] *La Quintessence des nouvelles historiques, politiques, critiques, morales et galantes*, no.17 (1725).

[107] *Mariamne, tragédie par Monsieur l'abbé Nadal* (Paris, Veuve Ribou, 1725). This edition bears an *approbation* from Gros de Boze dated 6 March 1725, and a *privilège* of 8 March 1725, registered on 13 March. Nadal's *Mariamne* must have been published rapidly, for the *Lettre de M' Tiriot à M' l'Abbé Nadal*, which is a reply to Nadal's Préface, is dated 20 March 1725.

[108] D226; 20 March 1725. (See below Appendix E.)

impartial audience. It was not to be answered before the following April, when the Comédie-Française gave the first performance of Voltaire's revised *Mariamne*.

In the meantime the rivalries of authors dramatising the story of Mariamne were kept before the public eye by a further *opéra comique*, *Les Quatre Mariamnes*, again attributed to Louis Fuzelier.[109] *Les Quatre Mariamnes* was played for the first time on 1 March 1725 at the Foire Saint-Germain. It received a favourable review in the *Mercure de France* of the same month,[110] and the text was published soon afterwards.[111] The *Mercure* records *Les Quatre Mariamnes* as having had 'un succès éclatant': 'C'est un Vaudeville naissant des contestations de quelques auteurs, au sujet de quelques tragédies nouvelles, toutes nommées Mariamnes, et travaillées sur le même fonds.'

The 'Mariamnes' in question are the play of unknown authorship refused by the Comédie-Française in 1723 ('Mariamne l'inconnue'), the failed *Mariamne* of Voltaire ('Mariamne l'étourdie'), the failed *Mariamne* of Nadal ('Mariamne la jeune') and the recently re-edited *La Mariane* of Tristan L'Hermite ('Mariamne la vieille'). Each of these characters presents in turn her claims for admission to the 'Hôtel de la Comédie'. Several of their exchanges make it plain that Voltaire's intention of bringing a revised *Mariamne* to the stage was by now common knowledge, but he is mocked for the fact that nothing had yet appeared,[112] and little

---

[109] See BnC; also Parfaict frères, *Mémoires pour servir à l'histoire des spectacles de la Foire*, vol.ii (1743), p.28.

[110] *Mercure*, March 1725, p.562-64. It is from the *Mercure* that we learn that *Les Quatre Mariamnes* was played at the Théâtre de l'Opéra Comique of the Foire St Germain, where it was added as an 'Acte nouveau' at the eighth performance of *Pierrot Perrette*.

[111] *Les Quatre Mariamnes, opéra comique représenté pour la première fois le jeudi premier mars mil sept cens vingt-cinq, à la suite de l'Audience du Temps et de Pierrot Perrette* (Paris, François Flahaut, 1725). It bears a *permis d'imprimer* dated 26 March 1725.

[112] Of 'Mariamne l'étourdie' we are told: 'Il y a plus d'un an qu'elle est à se rajuster, sans en pouvoir venir à son honneur.'

hope is held out for his success. [113] Much fun is made of the failure of the plays of both Voltaire and Nadal. In other exchanges Fuzelier's characters retail the suggestion that Voltaire was closely implicated in the disruption of Nadal's *Mariamne* ('Je ne serais pas tombée sitôt', says 'Mariamne la jeune', 'si vous et vos amis ne m'aviez pas poussée malignement'). 'Mariamne l'étourdie' admits that she was present at the première, 'où je jouissais délicieusement de vos affronts'. Within Voltaire's play Fuzelier focuses mainly on Mariamne and Varus. Mariamne is portrayed as a scatty lightweight ('l'étourdie'), Varus as her completely colourless appendage. The play was much admired by the *Mercure de France*: 'Cette pièce est semée de traits, qui séparés perdraient de leur grâce, qui consiste dans la liaison et la justesse des applications.' [114]

A final reaction to M24 is found in an anonymous tract, *Apologie de Monsieur de Voltaire adressée à lui-même*, published without place or date, attributed by BnC to the abbé Simon-Joseph Pellegrin, and by O. R. Taylor to the abbé Desfontaines. [115] From a reference to the 'première et dernière représentation' of *Mariamne*, we can infer that it was composed after the performance of M24 (6 March 1724), but before the first performance of M25 (10 April 1725). There are no references to it as a separate publication before March and April 1727, [116] but it was already circulating in handwritten form by 2 April 1725, [117] and it was printed in the July-August 1726 issue of the *Bibliothèque française*. [118] The main subject of this ironical *Apologie* is *La Henriade*,

[113] 'Mariamne l'étourdie' is warned that 'Le Parterre n'aime pas les beautés replâtrées'.

[114] *Mercure*, March 1725, p.564.

[115] *OC*, vol.2, p.56n.

[116] Its appearance 'depuis quelques jours' is mentioned in two reports from police informants dated 27 March and 16 April 1727 and cited from Arsenal ms. 10157, f.63v, by Foulet, *La Correspondance de Voltaire (1726-1729)*, appendice III: 'Voltaire et Desfontaines', p.245.

[117] BnF, mss. fonds fr. 25541, cited by O. R. Taylor (*OC*, vol.2, p.56n).

[118] P.257-80. It bears the date May 1725, and an editorial note names the author as 'l'abbé D...F...'. The *Apologie* is reprinted in *Les Voltairiens, 2ème série, Voltaire jugé*

but the final paragraphs contain sarcastic references to *Mariamne*: let Voltaire proceed to publish *Mariamne*. He has nothing to fear: since after its disastrous performance it would be impossible for the play to sink lower in general esteem, the public '*à la lecture* de *Mariamne ne rabattra rien des espérances qu'il a conçues* à la première et dernière *représentation* de cette pièce'. This sarcastic adaptation of La Motte's words in the 'approbation' for *Œdipe* is followed by a further wish: let Voltaire publish *Artémire* also – this would be revenge on an unappreciative *parterre*. It would also enable Voltaire to judge whether the public had committed a double injustice against him: 'car plusieurs prétendent qu'il n'en a commis qu'une, et que dans *Mariamne* il n'a condamné qu'*Artémire*'. The judgement implied by this heavy-handed irony that *Mariamne* was essentially no more than a repeat or copy of the earlier failed play does not withstand examination, as we have seen.

4. *Mariamne in 1725-1726*

i. *First performances and initial reactions*

At some time in early 1725 Voltaire set about organising the staging of the revised version of *Mariamne* at the Comédie-Française. Following the customary course he submitted the play to a reading by the actors. This event is recorded in the *Registres* of the Comédie: 'Aujourd'hui dimanche 12ᵉ fevr. 1725 La troupe s'est assemblée extraordinairement pour entendre la lecture d'une tragédie intitulée Mariamne de Monsieur de Voltaire laquelle sera jouée immédiatement après Pâques et les présents à lad. assemblée l'ont reçue.'[119] The signatures of ten actors are appended. Five among them (Mlle Dangeville, Mlle Lecouvreur, La Thorillière fils, Fontenay and Duchemin) had voted in

---

par les siens 1719-1749, ed. Jeroom Vercruysse, vol.ii (1724-1732) (New York 1983), p.217-36.

[119] Comédie-Française, *Registres* 361, p.109.

September 1723 to accept the earlier *Mariamne*. Only three of the signatories (Mlle Lecouvreur, La Thorillière fils and Du Chemin) were to have roles in the first performance of the revised play.

A notice in the *Mercure* of March 1725 provides an insight into the intensity of the emotions released at the reading:

Le 11. M. de Voltaire fit lire dans l'assemblée des Comédiens français sa tragédie de *Mariamne*, à laquelle il a beaucoup travaillé depuis la représentation qui en fut donnée l'année passée [...] Cette pièce a paru fort intéressante à la lecture; elle a même fait verser des larmes. Les Comédiens l'ont reçue pour la jouer après Pâques.[120]

The interval between acceptance and performance of the new *Mariamne* was brief. In the case of the first *Mariamne* some seven months had separated acceptance and performance; for Nadal's *Mariamne* the interval had been eight months. Yet the revised *Mariamne* received its first performance only one month after its acceptance. The annual recess of the Comédie-Française (from 18 March to 9 April in 1725) intervened during that period. The première of the new *Mariamne* took place on 10 April 1725, 'immédiatement après Pâques' as promised by the actors, opening the 1725-1726 season. The cast was as follows: Hérode: Quinault-Dufrêne / Mariamne: Mlle Lecouvreur / Varus: Maurice Quinault / Salome: Mlle de Seine[121] / Mazaël: Le Grand père / Nabal: Le Grand fils / Elise: Mlle Jouvenot / Albin: La Thorillière fils / Idamas: Duchemin.[122]

---

[120] *Mercure*, March 1725, p.566-67. The *Mercure* does not specify a month, but it is quite clear that it was March. The date given in the *Registres* of the Comédie is unsustainable: 12 February did not fall on a Sunday in 1725; furthermore the leaves preceding and following page 109 in register 361 refer to events which took place in March. Though in 1725 both 11 February and 11 March were Sundays, the February date is obviously incorrect, and almost certainly a simple error for 11 March.

[121] And not Mlle Duclos, as stated by Jean-Jacques Olivier, *Voltaire et les Comédiens interprètes de son théâtre* (Paris 1900), p.17-18, 397. On the basis of this error Olivier paints a vivid, but entirely imaginary, picture of tensions at the 1725 reprise of *Hérode et Mariamne* in an audience divided into two rival camps of partisans of Adrienne Lecouvreur and Mlle Duclos.

[122] *Mercure de France*, April 1725, p.801-802 (*extrait* of *Mariamne*).

According to Lancaster 1148 spectators paid to attend the première, an excellent house. Admission prices, however, were not increased, [123] a fact which the parodists and satirists were soon to seize upon.

The first performance aroused strong enthusiasm. It began a highly successful run of further performances that filled the following weeks. The play was given in all sixteen times, [124] and the attendance figures show that it was extremely popular. The eight performances which followed the première until 28 April each attracted an audience of over 1000 paying spectators. For the further seven performances from 30 April onwards numbers dropped below the 1000 mark, but if no longer excellent, they remained good, averaging around 800. [125] For all performances after the first the play appears in the records of the Comédie-Française as *Hérode et Mariamne*. This title was to be used for the next several years, and we may speculate that Voltaire adopted it principally to distinguish the successful version of 1725 from its failed predecessor.

Voltaire has left no direct account of his judgements or opinions concerning these performances. However, his dissatisfaction with Mlle de Seine's interpretation of the role of Salome is reported by the abbé Nadal. [126]

The early performances of *Hérode et Mariamne* attracted wide

[123] Lancaster, *The Comédie-Française*, p.683. Receipts for the première of *Mariamne* totalled 2487 *livres*, of which the author's share was 163 *livres* 10 *sous*.

[124] The performance dates were 10, 12, 14, 16, 18, 20, 22, 25, 28, 30 April and 2, 5, 9, 12, 16, 19 May (Lancaster, *ibid.*, p.683).

[125] Only one house fell significantly below this level, that of 12 May (578 paying spectators) (Lancaster, *ibid.*, p.683).

[126] For Nadal's *Observations critiques sur la tragédie d'Hérode et Mariamne de M. de V**** (Paris 1725) see the following section. Nadal, who writes (p.27): 'M. de V*** s'est pris à Mademoiselle de Seine du peu de succès du rôle de Salome', attributes this failure not to the inadequacies of the actress, but to defects in the role created for her: 'Il n'est pas possible à l'art d'une comédienne de dépayser l'esprit du spectateur sur le fond d'un caractère vicieux.' Georges Monval (*Lettres d'Adrienne Le Couvreur*, Paris 1892, p.31) describes tensions existing in May 1725 between this actress and other members of the company, especially Adrienne Lecouvreur.

acclaim. Marais noted in his diary entry for 10 April 1725: 'Nouvelle représentation de la *Mariamne* de Voltaire, qu'il a refaite et qui a très bien réussi. C'est le plus grand poète que nous ayons.' [127] Warm acclaim for Voltaire is evident in his letter of the same date to the président Bouhier: 'Voltaire a fait jouer sa *Mariamne* mardi: elle parut un chef-d'œuvre.' [128]

In an enthusiastic letter addressed to Voltaire from Normandy on 13 April Cideville reflects widespread favourable reaction and details features of the play especially appreciated by the public (D229):

Monsieur, Les applaudissements qu'on a donnés à votre Mariamne ont retenti jusqu'ici. Le public croyait qu'un sujet que vous aviez traité et qui n'avait pas réussi ne pouvait point être mis au théâtre, et il le croyait sans retour. Il n'appartenait qu'à vous de le convaincre du contraire. On nous assure ici que la réussite de votre pièce a été complète. Il en court plusieurs lettres qui en rapportant le simple fait sont pleines de vos louanges. Ceux qui les ont écrites parlent avec éloge et de la vérité des caractères et de l'élégance de la diction. Ils paraissent frappés entre autres endroits et du portrait ressemblant des femmes et des fureurs touchantes d'Hérode.

The *Mercure* of April 1725 devoted over twenty pages to an account of *Hérode et Mariamne* which is extremely sympathetic to Voltaire. [129] The *extrait* is a longer and more elaborate text than is usually found in the reviews of new plays published in the *Mercure* during this period, and it does not seem too fanciful to speculate that Voltaire, through a network of well-placed supporters and allies, may have had a hand in securing special treatment for *Hérode et Mariamne*. After a brief allusion to Voltaire's earlier failure with *Mariamne*, an introductory paragraph celebrates his present achievement: 'il a retravaillé sa pièce avec tant de soin qu'elle n'est pas reconnaissable; nous n'en avons guère vu sur

[127] Marais, *Journal et Mémoires*, iii.174.
[128] Marais, *Journal et Mémoires*, iii.317.
[129] *Mercure*, April 1725, p.800-26.

notre théâtre qui aient été si applaudies, les applaudissements étaient trop généraux et trop unanimes pour laisser aucun soupçon qu'ils fussent mandiés'. The *extrait* then gives a detailed synopsis of the play, into which are interspersed some twenty lengthy quotations from the text.

In several instances, most notably in the speech of Hérode which concludes the play,[130] the text quoted in the *extrait* is not identical with that of the first printed edition of the play authorised by Voltaire (25P), which was not to appear until August 1725, but is that found in three earlier unauthorised editions (25CH, 25X, 26H), and in an old manuscript copy held in the Fonds Rondel at the Bibliothèque de l'Arsenal (MS1). Many passages quoted in the *Observations critiques* of the abbé Nadal show the same provenance, with Nadal recognising furthermore that his remarks concern 'une tragédie qui n'a point été encore imprimée'. It is difficult to avoid the conclusion that these three editions and the manuscript copy, which differ only insignificantly from one another, preserve more closely than 25P the state of the text used for the first series of performances of *Hérode et Mariamne* in April and May 1725. We shall examine later the considerable number of changes introduced by Voltaire into this first version of M25 when preparing a more definitive version for publication and use in subsequent performances.

The 1725 *Mercure extrait* of *Hérode et Mariamne* also contains a small number of appreciations which reveal the impression produced on the minds of spectators by certain features of the play. We read that in act II scene v Varus's silence in response to Mariamne's request for help in fleeing to Rome 'donne lieu à une déclaration d'amour qui a paru très fine et très neuve', the journalist of 1725 using the same words as had been used in the *extrait* of M24 the previous year to describe Varus's declaration of love. The conclusion of act III, when Mazaël rushes in to inform Hérode that Mariamne is fleeing with the help of Varus, is judged

---

[130] V.228f; but see also I.43, 47, 183; V.13.

to be a 'grand coup de théâtre'. The act IV interview between Hérode and Mariame was particularly impressive: 'Cette scène a paru une des plus pathétiques de la pièce.' Hérode's change of mood at the end of this scene, when, on being informed that Varus has taken up arms against him, he abandons all willingness for reconciliation and returns to his violent hatred of Mariamne, gives rise to reservations, which however are only fleetingly maintained: 'Ce changement a paru un peu trop brusque, quoique pris dans le caractère d'Hérode.' Scene i of act V, in which Mariamne, now a captive on Hérode's orders, refuses the help of Varus, also attracted special admiration: 'Cette scene a paru la plus belle de la pièce', and the 'beaux vers' of Hérode's final speech are also singled out, before being quoted in the version found in MS1, 25CH, 25X and 26H.

The concluding paragraphs of the *extrait* offer general observations. Taking as his reference point the 1724 performance of the first *Mariamne*, the writer declares:

Les représentations d'aujourd'hui sont bien différentes de celle-là. Le concours est étonnant, les deux tiers des loges sont toujours loués d'avance. Le spectateur a le cœur attendri, l'esprit satisfait, et il est souvent en admiration. Au reste, cette pièce est très bien représentée; les acteurs voulant répondre à la beauté de l'ouvrage, et au plaisir qu'il fait au public, se surpassent à l'envi les uns des autres. [131]

In spite of a notice in the May issue of the *Mercure* (p.1007) announcing that the Comédiens had brought the run of perfor-

---

[131] *Mercure*, April 1725, p.825-26. That there was perhaps one mocking voice injecting a discordant note into the chorus of acclaim surrounding *Hérode et Mariamne* is suggested by an incident recorded by Grimm, who, in reporting (*Correspondance littéraire*, 15 August 1754) the 1754 revival of the play, looks back briefly at its earlier history: 'Cette pièce [*Hérode et Mariamne*] eut toutes sortes de malheurs dans sa nouveauté, le parterre était alors moins policé et moins tranquille; le rôle de Varus était rempli par un acteur fort laid; son confident lui dit: "Vous vous troublez, Seigneur, et changez de visage." [II.305] "Laissez-le faire", cria un plaisant du parterre.' This incident is not attested in any source closer to the first performances, and may be quite apocryphal.

mances to an end on 19 May and would not be restaging *Hérode et Mariamne* before the following winter, a further performance was added on Saturday, 9 June, attracting 705 paying spectators.[132] Voltaire sought the assistance of Mme de Bernières in securing this performance, writing to her from Versailles on 28 May: 'Allez-vous souvent aux spectacles, avez-vous fait dire à Dufrene et à la Couvreur de jouer Mariamne?' (D233). He expressed his intention of attending the performance himself in a further letter to Mme de Bernières on 4 June: 'Je verrai samedi Mariamne avec vous' (D238).

ii. *The reception of M25*

a) Parodies

Whereas in M24 it had been the failure of *Mariamne* that had brought the play to the notice of the satirists and parodists, in 1725 the success of *Hérode et Mariamne* at the Comédie-Française exposed it to their attentions. Two works followed in rapid succession.

The first was *Les Huit Mariamnes* by Alexis Piron, probably first performed at the Hôtel de Bourgogne by the Comédiens italiens on 27 or 28 April 1725, that is to say, at a time when Voltaire's revised *Hérode et Mariamne* had already received eight performances. Piron wrote quickly in order to exploit the topicality of his subject, and to outstrip a rival work being prepared by a 'Comédien français'.[133] A short account of *Les Huit Mariamnes* which appeared in the *Mercure de France* of May 1725,[134] tells us that Piron's comedy 'fut assez bien reçûë du

---

[132] Lancaster, *The Comédie-Française*, p.684.
[133] See the 'Avertissement de l'Auteur' to *Les Huit Mariamnes* in *Œuvres complettes d'Alexis Piron*, v.261. Piron's rival was doubtless Marc-Antoine Le Grand, whose parody of *Hérode et Mariamne*, written in conjunction with Dominique, was *Le Mauvais Ménage*, discussed in the next section.
[134] P.1007-1008.

Public' and that it was a work which 'fait honneur à l'imagination de son Auteur'.

Piron adopted the imaginative plan of casting the stock characters of the Comédie italienne as a series of allegorical personages each representing a play based on the Mariamne story. [135] Another character 'Le Public-Sultan' is seeking to stock his harem with new beauties, and in a series of comic encounters each Mariamne seeks to win his favours. He finally succumbs, somewhat reluctantly, to the persistent demands, rather than the charms, of Voltaire's second Mariamne.

Piron was not an impartial judge of Voltaire, as Pascale Verèb [136] makes clear. The insights of adversaries are often perceptive, however, and Piron was doubtless confident that the patrons of the Comédie italienne would recognise the pertinence of his satire. His main themes are clear. The attempts of Voltaire's second Mariamne to seduce the Sultan-Public, at whom she throws herself insistently, suggest an image of obstinate efforts by Voltaire to win over a reluctant public to the revised play. Piron seizes on the arrogance of Voltaire's first Mariamne revealed in her refusal to love her husband (sc.viii). As for the second Mariamne, who appears wearing 'un grand manteau de Reine tout couvert de clinquant' (sc.xiv), she may be dressed more gaudily than her predecessor, but Voltaire's efforts have not improved her appeal, even though he has clothed her in robes stolen from the great heroines of the past. But Piron's strongest satire is directed against the inconsistencies which he finds in the character and behaviour of the second Mariamne. He takes malicious pleasure in bringing into sharp focus the discrepancy between the uncom-

---

[135] Voltaire's two *Mariamnes* were fused into one. In order of appearance the eight *Mariamnes* are (1) the *Mariamne* of unknown authorship not accepted by the Comédie-Française, (2a) the first *Mariamne* of Voltaire (M24), (3) the *Mariamne* of the abbé Nadal, (4) *La Mariane* of Tristan L'Hermite, (2b) the second *Mariamne* or *Hérode et Mariamne* of Voltaire (M25), and (5-8) *Les Quatre Mariamnes* of Fuzelier.

[136] Verèb, *Alexis Piron, passim*, and in particular p.17-131.

promising integrity professed by Mariamne, and her equivocal conduct particularly in regard to Varus. [137]

The *Mercure* of May 1725, in addition to reporting that the first run of the performances of *Hérode et Mariamne* had come to an end on 19 May, also announced that on the same day the Comédiens italiens had given the first performance of 'une petite comédie en vers que le public applaudit, et qu'il va voir avec empressement. C'est une deuxième parodie critique de la nouvelle tragédie de *Mariamne*, intitulée *Le Mauvais Ménage*. Elle a paru fort ingénieuse.' [138] It seems unlikely that this coincidence in timing was due to chance, but we do not have evidence to elucidate the circumstances. The *Quintessence des nouvelles* notes that the parody had been well received, and gives the further information that it had been staged without advance publicity. [139]

In their much later notice on *Le Mauvais Ménage*, Clément and La Porte also record the absence of advance publicity, prompted (they suggest) by a desire to conceal the existence of the parody from Voltaire. [140] Voltaire's justifiable dislike for parodies of his works is well attested, and it is more than probable that had he been alerted to the existence of *Le Mauvais Ménage* he would have taken vigorous measures to suppress it.

[137] A footnote to sc.xxv of *Les Huit Mariamnes* in the *Œuvres complettes* of Piron describes a stratagem allegedly resorted to by Voltaire to curry favour with the *parterre* before the staging of the revised *Mariamne*: 'M. de Voltaire fit faire un compliment au Parterre avant de représenter sa seconde *Mariamne*, et dit qu'il la rendait par un juste respect pour l'empressement du public: on le désavoua tout haut.' This note suggests that Voltaire claimed to be bringing back his play in response to popular demand. Piron's last sentence curtly denies the existence of popular eagerness for the revival of *Mariamne*. There is no other record of this incident, though Mathieu Marais (iii.293-94; see above, p.46) relates that there were calls for Voltaire's *Mariamne* at Nadal's failed premiere. We have not been able to discover any text by Voltaire which could be taken as this 'Compliment au Parterre'.

[138] *Mercure de France*, May 1725, p.1008-1009.

[139] *La Quintessence des nouvelles historiques, politiques, critiques, morales et galantes*, no.44 (31 May 1725).

[140] Clément and La Porte, *Anecdotes dramatiques*, vol.i (1775), p.529. See also D'Origny, *Annales du théâtre italien depuis son origine jusqu'à ce jour* (1788), i.86.

No author is named for the parody. The following month's issue of the *Mercure* contains a six-page *extrait* of the new play,[141] from the opening paragraph of which readers would have readily divined that it was the work of Dominique (Pierre-François Biancolelli) and Marc-Antoine Le Grand, renowned already for their parody *Agnès de Chaillot* of La Motte's *Inès de Castro*. The *Mercure* journalist writes positively about *Le Mauvais Ménage*:

l'auteur a voulu suivre la tragédie de Mariamne pas à pas; jamais parodie n'est entrée plus de plain-pied dans la tragédie qu'elle a voulu tourner en comédie, que celle-ci et celle d'*Agnès de Chaillot*, et jamais deux parodies ne se sont mieux ressemblé que *Agnès de Chaillot* et *Le Mauvais Ménage*; aussi personne ne doute qu'elles ne soient toutes deux parties de la même main.[142]

Le Mauvais Ménage is a parody in the strict sense of the term, in that it takes the components of *Hérode et Mariamne* (plot, characters, situations, language) and subjects them to a systematic process of trivialisation and deflation.[143] As the title suggests, the parody succeeds in turning Voltaire's tragedy into a comical account of the misadventures of a 'mauvais ménage'. Many lines echo the text of Voltaire. They are sometimes quoted verbatim (or with only slight modification) and applied to a context which has

---

[141] *Mercure de France*, June 1725, p.1201-208.

[142] The new parody was published as *Le Mauvais Ménage, parodie, représentée sur le théâtre de l'Hôtel de Bourgogne par les Comédiens italiens ordinaires du Roi* (Paris, Flahaut, 1725). This edition seems to have appeared rapidly, if we may judge from the dates of the *cession* (dated 7 June 1725, registered 15 June) and the *permis d'imprimer* (10 June). An identical edition 'suivant la copie de Paris' was published the following year in Holland (La Haye, J. Néaulme, 1726). The Paris edition is reprinted in *Voltaire jugé par les siens, 1719-1749*, ed. Vercruysse, ii.127-78.

[143] 'Une Ville de Normandie sur le bord de la Mer' replaces Palestine as the scene of the action; stripped of their grandeur, the characters are now low-ranking unsophisticated provincial officials, with, apart from Mariamne, burlesque names; the secret order issued against Mariamne is not for her execution, but for her transportation to the Mississipi; the common language of the parody ridicules the elevated diction of the original; and so on.

lost all the elevation with which it was invested in the tragedy. More often significant changes made to the wording produce a comic effect of deflation.

The plot of the parody follows closely the lines of the action of the tragedy. The authors highlight what they perceived (and were confident audiences would also perceive) as weaknesses or improbabilities in Voltaire's play. Often no explicit criticism is made. Dominique and Le Grand seem then to work on the principle that 'l'action même porte sa critique avec elle'.[144] But on many other occasions they target explicitly identifiable features of the tragedy. The satire seizes on Varus's professions of disinterested love without desire for Mariamne. It evokes mockingly the ambivalences of Mariamne's conduct on receiving this declaration: the *Mercure de France* extrait shows that here the parody struck a responsive chord in audiences.[145] Further on the parody highlights the implausibility, for lack of adequate motivation, of Hérode's brusque change of attitude at the end of act IV, when, on the verge of reconciliation, he reverts to anger and threats. Here too the *Mercure* extrait reveals that spectators saw the pertinence of the satire.[146]

The popularity of *Le Mauvais Ménage* is confirmed by the much later (1769) account of J. Desboulmiers, who adds interesting comment: 'Cette parodie [...] fut très bien reçue, et eut dix-sept représentations. Elle a surtout le mérite d'avoir très bien saisi et très

[144] *Mercure de France*, June 1725, p.1205.

[145] 'On a trouvé que cette critique ne porte tout au plus que sur la bonté avec laquelle Mariamne dans la tragédie pardonne à Varus la témerité d'une déclaration d'amour, à une reine et à une reine mariée; ce que tout le monde a jugé peu digne de la majesté de la tragédie, et qu'on ne passerait pas même dans une comédie, tant le théâtre est épuré' (p.1205).

[146] 'C'est ici l'endroit de la tragédie qui a paru le mieux critiqué [...] Tout le monde a trouvé ce trait de critique très sensé. On avoit d'abord senti dans la tragédie le brusque de cette fin de scène, et peut-être n'avait-on pas d'abord approfondi la cause de cette impression générale. La parodie l'a mise en un plus grand jour, et il n'y a personne qui ne sente que le retour n'est déraisonnable que parce qu'il manque de nouveau motif' (p.1207).

agréablement critiqué les défauts de la tragédie; l'endroit surtout où Barbarin [i.e., Hérode], après avoir pardonné à sa femme, s'emporte contre elle au même instant sans en avoir de nouveaux sujets, est très judicieux: elle ne fit que confirmer l'opinion du Public, qui dès la première représentation de la tragédie, avait fort bien senti combien ce retour d'emportement était ridicule'. [147]

In addition to recording the end of the first run of performances of *Hérode et Mariamne* on 19 May and the première of *Le Mauvais Ménage* at the Comédie-Italienne on the same day, the *Mercure* of May 1725 carried an announcement (p.1009) that the Comédiens français were also to stage a parody of the tragedy. The *Registres* of the Comédie confirm that the company had resolved on the selfsame day of 19 May to accept a parody of *Hérode et Mariamne* entitled *Marie Torne* for performance at the earliest possible date. [148] The June issue of the *Mercure*, however, after the *extrait* of *Le Mauvais Ménage*, announced the cancellation of this project: 'Les Comédiens français ne joueront pas la parodie de *Mariamne*, qu'ils avaient commencé d'apprendre. L'auteur n'ayant pas jugé à propos que cette pièce parût.' [149] It would appear therefore that, even though the actors had begun to learn their roles, Voltaire's opposition ensured that this parody of *Hérode et Mariamne* was never performed. Writing in 1769, Desboulmiers attributes the decision to the actors themselves, daunted by 'le prodigieux succès' of *Le Mauvais Ménage*. [150] He also reports a claim that Voltaire

---

[147] Desboulmiers, *op. cit.*, p.377. D'Origny expresses a similar view (*op. cit.*, p.86).

[148] Archives de la Comédie-Française, *Registres*, R52G, p.8v: 'Aujourd'hui vendredi 19e mai 1725 la troupe s'est assemblée pour entendre la lecture d'une pièce intitulée Marie Torne ou la Parodie de Mariamne et les présents a la dite assemblée ont sign[é] pour la recevoir et être jouée le plutôt que faire se pourra.' The signatures of sixteen actors are appended. On this parody see also Monval, *Lettres d'Adrienne Lecouvreur*, p.30. It has not survived.

[149] *Mercure de France*, June 1725, p.1208.

[150] See Desboulmiers, *Histoire du Théâtre Italien*, vol.ii (1769), p.377-78: 'Les Comédiens français avaient aussi appris une parodie de la tragédie de Marianne; mais ils ne jugèrent pas à propos de la jouer, lorsqu'ils virent le prodigieux succès de celle-ci [*Le Mauvais Ménage*]'. Cf. Clément et La Porte, *Anecdotes dramatiques*,

himself was the author of this unperformed parody, and that in it he had not dealt harshly with his tragedy: 'On prétend [que la parodie] avait été faite par M. de Voltaire lui-même, qui, selon toute apparence, s'était ménagé, ce qui est assez naturel; lorsque l'on se châtie, on frappe à côté.' D'Origny makes a similar assertion.[151] Although these late texts do not warrant complete confidence, we cannot exclude the possibility that Voltaire might have adopted a strategy similar to that which he had pursued in 1719 concerning Œdipe. It will be remembered that then, in order to disarm criticism of his arrogance in seeking to rival Sophocles and Corneille, Voltaire appended to the first editions of his tragedy a series of Lettres sur Œdipe,[152] in which he undertook to examine with equal impartiality the three Œdipus plays (those of Sophocles and Corneille, and his own), and to be no less severe in his judgements on himself than on his illustrious predecessors. Although he proved in the event rather more indulgent towards the 'défauts' which he acknowledged in his own Œdipe than towards those which he discovered in the other plays, he may have calculated that a display of humility would win him public approval. It is possible that a similar motive may have inspired him to write his own parody of Hérode et Mariamne as a vehicle for mild criticism, all the more tolerable in as much as it originated from himself.

b) Other satirical and critical writings

After Les Huit Mariamnes and Le Mauvais Ménage, Hérode et Mariamne received further satirical treatment in Momus, Censeur des Théâtres, a one-act play by Jacques Bailly, first performed at the Théâtre de l'Opéra Comique on 6 June 1725.[153] In this work

---

i.529-30: 'Les Comédiens français avaient appris une parodie de Mariamne, mais ils ne jugèrent pas à propos de la jouer, quand ils virent le prodigieux succès de celle-ci.'

[151] Annales du Théâtre Italien, i.86.

[152] OC, vol.1A, p.285-385.

[153] Momus, censeur des théâtres was published in Bailly, Théâtres et Œuvres mêlées par M. Bailly (Paris, Nyon, 1768), i.63-112.

Momus, 'Dieu de la Satyre', has a conversation with 'La Comédie française', in which the latter confesses that she has had a poor season, and that, had it not been for *Mariamne*, the public would have abandoned her altogether: 'si je ne me fusse avisée de rhabiller Marianne de pied en cap, [le public] m'auroit laissée tout-à-fait là'. The revised *Mariamne* that Paris will now be able to see is 'plus brillante et plus gentille'. But her success is not due to her merits alone. It would not have been achieved without the support of a 'brigue' of Voltaire's supporters. Furthermore *Mariamne* has thrived on stolen beauties: 'Le public ne doit qu'au larcin / Ses beautés, ses délicatesses. / Ainsi qu'un habit d'Arlequin, / Elle est faite de toutes pièces'. Finally there is the fact that 'pour empêcher le trouble' admission prices were not doubled for the première of the renewed *Mariamne*.

The insinuation that the means by which Voltaire secured success for Mariamne were somehow illegitimate does not stand up to scrutiny. The *Extrait du Mercure* alone establishes that the enthusiastic response of audiences was prompted by what they perceived to be the genuine merits of the play.

At this early stage in its history *Hérode et Mariamne* attracted fierce criticism from two writers who had little sympathy for Voltaire. The first was J.-B. Rousseau, who in a letter of 11 August 1725 (D245)[154] attacked the play in language which in places becomes abusive. Rousseau, exiled in Brussels, did not attend any of the early (or for that matter later) performances of *Hérode et Mariamne*. His knowledge of the play must have derived from one of two editions printed without Voltaire's authorisation in 1725. If we strip away the personal animosity which fills this letter, it becomes possible to discern the main lines of Rousseau's objections. M25 in his opinion was not an improvement on M24: for all Voltaire's efforts to give the play a second birth, the revised version was no more 'régulière': the structure was disjointed, the

[154] Besterman's notes show that this letter was not published until 1749, but it was no doubt circulated widely at the time by its recipient (Laserré).

action hasty and implausible. Rousseau dismisses each of the characters with a quick disparaging description. [155] His principal attention is devoted to the conduct of the action. He criticises Mariamne's tardiness in carrying out her decision to flee, and has caustic words for Voltaire's handling of the first entrance of Hérode, and also for the bizarre behaviour attributed to Varus on Hérode's arrival. His main onslaught is reserved for the ending of the play, in particular the haste with which Mariamne is put to death: the scaffold which had just been torn down is re-erected and the end of Mariamne consummated, according to Rousseau, all within the space of twelve lines. After denouncing 'cette surpre- nante catastrophe', Rousseau turns to the portrayal of Hérode's final madness, alleging that the bereaved king's 'fureurs', which had been 'si animées et si touchantes' in Tristan's play, receive only the most perfunctory of presentations in Voltaire. [156]

Later in 1725 the abbé Nadal published his *Observations critiques sur la tragédie d'Hérode et Mariamne de M. de V****. [157] The *approbation* and *privilège* show that this 36-page tract cannot have been published before early September. [158]

---

[155] Mariamne is 'une idole froide et insipide', Varus 'un étourdi, qui prend aussi mal ses mesures sur le Jourdain que sur le Danube', Hérode 'la plus grande dupe et le plus imbécile personnage de la troupe'.

[156] Some eleven years later Rousseau published a long letter in the *Bibliothèque française* (printed by Besterman as D1078; May 1736) purporting to give a 'récit abrégé' of the history of his relations with Voltaire since their first meeting. Rousseau claims to have received a reply to his earlier letter: 'Je ne sais comment ma lettre vint à sa connaissance, mais elle m'en attira bientôt une autre anonyme et d'une écriture contrefaite où j'étais accommodé de toutes pièces, à laquelle je me contentai de répondre en huit lignes.' A different version of D1078 quoted by Besterman (D245n) attributes this reply specifically to Voltaire. No trace of it has been found. Besterman is sceptical of its existence, though he does not exclude the possibility that a subsequent letter from Rousseau (D248), which contains a scathing attack upon Voltaire as a blasphemer, may have been a riposte to such a reply.

[157] Paris, veuve de Pierre Ribou, 1725. Reprinted in Vercruysse, *Les Voltairiens*, 2ème série, ii.179-216.

[158] The *approbation* by Fontenelle is dated 12 August; the *privilège* granted on 2 September was registered on 9 September.

Although by then Voltaire's first authorised edition of the play (25P) had just appeared, [159] Nadal claims that he is dealing with 'une tragédie qui n'a point été encore imprimée' (p.36), well known nevertheless because it had been much performed and much discussed. The text which he discusses and quotes liberally is that of the first performances, that early state not identical with 25P, which is preserved in MS1 and in the unauthorised editions 25CH, 25X and 26H.

The *Observations critiques* present a lengthy and detailed examination of Voltaire's tragedy. Although Nadal claims in his introductory paragraph that his concern is with 'l'exposition seule des incidents qui la composent' and 'leur liaison entre eux', his criticisms tend to take on an inappropriate personal note directed with a measure of venom against Voltaire: [160] doubtless Nadal was still smarting from the rude treatment he had received at the hands of Voltaire in the latter's *Lettre de Mr Tiriot à M^r l'abbé Nadal*. [161] Praise for Voltaire is rare indeed. Nadal works his way minutely through the play, finding numerous implausibilities, inconsistencies and contradictions in the structuring of the plot and the presentation of situations.

Much of the content of the *Observations critiques* is no more than petty point scoring. From time to time, however, criticisms bear on matters of greater substance. He points out for example the ignorance in which the spectator is left regarding the reasons for Mariamne's condemnation: we are never told the nature of her crime (p.6). And how likely is it that Hérode's first action, after being spared by Augustus, would be to order her execution (p.7)? Nadal criticises the similarity, already noted by other commenta-

[159] 25P is first mentioned in D246, dated 20 August. This letter shows Voltaire actively engaged in distributing copies to his friends in Normandy.

[160] For instance the introductory paragraph, where Nadal comments sarcastically that *Hérode et Mariamne* was 'une pièce qui a fait beaucoup de bruit d'abord, et qui a semblé à quelques-uns mettre son auteur au-dessus de lui-même; ce qui a été pour M. de V*** le plus flatteur de tous les éloges'.

[161] Reproduced below, Appendix E.

tors, of the catastrophes which conclude acts III and IV, and reproaches Voltaire for bringing both about by the same device, namely dramatic interventions by Mazaël with alarming news for Hérode (p.21). In spite of the scorn which he sheds on Nadal in the *Lettre de Mr Tiriot à M^r l'abbé Nadal*, Voltaire may have been sensitive to this reproach, and may have sought to remove the grounds for criticism, when he later transferred the speech at IV.210-14, given to Mazaël in the text of the early performances, to a 'garde' introduced specifically for this purpose, and whose only function in the play is to speak these five lines.

Nadal finds fault, as do the *Mercure* review and the parodies, with the speed of Hérode's change of heart at the end of act IV: '[il] rentre tout à coup dans ses premières fureurs, et ne laisse aucun intervalle entre des mouvements aussi opposes' (p.21).

In several places Nadal accuses Voltaire of a lack of respect for the dignity of the tragic stage, in particular for the dignity which should surround the comportment of tragic characters. The Roman governor Varus especially offended Nadal in this regard. He objects to Varus's scorn for futile ceremonial, expressed in act III scene iii, and this reproach leads him to criticise severely one of the most important changes made by Voltaire when refashioning M24 into M25 (p.16):

Ce sentiment de Varus [...] ne peut être regardé que comme un faux-fuyant dont l'auteur se sert pour ne point faire paraître ensemble sur la scène Hérode et Varus, ce qui est une faute essentielle dans sa pièce, et qu'il ne saurait justifier, tant par l'importance et la dignité des Personnages que par la subordination établie des rois aux Romains, et est-il vraisemblable que Varus soit dans le palais d'Hérode, sans qu'il ait aucune entrevue ni entretien avec lui?

Voltaire devotes a significant paragraph of the Préface to 25P to defending the elimination of an on-stage encounter between Hérode and Varus. It is possible that his defence of this change was prompted by Nadal's remarks. For, although the publication of the *Observations critiques* was subsequent (albeit by a small

interval) to the first recorded references to 25P in D246, dated 20
August 1725, Nadal's tract must have been in existence for some
time before 12 August 1725 (the date of the *approbation* signed by
Fontenelle), and Voltaire may have been aware of its contents
when he was writing the Préface to 25P.

As for Mariamne, Nadal rejoins the parodists in considering
that her reply to Varus's declaration of love (II.v) lowers her
dignity: 'Je ne sais après tout s'il n'y a point un peu d'art dans la
réplique de Mariamne, et si sa sortie n'est point celle d'une
coquette' (p.15).

Nadal has several suggestions for the improvement of the play.
For instance, the mother of Mariamne, instead of having her
terrors and anguish reported by Mariammne (II.153-60), could
appear on stage to speak for herself in this crisis. Or perhaps it
might be 'plus raisonnable' to suppose her dead, in which case her
ghost could appear to Mariamne 'dans l'horreur de la nuit' (p.12)
and urge her to flee. Another suggestion is that Hérode's interview
with Mariamne on his return from Rome (reported at III.154-64),
should have taken place on stage (p.15).

Discussing the conclusion of the play, Nadal gives credit to
Voltaire for condensing the distraught ravings of Hérode at the
end of Tristan's *La Mariane*, but, Nadal continues, 'il est fâcheux
pour nous, qu'il ait négligé de faire usage de ces grands traits
prophétiques, qui terminent la pièce de ce poète célèbre' (p.24).
These 'grands traits prophétiques' are contained in Hérode's
major speech of act V scene ii of Tristan's tragedy, in which the
king in a frenzy of grief, after finding no response to his appeal to
his people to avenge the death of Mariamne by killing him, calls
down destruction upon the entire Jewish nation: may the Temple
be razed, may the Jews be dispossessed of their lands and dispersed
to the ends of the earth. Nothing reminiscent of the 'grands traits
prophétiques' of Tristan is to be found in the version of Voltaire's
Hérode et Mariamne which was produced in the first run of
performances in 1725, and of which we find a record in MS1,
25CH, 25X and 26H. In that text Hérode limits himself to calling

down destruction upon his own head. However Hérode's final speech in 25P contains a more generalised appeal for destruction and ruin, whose content closely echoes Tristan's 'grands traits prophétiques'. We find the same call for the destruction of the Temple and for the dispersal of the Jews, the same curses pronounced upon the nation of Israel. Were these changes prompted by Nadal's remark? The possibility cannot be excluded: we have just seen that though 25P was already in print before the appearance of the *Observations critiques*, Voltaire may have had some pre-publication knowledge of its contents.[162]

A further section (p.26ff.) contains Nadal's 'Réflexions sur le caractère des personages', all of whom are vigorously denounced: Varus is wanting in prudence and dignity, Hérode in self-control, Mariamne in restraint. Other general comments reproach Voltaire for infidelity to the writings of Josephus, and for excessive borrowings from Racine.

Nadal's final criticism in this section is directed at 'la négligence que [Voltaire] affecte pour la rime'. Only one precise example is cited: 'Quel est le Poëte, à l'exception de M. de V...., qui jusqu'ici ait fait rimer *enfin* avec *Asmonéen*' (p.28). The verses containing this rhyme appear in MS1, 25CH, 25X and 26H. They were replaced in 25P[163] and no doubt in all performances subsequent to the first run.

The concluding pages of Nadal's tract are occupied by *Remarques sur Quelques Vers*. This section contains some 30 short passages quoted with comments. They give the early text (MS1, 25CH, 25X, 26H) in cases where that differs from the later authorised text (25P and succeeding editions). Many of Nadal's remarks address petty points of detail; those of interest have been recorded in the notes to the text.[164] It is noteworthy that, in addition to the lines at I.126-30 discussed two paragraphs above, in

---

[162] See variants at V.229-42a.
[163] See I.126-30 and variants.
[164] See notes at I.28, 302; II.110, 215; V.37-38.

several further cases passages criticised by Nadal appear in an amended form in 25P. This fact lends support to the hypothesis that Voltaire had some sort of notice of Nadal's objections prior to the publication of the *Observations* and took them into account when retouching *Hérode et Mariamne* for the subsequent performances of 1725 and for publication.[165]

There is grudging recognition of Voltaire's skills in versification, but the *Observations* end on a rancorous note with the suggestion that *Hérode et Mariamne* will not withstand the test of time.

iii. *Further performances in 1725-1726*

Although the *Mercure* had announced in May 1725 that *Hérode et Mariamne* would not be staged again until the following winter, a further six performances took place in August 1725, in support of the initial stagings of *L'Indiscret*, Voltaire's first attempt in the comic genre. On these occasions a performance of *Hérode et Mariamne* preceded the one-act comedy. That a confident, if not ebullient, Voltaire had a large part in instigating this double billing seems to be implied by his remark to Thiriot in a letter from the beginning of the month: 'Je sors dans le moment pour faire jouer [*Hérode et Mariamne*], et pour la faire imprimer. J'ai un procès, un poème épique, une tragédie et une comédie sur les bras. Si j'ai de la santé je soutiendrai tous ces fardeaux gaiement. Si je n'en ai point que tout aille au diable' (D244, c.1 August).

The two plays were first given together on 18 August, and then on 20, 22, 24, 25 and 26 August.[166] Although the season was brief, the double bill attracted large attendances: 1362 paying spectators are recorded for the first performance, which was the première of

---

[165] See variants and notes at II.153-54; III.99; IV.203-204.

[166] Lancaster, *The Comédie-Française 1701-1774*, p.684. For all six performances the title of the play is given in the *Registres* as *Hérode et Mariamne*.

L'Indiscret. This was an excellent house, and may have been as much due to the novelty of the comedy as to the established reputation of the tragedy. Audience figures for the following performances, though on two occasions exceeding 900, averaged around 600. [167] Voltaire received the author's share of the receipts for the tragedy as well as for the comedy. [168] A brief notice in the August *Mercure* (p.1860) reported that both plays had been well received, and that *Hérode et Mariamne* had been performed 'avec quelques changements'. It seems reasonable to suppose that with these revisions the text of the play had now attained the form in which it was shortly to appear in the first edition to be authorised by Voltaire (25P).

The following month saw a further combined performance of the two plays before the court at Fontainebleau on 27 September, as part of the celebrations which followed the wedding of Louis XV and Marie Leszczynska on 5 September. [169] Voltaire was at this time resident at Fontainebleau in an apartment provided by Mme de Prie, mistress of the duc de Bourbon, the king's first minister, and in which he was able to stay for over two months. [170] René Pomeau has shown how Voltaire sought to use this lengthy sojourn at court to advance his financial and social situation. [171] In these efforts his plays became important strategic arms. Although he was particularly anxious to secure the favour of the new queen and especially to obtain her approval for performances of *Œdipe* and *Hérode et Mariamne*, the correspon-

[167] The exact figures are as follows: 20 August: 941 spectators; 22 August: 679 spectators; 24 August: 952 spectators; 25 August: 612 spectators; 26 August: 593 spectators.

[168] Lancaster, *The Comédie-Française*, p.686.

[169] This performance was noted without further comment in the *Mercure*, September 1725, p.2291.

[170] Voltaire may have gone to Fontainebleau as early as the last week in August, for he writes to Thiriot on 24 or 25 August: 'Je pars dans deux jours pour Fontainebleau' (D247). His last letter from Fontainebleau is dated 13 November (D255).

[171] Pomeau, *Voltaire en son temps*, i.148-49.

dence shows him biding his time before seeking to approach her. On 7 September he writes to Mme de Bernières (D249):

Au reste c'est ici un bruit, un fracas, une presse, un tumulte épouvantable. Je me garderai bien dans ces premiers jours de confusion de me faire présenter à la reine. J'attendrai que la foule soit écoulée et que sa majesté soit un peu revenue de l'étourdissement que tout ce sabbat doit lui causer. Alors je tâcherai de faire jouer Œdipe et Mariamne devant elle.

In the same letter he tells Mme de Bernières of his intention to dedicate both plays to the queen, and that she had already given her permission for him to do so. This was a first indication of royal favour. The graceful dedicatory letter subsequently written by Voltaire is found in only one of the eleven copies known to us of the first authorised edition of *Hérode et Mariamne* (25P). It may seem inappropriate, he writes, to dedicate this work to a queen 'qui fait le bonheur de son époux'. But his play is 'l'éloge de la vertu': that is what moves him to present it to the queen, who will find in it 'des sentimens de grandeur sans orgueil, de modestie sans affectation, de générosité et de bienséance'.[172]

Voltaire's tactical patience proved successful, and performances of both plays were given at Fontainebleau before the end of September, *Œdipe* on 20 September, and *Hérode et Mariamne*, followed by *L'Indiscret*, on the 27th.[173] There is no reference to these performances in Voltaire's correspondence before 17 October, when they are noted in a letter to Mme de Bernières (D252). A letter written to Thiriot the same day gives the queen's reactions: 'J'ai été ici très bien reçu de la reine, elle a pleuré à Mariamne, elle a ri à l'indiscret, elle me parle souvent, elle m'appelle mon pauvre Voltaire.'[174] Voltaire makes it plain that, however pleasing these

[172] The full text of the dedication to the queen is reproduced under the bibliographical description of 25P.

[173] *Mercure*, September 1725, p.2291.

[174] D253. It would appear that Thiriot had not been entirely happy with *Hérode et Mariamne*, for Voltaire refers to his friend's 'critiques' of the play. Cf. his letter of 13 November (D255), where he describes Thiriot as appearing 'dégoûté [...] de Mariamne'. We do not know the nature of Thiriot's criticisms.

expressions of approval may have been, they did not satisfy his essential need for an established position and material security.[175]

On 1 October, just a few days after the performance of *Hérode et Mariamne*, the Comédiens italiens put on a production of *Le Mauvais Ménage* before the king and queen at Fontainebleau.[176] Voltaire's reaction to this event is not recorded, though we might surmise that a performance of the parody before so august an audience was not to his liking.

As had been anticipated in the *Mercure* notice of May, the Comédie-Française gave further performances of *Hérode et Mariamne* the following winter. Previously in August, just before the second series of performances had begun, Voltaire had signed an agreement with the actors that they would give four performances of *Hérode et Mariamne* after their return from Fontainebleau, after which he would cede to them his interests in the play.[177] Although the actors who had gone to Fontainebleau were back in Paris by 26 November,[178] further performances of *Hérode et Mariamne* did not begin until late in December, when the play was staged five times between 27 December 1725 and 6 January 1726. At the first of these performances *Hérode et Mariamne* was followed by *Les Précieuses ridicules*, and an excellent attendance of 1177 paying spectators was recorded. Audiences for the following performances dwindled sharply (648, 476, 280 spectators). The last performance, on 6 January,

[175] Nevertheless Voltaire was able to report to Mme de Bernières before he left Fontainebleau, that the queen had granted him a pension of 1500 *livres* (D255, 13 November 1725).

[176] *Mercure*, October 1725, p.2493.

[177] This agreement is an addendum to the record of the meeting of actors held on 15 August 1725 which attracted an attendance of more than twenty members (Archives de la Comédie-Française, *Registres*, R52G, p.24). It reads as follows: 'Monsieur de Voltaire a demandé qu'après la reprise de Mariamne qui sera jouée jeudi prochain la troupe lui en donne quatre représentations aussi tôt que la ditte troupe sera de retour de Fontainebleau, après lesquelles représentations Mr de Voltaire abandonne la ditte tragédie à la troupe.' The signatures of Voltaire and four actors (the two La Thorillière, Duchemin and Armand) are appended to this text.

[178] Lancaster, *The Comédie-Française*, p.686.

at which *L'Indiscret* was again coupled with *Hérode et Mariamne*, saw the paying audience numbers rebound a little to 592.[179] It is hard to avoid the conclusion that all those interested in the play had by now seen it, and the potential public for *Hérode et Mariamne* had been exhausted.

Nevertheless the success of the revised *Hérode et Mariamne* in 1725-1726 cannot be regarded as other than remarkable. In the season of its creation it had achieved, in all twenty-eight performances at the Comédie, a total comparable with the success of *Œdipe*, staged thirty times in its first season.[180] The performances of *Hérode et Mariamne* had been spread over eight months, forming three distinct runs separated by considerable intervals when the play was not put on. They had not followed hard upon one another in the sort of unbroken sequence that had made *Œdipe* such an extraordinary success for Voltaire. Nevertheless this figure speaks for itself. Henri Lagrave has established that in the period 1715-1750 only seven other plays (three of them by Voltaire) received more performances in their first season. In Lagrave's opinion thirty performances would have been the mark of a 'triomphe'.[181] Although *Hérode et Mariamne* fell just short of this mark, and below the record forty-two performances achieved by La Motte's *Inès de Castro* in 1723-1724, it clearly exceeded the minimum of twenty performances required for a 'franc succès'. But Lagrave does not consider it inappropriate to regard *Hérode et Mariamne* as a 'triomphe exceptionnel', for he calculates that during the same period (1715 to 1750) this play is one of only six to have achieved more than 23,000 admissions in the season of its creation. In this élite *Hérode et Mariamne* holds fourth place, and is

---

[179] See Lancaster, *The Comédie-Française*, p.685. The title of the play is given in the *Registres* as *Hérode et Mariamne* for the first and last of this series of performances (27 December and 6 January), and as *Mariamne* for those of the intermediate days (31 December, 2 and 4 January).

[180] Established by Jory, *OC*, vol.1A, p.90.

[181] Henri Lagrave, *Le Théâtre et le public à Paris de 1715 à 1750* (Paris 1992), p.585.

exceeded only (in ascending order) by Voltaire's *Œdipe* and *Zaïre* and by La Motte's *Inès*. [182]

iv. *Publication*

The first editions of *Hérode et Mariamne* were published without Voltaire's authorisation. It is impossible to determine exactly when they first began to appear, but Voltaire was aware of them by late July 1725, and his letters at this time to Mme de Bernières (D243, 23 July) and to Thiriot (D244, *c.*1 August) attest the anger which they roused in him. The correspondence refers to three unauthorised editions of *Hérode et Mariamne*. The first is mentioned in D243, where Voltaire declares that a copy has come into his hands, and condemns it as 'pleine de fautes grossières et de vers qui ne sont pas de moi. J'en suis dans une colère de père qui voit ses enfants maltraités.' He saw a need for prompt counter measures. Suspecting that this book had been produced in Rouen, he sent instructions to Thiriot in the same letter to track down the publisher so that legal pursuit could be initiated. He writes also that the appearance of this publication now made it urgent for him to bring out an authentic edition, even though he considered that the moment was not appropriate, for so many poets were seeking just then to claim the attention of the public: 'Et cela m'oblige de faire imprimer ma Mariamne plus tôt que je ne l'avais résolu et dans un temps très peu favorable. Il pleut des vers à Paris.' In illustration of this poetic over-production Voltaire cites the *Œdipe* of La Motte, the comedies of Fontenelle, and the epic poems of 'tout le monde'.

A week later Voltaire returns to the question of publication (D244):

Voilà encore une autre édition de Mariamne qui paraît d'hier et une troisième dont on me menace. [183] Vous voyez que l'honneur qu'on a fait à

---

[182] Lagrave, *Le Théâtre et le public à Paris*, p.191.
[183] Cf. D246 (to Mme de Bernières, 20 August), where Voltaire alludes to 'trois éditions subreptices' of *Hérode et Mariamne*.

la Motte d'écrire son Inès pendant les représentations n'est pas un honneur si singulier qu'il le prétend. Je ne sais à cela que de donner ma pièce et d'y corriger le plus de choses que je pourrai, afin que l'air de la nouveauté soit joint à la correction dont elle avait besoin.

He goes on to consider himself 'assassiné d'éditions de tous les côtés', and promises to send Thiriot a copy of *Mariamne* as soon as the play is printed. The existence of these unauthorised editions, based, it would seem from Voltaire's words, on transcriptions made during performances, is evidence of the intense interest generated by *Hérode et Mariamne* and the great success which it had achieved. Voltaire refers again to these transcriptions in the opening sentence of the Preface to 25P. That publishers should resort to the expedient of using copyists to secure the text of a dramatic work, and that they should bring out pirated editions based on that text so quickly after the first performances, were signs that in their estimation the play could count on immense public favour and could appeal to a wide market. Only a small number of plays was honoured in this way.

Voltaire now made use of the rights conferred on him by the *privilège* which he had obtained for the publication of *Mariamne* the previous year, but had not exploited at that time. Fabrication of the first authorised edition of *Hérode et Mariamne* was achieved without delay, and Voltaire was able to write to Mme de Bernières on 20 August (D246): 'Mariamne est enfin imprimée de ma façon.' In a letter a few days later to Thiriot (D247, dated 24 or 25 August) he reveals that he himself had met the entire costs of the printing: 'J'ai été obligé de faire imprimer Mariamne à mes dépens. Il a fallu rompre le marché que j'avais fait avec les libraires, parceque les éditions contrefaites leur coupaient la gorge. Ainsi je me la suis coupée moi même par bonté et j'ai fait tous les frais.' No precise information about the costs met by Voltaire has come down to us, but his throat-cutting image suggests that these were not inconsiderable.

This edition was 25P, bearing the imprint of Pissot and Flahaut, printed by Louis Sevestre. [184] On 25 August Voltaire gave instructions for the delivery of 1000 copies to Pissot, and received from him a promissory note for 1250 *livres*, to secure payment of which he was obliged four years later to take Pissot's widow to court. [185]

The appearance of 25P was mentioned in the 'Nouvelles littéraires' section of the *Mercure* of September 1725 (p.2027-28), in a brief notice informing readers that this was a corrected version of the play, with the addition at the end of certain lines, quoted in full, which are the revised text of Hérode's final speech (act V, lines 229-42).

On 20 August (D246) Voltaire had told Mme de Bernières that he was sending her a parcel of copies, a bound one for herself, others unbound intended for his Rouen friends (Cideville, Brèvedent and others) and, at her discretion, for such other persons as she would like to see well disposed towards him. Other letters enable us to identify further recipients of presentation copies. Foremost among them was Marie Leszczynska, to whom Voltaire wrote a 15-line *Epitre* of lavish compliment. [186] A copy was sent to Mme de Villette (now Lady Bolingbroke) in England to be forwarded to Henrietta Howard for eventual presentation to Caroline of Ansbach, princess of Wales (D251, October 1725). Voltaire had by now formed the project of a visit to England and no doubt wished to draw himself to the attention of the princess and her circle as possible sources of support. [187] One

---

[184] Foulet has shown that Voltaire procured the paper for 25P from Coulange 'marchand papetier à Paris', and hazards an estimate of its cost at 325 *livres*: *La Correspondance de Voltaire*, p.283n.

[185] The affair of the promissory notes issued by Pissot is recounted in detail in Foulet, *La Correspondance de Voltaire*, appendix 8: 'Voltaire devant les juges-consuls'. Foulet judges that Voltaire probably achieved satisfaction in regard to *Hérode et Mariamne*. For this affair see also Voltaire's letters to Thiriot of 1, 3 and 5 July 1729 (D361, D362 and D363), and the accounts of Jacques Donvez, *De quoi vivait Voltaire?* (Paris 1949), p.37-38, and P. M. Conlon, *Voltaire's literary career*, *SVEC* 14 (1961), p.54.

[186] *Epitre à la Reine, en lui envoyant la tragédie de Mariamne*, M.x.259.

[187] See *OC*, vol.3B, p.128.

unlikely recipient was the abbé Couet, *grand vicaire* of the cardinal de Noailles, archbishop of Paris. [188] Voltaire probably also sent a copy at about the same time to Isaac Cambiague, former representative of the Republic of Geneva in France, along with a letter of compliments in which he sounds out the possibility of publishing *La Henriade* in Geneva. [189]

In 25P Voltaire introduces the text of the play with an important Préface in which he seeks to win over the goodwill of his readers before they tackle the work itself. The Préface treats three principal subjects. First Voltaire reviews the history of his play, received with such hostility in 1724, yet acclaimed in its revised form a year later, and explores the reasons for the failure of the first *Mariamne* and the success of the subsequent version. In the second section he declares the hesitations with which he approaches the publication of *Hérode et Mariamne*, for he is fully aware that for any play success on the stage does not guarantee that the published text will be well received. He cites the example of the *Phèdre* plays of Racine and Pradon: both had been successful in performance, but publication had revealed the distance separating them. The third main part is devoted to rebutting the criticism that the subject of *Hérode et Mariamne* is nothing more than the domestic difficulties of the two principals and as such does not constitute a theme for tragedy. Citing examples from Racine and Molière,

[188] This was in response to the gift which Couet had made to Voltaire of a copy of the Cardinal's *mandement* concerning the miraculous cure allegedly obtained by a certain Mme La Fosse, the wife of an ebonist of the Faubourg Saint-Antoine. R. Pomeau has given a detailed account of the circumstances leading to this exchange, which Voltaire used to declare his rejection of the claimed miracle. His incredulity is manifest in the mocking lines with which he accompanied his gift:

> Vous m'envoyez un mandement,
> Recevez une tragédie
> Et qu'ainsi mutuellement
> Nous nous donnions la comédie.

See Pomeau, *Voltaire en son temps*, i.154-55; also D246.

[189] D259, for which Besterman's suggested date is '*c*.December 1725'. But, with Pomeau, we prefer J.-M. Raynaud's conjecture of August 1725; see Pomeau, *Voltaire en son temps*, i.156 and note.

Voltaire argues that the same domestic situation can equally become the subject of a tragedy or of a comedy.

The Préface to *Hérode et Mariamne* is a substantial text, showing Voltaire at his persuasive best. It earned the praise of Matthieu Marais, a discerning commentator, who wrote to the président Bouhier in December 1725: 'J'ai lu la Préface de *Mariamne* et l'ai admirée comme vous: cela est digne des plus grands maîtres, et marque un beau génie, à qui tout est facile, prose, vers, etc.'[190]

The protest and disavowal which a robust Voltaire directs at the earlier unauthorised editions are worthy of some examination. His claim that his play is 'entièrement méconnaissable' as it appears in these 'trois mauvaises éditions' is a wild exaggeration. His further claims are that these early editions were defective copies, and that they had been brought out before the author had given his final touches to the work. Voltaire seems to be suggesting that in publishing this authenticated edition he is seeking on the one hand to correct the errors made by those who had mistranscribed his play during performances, and on the other hand to produce a definitive version of the text revised and retouched where necessary. In most cases where there is a divergence between the unauthorised editions and 25P, it seems to us that the material introduced in the latter edition derives from the second concern: we see the hand of Voltaire self-improving and enhancing his text, rather than correcting errors made by others.[191]

Voltaire had complained (D243) that the pirated edition which had come to his notice was full not only of gross errors but also of lines not composed by him. We might expect therefore that such inauthentic lines would have been removed by Voltaire when

---

[190] Marais, *Mémoires*, iii.379 (letter 42, 15 December 1725).

[191] There are some cases where 25P corrects evident blunders in the earlier editions which were probably not due to Voltaire: for examples see critical apparatus at I.303 (omitted line destroys couplet); III.230 (ditto); IV.103 (first hemistich absent); V.26 (omitted verse destroys couplet); V.117-18 (omitted couplet leaves four successive verses with feminine rhymes).

preparing 25P, and that there would have been a multitude of them. In fact the number of lines removed (and replaced by new lines) is quite low; 11 in act I, 10 in act II, 9 in act III, 8 in act IV and none in act V. [192] In many, if not most, cases the replacement lines give an improved version of the text: the 25P reading is better either stylistically or in expression, or sharper in relevance to the situation of a character or to the momentum of the action. A similar conclusion could be drawn from a detailed examination of the many instances (too numerous to list individually) where just a word or short phrase is changed in 25P.

The authorised edition also contains a significant number of longer passages which do not appear in the early editions. [193] Some of them are simple insertions; others replace a small number of lines with a larger number of new lines. In all, 85 lines appear for the first time in 25P; to make way for them 15 lines are sacrificed, leaving a net increase of 70, an appreciable augmentation in a play numbering in all 1424 lines. Yet the importance of the additions far outweighs their quantitative measurement. Each of them occurs at a critical point in the development of the tragedy and heightens the dramatic interest or enhances the dramatic tension in some way.

The first, which occurs at I.83-104 in the long opening scene, is devoted to Salome's account of the 'victoire' and the 'vengeance' which she has secured over Mariamne in obtaining Hérode's order for the execution of the queen. The twenty-two lines introduced at this point give a forceful presentation to Salome's bitter hatred of Mariamne, whom she regards as having defeated her repeated intriguing through her power over Hérode. The eight lines inserted at I.231-38 give additional emphasis to Varus's assertion to Albin of the purity of his motives in going to the defence of

[192] See variants at I.13-14, 126-30, 189-90, 193-94; II.126c-28, 153-54, 223-26; III.25-26, 45-48, 85-87; IV.162-70.

[193] See variants at I.83-104 (where 22 lines in 25P replace 2 in the earlier version), 231-38 (8 new lines); II.137-40 (4 new lines); III.7-21 (15 new lines), 121-32 (12 new lines), 225-26 (2 new lines); IV.51-58 (8 new lines replace 4); V.117-18 (2 new lines), 229-42a (14 new lines replace 6).

Mariamne. Critics and parodists had doubted the plausibility of this sentiment.

The next addition occurs at II.137-40, where in four inserted lines Elize describes the terrible power with which Hérode is now armed, and which he has obtained thanks to Mariamne. In act III scene i the fifteen lines (7-21) which replace three in the earlier versions contain a portrait of Idamas which emphasises the nobility of his character and clearly prepare his entrance in scene iii. The same passage also paints a vivid picture of the last-minute hesitations of Mariamne as she prepares to flee and finds herself torn between her 'austère vertu' and her mother's moving pleas. Scene iv is significantly recast by the twelve new lines which appear at 121-32 in 25P. In the earlier version Idamas took part in neither this nor the following scene. The inserted lines give him a major role: he appeals to Hérode to base his power on love rather than fear, and seeks to sway the king towards justice and virtue. In the following lines, already present in the earlier text, Mazaël attempts to influence him in the opposite direction, asking him to receive the evil Zarès. The intervention of Idamas intensifies the drama of this scene. Hérode is shown hesitating between two sets of contrary advice, both here and in the next scene v, where two lines (147 and 149), originally given to Mazaël, are transferred with slightly changed wording to Idamas. The two added lines at III.225-26 contain an explicit signal for the other characters to leave the stage, clearing it for the confrontation between Hérode and Salome which takes place in the next scene.

In eight inserted lines at IV.ii.51-58, which replace four in the earlier editions, Hérode doubts whether the Romans will endorse the execution of Mariamne, and receives reassurance from Salome. Hérode is made to hesitate, for purely political reasons, before giving the final order for the death of Mariamne. His irresolution expressed in the new lines seems calculated to heighten dramatic tension at this point.

In act V the six lines of Hérode's last speech in the earlier version, in which he gives himself up to self-recrimination and calls down destruction on his own head, are replaced by fourteen lines in 25P, perhaps in response to Nadal's complaint that Voltaire's play contained no equivalent to the 'grands traits prophétiques' in Tristan's tragedy. In the revised text the despairing Hérode turns on his people and calls for their ruin and dispersal, for having failed to avenge the death of Mariamne. In place of Hérode's calls for self-punishment the new ending sets the fate of Mariamne within a larger context of the subsequent history of the Jewish nation, inviting the spectator to view the diaspora as a punishment inflicted on the Jews for the death of Mariamne.

Another significant change, not however involving the insertion of new lines, comes at the end of act IV, where 25P introduces Le Garde to speak lines 210-14 which the first performances and the earlier editions had given to Mazaël, and which contain the dramatic news of Varus's attack on Hérode's palace. Voltaire had already used Mazaël in the role of messenger at the end of act III, where he rushes in to announce Mariamne's flight. The introduction of Le Garde at the end of act IV brings an element of variation into the final scenes of acts III and IV, which were very similar. In each case a situation which had been built up during earlier scenes was dramatically reversed at the last moment when Mazaël's announcement of sensational news caused a massive swing in Hérode's sentiments. Nadal and other commentators had perceived this similarity as a weakness. The changed messenger in act IV was perhaps Voltaire's response to their criticism.

It therefore seems clear that Voltaire's denunciation of the defects of the early editions serves him as a pretext for introducing into the text significant changes at important points. Such revisions may have been dictated by the experience of the first run of performances or by the reactions of critics and the public, or they may have been simply spontaneous, the result of authorial second thoughts.

v. *Critical writings after the publication of 25P*

The end of 1725 saw the appearance of an anonymous tract entitled
*Vérités littéraires sur la tragédie d'Hérode et de Mariamne adressées à
M. de Voltaire*.[194] According to the catalogue of the Bibliothèque
nationale, the authors of this 28-page tract were the abbés Pierre
Guyot Desfontaines, by now a declared adversary of Voltaire, and
François Granet.[195] In the final paragraph of the text, however,
Voltaire is advised to address himself to 'les deux auteurs de [son]
Apologie' if he wishes to discover the identity of the authors of this
piece. This suggests that Simon-Joseph Pellegrin, co-author with
Desfontaines of that *Apologie*,[196] may also have participated in the
composition of the *Vérités littéraires*. The friendliness of Voltaire's
letter of 13 November 1725 (D255) to his 'cher abbé Desfontaines'
can only be explained by supposing that Voltaire, still at
Fontainebleau, was as yet unaware of the highly antagonistic
stance generally adopted by this pamphlet.[197]

---

[194] Reprinted by Vercruysse in *Voltaire jugé pas les siens*, ii.97-126. The pamphlet
bears an *approbation* of 8 September 1725 and a *permis d'imprimer* of 12 September,
registered with the Chambre Syndicale des Libraires on 28 September. The first
record of its publication is not found however until November (*Journal de Trévoux*,
p.2104: 'Nouvelles littéraires'). This is the only reference to *Hérode et Mariamne* and
the writings which it prompted that we have discovered in the pages of the *Journal
de Trévoux* during the period between January 1724 and March 1726 when the play
was the object of intense interest in many other quarters.

[195] BnC, vol.39, col.289. On the title page of one of the BN copies of this work
(BN Yf 9555) an old hand has inscribed the words 'par Guyot Desfontaines et Sr
Granet'. The attribution to these two writers is confirmed by Cioranescu, i.650 and
ii.886. The long and productive journalistic collaboration of Desfontaines and
Granet is described in the articles devoted to them in the *Dictionnaire des journalistes*,
2nd edn, ed. J. Sgard (Oxford 1999).

[196] See above, p.49.

[197] D255 has three addressees: Mme de Bernières, Thiriot and Desfontaines, to
each of whom a separate section of the letter is addressed. The part intended for
Desfontaines contains the enigmatic sentence: 'Je vous suis presque également
obligé pour Mariamne et pour le héros de Gratien.' We do not know what (if any)
service Desfontaines had rendered to Voltaire in regard to *Hérode et Mariamne*. One

A mocking tone is established in the opening words, where Voltaire is maliciously accused of imitating La Motte in adding the ornament of a preface to his published tragedy, and ironically congratulated on a noble lack of concern for his reputation in offering to the public an edition of the play which by his own admission still contains faults, even if these are now only Voltaire's own. Mockery and sarcasm are maintained throughout this lengthy and unsparing pamphlet. Yet we find interspersed remarks which show a certain clarity of analysis and present useful insights into the difficulties of Voltaire's tragedy.

A first section is devoted to Voltaire's Préface. His account of the reasons for the failure of the 1724 Mariamne is discussed in detail. Voltaire is principally reproached for having shown an excessively servile fidelity to his historical sources. He had been unable to adapt the 'couleurs de l'historien' to the theatre; he had not yet seized 'l'art d'embellir les personnages'; he had failed to confer 'le lustre de la poésie' on the factual historical record (p.5). The parallel of Racine and Pradon receives praise: Voltaire is right to insist on the importance of versification, and is admired for his skill in this domain (p.7).

The main topic of the pamphlet is the authors' reflexions on the characters of Varus, Hérode and Mariamne. Varus comes in for several pages of sustained and vigorous criticism. Presented as a noble-minded hero, he behaves in a manner quite inconsistent with this character. The love which he declares for Mariamne

---

possibility may be that Voltaire had learnt that Desfontaines had written an essay on the play, and had assumed – in the light of his protégé's recent professions of friendship and gratitude for Voltaire's help in securing his release from imprisonment at Bicêtre (D235, 31 May 1725) – that its contents would be favourable. For the reference to 'le héros de Gratien' we are equally reduced to speculation. But there is a passage in the Vérités littéraires (p.15) where the authors declare that they do not share the view of an unnamed opponent of literary plagiarism that Voltaire had copied the character of Varus from the Spanish writer Baltasar Gracian y Morales's El Heroe, of which a French translation had appeared in 1724 (D255, n.9). Desfontaines may perhaps have claimed credit for defending Voltaire against this charge in a communication which does not survive.

cannot in the nature of things be disinterested. A major objection is to his 'inaction perpétuelle' (p.11); several examples of ineffectual conduct are cited. Voltaire is severely reprimanded for excluding a meeting with Hérode: 'Est-il vraisemblable que ces deux Héros n'aient rien à se dire?' (p.13). The greatest obstacle with Varus is his 'qualité d'amant, et d'amant imprudent, [qui] infecte entière- ment [son] caractère' (p.13). Voltaire's portrayal of Hérode receives more favourable treatment, but the brusqueness of his changes of heart at the conclusion of acts III and IV is criticised, as well as the repetition of this device. Voltaire is also rebuked for linking the dispersion of the Jews to the death of Mariamne: this was to introduce into sacred history 'un mélange d'idées profanes' (p.20), and Voltaire is sanctimoniously reminded that the Jewish nation had been destroyed in punishment for the death not of Mariamne but of Christ. The 'beautés' of the portrayal of Mariamne attract approval: 'Mariamne intéressera toujours par sa vertu, et par ses malheurs; vous avez substitué à son aigreur, une majestueuse fierté' (p.21). Yet she does not altogether escape criticism; in particular it is considered inadmissible that she should accept Varus's offer of assistance after his declaration of love.

The overwhelming balance of the observations contained in the *Vérités littéraires* is hostile and critical.[198] In the final pages lines or couplets from the play are quoted, with pedantic comments on Voltaire's versification and choice of language.

The April 1726 issue of Jean Frédéric Bernard's Amsterdam gazette *La Bibliothèque française, ou histoire littéraire de la France* carried an article reporting the 'Nouvelles littéraires de Paris' dated 2 January 1726, which contained notices recording the publication both of *Hérode et Mariamne* and of the critical writings to which it had given rise. In describing what he calls 'la fameuse tragédie de M. de Voltaire', the writer claims that the initial

[198] Cf. Foulet's comment on this brochure: 'Il y était surtout question de vérités désagréables' (*La Correspondance de Voltaire*, p.246). The contemporary judgement of Mathieu Marais on the *Vérités littéraires* had also been unflattering (Marais, *Mémoires*, iii.373).

version of the play had failed because 'M. de Voltaire copia servilement l'histoire, et le public demandait des caractères de théâtre. Rien n'est plus vrai, puisqu'il a applaudi dès qu'il a cru les apercevoir: ainsi les acclamations furent précisément refusées, parce que le poète s'était écarté des lois théâtrales.'

The Préface is commended, with special praise for the parallel of Racine and Pradon, and the overall judgement on the play is favourable: 'La docilité de l'auteur, à corriger autant qu'il a pu les défauts de sa pièce, n'a pas peu contribué à lui attirer des suffrages flatteurs, qu'on ne peut d'ailleurs refuser à la noble versification.' [199]

An *Examen de la tragédie d'Hérode et de Mariamne* also appeared early in 1726, in the first issue of the *Continuation des mémoires de littérature et d'histoire de Mr de Salengre*, edited by Pierre Desmolets, [200] who no doubt wished to inaugurate the periodical with articles of substance. No author is named for this *Examen*, and we have not been able to identify the writer. [201] The opening paragraphs strike an apparently conciliatory tone. Voltaire's anger at the appearance of the unauthorised editions of his play is understandable, the author begins, yet these 'éditions furtives' had done him a service in obliging him to bring out a definitive edition of his tragedy: otherwise there may well have been no end to his retouches and corrections. There follows a well developed and sustained analysis of the play, some forty pages in length.

[199] *Bibliothèque française*, April 1726, p.301.
[200] *Continuation des mémoires de littérature et d'histoire de Mr. de Salengre*, vol.i, part I (Paris, Simart, 1726), p.206-45. This volume reproduces an approbation dated 12 January 1726; it was published c.20 February 1726 (*Dictionnaire des journaux 1600-1789*, ed. J. Sgard, Paris and Oxford 1991, p.249).
[201] The many contributors to the *Continuation des mémoires* are listed in the *Dictionnaire des journaux*, p.226. There is no evidence for ascribing the *Examen* to any one of them in particular. And it would seem that two names need to be eliminated from consideration: Desmolets himself, who writes in the preface to volume iii that 'toutes les pièces que je publie me sont étrangères', suggesting that his role was that of editor rather than writer, and Jean-Jacques Bel, whose contribution to the criticism of *Hérode et Mariamne*, published in a later issue of the journal and discussed below, is quite different in manner and style.

The author attributes the great success of *Hérode et Mariamne* to the vivid portrayal of the passions of 'deux personnages qui nous intéressent d'une manière bien particulière', namely Mariamne and Hérode. But 'la conduite de la pièce' had many defects. Voltaire had not for example observed the basic principle of ensuring variety of dramatic structure. Thus three of the five acts (acts I, II and IV) open in the same way with conversations between Mazaël and Salome. But the greatest defect ('la faute la plus capitale') is the similarity in the endings of acts III and IV. The differences between the two scenes are minimal,[202] and the repetition of the same device is a serious weakness.

Varus is judged to be a failed creation, a failure all the more reprehensible in that Voltaire had free rein to construct this character as he wished. The principal complaint against Varus is his 'amour postiche' for Mariamne. Varus is demeaned throughout by this inappropriate sentiment, quite inconsistent with the established practice on the French stage of nobly portraying Roman nobles. It had the further disadvantage of compromising the character of Mariamne. This portrayal was inexcusable because it was completely unnecessary to suppose Varus in love. A Roman of his stamp would not need to be prompted by love in order to hasten to the defence of oppressed virtue: 'la genérosité naturelle aux Romains' (p.218) would have been ample motivation in itself. Furthermore, when it comes to action, Varus is singularly dilatory: after promising his help to Mariamne, he wastes valuable time in conversation with Albin (II.vi), and then with Nabal (III.i) and Idamas (III.iii). His decision to avoid a meeting with Hérode on the latter's return to Jerusalem is roundly condemned. It was urgent to confront Hérode, yet, to the writer's astonishment, nothing is heard

---

[202] We may note here that in the summary of the conclusion of act IV given by the author of the *Examen*, it is Mazaël who comes in to announce the overturning of the scaffold erected for Mariamne on the orders of Salome. This return to the earlier version of this scene is somewhat strange, for, as we have seen (see above. p.81), one of Voltaire's principal innovations in 25P was to introduce a new character (Le Garde) to bring this news.

of Varus between the end of act III and the end of act IV, and the *Examen* speculates ironically on what Varus may be supposed to have been doing during this interval: 'Peut-être était-il les bras croisés au milieu de ses troupes; peut-être en faisait-il la revue pour se désennuyer. Quoiqu'il en soit, on ne vit jamais une pareille indolence dans un homme qui avait des intérêts si pressants' (p.222-23). Varus proves to be no Roman hero but a mere scatterbrain, worthy to receive 'la palme de l'étourderie' (p.224). The strong censure of Varus is then turned against his creator Voltaire: 'Je ne sais si on a jamais mis sur la scène un personnage aussi extraordinaire. Plus j'examine son caractère, moins je puis me figurer comment un homme d'esprit qui a mis tant de temps à refondre son ouvrage, ne s'est pas aperçu de défauts si palpables' (p.226).

The portrayal of Mariamne was found to be deeply moving: 'Le caractère de Marianne plaira sans cesse: ses charmes, ses vertus, ses malheurs paraissent dans tout leur jour. A la place de l'aigreur on a substitué fort à propos la hauteur et la fierté' (p.226-27). Nowhere is Mariamne's virtue more apparent than in her decision in act V to place her life at the mercy of Hérode.

The character of Hérode, the author continues, was 'mieux approfondi'; his was the role which had no doubt cost most to Voltaire. Hérode's sudden emotional swings are criticised: 'Il eût été plus à propos de ne point passer si brusquement de l'amour à la haine, et de la haine à l'amour' (p.232). Not that the portrait of Hérode left to us by Josephus was not to be followed, but the transitions could have been more gradual: 'Mais enfin la pente ne pouvait-elle pas être plus douce? Ce n'eût pas été défigurer l'histoire, c'eût été l'embellir' (p.232). He points out the difficulty of gaining acceptance for Hérode's sudden changes of mood: '[Voltaire] n'a-t-il pas peché contre la vraisemblance, quand Hérode après avoir pardonné à son épouse, la condamne de nouveau à la mort, parce que Varus a renversé l'échafaud?' (p.233). A little later he returns to this idea: 'Pourquoi donc vouloir que Marianne soit comptable de l'imprudence du Proconsul? C'est à Varus seul à en porter la peine' (p.234).

The writer next suggests, using extremely tentative language, [203] that the dramatic principle of unity of action is violated by the conclusion of *Hérode et Mariamne*. He argues that at the end of the tragedy the action is not completed, for we are left ignorant of the final fate of Hérode. We can be certain that terrible punishment awaits him for the death of Varus, yet we do not know what form that will take. This makes for an unsatisfactory ending.

Like the *Vérités littéraires*, the *Examen* raises serious objections to the revised version of Hérode's final speech: 'La vengeance terrible que Dieu exerce contre les Juifs, peut-elle être détournée de la mort du Fils de Dieu à celle de Marianne?' (p.240). Voltaire is accused of a gross abuse of poetic licence in a manner shocking to religious sensibilities.

Brief comments follow on the characters of Mazaël and Salome. A last word of complaint is directed at act V scene vi, when the sudden appearance of Hérode brings to a brutal end, in an unacceptably brusque transition, all hope for Mariamne.

The final conclusion of the *Examen* is that for several reasons, chief among them 'la fuite mal concertée de Mariamne, l'emportement incroyable d'Hérode à la nouvelle du renversement de l'échafaud, et la conduite étourdie de Varus', Voltaire failed in his central task, which was to produce a plausible account of the death of Mariamne.

Three letters under the title *Lettres à Mr. de *** contenant quelques observations sur la tragédie de Mariamne, par M. de Voltaire* were published in Holland in the issue for May and June 1726 of Bernard's *Bibliothèque française* (p.94-110). An introductory editorial note proclaims the superiority of these letters to all previous reviews, estimable though some of these have been, and expresses regret that the author may not be named. However, when early in the following year these letters were

---

[203] 'Je ne hazarde qu'en tremblant la reflexion suivante' (p.234-35). This is perhaps an ironic echo of Voltaire's hesitations in the Préface of 25P: 'Je ne donne même cette édition qu'en tremblant' (lines 106-107). (This statement was to become the opening sentence of the preface from w38 onwards.)

reprinted in a revised and (in the case of the second letter) considerably expanded form in Paris in the *Continuation des Memoires de litterature et d'histoire*,[204] a preface revealed that they were the work of 'M. Bel Conseiller au Parlement de Bordeaux'.[205]

The letters make many statements critical both of *Hérode et Mariamne* and of Voltaire, but for the most part in generalised terms. The first letter, dated 7 September 1725, seeks to establish that *Hérode et Mariamne* cannot stand comparison with La Motte's *Inès de Castro*: 'Selon moi Mariamne ne vaut pas Inés de Castro' (p.43). Although it is true that Voltaire's tragedy contains 'quelques portraits assez brillants', these are most often 'des portraits de déclamateur' placed haphazardly in the text with no attention paid to their appropriateness to the character to whom they are given. A lengthier criticism alleges that there are frequent inconsistences between 'le caractère d'un personnage' and 'le sentiment que chaque circonstance doit produire en lui' (p.44). A further complaint is that there is no real dialogue in the play. Voltaire has assigned set speeches to his characters, who speak one after the other, but not to one another. However, Voltaire's versification receives qualified praise.

The second letter, dated 19 November 1725, is the longest of the three, and the text published in the *Continuation des mémoires* is considerably expanded from the first version which appeared in the *Bibliothèque française*. Bel begins by attacking the arguments with which in the Préface Voltaire had sought to demonstrate that

---

[204] *Continuation des mémoires de litterature et d'histoire de Mr de Salengre*, iii.1, p.43-75. This volume bears an *approbation* dated 29 December 1726.

[205] Jean-Jacques Bel was the friend of Montesquieu and of Desmolets. In 1726 he was the collaborator of Desfontaines in the production of the latter's *Dictionnaire néologique*. He was also at this time director of the *Bibliothèque française*, and may therefore have been unwilling to name himself as the author of the three letters, highly commended by him in his editorial introduction at the time of their initial publication in that journal. (See the article on Bel in the *Dictionnaire des journalistes*, ed. Sgard, p.69-70.)

the story of Hérode and Mariamne provided a fit theme for
tragedy.[206] Bel finds that the action of the play is 'vitieuse par la
bassesse et par le ridicule' (p.48), 'digne tout au plus du plus bas
comique' (p.49).

A long development, which in the *Continuation des mémoires*
expands a much shorter account in the *Bibliothèque française*, is
devoted to Salome. Voltaire, Bel alleges, had wanted to portray a
strong character, but fails in the attempt: Salome is merely vulgar
and odious. Bel is also irritated by Hérode's ministers. Their
presence raises unanswered questions about their motives and
aims, which give the play 'un air de langueur insupportable'
(p.62). The portrayal of Mazaël receives particular criticism: he
lacks a personal interest in the plot.[207] And as well the play has too
many confidants, five in all (Mazaël, Idamas, Nabal, Elize and
Albin).

The absence of an encounter between Hérode and Varus is
deplored by Bel. He refers the reader to the *Verités littéraires*,
whose arguments he regards as carrying much force. Such a
meeting is absolutely called for; the action of the play insistently
prepares it (p.63).

Bel ends by calling on Voltaire to give up hope of equalling
Racine. In a curious final section found in the 1727 *Continuations
des Mémoires* version of this letter, but which did not appear in the
earlier text published in 1726 in the *Bibliothèque française*, he
addresses an impassioned appeal to Voltaire to abandon writing
for the stage and to return to epic poetry, the genre in which he had
so finely begun his career.

A briefer third letter dated 22 December 1725 discusses the first
scene of act I. Bel argues that the first speech in the play should
have been given to Salome, not Mazaël. Salome would then have
been able to interrogate Mazaël actively, rather than simply
listening to his report, and her questions to him would have

[206] See Préface, lines 201f.
[207] The *Examen* had made a similar observation.

revealed the state of anxiety and fearful curiosity in which she had awaited his return. Bel contrasts Voltaire's treatment of this scene with the first scene in Racine's *Bajazet*, where Acomat takes the initiative. His questions to Osmin enable us to see the impact upon him of the information which he elicits little by little. The comparison with Racine proves for Bel the weakness of Voltaire's opening scene. The letter ends with a general eulogy of Racine.[208]

5. *Mariamne from 1728 to 1760*

i. *Performances*

The Comédie-Française was slow to make use of the discretion over further performances ceded by Voltaire in August 1725. *Hérode et Mariamne* was not staged again until mid-1728, when four performances were given (on 3, 5, 7 and 9 June), but they attracted only modest houses.[209]

Voltaire's return to France in the autumn of 1728, and to Paris in April 1729,[210] did not produce a reawakening of interest in *Hérode et Mariamne*. That had to wait until the 1732-1733 season, when in the wake of the triumph of *Zaïre* (performed first on 13 August 1732, and then more than thirty times before the

---

[208] The publication of Bel's three letters in the *Continuation des Mémoires* was noted in Bernard's *Bibliothèque française* in 1728 (tome xi, Première Partie, p.15-17), with the mention that 'M. Bel a retouché quelques endroits [...] mais le fond est demeuré le même'. The notice reprints Bel's exhortation to Voltaire to abandon the theatre and return to the epic.

[209] 509, 374, 239, and 376 paying spectators respectively. These statistics, as all others regarding performance dates and audience numbers at the Comédie-Française, are drawn from Lancaster, *The Comédie-Française 1701-1774*, p.694f. *Œdipe* fared scarcely better during the period of Voltaire's absence from France: it received eight performances in the 1727-1728 season but they were not well attended. Voltaire's theatre may have undergone an eclipse during the period following his quarrel with the chevalier de Rohan-Chabot, his imprisonment in the Bastille and his departure for England.

[210] Pomeau, *Voltaire en son temps*, i.203-204.

following January), there was a brief revival of *Hérode et Mariamne* in two performances on 26 and 28 October 1732, with excellent audience numbers. [211]

Shortly before this, on 14 October, the Comédiens français had performed *Hérode et Mariamne* before the court at Fontainebleau. Voltaire was present, and became involved in a dispute recounted by Mathieu Marais. The duc de Mortemart, *premier gentilhomme de la chambre*, had not been willing to allow its staging. Voltaire overcame his opposition by obtaining an order from the queen authorising the performance. In order to avenge this humiliation, Montemart then sought to have the Comédiens italiens[212] play 'la critique de Mariane' (probably *Le Mauvais Ménage*). Voltaire countered this by obtaining the queen's promise that the parody would not be performed. Unfortunately the queen forgot to give orders to this effect. The Italiens therefore performed their main play, and were on the point of playing the parody, when the queen stood up and left the theatre, thereby bringing the performance to an end. [213] This surprising action saved the situation for Voltaire, whose sense of triumph is evident in the letter which he wrote some days later to Mlle de Lubert: 'J'ai eu un crédit étonnant en fait de bagatelles, et j'ai remporté des victoires signalées où il ne s'agissait de rien du tout' (D532, 29 October 1732). The excellent attendances recorded, as we have seen, at the two performances in Paris on 26 and 28 October may have been due not only to the success of *Zaïre*, but in part also to the interest created by Voltaire's petty victory at court.

In the following season (1733-1734) *Hérode et Mariamne* was

[211] 1112 and 1054 paying spectators respectively. The house would seem to have been especially full on 26 October, for Michel Linant wrote next day to Cideville: 'On s'y crêvait, et il y eut plus d'une catastrophe au parterre' (D531, [27 Octobre 1732]).

[212] In 1732 actors from both the Comédie-Française and the Comédie-Italienne were in residence at Fontainebleau during the autumn sojourn of the court (*Mercure*, September 1732, p.2062).

[213] Marais, *Journal et mémoires*, letter to Bouhier of 28 October 1732, ed. Lescure, iv.438. This account is reproduced in a note to D532.

given once, on 9 January 1734, some ten days before the première of *Adélaïde du Guesclin*, before a good house. There were further revivals in 1735, with four performances on 31 October 1735, 2, 5 and 7 November, and three performances on 9, 11 and 13 June 1736. Houses on most of these occasions reached but did not exceed acceptable levels.[214] A brief notice in the *Mercure* (June 1736, p.1434) records that Mlle Conel received applause for her interpretation of the role of Mariamne. *Hérode et Mariamne* then disappeared from the repertoire of the Comédie-Française until 1746, when three performances were given before half-filled houses on 10, 12 and 15 January.[215]

Little trace of performances given in theatres other than the Comédie-Française, either in Paris or the provinces, has come down to us. The meticulous records kept by Lekain of the productions in which he participated provide evidence of a performance of *Hérode et Mariamne* at the Hôtel de Clermont-Tonnerre, a private theatre in Paris, on 14 September 1749,[216] when Lekain, then at the beginning of his career, took the role of Mazaël. Evidence of other productions during these years is lacking, but *Hérode et Mariamne* is likely to have been staged many times in several of the private theatres of Paris, especially in Voltaire's own theatre in the rue Traversière.

Voltaire met Lekain in February 1750 and, sensing his great potential, took him into his protection.[217] He advised him to rehearse a number of roles, including that of Hérode: he should shout parts of them out loudly, in order to correct the weakness of his otherwise impressive voice.[218] In 1753 Lekain gave his first

---

[214] Successively 419, 501, 422 and 295 paying spectators in 1735, and 648, 508 and 243 in 1736.

[215] 420, 663 and 536 paying spectators.

[216] BnF, mss. fonds fr. 12532: [Lekain], 'Journal exact de tous les rôles que j'ai joués en bourgeoisie depuis le 27 Xbre 1747', p.1.

[217] *Mémoires de Lekain* (Paris 1825), p.422f.

[218] See Voltaire's letter to d'Argental (D4163, 26 [June 1750]): Mme Denis is enjoined to make Lekain 'crier à tue-tête'. A little later Voltaire places *Hérode et Mariamne*, along with *Le Duc d'Alençon* and his own private theatre, under the

93

performances as Hérode, a role with which he was to become closely identified, in two productions outside Paris. The first, in September, was in a military camp at Gray, the second, undated, was at Rouen.[219]

Hérode et Mariamne returned to the Comédie-Française in August 1754 in a significant revival with Lekain and Mlle Gaussin in the leading roles. Five performances were given, and audience numbers were good for the first three.[220] This revival attracted highly favourable comment. The *Mercure*, in a short notice, commended both the play and the two leading actors for their roles 'bien rendus' (September 1754, p.186).

The *Correspondance littéraire* included a fuller and in most respects highly complimentary review in its issue of 15 August 1754:[221] 'On a reçu avec de grands applaudissements la tragédie de *Hérode et Mariamne*, remise au théâtre de la Comédie française [...] Le sujet est à mon gré un des plus beaux qui soient au théâtre, et, traité par M. de Voltaire, il est devenu plus beau encore'. There is admiration for the quality of the writing: 'C'est une beauté régulière et soutenue qui vous charme et vous enchante'. Voltaire is applauded for excluding a meeting between Hérode and Varus: this was the mark of 'un homme de génie'. He is sharply criticised however for removing the death of Mariamne from the stage in his

---

protection of the marquis de Thibouville, one of his amateur actors, and asks Thibouville to assure Lekain 'à quel point je lui suis dévoué' (D4178, 1 August [1750]).

[219] Lekain, 'Journal exact', p.39.

[220] 5, 7, 10, 17 and 21 August. These performances were due to begin on Saturday 27 July, but were postponed because of the indisposition of Lekain (D5892, Lekain to d'Argental, 26 July 1754). Two days before the first performance Voltaire had thanked d'Argental for an unspecified service in regard to *Hérode et Mariamne*, which perhaps had to do with supplying the actors with copies of their parts (D5899). There were 816, 693, and 990 paying spectators for the first two performances, but for the following two 494 and 443 (Lancaster, *The Comédie-Française*, p.778).

[221] *CL*, ii.397-98.

1724-1725 revisions. This had ruined the final act and indeed the whole play. On the cry from the pit that disrupted the performance of M24 the report comments: 'Une telle platitude suffit pour faire rire le parterre; mais elle ne doit pas suffire pour engager un homme supérieur à faire un mauvais changement'. The play would have concluded with a spectacular 'tableau effrayant et touchant' if Mariamne's blood-stained body had been the background to Hérode's frenzy. The notice mentions finally the 'applaudissement universel' with which Lekain's performance as Hérode was received, and expresses admiration for the 'génie supérieur' of this actor.

Lekain's records for the season 1754-1755 document two further performances of *Hérode et Mariamne* in which he took the role of Hérode: the first before the court at Fontainebleau on 16 October 1754, the second in Dijon.[222] He also played Hérode in a performance in Rouen in the following season (1755-1756). *Hérode et Mariamne* was not played at the Comédie-Française during the 1755-1756 season, although Voltaire (it seems from D6531) anticipated performances in November, in which Mlle Clairon would have replaced Mlle Gaussin as Mariamne, with Lekain continuing to play Hérode.[223]

---

[222] Lekain, 'Journal exact', p.54. The performance at Fontainebleau is noted without comment in the *Mercure* of December 1754, p.196. J.-J. Olivier (*Henri-Louis Lekain de la Comédie-Française*, Paris 1907, p.70-71) dates the Dijon performance to March 1755. We have not been able to establish the identity of Lekain's fellow actors on this occasion.

[223] D6531, addressed to Mlle Clairon on 8 August 1755: Voltaire suggests a course for the immediate future that would be preferable to staging *L'Orphelin de la Chine*, with which he was not yet satisfied: 'Voici ce que je vous conseillerais. Ce serait de jouer Mariamne à la rentrée de votre parlement [in November]. Ce rôle est trop long pour Mlle Gaussin, qui ne doit pas d'ailleurs en être jalouse. Vous feriez réussir cette pièce avec M Lekain, qui joue, dit-on, très bien Hérode. Vous joueriez après cela Idamé.' A later letter to d'Argental (D6680, 8 January 1756) raises the name of Mlle Hus, and discusses her suitability for the 'vilain rôle' of Salome. Although he has doubts, Voltaire agrees that she can have the part if this is what d'Argental wants. Later, in August 1756, Mlle Dumesnil accused d'Argental of relegating her to the role of Salome, which she considered 'misérable' (D6980).

The Comédie-Française did not, however, put on *Hérode et Mariamne* until the following season (1756-1757), which proved to be a remarkable one for Voltaire, during which no fewer than eight of his plays were staged, in a total of twenty-nine performances. [224] It was given on 31 August, 1 and 11 September 1756, with reasonable success. [225] A further performance was given at Fontainebleau before the court on 18 October. Two further performances took place three years later in the 1759-1760 season, again with significant success, on 29 August 1759 (759 paying spectators) and 1 September (677). On all these occasions the role of Hérode was taken by Lekain. [226]

Like Voltaire's other works, *Hérode et Mariamne* soon became known in the courts and intellectual circles of many German principalities. It is mentioned in a letter conveying the esteem of Queen Sophia Dorothea of Prussia for his writings which Voltaire received as early as 1728 (D369). As for performances, *Hérode et Mariamne* was included from 1747 in the repertory of the troupe of French actors in Frankfurt. [227] The margrave of Bayreuth maintained a troupe of French actors at his court, and during a visit by Lekain in the spring of 1756 two performances of *Hérode et Mariamne* were given, in which he played the role of Hérode, for which he was now well known. [228]

More vigorously perhaps than elsewhere in Germany, interest in the French theatre was cultivated at the court of Frederick II in Berlin. Frederick also maintained a troupe of French actors, but there is no record of performances by them of *Hérode et*

---

[224] Pomeau, *Voltaire en son temps*, i.847.

[225] Attracting successively 460, 596 and 796 paying spectators (Lancaster, *The Comédie-Française*, p.784). The 11 September performance was noted in the *Mercure*, October 1756, p.185.

[226] Lekain, 'Journal exact', p.54, 87, 139; Lancaster, *The Comédie-Française*, p.798.

[227] E. Mentzel, *Geschichte der Schauspielkunst in Frankfurt a.M.*, cited in J.-J. Olivier, *Les Comédiens français dans les cours d'Allemagne au XVIIIe siècle*, vol.iii (Paris 1903), p.95, n.10.

[228] Olivier, *Les Comédiens français dans les cours d'Allemagne au XVIIIe siècle*, and Lekain, 'Journal exact', p.71.

Mariamne. More is known about the private theatre composed of members of the royal family and privileged courtiers, of which Voltaire himself was a leading member during his stay in Berlin from 1750 to 1753. In the amateur theatricals of this select circle he not only took roles himself, but also acted as circumstances required as director, producer and coach. Voltaire's plays had pride of place in the repertory of this group, and *Hérode et Mariamne* is recorded by D. Thiébault in the list of plays which they prepared. The same writer recounts a quarrel which arose between Voltaire and Baculard d'Arnaud when the latter was cast as the Guard in *Hérode et Mariamne*, with only four or five lines to speak. Slighted by this minor role, Arnaud delivered his lines in an offhand manner, maintaining that they deserved no better. Voltaire, incensed, castigated him for his lack of talent, and set about proving to him 'que c'est sur ces deux mots que porte tout le nœud de la pièce, et qu'enfin c'est le rôle le plus important'.[229] It will be remembered that the Guard was added by Voltaire after the early performances of 1725, possibly in response to criticism, in order to make the the endings of acts III and IV less alike. It seems possible that more than twenty-five years later this change still remained a sensitive point for Voltaire.

ii. *Development of the text of M25*

Printing *Hérode et Mariamne* at his own expense had been a trying experience for Voltaire. Soon after the appearance of 25P he had complained to Thiriot that he was 'las du métier d'imprimeur', and intended to find another way to publish *L'Indiscret* (D247, 24 August [1725]). Shortly before the end of 1725, wishing perhaps to avoid further involvement in what had proved to be a bothersome business, he transferred to the widow of Pierre Ribou the

[229] Dieudonné Thiébault, *Mes souvenirs de vingt ans de séjour à Berlin*, 2nd edn (1805), v.253-54.

privilège for *Hérode et Mariamne*. [230] In the next and following year further copies of the sheets printed by Sevestre were released to form 26P and 27, which therefore present an unchanged text, with new title pages only.

A further release of the 25P sheets took place in 1730, but Voltaire's Préface was trimmed of its final three paragraphs in this edition (30), and, more significantly, gathering D was reprinted, introducing important changes from III.139 to IV.52. These changes were to become permanently embedded in the text. In the first, at III.185, nine lines are introduced spoken principally by Idamas. His words, stressing the ennobling power of love, act as a counterweight to the promptings of Mazaël, who seeks to fan Hérode's hatred for Mariamne. Idamas' plea for reconciliation heightens Hérode's remorse, highlighted in the new lines added to his role. Voltaire also expanded Hérode's speech to Salome in scene vi by inserting ten lines to replace III.291-92. These have the effect of prolonging Hérode's struggle with the jealousy that sweeps over him when Salome accuses Mariamne of loving another. They show him striving to hold on just a little longer to his desire for reconciliation with Mariamne and to his restored belief in her virtue. Voltaire may have wanted to give greater plausibility to Hérode's change of heart at the end of act III by slowing it down in this way. This may have been his response to the many voices raised in protest against the brusqueness of Hérode's swings of emotion. The last line of the same scene (296) also undergoes expansion. In four added lines Hérode gives free rein to his rage. His desire for vengeance is extended to encompass even his informant Salome, and he melodramatically invites her to strike his heart. The last new line heightens the suspense already

---

[230] Voltaire's *cession* of the *privilège* was transcribed into the *Registres de la Libraire* on 8 January 1726 (BnF, mss. fonds fr. 21953, p.284) and was included as an addendum to the *privilège* when this was reprinted for the next editions (26P and 27). It reads: 'Je cède à Madame Ribou le Privilège de six années obtenu pour moi pour la *Tragédie de Mariamne*. Fait à Paris ce 12. Décembre 1725. VOLTAIRE.'

present in 25P, as Hérode presses Salome to reveal the name of Mariamne's lover.

At IV.30 Voltaire also inserts a new speech for Mazaël, in which Hérode is warned of the danger which Varus presents for him.[231]

a) Changes introduced in 1731

The Amsterdam, Ledet / Desbordes edition of 1731 (31) is the first edition in which the play appears under the shortened title *Mariamne* which it bears in about two-thirds of the subsequent editions of the version with Varus and in all editions of the version with Sohème.

The Préface is given in the complete original form as in 25P. In the body of the play 31 introduces many changes which became part of the standard text and re-appear therefore in all subsequent editions. The most important of these changes affect the later parts of the play. The last two scenes of act IV were reworked so that at the end of scene v Mariamne is not taken away by the guards but remains on stage for scene vi, which is revised to include a brief exchange with Hérode.[232] Her continued presence until the end of the act and her plea to Hérode heighten the dramatic tension and procure a strong ending to act IV.

Significant changes were also made in act V. In scene i, lines 9-12 are new and introduce a change of emphasis. In 25P Mariamne laments that she has never known anything but unhappiness throughout her entire life. Edition 31 suggests rather that earlier illusions now lie shattered. Scene v was substantially reworked. In 25P this is a brief transitional scene, dramatically weak: two minor characters only are present on stage, and their dialogue contributes little to maintaining dramatic intensity at this critical point. In addition, it seems improbable that Hérode should appear on stage

---

[231] See variants at IV.27-28.
[232] See variants at IV.210c-19 and 224-25.

so soon after Mariamne has gone off to look for him. He must have already been close by at the end of scene iv, but how then did Mariamne miss him? This is a weakness which the authors of *Le Mauvais Ménage* had already seized upon, and which the *Examen de la tragédie d'Hérode et de Mariamne* had also criticised. In 31 Hérode enters before Mariamne departs, thereby transforming scene v. The chain of events is made to appear more plausible, and an occasion is provided for a last brief confrontation between Hérode and Mariamne (IV, 115-19 and variants).

Hérode's final speech (V.vii) was also revised in 31. Voltaire removed the lines introduced in 25P, which contain Hérode's call for the destruction of the Jewish nation in punishment for the death of Mariamne. He retained only those lines (231-34) calling for the destruction of his own palace and of Mariamne's place of execution, and restored around them the six lines of the earlier version preserved in MS1, 25CH, 25X and 26H, in which Hérode's calls for punishment are directed against himself alone. [233] All reference to Israël, the temple and the Jewish nation disappears. Voltaire's bid in 25P to link the diaspora with the death of Mariamne had been attacked in both the *Vérités littéraires* and the *Examen de la tragédie d'Hérode et de Marianne*. These critics had denounced Voltaire's apparent mingling of secular and sacred history. His revision in 31 of Hérode's final speech may perhaps therefore have been prompted by a desire to remove this ground of objection.

In addition to the above changes one small but significant amendment occurs at I.298, where the word 'espoir' in Varus's account of his love for Mariamne is replaced by 'amour', perhaps to remove any implication that Varus's motives might be less than perfectly noble. Varus's explanation of his motivations had been ridiculed by the parodists and attacked in the critical writings, either on the grounds of their implausibility (*Vérités littéraires*), or because they stripped Varus of the dignity appropriate to the portrayal of Roman nobles on the tragic stage (*Observations*

[233] See variants at V.229-42a.

critiques, *Examen*). The variant 'amour' introduced at this point may indicate a sensitivity on Voltaire's part to the widespread disapproval and mockery bestowed on Varus.

A complete line is replaced at IV.209, where the new text implies that Hérode sees Mariamne as sharing the responsibility for his crimes. A further line is replaced at V.26: Mariamne now pleads that she herself, rather than abstract virtue, be honoured after her death, and that no vengeance be sought. The remaining variants presented by 31 are minor.[234]

b) Subsequent changes: w38 to w57p

With 31 the Varus version of *Hérode et Mariamne* attains a shape that we can qualify as definitive, even though Voltaire was to introduce variant readings into some of the later editions. Although most of these affect only a word or phrase, a single line or at most two, they are nevertheless significant.[235]

The Préface, however, was to undergo considerable shortening. The Amsterdam, Ledet/Desbordes 1738 edition of the *Œuvres* of Voltaire (w38) saw the removal of the first twelve paragraphs, containing Voltaire's discussion of the failure of the 1724 *Mariamne*. Edition w38 also maintained the suppression, first seen in w37, of the final paragraph of the 25P Préface, which contained an announcement for subscribers to the 1724 edition of *La Henriade*, now quite out of date.[236] Further cuts were made in

[234] Slight changes of wording or in forms of words are observed at several points in the Préface and also in the list of actors, and at I.204 and 290; II.11, 29 and 33; III.81; V.170 and 189. These changes do no more than make the expression more felicitous or remove minor blemishes. At the points which occur in the body of the play the readings of 31, some of which correct errors found in 25P, re-establish in all cases forms which had already been part of the earlier version of the text represented by MS1, 25CH, 25X and 26H, but which are not found in 25P or the other editions formed from the same sheets.

[235] There was a further release of the sheets printed for 25 and 30 in 1736: see below, bibliographical description of 36P.

[236] For these changes see variants to the Préface, lines 1-105 and 277, and also, for

the London, Jean Nourse 1746 edition of Voltaire's *Œuvres diverses* (w46), when two more paragraphs at the end of the Préface were suppressed and replaced with a quotation from the *Amphitryon* of Molière.[237] With w46 the Préface attains its definitive form: the small number of subsequent changes concern slight details only.

The changes to the text of the play after w38, though small, were retained in subsequent editions, and seem therefore to have been intended by Voltaire. This is the case for the three new readings which appear in w40 at III.116, III.134 and IV.16. The instruction in the errata of w42 to restore the base text reading at V.26 must equally have emanated from Voltaire. In the errata of w46 at I.296 the subjunctive 'détruise' is substituted for the indicative 'détruit', bringing into the textual canon a delicate shading of the meaning of this line. Lines II.125-26 are replaced in the same edition by a variant couplet which introduces a nuance into Salome's reaction to Mariamne's rejection of her advances: she will seek now not so much to avenge herself as to punish Mariamne. Slight though the difference of meaning may be, the new couplet is retained in all but two of the subsequent editions of the Varus version of the play.

The Dresden, Walther 1748 edition of Voltaire's *Œuvres* (w48D) introduces several important changes into the textual canon. A revised line at III.275 somewhat reduces the gravity of Hérode's accusation against Salome. The new couplet which replaces IV.71-72 throws into sharper relief Hérode's sadistic imaginings of the sufferings of Mariamne. Changed readings also appear at line 245 of the Préface, I.298 and V.15. The most interesting of these small changes is I.298, where Voltaire grapples with the still unresolved difficulty of finding a plausible statement

---

the suppression of a further short sentence, at line 266. In w38 the Préface is preceded by an Avertissement (see Appendix C), which, though reprinted in a number of subsequent editions, was eventually to disappear from the textual canon.

[237] See variants to line 261.

for Varus that will explain his love for Mariamne: 'les sens' replaces the 1731 reading of 'l'amour', which had itself replaced the 25P reading of 'l'espoir'.

The Paris, M. Lambert 1751 edition of Voltaire's *Œuvres* (w51) corrected the error in the Préface regarding Iphigénie which had persisted since 25P (line 213). It otherwise contributed little to the development of the text, and even this correction was not generally adopted until w68.

For the Dresden, Walther 1752 edition (w52) Voltaire abandoned the Avertissement which had first appeared in w38. He also reworked significantly three points in the part of Salome at II.18, II.67-72 and IV.67-68. These changes combine to reduce just slightly the importance of Salome's influence in the unfolding of the action. [238]

The first printing of the Cramer *Collection complette* of the works of Voltaire (w56) reproduces the text of *Mariamne* almost without variation from w52, in spite of an assertion in the *Préface des éditeurs* (vol.i, p.ii) that this edition contains 'de grands changements' affecting the plays. For *Mariamne* w56 introduces no more than a few retouches, affecting only single words, mainly in the Préface, [239] but also at II.73 and V.181, and it restores a pre-w42 reading at IV.16. These changes are retained in the subsequent Cramer editions w57G1 and w57G2. The small number of further retouches introduced in the Paris editions of 1757, 1762, 1764 and 1767 (see w57P, 62, T64P and T67) did not become part of the textual canon.

It can be said therefore that Voltaire's definitive statement concerning the text of the Varus version of *Hérode et Mariamne* is to be found in w52. Although he had reworked many significant points in his successive revisions, these had not affected the overall structure and balance of the play, which had remained unchanged

[238] In addition w52 presents single word retouches at I.181 and II.73 which became permanently embedded in the text.
[239] See variants to lines 147, 227, 261.

since 25P. The W52 text was the version which the Comédie-Française performed in its successful revivals of *Hérode et Mariamne* in 1754 and the following years, with Lekain in the role of Hérode.[240]

6. *The Mariamne of 1762*

i. *The genesis of M62*

We can only speculate on the reasons which led Voltaire in 1762, a year in which his activities were, in H. T. Mason's phrase, 'bewilderingly multifarious', to undertake a substantial revision of *Mariamne*.[241] A first reference can be found, however, in a letter of 21 July 1762 (D10597), in which he thanks the cardinal de Bernis for forwarding suggestions for corrections to his new play *Olympie*: 'Malheur à qui ne se corrige pas, soi, et ses œuvres. En relisant une tragédie de Mariamne que j'avais faite il y a quarante ans, je l'ai trouvée plate et le sujet beau. Je l'ai entièrement changée. Il faut se corriger eût on quatrevingt ans. Je n'aime point les vieillards qui disent, j'ai pris mon pli'.

Voltaire's dissatisfaction with the play in its previous form is plain. There may have been a further reason for his returning to it at this particular time: 1762 was the year of the commencement of the Calas affair, the dominant theme of Voltaire's correspondence from June onwards. He is particularly preoccupied with the fate of

---

[240] In 1760 *Hérode et Mariamne* appeared as a character in Cailleau's parody *Les Tragédies de Voltaire ou Tancrède jugée par ses sœurs*, in which *Œdipe* presents the tragedies of Voltaire in order of their composition to the newest arrival *Tancrède*, with a brief comment on each. In introducing *Hérode et Mariamne* after *Artémire*, *Œdipe* observes: '[Elle] n'aurait pas été plus heureuse [qu'*Artémire*], mais à force de corrections notre Père l'a rendue meilleure: effectivement elle a des beautés' (cited in Grannis, *Dramatic parody*, p.345).

[241] Preface to *OC*, vol.56A, p.xix. Mason shows Voltaire dividing his astonishing energies between works in a wide range of fields, which, in addition to polemical writings prompted by the Calas affair, numbered theatrical works, the massive *Histoire de Pierre le Grand*, and the equally weighty *Commentaires sur Corneille*.

Mme Calas. His letters abound in compassionate references to 'cette veuve infortunée', who was no stage heroine, but victim of a terrible tragedy in real life. It may be that this image of persecuted innocence led Voltaire back to his heroine of the 1720s, and induced him to focus his attention once more on *Mariamne*.[242]

The letter to de Bernis shows that the reworking of *Mariamne* was accomplished in the summer of 1762. Writing to the d'Argentals on 7 August (D10636), Voltaire promises to send them without delay the new version, and describes the principal change which he has made: 'Vous y verrez une espèce de janséniste, essénien de son metier, que j'ai substitué à Varus [...] Ce Varus m'avait paru prodigieusement fade.' In September he proposes that *Mariamne* could well be played at Fontainebleau, as ill health prevents him from producing a new work for the court (D10702, 14 September). This would suggest that he regarded the revision as complete. Yet the final touches had not yet been applied, for in October he tells the d'Argentals that he has not been well enough to work on three plays simultaneously: 'Vous pensez bien qu'en refaisant Olimpie je n'ay pu songer ni à Mariamne ni à Œdipe. Je ne me porte pas assez bien pour avoir à la fois trois tragédies sur le métier' (D10754, 10 October).

Discussion of the details of the revision seems to have taken place between Voltaire and d'Argental, to whose criticisms Voltaire responds a little later in a letter revealing his uncertainties concerning the new version of *Mariamne* (D10777, 25 October): 'Je ne sais plus où j'en suis pour Mariamne [...] Vous me disiez que le second acte n'était pas fini. Cependant Marianne sort pour aller *consulter dieu, l'honneur et le devoir*.[243] N'est-ce pas une raison de sortir quand on a de telles consultations à faire? et ne voilà t'il pas l'acte fini?' There seems nevertheless to be an assumption that

---

[242] The correspondence makes it clear that even among his dramatic works *Mariamne* was not the sole object of Voltaire's attentions at this amazingly productive point in his career. His letters contain abundant discussion of *Olympie*, on which he was then working; *Zulime* and even *Œdipe* are also mentioned.

[243] See variants at II.304a-34.

performance of the revised play was imminent. Casting is discussed, and Voltaire gives d'Argental complete discretion in the matter: 'Vous parliez mon divin ange de distribution de rôles. Je ne m'en souviens plus [...] Mais voici mon blanc seing tragique que vous ferez remplir comme il vous plaira et que vous appuierez de votre protection.'

In December Voltaire complains that his other works have distracted him from attending to his plays: 'Je reverrai Mariamne et Zulime quand je r'aurai ma tête, j'entends ma tête poétique. A présent je suis tout prose, me voilà cunctateur. Attendons: Zulime, Mariane, Olimpie, tout cela viendra, si je vis' (D10831, 10 December). For the time being let the Comédiens neglect *Mariamne* and *Le Droit du Seigneur*, and, if they so wish, put on 'des Eponimes' [244] instead (D10836, 13 December). Voltaire's prose works remain his first priority. He therefore has no new play for the actors, but offers the suggestion that, if their other productions were to fail, 'les comédiens pourraient trouver quelque ressource dans le droit du seigneur et dans Mariamne telle qu'elle est [...] Qu'ils jouent le droit du seigneur et Mariane, s'ils n'ont rien de nouveau ce carême' (D10855, 23 December). This is presumably the revised *Mariamne*, with which Voltaire seems pleased: 'Car je trouve très bon que la Salome dise à Mariamne qu'elle ne la regarde plus que *comme une rivale*. [245] C'est précisément cette rivalité dont il s'agit, c'est de quoi Salome est piquée, et une femme à qui on joue ce tour, dit volontiers à son adverse partie, ce qu'elle a sur le cœur.' Voltaire further recommends *Mariamne* to the Comédiens in early January (D10874, to Mme d'Argental).

Eager as Voltaire now is, in January 1763, to have the play produced, he is at the same time also pressing for early publication.

[244] The reference is probably to *Eponine* or *Sabinus* by Chabanon, not performed until 1764.

[245] In M25 Salome sees Mariamne as her rival for authority over the Hebrews (I.37) or for influence with Hérode (II.19). What is new in M62 is Salome's perception of Mariamne as her rival for the love of Sohème (II.124a-26, variant).

His letter to Cramer of 4 January (D10881) contains instructions on several points concerning the new edition of his works (presumably w64G) then in preparation: 'Il serait essentiel de réimprimer Mariamne selon la nouvelle leçon, en observant de mettre autant de pages pour la nouvelle Mariamne que pour l'ancienne, ce qui est très aisé, et ce qui ne nuira pas à l'édition.' A little later he comments with feigned despair on gossip from the Comédiens concerning the casting for *Mariamne*. 'On dit que la très sublime Clairon ne veut pas ôter le rôle de Mariamne à la très dépenaillée Gossin. Que voulez-vous? Ce n'est pas ma faute, je ne peux rendre ni les hommes ni les filles raisonnables; qui est-ce qui se rend justice?' (D10989, to Mme d'Argental, 9 February 1763).

A few days later Voltaire suggests that *Mariamne* should be included in a small volume of his plays to be offered, along with a respectable sum of money from a publisher (Cramer or another), to Mlle Clairon and Lekain (D10999). He is becoming impatient with publishing delays affecting both *Mariamne* and other works; on 21 February he expresses satisfaction with his play: 'Pour Mariamne je la trouve assez bonne, je crois qu'elle fera effet' (D11034), and writes to Cramer the next day (D11036): 'Quand glisserez-vous la nouvelle Mariamne à la place de l'ancienne dans les œuvres? [...] Mais dépêchons un peu, je vous prie, la vie est courte.' He renews this request in a further letter to Cramer (D11055, February/March 1763): 'Je prie instamment monsieur Caro de me faire l'amitié, d'imprimer la nouvelle Mariamne à la place de l'ancienne.'[246] Yet four days later confidence has disappeared, and a depressed Voltaire writes again to the d'Argentals: 'Mariamne est médiocre, malgré mon Essénien. Olimpie est prodigieusement supérieure à cette Mariamne, et n'est pas encore trop bonne, tout m'humilie et me chagrine, je suis difficile pour moi même comme pour les autres. Il est dur de

---

[246] Voltaire's eagerness may have been inspired by a wish to see the play in print before it was staged, in order to eliminate all risk that the text might be mutilated in performance by Lekain and Mlle Clairon: see D11174 (to d'Argental, 25 April 1763), where he explicitly expresses this fear concerning *Olympie*.

sentir la perfection, et de n'y pouvoir atteindre.'[247] In early March there was a further exchange of correspondence with Cramer, Voltaire promising to fetch from Ferney his only remaining copy of *Mariamne* (D11075, D11082).

Late in May Voltaire asked Cramer, in a note that suggests that the intended recipients were to be the d'Argentals in Paris, to send 'une demi-douzaine d'exemplaires de la nouvelle Mariamne' (D11230, c.25 May 1763). He sent another request to Cramer the next day to send a 'cargaison' of six copies each of *Mariamne*, *Olympie*, *Zulime* and *Le Droit du Seigneur* for the actors of his theatrical performances at Ferney (D11232). The correspondence between Voltaire, Cramer and the d'Argentals in the following months contains many allusions to the sending and receiving of the copies of *Olympie* and *Zulime*. No mention is made, however, of copies of *Mariamne*, and this must certainly have been because none were to hand, as the revised play had not yet been printed. Publication of M62 came with its incorporation into w64G, and was thus well subsequent to the performances given by the Comédie-Française in September 1763.

M62 represents a substantial revision of the earlier parts of the M25 version of the play. As already mentioned, the chief change made by Voltaire was the replacement of the Roman general Varus, by Sohème, a Jewish prince, belonging to the Asmonean family, and so a relative of Mariamne. He is the ruler of Ascalon, an independent kingdom not under the power of Hérode. Sohème is a member of the sect of the Essenians, 'stoïques de Judée',[248] a group who live contemplatively in withdrawal from society and who practise an austere moral code of temperance and mastery of the passions. As the play begins he is betrothed to Hérode's sister

[247] (D11042, 25 February). This last sentence echoes perfectly Voltaire's thoughts expressed in the Préface to *Mariamne*, written almost forty years earlier: 'Dans tous les arts il y a un terme par delà lequel on ne peut plus avancer. On est resserré dans les bornes de son talent: on voit la perfection au delà de soi, et on fait des efforts impuissants pour y atteindre' (lines 197-200).

[248] M62, I.135 (see Appendix D).

Salome. Voltaire radically revised the opening of M25 in order to accommodate this new character. He kept only the first 62 lines of act I, making some amendments and introducing, at line 35, a change of speaker. After that he rewrote altogether the remainder of the act, comprising some 250 lines, from line 63 onwards, retaining only seven lines (148, 232 to 236 and 301 to 302) from M25.[249] Salome's opening conversation with Mazaël is consequently much changed, as she tells him that she believes that Mariamne has eclipsed her in the affections of Sohème, and evokes with bitterness her chagrin at this betrayal. Sohème appears in scene ii and announces that, having become disenchanted with Hérode's ambitions for political ascendancy, he has decided to break off his plans for marriage and withdraw to his own kingdom. He denies that he is in love with Mariamne, but his evident compassion for her sufferings arouses the jealousy and anger of Salome, who is thus given considerably stronger motivation for hating her sister-in-law in the revised text than in the earlier version. In conversation in scene iii with his confidant Ammon, Sohème professes himself shocked by the insinuation that he is in love with Mariamne, denying that his 'austère amitié' for her could hide a 'feu profane', and rejecting the notion that the 'faiblesses d'amour' could have any hold over him (M62, I.127-30). A brief scene iv takes Sohème off the stage to answer a call for help from a distressed Alexandra, mother of Mariamne.

Although he invented the role of Sohème, Voltaire took the opportunity afforded by the revision of the play to bring one important element of the plot into closer alignment with the historical account found in Josephus. Hérode's secret order for the death of Mariamne, recounted by Sohème (M62, I.153-60), and referred to a little later by Elize (M62, I.194-95), now follows substantially the Josephan narrative. With only a few differences of detail,[250] Sohème describes how Hérode, departing for his

[249] The full text of the revised sections of act I is given in Appendix D.
[250] The meeting between Hérode and Octavian is located in Rome, rather than Rhodes. The minister charged to carry out this order (Soeme or Sohème in Arnauld

interview with Octavian, had left an order that in the event of his failure to return she too should be put to death so that she would not fall into another's hands. Voltaire wrote out of the play the order which in the Varus version Hérode sends back from Rome for the summary execution of Mariamne.

The introduction of Sohème and the changed nature of Hérode's order necessitated adjustments to the rest of the play, but these were more limited in extent. The principal changes to act II are not numerous. The first nineteen lines of scene i are replaced by 38 new verses, and the final forty-four lines were removed.[251] These changes refer to Hérode's new order against Mariamne in place of the earlier one, but their main effect is to intensify Salome's forebodings already present in M25, her sense that power is slipping away from her. In scene ii, lines 81-84, with their now inappropriate allusion to Hérode's order sent from Rome, are omitted, and lines 125-26 are replaced by six lines spoken by Salome,[252] which contain an explosion of jealousy against Mariamne, whom she sees as having defeated her in rivalry for the affections of Sohème. In scene iii Elize's warning speech is revised to take account of the fact that Mariamne will shortly lose the protection not of Varus but of Sohème.[253] In Mariamne's speech in scene iv to Narbas (the former Nabal of M25) six lines are changed to remove reference to Varus,[254] and eight verses devoted to the praise of Augustus (II.257-64) disappear from her long plea in scene v.

More important than these is the change made at the end of act II, where the final scene vi is replaced by thirty-eight lines added to scene v.[255] These contain Sohème's dramatic declaration

d'Andilly's translation of Josephus) is now named Phérore (thus avoiding confusion with the character created by Voltaire to replace Varus).

[251] The full text of the revised scene i of act II is given in Appendix D.
[252] See variants at II.124a-26.
[253] See variants at II.135-49.
[254] See variants at II.159-64. See also variants and notes at II.186.
[255] See variants at II.304a-34.

that Mariamne's virtues have inspired him to overcome the temptation of selfish passion. He will henceforth devote himself disinterestedly to her service, even at the cost of sacrificing everything of value to himself. Mariamne, who remains on stage, admires this noble conduct. She is conscious of the dangers which lie ahead. But Sohème reassures her: they are worthy of each other, and will be joined not in love, but in shared virtue. Act II comes to an end on this sublime note.

Act III was little changed. There are several minor modifications of wording, mostly dictated by the substitution of Sohème for Varus. In scene ii, whereas Varus in M25 excludes the notion of fleeing with Mariamne, a slight rewording of lines 45-48 in M62 shows Sohème briefly questioning whether that course is really denied him. Voltaire rearranged Idamas's speech in scene iii. [256] He also dropped twelve lines from the following scene (III.133-44), eliminating a mention of the sinister Zarès, who was to have executed Hérode's original order for the death of Mariamne, and Hérode's brief evocation of his glorious past. There is also an expansion from two lines to eight of the opening of the former scene vi (now scene v in M62), which gives Salome an opportunity to make hostile insinuations against Sohème and Mariamne. [257] Line 258 was also modified to reflect the change in Hérode's order against Mariamne.

In act IV Voltaire's revisions were limited to scenes i and ii. He added eight lines, between lines 22 and 23, to Salome's speech in scene i. In these she laments bitterly the fact that she has alienated Sohème, and that Hérode seems bent on reconciliation with Mariamne. [258] The beginning of scene ii, which had been considerably extended in 1730, was further augmented by 11 new lines, in which Mazaël accuses Sohème of plotting to take Hérode's life. [259] Later in this scene Voltaire dropped lines 51-58, no longer

---

[256] See variants and notes at III.59-87.
[257] See variants at III.225a-28.
[258] See variants at IV.23-24.
[259] See variants at IV.27-31.

appropriate in the context of Sohème:[260] in the revised play Hérode has no need to fear an adverse reaction from Rome to his treatment of a Roman governor. Finally in the same scene lines 67-68 are replaced in M62 by ten lines in which Hérode, though reciting the wrongs which he has suffered at the hands of Mariamne, questions whether her real attention was to dishonour him.[261] Apart from the replacement of the name Varus by Sohème, no further changes were made to act IV. The remainder of the act, containing the great confrontation between Hérode and Mariamne in scene iv and its brusque interruption in the following scenes v and vi, reads in M62 exactly as it did in the final state of M25.

Act V was also left untouched, apart from changes to the names of the characters, with the single exception of lines 121-27, where two short speeches by Idamas are reworked to eliminate references to the Romans and their likely anger at the death of Varus.[262] Thus the account given by Narbas of the execution of Mariamne is identical with the earlier account given by Nabal in the final state of M25.

Voltaire's claim in D10597 that he had entirely changed *Mariamne* is therefore in need of some qualification. He certainly seems to have begun the reworking of the play with considerable gusto. Rewriting act I almost completely was radical surgery. Interventions at the end of act II were also major. But thereafter treatment becomes intermittent in act III and the initial scenes of act IV, and ceases altogether in the remaining scenes of act IV and in act V in its entirety. Voltaire did not alter important features of the play which had attracted adverse comment from the critics and mockery from the parodists, such as the similarity of the endings of acts III and IV, and the brusque change of Hérode's attitude in the last scenes of act IV. Moreover Voltaire left intact the much criticised romantic sub-plot, and probably aggravated its improbability, since, however indirect, a declaration of love for the

[260] See variants at IV.50-59.
[261] See variants at IV.67-69.
[262] See variants at V.122-27.

virtuous Mariamne would be unlikely in the extreme from the austere Sohème, who claims to practise a lofty moral code. Sohème uses the same words as Varus, much ridiculed and much criticised although they had been, to describe the purity of his intentions towards Mariamne, M25 I.302-304 reappearing, with only a change of tense, as M62, I.171-72: these lines are among the very few from act I of M25 which reappear in the lengthy rewritten section of act I of M62. Sohème's dramatic function is in fact little different from that of Varus. Each is the champion and protector of Mariamne. Each falls in love with her, yet is inspired by the example of her virtue to solve nobly the moral problem which this creates. Sohème may be said to achieve this in a more declamatory and even histrionic fashion in his speech in the rewritten conclusion to act II than Varus in his dialogue with Albin in the last scene of the act in M25, but the differences do not go beyond that.

The Kehl editors describe the reasons which they claim led Voltaire to replace Varus (K85, i.201). They list the numerous contradictions between the events featured in the play and the real historical record: Varus's defeat and death in Germany were too well known for anyone to suppose that he was killed in Judea, a Roman praetor would never have stirred up a revolt in Jerusalem, he would have forbidden Hérode to threaten his wife's life, and Hérode would have obeyed. The original play also contravened accepted views about the Romans: except in special cases such as Racine's *Bérénice*, a Roman who loved a queen was not an interesting subject. In the presence of Varus Hérode had to be portrayed in a demeaning light: for all his kingly status, he was a mere subject in Roman eyes. These reasons are all plausible enough, but there is no evidence for ascribing them to Voltaire himself.

ii. *Performances, reception and publication*

The revised *Mariamne* with Sohème was given two performances only at the Comédie-Française, on 7 and 10 September 1763, attracting houses of respectively 759 and 677 paying spectators. [263] These houses were no more than average for this time. The *Mercure de France* reported this event as follows in its October issue (p.194):

Le 7 septembre on a représenté HERODE, tragédie de M. de Voltaire, avec les changements jugés nécessaires. Les acteurs ont très bien joué dans cette pièce, qui a été fort applaudie dans un grand nombre d'endroits. Beaucoup de spectateurs ont regretté de grandes beautés de détails supprimés dans les changements faits à cette tragédie.

Other appreciations were less favourable. Favart wrote to the comte de Durazzo on 18 September 1763: 'On a représenté la semaine dernière au Théâtre français *Hérode et Mariamne*, tragédie de M. de Voltaire, avec des corrections; on a retranché le rôle de Varus pour en substituer un autre; le public n'a point applaudi à ces changements.' [264] And Collé, who apparently did not attend a performance, noted in his *Journal*:

Dans tout le commencement de ce mois, l'on a donné *Hérode et Mariamne*, de M. de Voltaire; cela n'a point fait sensation. Les changements qu'il y a faits n'ont rien changé, m'a-t-on dit, au peu d'intérêt de cette tragédie, si l'on peut appeler ainsi des tracasseries de ménage mises en action. Voltaire a eu beau ôter le rôle impertinent de Varus, Sosime [*sic*] qui a pris sa place, n'en a pas moins ennuyé les spectateurs. Cette drogue a été donnée trois fois [*sic*] à Paris, et sera jouée le mois prochain à Fontainebleau. [265]

The *Mémoires secrets* of Bachaumont had mentioned Voltaire's revision of the play as early as February 1763, and given it a further notice on the eve of the first performance. Their report after the performance was unenthusiastic:

[263] Lancaster, *The Comédie-Française*, p.808.

[264] C.-S. Favart, *Mémoires et correspondance littéraires dramatiques et anecdotiques* (1808), ii.144-45.

[265] Charles Collé, *Journal historique ou mémoires critiques et littéraires* (Paris 1809), iii.57. *Mariamne* does not appear in the *Mercure de France* reports of performances before the court at Fontainebleau in 1763 and 1764.

On a repris aujourd'hui *Mariamne*, avec les changements qui ont paru nécessaires, disait l'affiche. Le concours n'a pas été nombreux, comme il l'est aux pièces de M. de Voltaire, et tout cet appareil n'a point fait, ainsi qu'on l'espérait, la sensation d'une pièce nouvelle. Les innovations se réduisent au rôle de Varus, auquel l'on en a substitué un autre. Il se trouve dans la même position, et dit à peu près les mêmes choses et les mêmes vers.

Attendance was not good. Voltaire had not succeeded in renewing his play, for there was little apparent difference between Varus and Sohème not only in their situations but even in the lines which they were given to speak. Like the *Mercure*, the *Mémoires secrets* registered the disappointment of many spectators at the loss of 'de grandes beautés de détail' from the earlier version.[266]

The most interesting account of these performances of the revised *Mariamne* comes from La Harpe, who, in a passage of his *Cours de littérature* in which he seeks to account for the failure of Voltaire's *Mariamne* to achieve durable success despite the acclaim that had surrounded it in 1725, writes as follows:

Je fus témoin de la reprise de cette pièce en 1762, et, quoique fort jeune, je fus assez frappé de ce qui s'y passa pour ne l'avoir jamais oublié. Le vide d'action dans les trois premiers actes les fit accueillir froidement: les beautés du style avaient pu les faire applaudir dans la nouveauté, mais alors la pièce était connue depuis longtemps; et il faut observer que ces sortes de beautés, qui attirent d'abord beaucoup d'applaudissements lorsqu'elles sont nouvelles, perdent bientôt de leur effet au théâtre, si elles ne sont pas attachées à un fond tragique [...] Au quatrième acte, la scène [quatre], jouée par l'inimitable Lekain, et par une actrice digne de jouer avec lui, mademoiselle Clairon, fit un plaisir général.

But when the guard rushed in to announce that the scaffold prepared for Mariamne had been overthrown by the people, now commanded by Sohème, 'il s'éleva un murmure universel à cet endroit, qui montrait tout le faible de l'ouvrage, et de quel frivole

---

[266] [Bachaumont], *Mémoires secrets pour servir à l'histoire de la République des Lettres en France depuis* [*1762*] (London 1780-1789), i.303-304 (entry for 7 September 1763).

prétexte l'auteur se servait pour amener la mort de Mariame, commandée par le sujet'. The overturning of the scaffold, for which Mariamne was not responsible, was a totally inadequate justification for the return of Hérode's anger: 'Plus on venait d'être ému de la scène des deux époux, plus cette révolution invraisemblable dut refroidir tout le reste de la pièce, où l'on ne voyait plus dans Hérode qu'une barbarie gratuite.' This ruined the rest of the play. Hérode appeared unrelievedly odious from that point, and the capacity of spectators to be moved by the nobility of Mariamne's subsequent actions was adversely affected, for it became difficult to accept that she should refuse Sohème's aid, and finally sacrifice her life altogether, for the benefit of so unworthy a personage: 'La pièce, dans les deux [sic] représentations suivantes, ne se releva pas, et depuis elle n'a pas reparu.'[267]

The revival of *Mariamne* is also discussed in Grimm's *Correspondance littéraire* under the date of 15 September 1763.[268] Grimm states that Voltaire had bowed to widespread criticism of the role of Varus in replacing him with the austere Sohème. This personage however had fallen passionately in love with Mariamne ('ô étrange faiblesse du stoïque Sohème et de son poëte!'). He allows himself to reveal his feelings to Mariamne only once, assuring her that he will never speak about them again, but will be content to adore her virtues far away from her and a hateful court unworthy of possessing her. This, Grimm says, is 'le principal défaut de ce rôle substitué au personnage de Varus, dont Sohème ne fait plus que réciter les vers mot pour mot, dès qu'il nous a appris une fois qu'il est parent de Mariamne, et qu'il suit les principes des Esséniens'. To be sure, a Roman praetor 'amoureux comme un roman' was quite out of place and absurd in this tragedy, 'mais un Juif stoïcien qui succombe aux charmes de sa parente ne l'est guère moins, et nous n'avons rien gagné au change'. Grimm expresses astonishment that Voltaire had not

[267] La Harpe, *Cours de littérature*, ii.207-208.
[268] *CL*, v.383-87.

perceived 'combien cet amour est oisif et inutile'; all it produced was 'une froide et insipide déclaration'. Voltaire, he suggests, had been the prisoner of conventions prevailing in an earlier time: 'Lorsque M. de Voltaire entreprit dans sa jeunesse de traiter ce sujet, le théâtre français était infecté de cet insipide amour qui y a régné si longtemps. Il était de l'essence d'une tragédie française, et c'était un usage convenu, qu'outre le principal amour il y eût encore un amour postiche. [...] M. de Voltaire n'osa s'écarter d'un usage qui était devenu loi.' How extraordinary it was that, having realised that the role of Varus had to be changed, he had not removed what disfigured it most, namely 'cet amour déplacé et inutile'!

Grimm was surprised that Voltaire had not taken advantage of this revival to restore the final act to the original form which it had been given in the *Mariamne* of 1724. He recounts the incident which had brought the end of the play down in ruin, and, reiterating his criticism of 1754,[269] comments as follows:

Ce n'est pas la première fois qu'un mauvais plaisant a gâté de belles choses; mais depuis trente ans que cette pièce a paru pour la première fois, nous avons fait quelques progrès en fait de goût; l'esprit philosophique nous a guéris de quelques puérilités, et M. de Voltaire aurait pu rétablir sans danger une action si intéressante et si pathétique.

Grimm's overall judgement was that the revival had failed. There had been only two performances. The public had been led to expect great changes, but discovered that these amounted to no more than the change of the name of one character. Furthermore the play had been poorly performed. Mlle Dubois had been weak as Salome, Mlle Clairon poorly cast as Mariamne.[270]

Grimm finally asks how it was that *Mariamne* was such a disappointing play. The subject, 'plein d'intérêt et de pathétique'

---

[269] See above, p.95.
[270] *Mariamne* was not staged again at the Comédie-Française until 1817, when it received three performances, the first of which was a retirement benefit for Mlle Emilie Contat.

offered great promise from the very first scene. What was lacking was 'ce souffle de vie qui anime tout, et que rien ne peut remplacer; c'est cette force vivifiante de l'homme de génie, qui se répand sur la totalité de sa production, et qui donne à chaque partie le degré de vie qui lui est nécessaire'.

These last comments seem to condemn not only the 1762 revival but the totality of the Voltairean enterprise in regard to the story of Mariamne:

Il faut que le dessein de traiter ce sujet ait saisi le poète dans un mauvais quart d'heure, car tout y languit [...] M. de Voltaire a bien prouvé par ses ouvrages postérieurs qu'il ne manquait point de ce souffle de vie qu'on désirerait à *Mariamne*. Ce défaut est irréparable. Lorsqu'un homme de génie a traité un sujet sans chaleur, il faut qu'il y renonce; il aurait beau y revenir, se buter, il ne ferait que se fatiguer inutilement. C'est dommage, car le sujet de *Mariamne* était bien digne de l'auteur de *Zaïre*.

Voltaire's reaction to the lack of acclaim for the revised *Mariamne* is expressed in a letter to the d'Argentals of 18 September 1763 (D11422):

Je me doutais bien, mes divins anges, que mademoiselle Clairon n'était guère faite pour jouer Mariamne. Je ne me souviens plus du tout des anciennes imprécations qui finissaient le cinquième acte, et en général, je crois que ces imprécations sont comme les sottises, les plus courtes sont les meilleures. Je vous avoue que je serais bien plus sûr d'Olympie.

Voltaire accepts then the criticism that had been directed against Mlle Clairon. But from this letter we receive above all the impression that he has begun to distance himself from *Mariamne*, perhaps in a defensive reaction after the failure of the revival. He seems now to pin hopes for a success in Paris on *Olympie*, which, the continuation of the letter informs us, provided wonderful spectacle and had been very successfully performed in the provinces and abroad.

The lack of success of the performances did not lead Voltaire to modify his desire to include the revised version of *Mariamne* in the new edition of his complete works then under preparation, in which he intended that it should replace the Varus text. The Sohème version was published for the first time in w64G. The Varus version was not completely abandoned, however, for the longer passages discarded from the earlier text were included in an appendix. Subsequent editions of the works of Voltaire reprint the text of w64G with little change, and most of them also reproduce the appendix of passages from the Varus version. At the time when Cramer was preparing the publication of the great quarto edition of Voltaire's works (w68), Voltaire asked him to consider whether both versions of the play might not be printed together, either on the same pages, with the Sohème version as the main text and the Varus text in footnotes, or one after the other (D13331, May/June 1766). Neither suggestion was implemented, and the same compromise was adopted as for w64G.

A letter to d'Argental in 1769 provides evidence that, despite its failure at the Comédie-Française, the revised *Mariamne* was enjoying some years later a better fate in the provinces. Voltaire reports that Lekain, with the help of a troupe of local actors, had had great success in staging it, along with other tragedies by Voltaire, at Toulouse, that former stronghold of obscurantism and bigotry: 'Les spectacles adoucissent les mœurs, et quand la philosophie s'y joint la superstition est bientôt écraseé. Il s'est fait depuis dix ans dans toute la jeunesse de Toulouse un changement incroyable' (D15897, 16 September 1769).

Voltaire no doubt derived much encouragement from this development. Yet in his last years Voltaire came to look back upon his involvement with the story of Mariamne with very mixed feelings. A sense of regret, and even of time wasted, is evident in a further report from La Harpe: 'J'ai vu Voltaire se reprocher le temps qu'il croyait avoir perdu en s'obstinant à un sujet qui n'était pas heureux. Son âme, insatiable de gloire, eût voulu ne pas laisser une trace des pas qu'il avait faits dans la carrière qui ne fût marquée par des lauriers: mais il se jugeait trop sévèrement.' But, La Harpe continues, Voltaire had not wasted his time: '*Mariamne* est une des pièces où il s'est le plus approché de la pureté, de l'élégance et de l'harmonie de Racine. Voltaire en a fait plusieurs bien supérieures à celle-ci pour l'intérêt, mais dont la diction est moins soignée.' *Mariamne* was a play in which superior diction made up for 'le vide de l'action' and for 'le défaut d'intérêt. [271]

Voltaire's last words on *Mariamne*, however, contain a note certainly of disappointment and almost of disavowal. They appear in an autograph note inserted on the title page for *Mariamne* in the copy of w75G which, shortly before leaving Ferney for his final journey to Paris in 1778, he marked up for the proposed Panckoucke edition of his works: [272]

les gens de lettres qui ont presidé a cette edition complette ont cru devoir rejetter cette tragedie de mariamne parmy les pieces de lauteur qui ne sont pas représentees au teatre de paris, et qui ne sont pour la plus part que des pieces de societé. mariamne fut composee dans le temps de la nouvauté d'œdipe. il ne la jamais regardee que comme une declamation.

7. *Manuscripts and editions*

i. *Manuscripts*

No original manuscripts of any of the versions of *Hérode et Mariamne* are known. Surviving manuscript material of any description is meagre in quantity.

MS I

Herode / ET / Mariane / Tragedie.
Old copy, by one professional hand; 28.5 x 18 cm; 41 leaves.
[*1*]*r* title; [*1*]*v* Personnages; 1*r*-40*r* Hérode et Mariane, tragédie.

This manuscript gives the text of the play found in the editions 25CH, 25X and 26H, which we consider to be that of the earliest performances of the 1725 version.

Paris, Arsenal: Rondel ms 337.

271 La Harpe, *Cours de littérature* (Paris 1840), p.204.
272 The 'Leningrad encadré', see w75G* in the list of editions.

MS2

A copy in the hand of Lekain of the role of Hérode. Contained in a volume of copies of roles played by Lekain between 1754 and 1759.

[1] 'Année 1754 / Second Rosle. Herode / Dans Herode et Mariamne. / Tragédie de M^r De Voltaire.'; [2] Acteurs (gives cast lists for performances in 1763 and in 1754, in that order); 1-17 Rôle d'Hérode.

Lekain copied out the part of Hérode in the Varus version, leaving a large left margin, in which he wrote notes for his own guidance on questions of diction and interpretation. Later, no doubt in preparation for the 1763 performances, another hand using darker ink introduced the changes made to the role of Hérode in the Sohème version: rejected lines were crossed out and the new versions written in above or below the line; in some cases longer passages were transcribed onto slips of paper which were then pasted over the original text, still discernible in most cases beneath the pasted insert.

The Lekain transcript of the role of Hérode follows the printed sources for both versions. Variants affect points of detail and have been recorded, as they probably reflect Lekain's performances of the role. (The cue lines for Hérode are on occasion quoted rather approximately in the transcript and have been ignored.)

Paris, Comédie française: Lekain 1754-1759, no. 2.

MS3

A copy in the hand of Henri Rieu of the surviving parts of the 1724 version of *Hérode et Mariamne* (act III, scenes iii and iv). This copy, evidently dating from the Ferney period, is found in a manuscript annex to one of the 'recueils factices' (convenience bindings of short printed works by Voltaire) which form part of Voltaire's library held in St Petersburg (see BV, annexes manuscrites, no. 56). The manuscript has the following heading: 'Scenes de la Tragedie de Mariamne de Mr D.V. qui ne se trouvent dans aucune édition de ses œuvres'.

ii. *Editions*

All the editions of *Hérode et Mariamne* or *Mariamne*, whether published separately or included in collections of his works, which appeared during Voltaire's lifetime are described below.[273] To these we have added Kehl.

Collation shows that the texts fall into three groups, as follows:

(1) a small group of editions (25CH, 25X and 26H) published without Voltaire's approval, and giving the first state, used in the earliest performances, of the 1725 version with Varus.[274]

(2) a much larger group of editions which give the Varus version of the play in the text authorised by Voltaire. This first appeared in 1725 (25P). Of the many subsequent re-editions, several (30, 31, W38, W42 W46, W48D, W51, W52, W56, W57P and W57G) benefited from the collaboration of Voltaire, who over the years introduced significant revisions and additions. These variants have been recorded in the critical apparatus and discussed in the introduction and commentary.

(3) a group of editions (W64G, W68, W70G, W70L, W71, 72P, 72X, W72P, W72X, W75G, W75X, T76G, T76X, K) which give the 1762 Sohème version of the play. Voltaire participated in W64G, and subsequently in W68, W70L and W75G, and in the preparation of Kehl. We have recorded variants from these editions, but none of them shows extensive variation from W64G.

25CH

HERODE / ET / MARIAMNE, / TRAGEDIE. / PAR M. DE VOLTAIRE. / [woodcut, sphere in ornamental frame, 50 x 35 mm] / A AMSTERDAM, / Chez FRANÇOIS CHANGUYON. / [rule, 38 mm] / M. DCC. XXV.

6°. sig. A-E⁶; pag. 60 (p.3 numbered 'I'); $3 signed, roman (-A1); sheet catchwords.

[1] title; [2] Acteurs; [3]-60 Hérode et Mariamne, tragédie.

In the only copy known to us of this edition, the volume has been taken apart, and the pages separated (and perhaps trimmed) and remounted in

273 The only exceptions are four late editions of the dramatic writings in which he did not participate (T66, T73L, T73R, T77). Copies of these editions exist, at Aberdeen, Detmold, Beaune and Stockholm respectively, but we have not had access to them.

274 With MS1 we thus have four sources for the first state of the 1725 *Mariamne*. Two sub-groups are apparent: MS1 and 25CH, and 25X and 26H.

frames cut in the leaves of a blank volume made up from 6° gatherings of heavier paper. Each of the original pages thus appears surrounded by a large border of stouter material. The reassembly must have taken place at an early date, as the paper used to make the framing volume is old. Edition denounced by Voltaire in the preface to 25P.

Paris, Arsenal: Rf 14138.

25X

IIERODE / ET / MARIAMNE, / *TRAGEDIE.* / Par Monsieur DE VOLTAIRE. / Revuë & corrigée par l'Auteur. / [*woodcut, mask with flowers and foliage, 60 x 48 mm*] / [*single rule, 80 mm*] / M. DCC. XXV.

4°. sig. A-G⁴; pag. 55; $2 signed, roman (not A1, G2); no catchwords.

[1] title; [2] blank; [3] Avertissement; [4] Acteurs; 5-55 Hérode et Mariamne, tragédie.

Probably not the edition produced in Rouen and disavowed by Voltaire in D243, though it could be one of two editions 'sans nom d'imprimeur' denounced in the Préface, or one of two editions mentioned in D244. Probably produced in Holland by Jean Néaulme, for it shows close similarities with 26H, with which it shares errors. The Avertissement states that the text is 'une copie corrigée' of the play 'telle qu'on l'a représentée en dernier lieu sur le Théâtre de Paris', supplied not by Voltaire but by 'un de ses intimes amis'.

Toronto, University of Toronto Library, Harcourt Brown Voltaire Collection, pamphlets V65 M375 1725d.

25P

HERODE / ET / MARIAMNE, / *TRAGEDIE,* / DE M. DE VOLTAIRE. / . . . . *Æstuat ingens / Imo in corde pudor, mixto quae insania luctu, / Et furiis agitatus amor,* &c.[275] / Le prix est de 30. sols. / [*typographic ornament*] / A PARIS, QUAY DES AUGUS-TINS, / Chez [*accolade*] / NOEL PISSOT, à la descente du Pont- / Neuf, à la Croix d'Or, / ET / FRANÇOIS FLAHAUT, du / côté du Pont. S. Michel, au Roy de / Portugal. / [*rule, 43 mm*] / M. DCC. XXV. / *AVEC PRIVILEGE DU ROY.*

[275] *Aeneid,* XII.666-68. In Virgil the second line begins: 'Uno in corde.'

HERODE

ET

MARIAMNE,

TRAGEDIE.

Par Monſieur De Voltaire,

Revuë & corrigée par l'Auteur,

Et orig.   *Lagravere*

M. DCC. XXV.

1. *Hérode et Mariamne*, title page of 25x, one of the early editions denounced by Voltaire.

HERODE
ET
MARIAMNE,
TRAGEDIE,
DE M. DE VOLTAIRE.

,. . . . . Æftuat ingens
Imo in corde pudor, mixto quæ infania luctu,
Et furiis agitatus amor, &c.

Le prix eft de 30. fols.

༄

A PARIS, QUAY DES AUGUSTINS,

Chez {
NOEL PISSOT, à la defcente du Pont-
Neuf, à la Croix d'Or.
ET
FRANÇOIS FLAHAULT, du
côté du Pont. S. Michel, au Roy de
Portugal.

M. DCC. XXV.

AVEC PRIVILEGE DV ROY.

2. *Hérode et Mariamne*, title page of 25P (the base text).
Oxford, Taylor Institution Library.

3. *Hérode et Mariamne*, act IV, scene iv, Mariamne's entry
for her confrontation with Hérode.
(From a drawing by Desenne, reproduced in κ85.)

Act. 5.   *MARIAMNE*   Scene 7.

*Quoi. Citoyens perfides
Vous arrachés ce fer à mes mains parricides !*

4. *Hérode et Mariamne*, act V, scene vii, Hérode's remorse.
(From a drawing reproduced in w75G.)

127

8°. sig. π^2 (π1 + ã⁸) A-F8 [ ]²; pag. [20] 96 [4]; \$4 signed, roman; sheet catchwords (not ã, C).

[1] title; [2] blank; [3]-[19] Préface; [20] Acteurs; 1-95 Hérode et Mariamne, tragédie; [96] [within ornamented frame] 'De l'Imprimerie de LOUIS SEVESTRE, / Pont S. Michel.'; [1]-[4] Privilège.

The first edition of *Hérode et Mariamne* authorised by Voltaire, and taken as the base text of this edition. Eleven copies have been collated: BnF 8° Yth. 8459, 8° Yth. 8461, Rés. p. Yf. 393, Rés. Z Beuchot 338, Rés. Z Bengesco 9, and Rés. Rothschild 5230; Arsenal GD 11550 (in which *Hérode et Mariamne* is bound with Nadal's *Observations critiques*), Rf. 14137; Taylor V3 H5 1725; BL 11736.c.28 (1) (in which *Le Mauvais Ménage, parodie* by Dominique and Legrand, Paris, Flahaut, 1725, is bound in the same volume); ANL RB PEL 1218.

The *Privilège* is found in 8 copies: BnF Z Bengesco 9, Rés. p. Yf 393 and Z Rothschild 5230, Arsenal GD 11550 and Rf 14137, Taylor V3.H5.1725, BL 11736.c.28 (1) and ANL RB PEL 1218. The title of the play appears as *Mariamne*.

The following differences have been observed between the individual copies of 25P which we have examined:

(a) *Preliminaries*: Two copies (BnF 8° Yth. 8459 and ANL RB PEL 1218) present a revised setting of the preliminary bifolium. On the title page they read the correct Latin *mixtoque* in place of the defective *mixto quae* found in all other copies. The list of actors given on p.[20] is augmented by the inclusion of 'Un Garde d'Hérode, parlant' and 'Une Suivante de Mariamne, muette'.

(b) *Gathering ã*: The same two copies and also BL 11736.c.28 (1) correct two of the spelling errors and misprints observed in other copies, reading 'conservant' (not 'conservaut') at Préface, line 64 (page not numbered; sig. ã2v) and 'Mithridate' (not 'Mithidate') at Préface, line 216 (page not numbered; sig. ã7v).

(c) *Gathering C*: One copy (BnF Z Beuchot 338) corrects the misprint 'reconnuossance' at II.298 (p.36; sig. C2v).

(d) *Gathering F*: Two copies (BnF 8° Yth 8459 and ANL RB PEL 1218) introduce at two points textual variations not found in the other copies. The first is in the list of characters on stage at the beginning of act V, scene iv (p.84; sig. F2v), where the words 'Une Suivante' appear on a separate line inserted after V.82b; the second comes at the beginning of act V, scene vii (p.89; sig. F5r), where 'Gardes' is inserted on a separate line inserted after V.144b. In the same gathering these copies also correct two small errors found in other copies of 25P. At V.96 (p.85; sig. F3r) they print in correct alignment the final *t* of the initial word 'Tout', which is printed upside down elsewhere, and they remove the exclamation mark found in mid-sentence after 'nuage' at the end of V.208 (p.93; sig. F7r). In addition the same copies give a corrected version of V.103 (p.85; sig. F3r), which reads in the other copies 'Si j'avais un moment en secret souhaité ma vengeance'. BnF 8° Yth 8459 and ANL RB PEL 1218 omit 'en secret', thereby reducing the verse to a regular alexandrine.

The differences between individual copies suggest that corrections were made to at least some sheets while this edition was in the press: corrected sheets for the preliminaries and gatherings ã and F seem to have been used to make up 8° Yth 8459 and ANL RB PEL 1218, while other copies were composed from the earlier sheets. Further use of the corrected sheets is discussed under 27 and 30 below.

BnF Rés. p. Yf 393 presents special features. It contains an unsigned and unpaginated bifolium inserted between leaves π1 and ã1, the collation of the preliminaries therefore being π^2 ($\pi1 + 2\pi^2 + \tilde{a}^8$). The first added leaf is blank both recto and verso, as is the verso of the second leaf. The recto carries a woodcut,[276] and beneath it a dedication to Marie Leszczynska: 'A LA REINE. / MADAME, [the initial M is a woodcut] Il paraîtra peut-être peu convenable de dédier Mariamne à une Reine qui fait le bonheur de son époux; mais je dois présenter cet ouvrage à Votre Majesté parce qu'il est l'éloge de la vertu. Vous y trouverez des sentiments de grandeur sans orgueil, de modestie sans affectation, de générosité et de bienséance. C'est par là seulement que cette pièce peut trouver grâce devant vos yeux.' This copy is described by Bengesco (i.6) and is the only one known which contains the dedication. It is bound in leather and considerable traces of gilt are visible on the page edges. A manuscript annex of 4 leaves is included in the same binding, containing the *Lettre critique sur Mariamne par* [*J.-B.*] *Rousseau* (D245), with some minor variations in wording.

---

[276] Within a rectangular frame 85 x 24 mm a covered vase is depicted, bordered on both sides with fronds and vegetation, with the letters 'V.LS' in the lower left corner. A woodcut of this design is found at the head of the preface and each of acts I to IV in all copies of 25P.

There are minor handwritten annotations in three copies (Arsenal GD 11550, BnF Z Rothschild 5230 and BL 11736.c.28(1)).

Bengesco 19; BnC 927-930.

Canberra, ANL: RB PEL 1218. London, BL: 11736.c.28 (1) (bound with *Le Mauvais Ménage, parodie* by Dominique and Legrand, Paris, Flahaut, 1725). Oxford, Taylor: V3 H5 1725. Paris, Arsenal: GD 11550 (bound with Nadal's *Observations critiques*), Rf. 14137; BnF: 8° Yth. 8459, 8° Yth. 8461, Rés. p. Yf. 393, Rés. Z Beuchot 338, Rés. Z Bengesco 9, Rés. Rothschild 5230.

25P^c

HERODE / ET / MARIAMNE, / *TRAGEDIE,* / DE M. DE VOLTAIRE. / . . . . *Æstuat ingens / Imo in corde pudor, mixto quae insania luctu, / Et furiis agitatus amor,* &c. / Le prix est de 30. sols. / [*typographic ornament*] / A PARIS, QUAY DES AUGUSTINS, / Chez [*accolade*] / NOEL PISSOT, à la descente du Pont- / Neuf, à la Croix d'Or, / ET / FRANÇOIS FLAHAUT, du / côté du Pont S. Michel, au Roy de / Portugal. / [*rule, 54 mm*] / M. DCC. XXV. / *AVEC PRIVILEGE DU ROY.*

8°. sig. π² (π1 + ã⁸) A-F8 [ ]²; pag. [*20*] 96 [4]; $4 signed, ã arabic, A-F roman; sheet catchwords (incl. ã, C).

[*1*] title; [*2*] blank; [*3*]-[*19*] Préface; [*20*] Acteurs; 1-95 Hérode et Mariamne, tragédie; [96] [within ornamented frame] 'De l'Imprimerie de LOUIS SEVESTRE, / Pont S. Michel.'; [1]-[4] Privilège.

Imitates 25P, which it reproduces line by line and page by page. With the exception only of the first 12 lines of the Préface and the first 6 lines of the *privilège* (which have been rearranged to accommodate the woodcuts used for the first letter of each text), type, ornaments and woodcuts have been placed in the same positions on corresponding pages. Both editions have the same collation. The typefaces are very similar when not identical. The typographical ornaments are different, but in most cases not widely dissimilar. Clear differences exist however between the woodcuts of the two editions, though often based on similar motifs, and 25P^c sometimes lacks woodcuts in places where they appear in 25P.

25P^c corrects most of the misprints and errors observed in 25P (retaining 'void' however) and introduces a few new ones (at II.317, for instance, we find 'Dienx' for 'Dieux'). There are a few small variations in spelling, but more numerous differences are found in accentuation, 25P^c tending to use accents more liberally than 25P. No variants of significance have been found in 25P^c.

The two editions can be distinguished by the title page, which has a longer rule in 25P^c, and on which the accolade, almost rectilinear in 25P, has a more curved conformation in 25P^c, and by the woodcuts placed at the head of the Préface and of each act; in 25P these fill elegantly the whole width of the page and bear the initials V.LS for the preface and acts I-IV (all of which have the same design) and PIR (or PIB) for act V, whereas in 25P^c the woodcuts are smaller, more cramped, do not extend to the print margins and are without initials.

It is unlikely that Pissot and Flahaut would have published two distinct settings of *Hérode et Mariamne* with a 1725 imprint. No evidence is available to determine the publisher of 25P^c.

BnC 931.

Oxford, Bodley: Vet. E4. e. 29. Paris, Arsenal: Rf 14136 (2) (in which *Hérode et Mariamne* is bound with *Le Mauvais Ménage* and Nadal's *Observations critiques*); BnF 8° Yth 8460 (which lacks the *privilège*).

25A

HERODE / ET / MARIAMNE, / *TRAGEDIE*. / Par M. DE VOLTAIRE. / *Æstuat ingens / Imo in corde pudor, mixtóque insania luctu, / Et furiis agitatus amor, &c.* / [woodcut, basket of flowers surrounded by wreath, 52 x 38 mm] / A AMSTERDAM, / Chez la Veuve DESBORDES, / [rule, 32 mm] / M. DCC. XXV.

6°. sig. ã^6 ẽ^6 A-F^6 G^4 (E2 signed 'Dij'); pag. [4] XXI [2]-80 (p.VIII numbered 'XII'); $3 signed, roman (-ã1, ã2); sheet catchwords (not D). [1] blank; [2] Le Libraire au Lecteur; [3] title; [4] blank; I-XXI Préface; [2] Acteurs; 3-80 Hérode et Mariamne, tragédie.

Voltaire is not known to have participated in this edition, though given his association with the Desbordes publishing house in Amsterdam he may not have disapproved of it. 25A gives the text of 25P with several variants which have been recorded in the critical apparatus. Where 25A departs from 25P, it is often the readings of MS1, 25CH, 25X and 26H which appear. One particularly important variant at Préface, line 213 corrected the error of 25P concerning Iphigenia, but was not maintained in following editions.

In some copies (BnF Ye 35028 and Taylor V3 H5 1725 (2)) leaves ã1/6 and ã2/5 are bound in reverse order. In these copies the title page is followed by two blank pages and then by the notice 'Le Libraire au Lecteur';[277] and pages VII/VIII (numbered 'XII') precede pages V/VI.

Bengesco 20; BnC 932-934.

Oxford, Taylor: V3 H5 1725 (2). Paris, BnF: Ye 35028, Rés. Z Bengesco 10, Rés. Z Beuchot 531 (3). Comédie française: 1 MAR Vol

25A^C

HERODE / ET / MARIAMNE, / *TRAGEDIE*. / Par M. DE VOLTAIRE. / *Æstuat ingens / I'mo in corde pudor, mixtóque insania luctu, / Et furiis agitatus amor, &c.* / [*woodcut, mask surrounded by garlands and other decoration, 42 x 41 mm*] / A AMSTERDAM, / Chez la Veuve DESRORDES [*sic*], / [*rule, 40 mm*] / M. DCC. XXV.

6°. sig. ã⁶ ẽ⁶ A-F⁶ G⁴; pag. [4] XXI [2]-80; $3 signed, roman (-ã1,ã2); sheet catchwords.

[*1*] blank; [*2*] Le Libraire au Lecteur; [*3*] title; [*4*] blank; I-XXI Préface; [2] Acteurs; 3-80 Hérode et Mariamne, tragédie.

An imitation of 25A, which it reproduces line for line with only slight differences in the arrangement of the text on the pages, but using different

---

[277] 'Comme il a paru deux ou trois éditions de cette pièce très défectueuses, où il manquait quantité de vers outre un nombre considérable de fautes contre la poésie et même contre le bon sens; j'ai cru qu'il était à propos d'avertir mon acheteur, que celle-ci a été imprimée sur un Manuscrit original de l'auteur, avec sa Préface en tête; qu'il y a quantité de vers ajoutés, beaucoup de mots changés, et autres fautes corrigées, en un mot qu'elle est dans la perfection, où un auteur d'un si grand génie, peut mettre une semblable pièce.'

fleurons and ornaments. Typographically it is inferior to 25A: letters are frequently misaligned, lines often scarcely straight.

Bengesco 21; BnC 936.

Paris, BnF: Rés. Z Bengesco 11.

26H

HERODE / ET / MARIAMNE, / *TRAGEDIE.* / Par Mr. DE VOLTAIRE. / *Revuë & corrigée par l'Auteur.* / [*decorative ornament, 30 x 24 mm*] / *A LA HAYE,* / Chez JEAN NEAULME. / M. DCC. XXVI.

12°. sig. A-E¹², F⁴; pag. 128; \$7 signed, arabic (not A1, A7, D5, F4); page catchwords (in many cases first syllable only).

[1] title; [2] blank; 3 Avertissement; 4 Acteurs; 5-79 Hérode et Mariamne, tragédie; [80] blank; [81] D5r 'LE MAUVAIS / MENAGE, / PARODIE. / REPRESENTÉE SUR LE THEATRE / DE L'HÔTEL DE BOURGOGNE, / *PAR LES COMEDIENS ITALIENS* / *Ordinaires du Roi.* / [*woodcut, printer's ornament, 39 x 33 mm*] / *Suivant la Copie de Paris.* / A LA HAYE, / Chez JEAN NEAULME. / MDCCXXVI.'; [82] Acteurs; 83-128 Le Mauvais Ménage, parodie.

Gives text of first performances (cf. MS1, 25CH, 25X). The Avertissement is identical with that of 25X.

Bengesco i.7, n.1; BnC 942.

Paris, Arsenal: Rf 14139; BnF: Rés. Z Beuchot 1 (2); [in this volume *Hérode et Mariamne* is bound with *Œdipe* (La Haye, Gosse et Néaulme, 1728); the spine bears the inscription: *Œuvres de M. de Voltaire, t. II.*]

26P

HERODE / ET / MARIAMNE, / *TRAGEDIE,* / DE M. DE VOLTAIRE. / . . . . *Æstuat ingens* / *Imo in corde pudor,* / *mixtoque insania luctu,* / *Et furiis agitatus amor, &c.* / Le prix est de 30. sols. / [*woodcut, leaves and fronds, with shield placed in centre showing human face with rays, 48 x 39 mm*] / A PARIS, / Chez la Veuve de PIERRE RIBOU, seul Libraire de l'Académie / Royale de Musique;

Quai des Augustins, à la descente / du Pont-Neuf, à l'Image Saint Loüis. / [rule, 66 mm] / M. DCC. XXVI. / AVEC PRIVILEGE DU ROY.

8°. sig. π^2 (π1 + X + ã⁸) A-F⁸; pag. [22] 96; $4 signed, roman; sheet catchwords (not ã, C).

[1] title; [2] blank; [3]-[4] Privilège and Cession; [5]-[21] Préface; [22] Acteurs; 1-95 Hérode et Mariamne, tragédie; [96] [within ornamented frame] 'De l'Imprimerie de LOUIS SEVESTRE, / Pont S. Michel.'

A new release of the sheets printed by Sevestre for 25P, in which the original title page was replaced by a bifolium containing the new title (on π1r) and (on π2r and v) pages [21] (end of Préface) and [22] (Acteurs). The list of actors is the augmented version already found in two copies of 25P. An inconjugate leaf added after π1 contains the privilège and Voltaire's cession to Madame Ribou (see above, section 4.ii).

Bengesco 22.

Paris, Arsenal 8° B 13066 (in which Hérode et Mariamne is bound with separate editions of two other plays by Voltaire).

27

HERODE / ET / MARIAMNE, / TRAGEDIE / DE M. DE VOLTAIRE. / . . . . Æstuat ingens / Imo in corde pudor, mixtoque insania luctu, / Et furiis agitatus amor, &c. / Le prix est de 30. sols. / [woodcut, sun with rays surrounded by decorative motifs, 55 x 42 mm] / A PARIS, / Chez la Veuve de PIERRE RIBOU, seul Libraire de l'Académie / Royale de Musique; ruë & vis-à-vis la Comedie Françoise, / à l'Image Saint Louis. / [rule, 80 mm] / M. DCC. XXVII. / AVEC PRIVILEGE DU ROY.

8°. sig. π^2 (π1 + X + ã⁸) A-F⁸; pag. [22] 96; $4 signed, roman; sheet catchwords (not ã, C).

[1] title; [2] blank; [3]-[4] Privilège and Cession; [5]-[21] Préface; [22] Acteurs; 1-95 Hérode et Mariamne, tragédie; [96] [within ornamented frame] 'De l'Imprimerie de LOUIS SEVESTRE, / Pont S. Michel.'

A further issue of the sheets printed for 25P, in which (as in 26P) the original title page has been replaced by a bifolium containing the new title (on π1r) and (on π2r and v) pages [21] (end of Préface) and [22]

(Acteurs). The list of actors is the augmented version already found in two copies of 25P. An inconjugate leaf contains the *privilège* and *cession*. In three of the four copies seen this leaf is added after π1, as indicated in the collation above; in the fourth (BL 1608/4916) it is placed between π2 and A1.

Four copies bearing this 1727 imprint have been collated with one another and with 25P and 26P. They are Arsenal: 8° B 13071, Rf 14140, Rf 14141, and BL: 1608/4916.

Apart from differences in the prelimaries all copies seen of the three editions 25P, 26P and 27 are identical, [278] formed from the one stock of sheets. [279] Comparison of the several copies of 26P and 27 reveals the variations already noted between different copies of 25P: it seems therefore that both corrected and uncorrected sheets were used to make up these reissues. Curiously, however, in the case of one correction no modified sheets appear to have been issued in 1725, and only corrected sheets seem to have been used for the subsequent editions: at III.287 (p.58; sig. D5v) all copies seen of 25P read 'charmé', corrected to 'armé' in every copy examined of 26P and 27, and also in all copies of 30 and 36P.

In another case it would appear that few corrected sheets were issued in 1725: as we have seen, nine of the eleven copies collated of 25P give at V.103 (p.85; sig. F3r) the faulty reading 'Si j'avais un moment en secret souhaité ma vengeance'. The corrected line omitting 'en secret', already found in two copies of 25P, is present in all copies seen of 26P and 27, and also in all copies of 30 and 36P.

Other errors appearing in most copies of 25P are corrected in some (but not all) copies of 26P and 27: Arsenal 8° B 13071 (27) and Rf 14140 (27) correctly have 'conservant' at Préface, line 64 (sig. ã2v), and '*Mithridate*, at Préface, line 216 (sig. ã7v), while Arsenal 8° B 13066 (26P) and Rf 14141 (27) have 'reconnoissance' at II.298 (p.36; sig. C2v). In gathering F all copies seen of 26P and 27, except Arsenal RF 14040, present the variations and corrections noted in two copies of 25P.

In Arsenal RF 14040 the *privilège* in the original four-page setting of

---

[278] BL 1608/4916 is a special case: although it bears the 1727 imprint, it gives the revised version of gathering D not found in other copies before 1730. The most likely explanation is that unused preliminaries from 1727 were used to make up a few copies of the later edition.

[279] For further releases of the same sheets see below 30 and 36P.

25P has been bound after the play, which thus has the particularity of giving the *privilège* twice, both in the preliminaries (with the *cession*) and at the end.

w28

Œuvres de M. Arouet de Voltaire. La Haye: Gosse et Néaulme, 1728. 8°.

Volume i consists of separate editions of three works by Voltaire, each with its own pagination, bound together. The works are *Œdipe* (La Haye, Gosse et Néaulme, 1728), *Hérode et Mariamne* (La Haye, Néaulme, 1726) and *La Henriade* (Londres, Woodmans et Lyons, 1728). The edition of *Hérode et Mariamne* found here is 26H, including *Le Mauvais Ménage*.

No evidence of Voltaire's participation.

Bengesco 2117; Trapnell 28; BnC 1.

Paris, BnF: Rés. Z Bengesco 46.

30

HERODE / ET / MARIAMNE, / *TRAGEDIE* / DE M. DE VOLTAIRE. / . . . . *Æstuat ingens* / *Imò in corde pudor,* *mixtoque insania luctu,* / *Et furiis agitatus amor, &c.* / Le prix est de 30. sols. / [*typographic ornament*] / A PARIS, / Chez la Veuve de PIERRE RIBOU, seul Libraire de / l'Académie Royale de Musique; ruë & vis-à-vis la / Comédie Françoise, à l'Image Saint Loüis. / [*rule, 62 mm (or 80 mm: Z Bengesco 12)*] / M. DCC. XXX. / *AVEC PRIVILEGE DU ROY.*

8°. sig. π^2 (π1 + $\tilde{a}^8$ (-$\tilde{a}$8)) A-F^8; pag. [*18*] 96; $4 signed, roman; sheet catchwords (not $\tilde{a}$, C).

[*1*] title; [*2*] blank; [*3*]-[*17*] Préface; [*18*] Acteurs; 1-95 Hérode et Mariamne, tragédie; [96] [within ornamented frame] 'De l'Imprimerie de LOUIS SEVESTRE, / Pont S. Michel.'

A reissue of the sheets of 25P, except for gathering D (p.49-64), which is a new setting of the text from III.139 to IV.52, introducing important changes which became permanently embedded (see above, section 4.ii).

The three final paragraphs of the Préface were removed, and the preliminary gathering (sig. π^2) was reset to accommodate both the new title page and the shortened end of the Préface. At the same time leaf ã8 was removed, eliminating the text no longer required at the conclusion of the Préface. The reset preliminary gathering exists in two forms (see below), but both are composed as follows: $\pi 1r$ title; $\pi 1v$ blank; $\pi 2r$ new end of Préface; $\pi 2v$ Acteurs.

Seven copies of 30 have been collated with one another and with 25P, 26P and 27: BnF Yf 6456 (in which *Hérode et Mariamne* is bound with Nadal's *Observations critiques*), 8° Yth 8462, Z Bengesco 12 and Z Beuchot 339; Arsenal: 8° B 13070; Taylor: V3 M7 1736 (in which *Hérode et Mariamne* is bound with four other plays by Voltaire) and V3 03 1730 (in which the play is bound with three other dramatic works by Voltaire).

Z Bengesco 12 presents a different setting of the preliminary gathering (sig. π^2) from the other copies seen. On the title page the rule is longer (70 mm. compared with 62 elsewhere), and there is a wider gap (15 mm. as against 11 mm.) between the typographic ornament and / A PARIS. /. At the end of the preface ($\pi 2r$), there is a smaller gap (8 mm. as against 11 mm.) between the last line of the text and / FIN. /. The clearest differences appear in the list of actors ($\pi 2v$), which reads 'Roy', not 'Roi', (line 2) and 'Servante', not 'Suivante' in the line added after line 12.

The actors are given in the augmented list already present in some copies of 25P and in 26P and 27, and appear in both settings of the page beneath a broad ornamented rule of different design from that found in all copies of the earlier editions.

Two of the errors found in 25P are corrected in all copies of 30, which read 'armé' at III.287, and 'Si j'avais un moment souhaité ma vengeance' at V.103. In other places some (but not all) copies of 30 give the corrected readings already observed in certain copies of 25P, 26P and 27. Thus six of the seven copies collated (excluding only Taylor V3 M7 1736) have 'conservant' at Préface, line 64 and '*Mithridate*' at Préface, line 216; three copies (Arsenal 8° B 13070, Taylor V3 M7 1736 and V3 03 1730 correctly read 'reconnoissance' at II.298.

In gathering F four of the seven copies seen (BnF Z Bengesco 12 and Z Beuchot 339, Arsenal 8° B 13070 and Taylor V3 M7 1736) give the textual variations and corrections found in some copies of 25P, 26P and 27.

Variations affecting the composition of the preliminaries are apparent in several copies of 30: Arsenal 8° B 13070 and BnF 8° Yth 8462 present a double blank opening between p.[*17*] (end of Préface) and [*18*] (actors). This is no doubt due to the use of an unbacked up sheet to form the preliminary gathering. This would have consisted originally of four leaves, of which the second, blank on both sides, was probably removed. On this assumption the collation of the preliminaries would be π^4 ($-\pi 2$) ($\pi 1 + \tilde{a}^8$ ($-\tilde{a}8$)).

In Z Beuchot 339 the last leaf of the first gathering was not removed; this copy therefore gives both the original version (as in 25P) of most of the last three paragraphs of the preface and the shortened version (new in 30) of the conclusion, the preliminaries collating as π^2 ($\pi 1 + \tilde{a}^8$).

In one of the Taylor copies (V3 M7 1736) a wide (2-3 cm.) stub was left when the last leaf of gathering ã was removed; on it can be distinguished the initial letters of each line of ã8*r* and the final letters of each line of ã8*v*.

Bengesco 23; BnC 937-940.

31

MARIAMNE, / *TRAGEDIE*, / DE MONSIEUR / DE VOLTAIRE. / . . . . *Æstuat ingens* / *Imo in corde pudor*, *mixtoque insania luctu*, / *Et furiis agitatus amor*, *&c.* / NOUVELLE EDITION / Revûe & corrigée. / [*woodcut, 2 cupids or cherubs crouching, with a bust or mask on ground between them, 42 x 35 mm*] / *A AMSTERDAM*, / Chez E.J. LEDET & COMPAGNIE, / ET / JAQUES DESBORDES. / M. DCC. XXXI.

8°. sig. A-F⁸ G⁴ (±F3, F4, F8); pag. 104; $5 signed, roman (-F4,G4); page catchwords (not p.1, 2; often first syllable only).

[1] title; [2] blank; [3]-15 Préface; [16] Acteurs; [17]-104 Mariamne, tragédie.

The first edition with the shortened title *Mariamne*. The Préface is as in 25P. For the changes introduced in this edition see above, section 4.ii.

In all copies seen leaves F3-F4 (p.85-88) and F8 (p.95-96) are cancels. The first contains the text comprised between IV.202 ('MARIAMNE. / Ah! barbare,') and V.12 (var.) ('Vaine ombre de bonheur que vous m'avez trompée! / Sous [Catchword]') and therefore includes the variants introduced in act IV scenes v and vi, and in act V scene i. The second cancel contains a later section of act V, beginning at line 85 ('Unique et triste objet de ses transports jaloux') and ending at 117 (var.) ('Ils se sont vus! Ah Dieu...... perfide, tu mourras. / MA- [Catchword.]'). It thus includes the first three verses of the variant introduced in scene v. This variant extends on to the next page (97), the first of the following gathering (sig. G), which contains no cancels.

Most copies seen (but not BnF 16° Yf 332 (2)) contain a plate which shows Hérode with sword raised about to kill himself while a soldier to his right seeks to restrain him. Numerous guards and soldiers are depicted on both sides; the setting is the interior of a Roman style building with lofty arches and massive supporting structures. The caption reads 'MARIAMNE TRAGEDIE.', beneath which appears on the left 'L.F.D.B. inv.' and on the right 'I.C.Philips fecit 1731'. The plate size is 98 x 150 mm, image 91 x 139 mm.

In Arsenal Rf 14142 and Taylor V3 A2 1764 (13) the plate is bound before the title page, in BnF Z Beuchot 2 (2) and Z Bengesco 467 (2) it faces the title page; in BnF Ye 9208 and Z Bengesco 13 it is bound between gatherings A and B, facing p.[17].[280]

Bengesco 24; BnC 943-944.

Oxford, Taylor: V3 A2 1764 (13). Paris, Arsenal: Rf 14142, BnF: 16° Yf 332 (2), Rés. Z Bengesco 13, and (as part of w32) Ye 9028, Rés. Z Beuchot 2 (2) and Rés. Z Bengesco 467 (2). Comédie française: 1 MAR Vol.

w32

Œuvres de M. de Voltaire. Amsterdam: Ledet *or* Desbordes, 1732. 2 vols. 8°.

Based in part upon material supplied by Voltaire, but in D438 (November 1731) he asks for the edition to be suppressed.

---

[280] The binding in of the plate was at this time independent of the printing process. The position of the plate can therefore vary from copy to copy of the same edition.

Separate editions by Ledet and Desbordes of plays by Voltaire were bound together to form volume ii of w32: *Œdipe* (1731), *Mariamne* (our 31), *Brutus* (1731), *L'Indiscret* (1732). One copy (Z Beuchot 2 (2)) also contains *Le Temple du goût* (Amsterdam, J. Desbordes, 1733) and *Zaïre* (Amsterdam, E. Ledet, 1733). Each work has a separate pagination.

Bengesco 2118; Trapnell 32; BnC 2-6.

Paris, BnF: Rés. Z Beuchot 2 (2) (Desbordes imprint), Ye 9208, Rés. Z Bengesco 467 (2) (Ledet imprint]).

36A

MARIAMNE, / *TRAGEDIE* / DE MONSIEUR / DE VOLTAIRE. / . . . . *Æstuat ingens* / *Imo in corde pudor, mixtoque insania luctu,* / *Et furiis agitatus amor, &c.* / NOUVELLE EDITION. / Revûë & corrigée. / [*decorative ornament, 45 x 32 mm*] / *A AMSTERDAM,* / Chez [*accolade*] / E.J. LEDET & COMPAGNIE, / ET / JAQUES DESBORDES. / [*rule, 60 mm*] / M. DCC. XXXVI.

12°. sig. π¹ A⁸ B-D¹² E⁴; pag. [2] 96; $4 signed in gathering A, $6 signed in gatherings B-D, $2 signed in gathering E, all roman; sheet catchwords (usually first syllable only).

[*1*] title; [*2*] blank; [*1*]-15 Préface; 16 Acteurs; 17-96 Mariamne, tragédie.

Reproduces 31. There is no evidence to connect Voltaire with this edition. See w36 below.

Geneva, ImV: A 1736 / 1 (2-2).

36P

HERODE / ET / MARIAMNE, / *TRAGEDIE* / DE M. DE VOLTAIRE. / . . . . *Æstuat ingens* / *Imò in corde pudor,* *mixtoque insania luctu,* / *Et furiis agitatus amor, &c.* / Le prix est de 30. sols. / A PARIS; / [*engraving, terrace, with (at right) three dancing figures; the terrace overlooks a formal garden reminiscent of Villandry; in the distance brilliant rays of sunshine issue from behind a mountain top, 75 mm x 53 mm*] / Chez PRAULT fils, Quay de Conti, vis-à-vis la descente du / Pont-

Neuf, à la Charité / [*rule, 56 mm.*] / M. DCC. XXVI. / *Avec approbation & Privilege du Roy.*

8°. sig. p A-F⁸; pag. [*2*] 96; $4 signed, roman; sheet catchwords (not C). [*1*] title; [*2*] blank; 1-95 Hérode et Mariamne, tragédie; [96] [within ornamented frame] 'De l'Imprimerie de LOUIS SEVESTRE, / Pont S. Michel.'

A reissue of the sheets used to produce 30, but without gathering ã (Préface and Acteurs). 36P takes no account of the changes introduced in 31. Voltaire seems to have agreed that Prault should publish an edition of *Hérode et Mariamne*, *Œdipe* and *Brutus* (see D1817 where Prault writes that Voltaire had given him these plays for this purpose). That does not mean that Voltaire would necessarily have been content to see the new edition of *Hérode et Mariamne* made up from stocks of unused sheets from an earlier edition now somewhat out of date. He has however left us no comments on 36P. Prault's *privilège* for the three plays is dated 12 July 1736 (*OC* 1A, p.140).

Three copies have been seen and collated with 30. They present the same range of textual variations and corrections noted in that edition.

Bengesco 25; BnC 941.

Oxford, Taylor: V3 H5 1736. Paris, BnF: Rés. Z Beuchot 78 (2); 8° Yth 8463.

w36

Œuvres de Voltaire. Amsterdam [Rouen], 1736. 4 vol. 12°.

Separate editions, each with its own pagination, of five plays by Voltaire, were bound together under the above title. Ch. Wirz plausibly suggests that the components are imitations probably produced in Rouen of editions published in Amsterdam by Ledet and Desbordes.[281] W. H. Trapnell suggests Jore as the publisher.[282] w36 may be the edition referred to by Voltaire in D1160.

[281] 'L'Institut et Musée Voltaire en 1981', *Genava* n.s. 30 (1982), p.187-89.
[282] 'Survey and analysis of Voltaire's collective editions, 1728-1789', *SVEC* 77, p.111-12.

The text of *Mariamne*, in volume i, is 36A.

Geneva, ImV: A 1736/1.

W37

Œuvres de monsieur de Voltaire. Basle: Brandmüller, 1737. 3 vols. 8°.

No evidence of Voltaire's participation.

Mariamne is at vol.ii, p.[107]-208. W37 makes almost no changes to the text. The last paragraph of the preface is omitted. In other respects W37 reproduces 31.

Mariamne appears with an independent and complete title page,[283] as if for a separate edition, although the pagination of the play is incorporated into that of the volume. If a separate edition exists, no copies of it are known to us.

Bengesco iv.6n; BnC 15; Trapnell 37.

Stockholm, Kungliga Biblioteket.

38

MARIAMNE, / *TRAGEDIE* / DE MONSIEUR / DE VOLTAIRE. / ....*Æstuat ingens* / *Imò in corde pudor, mixtoque insania luctu.* / *Et furiis agitatus amor, &c.* / NOUVELLE E'DITION. / Revûë & corrigée. / [*decorative ornament, 44 x 32 mm*] / A PARIS. / [*rule, 59 mm*] / M. DCC. XXXVIII.

4°. sig A-F⁴ G³; pag. 54 (p.17 numbered '71'); $2 signed, roman (-A1, C2, E2); sheet catchwords (E first syllable 'Res-' only).

[1] title; [2] Acteurs; 3-54 Mariamne, tragédie.

The Paris imprint is spurious. The Préface is absent, the text of the play is that of 31. There are some indications that this edition may have come from the presses that produced 36A. In addition to an overall typo-

---

[283] MARIAMNE, / *TRAGEDIE* / DE MONSIEUR / DE / VOLTAIRE. / ....*Æstuat ingens* / *Imo in corde pudor, mixtoque insania luctu,* / *Et furiis agitatus amor, &c.* / NOUVELLE EDITION / Revûe & corrigée. / [*decorative ornament, 48 x 35 mm*] / A BASLE / [*rule*] / M.DCC.XXXVII.

142

graphical similarity, both editions have the same ornament on the title page, and at a few points where forms of words are given differently in 31 and 36A, 38 follows the readings of the latter.

Paris, Arsenal: Rf 14143.

w38

Œuvres de M. de Voltaire. Amsterdam: Ledet [or] Desbordes, 1738-1756. 9 vol. 8°.
Volume ii: [*1*] title; [*2*] blank; [*3*]-[*4*] Pièces contenues dans le Tome II; [1]-120 other texts (*Œdipe* and annexes); [121] H5*r* 'LA / MARIAMNE, / *TRAGÉDIE.* / H5'; [122] blank; [123]-[124] Avertissement; [125]-133 Préface; [134] Acteurs; [facing p.135] plate; [135]-228 Mariamne, tragédie; [229]-366 other texts (*Brutus* and annexes).

Volumes i-iv of this edition are known to have been produced under Voltaire's supervision, although they were later denounced by him. *Mariamne* is preceded by an Avertissement (reproduced in Appendix C). For *Mariamne* w38 reproduces the text of 31. Important changes were made to the Préface: see above, section 4.ii. w38 is the first edition in which the form 'Salomé' appears: see variants at Acteurs line 4.

The plate facing page 135 shows the same scene as appears in 31. Underneath is the caption 'MARIAMNE TRAGEDIE.', and below that on the left 'L.F.D.B. inv.' and on the right 'I.C.Philips fecit 1731'. The plate size is 98 x 150 mm, image 91 x 139 mm. This plate appears identical with that appearing in 31, except that the caption appears against a background of parallel vertical strokes, whereas in 31 the background is plain.

Bengesco 2120; Trapnell 39A; BnC 7-11.

Paris, Arsenal: Rés. 8° BL 34043 (2) [Desbordes imprint], Rés. 8° BL 34042 (2) [Ledet imprint]; BnF: Z 24564 [Desbordes], Ye 9212, Rés. Z Beuchot 4 (2), Rés. Z Bengesco 468 (2) [Ledet].

w39

Œuvres de M. de Voltaire. Amsterdam [Rouen]: Compagnie, 1739. 3 vol. 8°.
Volume i: [*1*] title; [*2*] blank; [1]-90 other texts (*Œdipe* and annexes); [91]

F6r 'MARIAMNE, / TRAGEDIE.'; [92] blank; 93-105 Préface; 106
Acteurs; [facing p.107] plate; 107-178 Mariamne, tragédie; [179]-431
other texts (Brutus and annexes, L'Indiscret, Zaïre and annexes).

Voltaire mentions this edition in D1907 and D1985 ('mes prétendues
œuvres'), but it was produced without his participation. The text
followed for Mariamne seems to be 31 rather than w38: the title of the
play is given as Mariamne, there is no Avertissement, and the Préface
appears in the full original version as in 31.

The plate facing p.107 is a new engraving, 77 x 132 mm, without
indication of the names of the artist and the engraver, of the scene depicted
in the plate of 31. Beneath it is the caption 'MARIAMNE TRAGEDIE.'

Bengesco 2121; Trapnell 39R; BnC 16-17.

Paris, BnF: Rés. Z Bengesco 470 (1), Rés. Z Beuchot 5 (1).

---

w40

Œuvres de M. de Voltaire. Amsterdam [Rouen?]: Compagnie, 1740.
4 vol. 12°.

Volume ii: [1] title; [2] blank; [1]-122 other texts (Œdipe and annexes);
[123] F2r 'LA / MARIAMNE, / TRAGÉDIE. / F2'; [124] blank; 125-126
Avertissement; [127]-135 Préface; [136] Acteurs; [facing p.137] plate; 137-
230 La Mariamne, tragédie; [231]-356 other texts (Brutus and annexes).

Under the title La Mariamne w40 reproduces the text of w38, with the
Préface in the shortened form. There is no evidence that Voltaire
participated in this edition, yet new readings at III.116 and III.134 re-
appear in almost all subsequent editions, and a new reading at IV.16 is
seen in most following editions before w56 and in some thereafter. The
form 'Salomé' is found at several points in the verse, even though it
creates hiatus and metrical irregularity.

The plate facing p.137 is identical with that found in w39.

Bengesco 2122; Trapnell 40R.

Paris, Arsenal: 8° BL 34045 (2), in which a handwritten note is added at
the end of the Avertissement on p.126 (see Appendix C).

W41R

Œuvres de M. de Voltaire. Amsterdam [Rouen?]: Compagnie, 1741. 4 vol. 12°.

[*1*] title; [*2*] blank; [1]-122 other texts (*Œdipe* and annexes); [123] F2*r* 'LA / MARIAMNE, / *TRAGE'DIE*. / F2'; [124] blank; 125-126 Avertissement; 127-135 Préface; 136 Acteurs; [facing p.137] plate; 137-230 Mariamne, tragédie; [231]-[360] other texts (*Brutus* and annexes).

There is no evidence that Voltaire participated in this edition. The text of *Mariamne* appears to be directly derived from w40.

The plate facing p.137 is identical with that found in w39 and w40. The same plate is thus found in the three editions w39 w40 and w41R all ostensibly published at Amsterdam 'aux dépens de la Compagnie' but in reality probably produced at Rouen.

Bengesco 2123; Trapnell 41R; BnC 19.

Paris, BnF: Rés. Z Beuchot 6 (1).

W41C (1742)

Œuvres de M. de Voltaire. Amsterdam [Paris: Didot, Barrois]: Compagnie, 1741-1742. 5 vol. 12°.

Volume ii: [*1*] half-title; [*2*] blank; [*3*] title; [*4*] blank; [1]-96 other texts (*Œdipe* and annexes); [97] E1*r* 'LA / MARIAMNE, / *TRAGÉDIE. / Tome II*. E'; [98] blank; 99-100 Avertissement; 101-107 Préface; [108] Acteurs; [facing p.109] plate; 109-180 La Mariamne, tragédie; [181]-285 other texts (*Brutus* and annexes); [286] blank.

No evidence of Voltaire's participation. The edition was suppressed at his request, and reissued as w42.

The plate facing p.109 is identical with that found in w42.

Bengesco 2124; Trapnell 41C; BnC 20-21.

Paris, BnF: Rés. Z Bengeso 471 (2).

W42

Œuvres mêlées de M. de Voltaire. Genève: Bousquet, 1742. 5 vol. 12°.

Volume ii: [*1*] title; [*2*] blank; [1]-96 other texts (*Œdipe* and annexes); [97]

E1r 'LA / MARIAMNE, / *TRAGÉDIE. / Tome II.* E'; [98] blank; 99-100 Avertissement; 101-107 Préface; [108] Acteurs; [facing p.109] plate; 109-180 La Mariamne, tragédie; [181]-293 other texts (*Brutus* and annexes, *Lettre sur les inconvénients attachés à la littérature*); 294-296 Errata pour le second Volume.

The sheets of w41c were re-issued for this edition, which was produced with Voltaire's participation. Though cancels and other changes were introduced in other works, the text of *Mariamne* is identical with w41c and w42. Several amendments affecting *Mariamne* appear in the *errata* of w42. w41c and w42 follow the textual tradition established by w38. For *Mariamne* they reproduce the text of w40, almost without change.

The changes suggested in the *errata* are recorded below in the critical apparatus at A 4, I.9, I.134, III.46, III.116 and V.26. One (A 4) prescribes the use of the name Salome throughout the text; another indicates that the reading of the base text is to be restored at V.26. The others are of lesser importance. Nevertheless it is highly probable that all these changes correspond to wishes expressed by Voltaire.

The plate which appears facing p.109 in both w41c and w42 is a further engraving, without indication of the names of the artist and the engraver, of the scene depicted in the plate of 31. Beneath it is the caption 'MARIAMNE TRAGEDIE'. The plate size is 67 x 113 mm.

Bengesco 2125; Trapnell 42G; BnC 22-24.

Paris, BnF: Rés. Z Beuchot 51 (2).

w43

Œuvres de M. de Voltaire. Amsterdam [or] Leipzig: Arkstée et Merkus, 1743-1745. 6 vol. (vol.5, 1744; vol.6, 1745). 8°.

Volume ii: [*1*] title; [*2*] blank; [*3*]-[*4*] Pièces contenues dans le Tome II; [1]-120 other texts (*Œdipe* and annexes); [121] H5r 'LA / MARIAMNE, / TRAGÉDIE. / H5'; [122] blank; [123]-[124] Avertissement; [125]-133 Préface; [134] Acteurs; [135]-228 Mariamne, tragédie; [229]-366 other texts (*Brutus* and annexes).

The text of *Mariamne* is identical with w38, this volume of w43 being a reissue, under a new title page, of the sheets of the earlier edition. There is no evidence of Voltaire's participation in this reissue.

Bengesco iv.23; Trapnell 43.

Köln, Universitäts- und Stadt-Bibliothek.

w46

Œuvres diverses de M. de Voltaire. Londres [Trévoux]: Nourse, 1746. 6 vol. 12°.

Volume ii: [*1*] half-title; [*2*] blank; [*3*] title; [*4*] blank; [I]-[XXIV], [1]-85 other texts (*Œdipe* and annexes); [86] blank; [87] D8*r* 'HERODE / ET / MARIAMNE, / *TRAGEDIE* / Représentée pour la premiere fois / le 6. Mars 1724.'; [88] blank; [89]-90 Avertissement; [91]-98 Préface; [99] blank, except for woodcut (foliage and flowers, 47 x 39 mm), and direction line and catchword ('*Tome II.* E2 ACTEURS'); [100] Acteurs; [101]-183 Mariamne, tragédie; [184] blank; [185]-477 other texts (*L'Indiscret*, *Brutus* and annexes, *Mahomet* and annexes, *Sur la police des spectacles*); 477-[478] Fautes à corriger.

This edition was produced at Trévoux, and there is some evidence that it was produced with Voltaire's approval (see *Lettres philosophiques*, ed. G. Lanson and A M Rousseau, Paris 1964, i.xviii). The text of *Mariamne* follows the tradition established by w38, and most closely resembles w42, though the title *La Mariamne* was abandoned. For the small number of significant changes introduced in w46, see above, section 4.ii.

Bengesco 2127; Trapnell 46; BnC 25-26.

Paris, BnF: Rés Z Beuchot 8 (2).

w48D

Œuvres de M. de Voltaire. Dresde: Walther, 1748-1754. 10 vol. 8°.

Volume iv: [*1*] title; [*2*] blank; [*3*] Table des pièces contenues dans le tome IV; [*4*] blank; [1]-106 other texts (*Œdipe* and annexes); [facing p.106] plate; [107] G6*r* 'HERODE / ET / MARIAMNE, / *TRAGEDIE* / *Représentée pour la premiere fois le 6. Mars / 1723.*'; [108] blank; 109-110 Avertissement; [111]-117 Préface; [118] Acteurs; [119]-196 Mariamne, tragédie; [197]-464 other texts (*L'Indiscret*, *Brutus* and annexes, *Mahomet* and annexes, *Sur la police des spectacles*).

This edition was produced with Voltaire's participation. The text of *Hérode et Mariamne* follows the tradition set by w38, as modified by w42 and w46, which latter it most closely resembles. w48D introduces several important modifications into the textual canon: see above, section 4.ii. The date of first performance on the half-title page is incorrect. This error is repeated in several subsequent editions (w50, w51, T53, OC56, 62, T62, T64A, T64G, T64P and T67). w48D is the first edition to introduce -*ai*- into words hitherto spelt with -*oi*-, though not into the endings of the imperfect and conditional tenses.

The plate facing p.106 is a new engraving of the scene depicted in 31. At the bottom within a decorated scroll there is a two-line caption: 'MARIAMNE / *TRAGEDIE*.' Beneath the image we read: 'Bernigeroth sc. Lips. 1747.' Image size, 87 x 157 mm, plate size 110 x 185 mm.

Bengesco 2129; Trapnell 48D; BnC 28-35.

Oxford, Taylor: V1 1748 (4). Paris, BnF: Z 24572, Rés. Z Beuchot 10 (4), Rés. Z Beuchot 12 (4).

w48R

Title unknown. Amsterdam: Compagnie [Rouen: Machuel], 1748. 12 vol. 8°.

Volume ii: [*1*] title; [*2*] blank; [1]-120 other texts (*Œdipe* and annexes); [121] F1r 'LA / MARIAMNE / *TRAGÉDIE*. / *Tome II*. F AVER-'; [122] blank; 123-124 Avertissement; 125-133 Préface; 134 Acteurs; [facing p.135] plate; [136]-224 Mariamne, tragédie; 225-400 other texts (*Brutus* and annexes; *Critique de l'Œdipe de Monsieur de Voltaire par M. le G****).

This edition, printed in Rouen by Machuel in or before 1748, was suppressed at Voltaire's instigation (see D3667, D3677, D3669, D3884): no copy of the original issue is known, but the sheets re-appeared in 1764, under new titles, as part of w64R. The description given above is that of the 1764 issue.

The sheets of *Mariamne* are printed on paper bearing watermark dates of 1743 and 1744 (see BnC 214, col. 130).

The text is that of the earlier imitations of w38 produced in Rouen under the imprint of Amsterdam, aux dépens de la Compagnie (w39, w40 and w41R): w48R is almost identical with the last of these (w41R). None of the changes introduced in w46 or first found in w48D appears in w48R.

The plate facing p.138 is a further engraving of the scene depicted in 31, without indication of artist or engraver. At the bottom appears the caption: '*MARIAMNE / TRAGEDIE*.' Plate size 84 x 148 mm, image size, 70 x 128 mm.

Bengesco 2128, 2136; Trapnell 48R; BnC 27, 145.

w50

La Henriade et autres ouvrages. Londres [Rouen]: Société, 1750-1752. 10 vol. 12°.

Volume iv: [*1*] half-title; [*2*] blank; [*3*] title; [*4*] blank; [*5*]-[*8*] Table des pièces et titres contenus au tome quatrième; [1]-124 other texts (*Œdipe* and annexes); [125] F3*r* 'HERODE / ET / MARIAMNE, / *TRAGÉDIE*, / *Représentée pour la premiére fois le 6. Mars. 1723* / F3 AVER-'; [126] blank; 127-128 Avertissement; [129]-137 Préface; 138 Acteurs; [facing p.138] plate; 139-228 Mariamne, tragédie; [229]-315 other texts (*L'Indiscret* and annexes, *Brutus* and annexes, *Mahomet* and annexes).

Voltaire is not known to have participated in this edition, which was produced at Rouen. For *Hérode et Mariamne* w50 reproduces with little variation the text of w48D in a setting modelled on w48R. Pages have the same composition (extending even to the placing of ornaments), many of the same practices are observed in spelling and punctuation, and there is strong typographical similarity.

The plate facing p.138 is identical with that found in w48R. Both were evidently printed from the same engraving.

Bengesco 2130; Trapnell 50R; BnC 39.

Geneva, ImV: A 1751/1 (4)

w51

Œuvres de M. de Voltaire. [Paris: Lambert], 1751. 11 vol. 12°.

Volume iv: [*1*] half-title; [*2*] blank; [*3*] title; [*4*] blank; [1]-106 other texts

(*Œdipe* and annexes); [107] I6*r* 'HÉRODE / ET / MARIAMNE, / *TRAGÉDIE,* / Représentée pour la premiére fois / le Mardi 10. Avril 1723.'; [108] blank; [109]-110 Avertissement; 111-119 Préface; 120 Acteurs; [facing p.121] plate; [121]-193 Mariamne, tragédie; [194] blank; [195]-359 other texts (*Brutus* and annexes, *L'Indiscret*).

This edition was produced in Paris by Michel Lambert, with Voltaire's collaboration. The text of *Hérode et Mariamne* closely follows w48D, but varies from it in a small number of instances. At Préface, 213 the error concerning Iphigenia found in all preceding editions except 25A and 25A^c is corrected. The form *Salomé* occurs, but once only, in the dramatis personae (see critical apparatus at A.4). w51 retains earlier readings at I.296 and III.134, and introduces a variant at III.96b. The half-title page for the play repeats the error concerning the date of first performance which first appears in w48D.

In the plate facing p.121 a central character in military clothing, with a plumed hat and swirling cloak makes a sweeping gesture with his right hand. His head is turned to the left and looks at two other figures, soldiers or guards, one of whom holds a sheathed sword in his hands. Behind them, to the left, two military figures are carrying away the body of a third. The background consists of pillars, a colonnade and drapes. Below the image on the left is 'C. Eisen jnv.' and on the right 'D. Sornique sculp.' At the bottom there is the caption: 'MARIAMNE'. Image size, 60 x 104 mm. This plate is probably inspired by V.203-204.

Bengesco 2131; Trapnell 51P; BnC 40-41.

Oxford, Taylor; V1 1751 (5). Paris, Arsenal: 8° B 13057 (1); BnF: Z 28786, Rés. Z Beuchot 13 (4).

w52

Œuvres de M. de Voltaire. Dresde: Walther, 1752. 9 vol. 8°.

Volume iii: [*1*] title; [*2*] blank; [*3*]-[*4*] Table des pièces contenues dans le tome III; [1]-312 other texts (poetical works and letters); [facing p.313] plate; [313] Dd1*r* 'MARIAMNE, / TRAGEDIE. / VOLT. Tom. III. Dd'; [314] blank; 315-319 Préface; [320] Acteurs; [321]-384 Mariamne, tragédie; 385-424 other texts (*L'Indiscret*).

w52 is a new edition by the publisher of w48D, and was produced with the participation of Voltaire. For *Mariamne* it reproduces the text of w48D, but a number of significant changes occur. The title of the play is given as 'MARIAMNE' on the half-title page, from which the incorrect date of first performance disappears. The Avertissement which had first appeared in w38 is abandoned. w52 introduces into the text several modifications which proved permanent: see above, section 4.ii. The use of forms in *-ai-* is extended to the imperfect and conditional tenses.

The plate facing p.313 shows the scene depicted in 31. The image in the engraving is identical with that which appears in w48D. The only differences between the two plates are found below the image in the caption ('MARIAMNE TRAGEDIE.'), which occupies only one line, and beneath the caption in the words 'Bernigeroth sc. Lips. 1752'.

Bengesco 2132; Trapnell 52 and 70x; BnC 36-38.

Geneva, ImV: A 1752/1. Paris, BnF: Rés. Z Beuchot 14 (3).

T53

Le Théâtre de M. de Voltaire. Amsterdam: Richoff, 1753. 4 vol. 8°.
Volume i: [*1*] title; [*2*] blank; [*3*]-[*6*] Préface (a general preface to the collection); [*7*]-[*8*] Table des pièces contenues dans le premier volume; [1]-86 other texts (*Œdipe* and annexes); [87] F4r 'HERODE / ET / MARIAMNE, / *TRAGEDIE* / *Représentée pour la premiere fois le 6. / Mars 1723.* / F4'; [88] blank; 89-90 Avertissement; 91-97 Préface; 98 Acteurs; 99-158 Mariamne, tragedie; [159]-404 other texts (*L'Indiscret*, *Brutus* and annexes, *Mahomet* and annexes).

Voltaire had no part in this edition. For *Hérode et Mariamne* it follows w48D closely throughout.

Bengesco 307.

Paris, Arsenal: Rf 14090 (1).

54P

MARIAMNE, / *TRAGÉDIE* / DE MONSIEUR / DE VOLTAIRE. /
............*Æstuat ingens / Imò in corde pudor, mixtoque insania luctu. /
Et furiis agitatus amor,* &c. / *NOUVELLE ÉDITION* / Revûë &

corrigée. / [*woodcut, vase with decorative foliage, 58 x 37 mm*] / A PARIS, / Aux dépens de la Compagnie. / [*thick-thin rule, 57 mm*] / M. DCC. LIV. / *Avec Aprobation & Privilége du Roi.*

4°; sig. [A]-F⁴; pag. 47 (p.[48] unnumbered); $1 signed (-A1); sheet catchwords.

[1] title; [2] Acteurs; [3]-47 Mariamne, tragédie; [48] blank.

The Paris imprint is certainly spurious. This edition was probably produced in Rouen. Through 38, which it reproduces exactly, 54P can be traced back to 31, with 36A perhaps serving as an intermediate link in the process of transmission.

Paris, Bibliothèque de la Sorbonne: R 874(3) 8° (bound in one volume with eight other plays, six of them by Voltaire).

54V

HERODE / ET / MARIAMNE, / *TRAGEDIE* / EN CINQ ACTES, / ET EN VERS. / PAR MONSIEUR / DE VOLTAIRE. / [*decorative ornament, 37 x 38 mm*] / *VIENNE EN AUTRICHE* / Chez Jean Pierre van Ghelen, Imprimeur de la / Cour de sa Majesté Imperiale & Royale. / [*rule, 58 mm*] / M D CC L IV. /

A-F⁸; pag. [1]-96; $5 signed, arabic (-A1; B4 signed 'B5'); page catchwords.

[1] title; [2] Acteurs; [3]-96 Mariamne, tragédie.

Reprints the text of w48D, without the Avertissement and without the Préface.

Prague, Narodni Knihovna: 9 H 4584.

OC56

Œuvres choisies de Monsieur de Voltaire. Genève, 1756.

Volume ii: [*1*] title; [*2*] blank; [*3*] Tables des pièces contenues dans le Tome II; [*4*] blank; [1]-99 other texts (*Œdipe* and annexes); [100] blank; [101] F1r 'HÉRODE / ET / MARIAMNE, / *TRAGÉDIE*. / *Représentée pour la prémière fois le 6 / Mars 1723. / Tome. II.* F'; [102]

Avertissement; 103-109 Préface; [110] Acteurs; 111-184 Mariamne, tragédie [185]f. other texts (*Brutus* and annexes, *Zaïre* and annexes).

Derived from w48D, which it follows closely throughout.

Geneva, ImV: BA 1756/1.

[T56]

The four volumes of w56 which contain Voltaire's dramatic works were issued as a separate collection without the half-title page. *Mariamne* is in volume i; the text and setting are identical with w56.

Paris, Arsenal Rf 14091 (1).

w56

Collection complette des œuvres de Mr. de Voltaire. [Genève: Cramer], 1756. 17 vol. 8°.

Volume vii: [*1*] half-title; [*2*] blank; [*3*] title; [*4*] blank; [*1*]-102 other texts (*Œdipe* and annexes); [103] G4*r* 'MARIAMNE, / TRAGEDIE. / G4 PRE-'; [104] blank; 105-111 Préface; [112] Acteurs; [113]-186 Mariamne, tragédie; [187]-445 other texts (*Brutus* and annexes, *La Mort de César* and annexes, *Samson*, *Pandore*); 446 Ouvrages dramatiques contenus en ce volume.

The first printing of the Cramer *Collection Complette*, produced under Voltaire's supervision. Reproduces w52, with only a small number of retouches: see above, section 4.ii.

Bengesco 2133; Trapnell 56; BnC 55-66.

Paris, Arsenal: 8° BL 34048 (7); BnF: Z 24582.

W57G1

Collection complette des œuvres de Mr. de Voltaire. [Genève: Cramer], 1757. 10 vol. 8°.

Volume vii: [*1*] half-title; [*2*] blank; [*3*] title; [*4*] blank; [*1*]-102 other texts

(*Œdipe* and annexes); [103] G4*r* 'MARIAMNE, / TRAGÉDIE. / G4
PRE-'; [104] blank; 105-111 Préface; [112] Acteurs; [113]-186 Mariamne,
tragédie; [187]-445 other texts (*Brutus* and annexes, *La Mort de César* and
annexes, *Samson*, *Pandore*); 446 Ouvrages dramatiques contenus en ce
volume.

A revised edition of w56. For *Mariamne*, though many variations appear
in typographical matters (spelling, accentuation and punctuation), the
text of w56 is reproduced without change line for line and page for page.
w57G1 displays a noticeable tendency to use double consonants (roughly
in conformity with modern usage) where w56 regularly uses single
consonants (e.g. w56 apas, couroux, falu; w57G1 appas, courroux, fallu).

This printing may be distinguished from that next below by the
presence, on p.111, of a woodcut of military emblems, 53 x 35 mm.

Bengesco 2134; Trapnell 57G; BnC 67.

Oxford, Taylor: V1 1757 (7). Paris, BnF: Rés. Z Beuchot 21.

W57G2

A reissue of w57G1.

Volume vii: [*1*] half-title; [*2*] blank; [*3*] title; [*4*] blank; [1]-102 other texts
(*Œdipe* and annexes); [103] G4*r* 'MARIAMNE, / TRAGÉDIE. / G4
PRE-'; [104] blank; 105-111 Préface; [112] Acteurs; [113]-186 Mariamne,
tragédie; [187]-445 other texts (*Brutus* and annexes, *La Mort de César* and
annexes, *Samson*, *Pandore*); 446 Ouvrages dramatiques contenus en ce
volume.

Another Cramer printing, the date of which is open to question: see *OC*,
vol.8, p.134. The woodcut on p.111, measuring 40 x 32 mm, depicts an
animal skin draped over a club.

For *Mariamne* the text of w56 is reproduced without change. Some
variation is apparent in the typography, affecting spelling, accentuation
and punctuation, but w57G2 follows the usage of w56 more closely than
does w57G1.

Bengesco 2134; Trapnell 57G; BnC 67-69.

Oxford, Taylor: V1 1757 (7A); Paris, BnF: Rés. Z Beuchot 21 (7).

w57P

Œuvres de M. de Voltaire. [Paris: Lambert], 1757. 22 vol. 12°.

Volume ii: [*1*] half-title; [*2*] blank; [*3*] title; [*4*] Pièces contenues dans ce volume; [1]-93 other texts (*Œdipe* and annexes); [94] blank; [facing p.95] plate; [95] H4*r* 'MARIAMNE, / *TRAGEDIE.*'; [96] blank; 97-105 Préface; 106 Acteurs; [107]-172 Mariamne, tragédie; [173]-431 other texts (*L'Indiscret*, *Brutus* and annexes, *Zaïre* and annexes).

The second edition published by Michel Lambert, and produced with Voltaire's participation. The text follows w51, but diverges from it at several points to incorporate readings found in w52 and w56. See critical apparatus at I.181, I.296, II.18, II.67-72, III.134 and IV.67-68. w57P presents readings not hitherto seen at Préface, lines 198, 254 and V.196. Though echoed in the following Duchesne editions, these variants did not secure a permanent place in the textual canon.

The plate facing p.95 is identical with that found in w51, and was certainly printed from the same engraving.

Bengesco 2135; Trapnell 57P; BnC 45-54.

Paris, BnF: Z 24643.

62

HÉRODE / *ET* / MARIAMNE, / *TRAGÉDIE*, / *Représentée pour la première fois, par / les Comédiens ordinaires du Roi, / le 6 Mars 1723.* / [*typographic ornament, 21 x 24 mm*] / *A PARIS,* / Chez DUCHESNE, Libraire, rue Saint Jacques, / au Temple du Goût. / [*thick-thin rule, 45-42 mm*] / M. DCC. LXII. /

12° sig. A-C¹²; pag. 72; $6 signed (-A1); sheet catchwords.
[1] title; [2] blank; [3]-9 Préface; 10 Acteurs; [11]-72 Hérode et Mariamne, tragédie.

Reproduces, without variation, the text of w57P.

Paris, Arsenal: GD 8° 11549.

T62

Le Théâtre de M. de Voltaire. Amsterdam: Richoff, 1762-1763. 5 vol. 8°.

Volume i: [*1*] title; [*2*] blank; [*3*] Table des ouvrages dramatiques contenus en ce volume; [*4*] blank; [*5*]-[*8*] Préface (a general preface to the collection, text as in T53); [1]-86 other texts (*Œdipe* and annexes); [87] F*4r* 'HERODE / ET / MARIAMNE, / *TRAGEDIE*. / *Représentée pour la premiere fois le 6. / Mars 1723*. / F4'; [88] blank; 89-90 Avertissement (as in w38); 91-97 Préface; 98 Acteurs; 99-158 Mariamne, tragédie; [159]-412 other texts (*L'Indiscret, Brutus* and annexes, *La Mort de César* and annexes, *Samson, Pandore*).

For *Hérode et Mariamne* T53 is reproduced without variation.

Bengesco 309; BnC 619.

Paris, BnF: Rés. Z Bengesco 123 (1).

T64A

Le Théâtre de M. de Voltaire. Amsterdam: Richoff, 1764. 5 vol. 8°.

Volume i: [*1*] title; [*2*] blank; [*3*] Table des ouvrages dramatiques contenus en ce volume; [*4*] blank; [*5*]-[*7*] Préface (a general preface to the collection, text as in T53); [*8*] blank; [1]-86 other texts (*Œdipe* and annexes); [87] G*8r* 'HERODE / *ET* / MARIAMNE, / *TRAGEDIE*. / *Représentée pour la première fois le 6. / Mars 1723*.'; [88] blank; 89-90 Avertissement (as in w38); 91-97 Préface; 98 Acteurs; 99-162 Mariamne, tragédie; [163]-416 other texts (*L'Indiscret, Brutus* and annexes, *La Mort de César* and annexes, *Samson, Pandore*).

For *Hérode et Mariamne* the text of T53 and T62 is reproduced without variation in a new setting.

Geneva, ImV: BC 1764/1 (1). London, BL: 11735.aa.1.

T64G

Le Théâtre de M. de Voltaire. Genève: Cramer, 1764. 5 vol. 8°.

Volume i: [*1*] title; [*2*] blank; [*3*]-104 other texts (*Œdipe* and annexes); [106] I*5v* 'HERODE / ET / MARIAMNE, / *TRAGEDIE* / *Représentée pour la premiere fois le 6 / Mars 1723*.'; [107]-[108] Avertissement;

[109]-117 Préface; 118 Acteurs; [119]-186 Mariamne, tragédie; [187]-332 other texts (*L'Indiscret*, *Brutus* and annexes).

The imprint is spurious. The text of w48D, but may be derived more immediately from T53. The variants of w52 and w56 are not found.

Paris, Arsenal: Rf 14092 (1).

T64P

Œuvres de théâtre de M. de Voltaire. Paris: Duchesne, 1764. 5 vol. 12°.

Volume i: [*1*] title; [*2*] blank; [*3*] Avis du libraire; [*4*]-[*6*] Approbation and Privilège; [*7*] Table des pièces qui composent le Théâtre de M. de Voltaire; [*8*] Catalogue des ouvrages de M. de Voltaire, qui se trouvent chez Duchesne, libraire; [1]-96 other texts (*Œdipe* and annexes); [97] E1r 'HÉRODE / ET / MARIAMNE, / TRAGÉDIE, / Représentée pour la premiere fois, par / les Comédiens ordinaires du Roi, / le 6 Mars 1723. / Tome I. E'; [98] blank; [99]-105 Préface; [106] Acteurs; [107]-168 Hérode et Mariamne, tragédie; [169]-420 other texts (*L'Indiscret*, *Brutus* and annexes, *Zaïre* and annexes).

This Duchesne edition of the theatre was much decried by Voltaire, and was reissued in 1767 (see T67). The text of *Hérode et Mariamne* is identical with that found in 62. The three issues (62, T64P and T67) seem in fact to have been printed from the same setting of type.

Bengesco 311.

Luzern, Zentralbibliothek: B 2172 (1).

[T64G]

The five volumes of w64G which contain Voltaire's dramatic works were issued as a separate collection without the half-title page. *Mariamne* is in volume i, text and setting as in w64G below.

Oxford, Taylor: V1 1764.

w64g

Collection complette des œuvres de M. de Voltaire. [Genève: Cramer], 1764. 10 vol. 8°.

Volume vii: [1] half-title; [2] blank; [3] title; [4] blank; [5]-148 other texts (*Œdipe* and annexes); [149] K3*r* 'MARIAMNE, / *TRAGÉDIE.* / Revûe et corrigée par l'auteur en 1762. / K3'; [150] blank; 151-157 Préface; [158] Acteurs; [159]-223 Mariamne, tragédie; [224]-246 Passages discarded from text with Varus; [247]-403 other texts (*Brutus* and annexes, *La Mort de César* and annexes); 404-405 Table des pièces contenues dans ce volume.

A new edition published by Cramer and the first to give the revised version of the play, substituting Sohème for Varus. For Voltaire's correspondence with Cramer regarding this edition see above, section 5.i. In spite of his request (D10881) that the same number of pages be used for the new version as for the former, *Mariamne* occupies much more space in w64g than in the earlier Cramer editions, as it is lengthened by the appendix giving the longer passages discarded from the Varus version, which are printed in italic and introduced by the following note on p.[224]: 'On a beaucoup regretté de très beaux vers que Mr. de Voltaire a supprimés dans les changements qu'il a faits en dernier lieu à sa tragédie de MARIAMNE; on a cru devoir les restituer ici, en y joignant les principales variantes, etc.' Most (but not all) editions after 1764 reprint the Sohème version with almost no change from w64g. All the variants of w64g are recorded in the critical apparatus; the label 'Sohème texts' denotes both this edition and those derived from it (w68, w70g, w70l, w71, 72p, 72x, w72p, w72x, w75g, w75x, t76g, t76x, k84, k85).

Bengesco 2133; Trapnell 64; BnC 89.

Oxford, Merton College: 36 f 9.

w64r

Collection complette des œuvres de M. de Voltaire. Amsterdam: Compagnie [Rouen: Machuel?], 1764. 18 vol. 12°.

The volume containing *Mariamne* was produced for publication as part of w48r. Although the edition was suppressed at that time, the sheets were reissued under a new title in 1764. See above, w48R. The text given is naturally the Varus version.

Benesco 2136; Trapnell 64R; BnC 145-148.

Paris, BnF: Rés. Z Beuchot 26 (2).

65

MARIAMNE, / *TRAGÉDIE* / EN CINQ ACTES. / *Par Mr. de* VOLTAIRE. / [*decorative ornament, flowers*] / A AVIGNON, / Chez *LOUIS CHAMBEAU, Imprimeur-Libraire* / *près les RR. PP. Jésuites.* / [*thin-thick-thin rule*] / M. DCC. LXV. /

4°. sig. A-E⁴ F²; pag. 44 (21, 34 numbered '2', '53'); $2 signed, arabic (-A1); sheet catchwords.

[1] title; [2] Acteurs; [3]-44 Mariamne, tragédie.

Gives the Varus version. The text is that of w48D, but this edition may be derived more immediately from a 'Richoff' edition (T53, T62 or T64A). No copies have been identified of another edition of 1765 listed by Bengesco (no.26): Paris, aux dépens de la Compagnie. In 8° 56 p.

Geneva, ImV D; Hérode 1765/1

T67

Œuvres de théâtre de M. de Voltaire. Paris: Duchesne, 1767. 7 vol. 12°.

Volume i: [*1*] title; [*2*] blank; [*3*] Avertissement [publisher's prefatory notice to this edition]; [*4*] Table des pièces contenues dans ce premier volume and Errata de ce premier volume; [1]-96 other texts (*Œdipe* and annexes); [97] E1r 'HÉRODE / ET / MARIAMNE, / *TRAGÉDIE,* / *Représentée pour la premiere fois, par* / *les Comédiens ordinaires du Roi,* / *le 6 Mars 1723.* / *Tome I. E*'; [98] blank; [99]-105 Préface; [106] Acteurs; [107]-168 Hérode et Mariamne, tragédie; [169]-420 other texts (*L'Indiscret, Brutus* and annexes, *Zaïre* and annexes).

A claim advanced on the title page to link this edition with the Geneva quarto edition of 1768 (see w68 below) is reiterated in the Avertissement: 'Et nous osons dire qu'elle [= cette édition] est aussi complète que l'Edition in-4° faite à Genève sous les yeux de M. de Voltaire. Il ne faut qu'y jeter un coup d'œil pour s'en convaincre.' This claim, in addition to raising questions concerning the actual date of publication of T67, is patently untrue in the case of *Hérode et Mariamne*, for which T67 is simply a reissue of the sheets of T64P, giving the Varus version of the play, whereas w68 reprints the version with Sohème.

Bengesco 312; BnC 622-625.

Paris, BnF: Rés Yf 3387.

T68

Le Théâtre de M. de Voltaire. Amsterdam: Richoff, 1768.

Volume i: [*1*] title; [*2*] blank; [1]-86 other texts (*Œdipe* and annexes); [87] D8*r* 'MARIAMNE, / *TRAGÉDIE* / *Représentée pour la premiere fois le 6 / Mars 1723.*'; [88] blank; 89-90 Avertissement (as in w38); 91-97 Préface; 98 Acteurs; [facing p.99] plate; 99-[158] (numbered '138') Mariamne, tragédie; [159]-371 other texts (*Brutus* and annexes, *La Mort de César* and annexes, *Samson, Pandore*); 372 Table des pièces contenues dans ce premier volume.

This edition seems to be the product of a revision of the earlier 'Richoff' editions (T53, T62, T64A) in the light of w56, w57G1 and w57G2, which it follows for the most part, and so gives the final state of the Varus version of *Mariamne*.

The plate facing p.99 is a careful copy of that found in w51 and w57P. The ressemblance is close and includes the names of the artist and the engraver. Differences of detail distinguish the two engravings. Image size 59 x 103 mm.

Bengesco 313; BnC 626.

Paris, BnF: Yf 4257.

[T68]

The five volumes of w68 which contain Voltaire's dramatic works were issued as a separate collection without the half-title page. *Mariamne* is in volume i, text and setting as in w68 below.

Paris, Arsenal: Rf 14093 (1).

w68

Collection complette des œuvres de M. de Voltaire. [Genève: Cramer; Paris: Panckoucke], 1768-1777. 30 vol. 4°.

Volume ii: [*1*] half-title; [*2*] blank; [*3*] title; [*4*] blank; [1]-5 Avertissement [a general preface to Voltaire's dramatic works, beginning: 'Nous donnons ici toutes les piéces de Théâtre de Monsieur *de Voltaire*, avec les variantes que nous avons pû recueillir...]; [6]-124 other texts (*Œdipe* and annexes); [facing page 125] plate; [125] Q3*r* '[ornamented capitals] MARIAMNE, / *TRAGÉDIE.* / [rule, 117 mm] / *Représentée pour la première fois le 6. Mars 1724. / Revuë & corrigée par l'Auteur en 1762.* / [rule, 117 mm] / Qiij'; [126] blank; 127-131 Préface; [132] Acteurs; 133-196 Mariamne, tragédie; [197]-[219] (numbered '223') Passages discarded from text with Varus; [220]-544 other texts (*Brutus* and annexes, *La Mort de César* and annexes, *Zaïre* and annexes, *Alzire* and annexes); 545-546 Table des pièces contenues dans ce troisième volume.

See *OC*, vol.8, p.141, for an explanation of the numbering of this, the first volume of the theatre in the Cramer quarto edition, as either volume 2 or volume 3 of the *Collection complette*.

The text of *Mariamne* is as in w64G, the only changes being the erroneous expansion of the title of the Préface noted in the variants at Préface, a, the correction of the error at Préface, 213 (w68 reads 'de la fille d'Agamemnon'), and the description of Mariamne's servant in the list of actors as a 'personnage muet' (A a-10). In addition the following note has been added to the explanatory paragraph which introduces the text discarded from the Varus version: 'N.B. Dans la MARIAMNE corrigée, telle qu'on vient de la lire, *Sohème* prince de la race des Asmonéens a été substitué à *Varus* préteur romain, gouverneur de Syrie; et *Amnon* confident de *Sohème*, à *Albin* confident de *Varus*.'

The plate is missing from some copies seen; in others it is bound facing a different page. The plate has high artistic qualities. It depicts Hérode about to stab himself, while two other figures seek to restrain him. All are dressed in richly worked Roman military clothing. The setting is an imposing room in Hérode's palace, with lofty columns and pillars, a classical frieze, and sumptuous drapes suspended above and behind Hérode's throne. Consumate craftsmanship is shown in the fineness of detail of all aspects of the engraving. Below the image we read on the left

'H. Gravelot inv.' and on the right 'N. De Launay Sculp. 1769'. Beneath this has been placed a quotation from one of Herod's act V speeches: 'Quoi! Citoyens perfides, / Vous arrachez ce fer à mes mains parricides!' (V.203-204).

Bengesco 2137; Trapnell 68; BnC 141-44.

Canberra, Australian National Library: RB De Vesci 853 (3). Paris, BnF: Rés. m Z 587 (3), Rés. Z Beuchot 1882 (3), Z 4930.

т70

Le Théâtre de M. de Voltaire. Amsterdam: Richoff, 1770. 6 vol. 12°.

Volume i: [*1*] title; [*2*] blank; [1]-86 other texts (*Œdipe* and annexes); [87] D8r 'MARIAMNE, / *TRAGÉDIE* / *Représentée pour la premiere fois le 6 / Mars 1723.*'; [88] blank; 89-90 Avertissement (as in w38); 91-97 Préface; 98 Acteurs; [facing p.99] plate; 99-158 Mariamne, tragédie; [159]-371 other texts (*Brutus* and annexes, *La Mort de César* and annexes, *Samson, Pandore*); 372 Table des pièces contenues dans ce premier volume.

A reissue of т68. *Mariamne* is reproduced line for line and page for page, with only minor typographical variations. The plate facing p.99 is identical with that found in т68 and was produced from the same engraving.

Bengesco 313; BnC 627.

Paris, BnF: Yf 4263.

w70G

Collection complette des œuvres de M. de Voltaire. [Genève: Cramer], 1770. 10 vol. 8°.

Volume vii: [1] half-title; [2] blank; [3] title; [4] blank; [5]-148 other texts (*Œdipe* and annexes); [149] K3r 'MARIAMNE, / *TRAGÉDIE*. / Revûe & corrigée par l'auteur en 1762. / K3'; [150] blank; 151-157 Préface; [158] Acteurs; [159]-223 Mariamne, tragédie; [224]-246 Passages discarded from text with Varus; [247]-403 other texts (*Brutus* and annexes, *La Mort de César* and annexes); 404-405 Table des pièces contenues dans ce volume.

The text of *Mariamne* is a new setting of w64G, which it follows rigorously line for line and page for page.

Bengesco 2133; Trapnell 64, 70G; BnC 90-91.

Oxford, Taylor: V1 1770G/1 (7). Paris, BnF: Z 24750.

W71

Collection complette des œuvres de M. de Voltaire. Genève [Liège: Plomteux], 1771. 32 vol. 8°.

Volume i: [*1*] half-title; [*2*] blank; [*3*] title; [*4*] blank; [1]-5 Avertissement [general preface, text as in w68]; [6]-115 other texts (*Œdipe* and annexes); [116] blank; [117] E11r 'MARIAMNE, / *TRAGÉDIE*. / [*ornamental rule, 75 mm*] / *Représentée pour la première fois le 6. Mars 1724. / Revuë & corrigée par l'Auteur en 1762. / [ornamental rule, 75 mm*].'; 118-123 Préface; [124] Acteurs; [facing p.125] plate; 125-173 Mariamne, tragédie; [174]-192 Passages discarded from text with Varus; [193]-462 other texts (*Brutus* and annexes, *La Mort de César* and annexes; *Zaïre* and annexes; *Alzire* and annexes).

Published by Plomteux at Liège, this edition reprints without variation the w68 text of *Mariamne*. The plate is a new engraving of the scene depicted in the w68 plate, with the same epigraph. The names of the artist and engraver are not shown.

Bengesco 2139; Trapnell 71; BnC 151.

Geneva, ImV: A 1770/1.

W70L(1772)

Collection complette des œuvres de M. de Voltaire. Lausanne: Grasset, 1770-1781. 57 vol. 8°.

Volume xiv: [i] half-title; [ii] blank; [iii] title; [iv] blank; V-VI Table des pièces contenues dans ce volume; VII-XII Avertissement [general preface, text as in w68]; XIII Avertissement des éditeurs de cette nouvelle édition; XIV-[xl] and [1]-121 other texts (*Œdipe* and annexes); [122] blank; [123] H6*r* 'MARIAMNE, / *TRAGÉDIE*. / Revue et corri-gée par l'Auteur / en 1762 et en 1771.'; [124] blank; 125-131 Préface; [132] Acteurs; 133-199 Mariamne, tragédie; [200]-232 Passages discarded from text with Varus; [233]-383 other texts (*Brutus* and annexes; *La Mort de César* and annexes).

The theatre section of Grasset's edition was produced with Voltaire's participation. The text of *Mariamne* follows w68, with the introduction of a small number of variants: see critical apparatus at I.74-75 in Appendix D (act I, Sohème version), III.131, IV.23 and 220, V.95-96 and 122. Four of these six changes substitute for the terms *tout Israël, aux Hébreux, Tout Juda, Les Hébreux*, all of which have strong connotations of religion and ethnicity, less specific, more 'neutral' words which belong to the secular vocabulary of politics: *le peuple, aux citoyens, Ils* (for 'nos Hébreux et nos prêtres'), *votre peuple*. These variants were not retained in subsequent editions.

Bengesco 2138; Trapnell 70L; BnC 149 (1-6, 14-21,25).

Oxford, Taylor: V1 1770L (14). Paris, BnF: Rés. Z Bengesco 124 (1).

72P

MARIAMNE, / *TRAGÉDIE*. / De M^R. DE VOLTAIRE. / ....
.... *Æstuat ingens* / *Imò in corde pudor, mixtoque insania luctu.* / *Et furiis agitatus amor, &c.* / Conforme à l'Édition in-4°. donnée par / l'Auteur. / [*woodcut, branches with flowers and fruit, 48 x 34 mm*] / A PARIS, / Aux dépens de la Compagnie. / [*thick-thin rule, 50-47 mm*] / M. DCC. LXXII. / *Avec Approbation & Privilége du Roi.*

4°. sig. A-F⁴ (F4 blank); pag. 46 (p.45 and 46 appear in reversed order); $2 signed, roman (-A1); sheet catchwords.

[1] title; [2] Acteurs; [3]-46 Mariamne, tragédie.

This separate edition is based on w68, the text of which it generally follows, omitting however both the Préface and the passages discarded from the Varus version.

72P is a curious hybrid, in that it retains readings of the earlier Varus version at several points where all the other Sohème editions vary the text. It shares some readings with 54P. There are further resemblances with 54P in typography and general presentation, and more specifically in the composition and layout of the title page. Both editions include the Latin epigraph not found in the intervening separate editions. These similarities lead us to suspect that the two editions may share a common origin, and that 72P, like 54P, is likely to have been produced in Rouen.

Paris, Arsenal: Rf 14145.

72X

[*all within a frame, 100 x 155 mm, consisting of ornamented and filled double rule, 8 mm in width:*] MARIAMNE, / *TRAGÉDIE.* / Par M. DE VOLTAIRE. / [*woodcut, foliage in vase surrounded by decorative motifs, 48 x 44 mm*] / [*ornamented rule, 40 mm*] / M. DCC. LXXII.

8°. sig. A-D⁴, E² (E2v blank); pag.67; $4 signed, roman (-A1, E2); sheet catchwords.

[1] title; [2] Acteurs; [3]-67 Mariamne, tragédie.

Nothing is known about the production of this edition. The text follows w68, but does not include the Préface or the text discarded from the Varus version.

Paris, Arsenal: Rf 14144.

W72X

Collection complette des œuvres de M. de Voltaire. [Genève: Cramer?], 1772. 10 vol. 8°.

Volume vii: [1] half-title; [2] blank; [3] title; [4] blank; [5]-144 other texts (*Œdipe* and annexes); [145] K1r 'MARIAMNE, / *TRAGÉDIE.* / Revue & corrigée par l'auteur en 1762. / *Théâtre.* Tom. I.K'; [146] blank; 147-153 Préface; [154] Acteurs; [155]-[216] (numbered '116') Mariamne, tragédie; [217]-239 Passages discarded from text with Varus; [240] blank; [241]-388 other texts (*Brutus* and annexes, *La Mort de César* and annexes); 389-390 Table des pièces contenues dans ce volume.

This edition was probably printed for Cramer. There is no evidence of Voltaire's participation. For *Mariamne* it reprints the text of w70G in inferior typography.

Bengesco 2133; Trapnell 72X; BnC 92, 105.

Canberra, ANL: RB PEL 1221 (7). Paris, BnF: 16° Z 15081 (7).

w72p(1773)

Œuvres de M. de V.... Neufchâtel [Paris: Panckoucke], 1771-1777. 34 or 40 vol. 8° and 12°.

Volume iv: [*1*] title; [*2*] blank; j-ij Avertissement des Libraires Associés; [1]-178 other texts (*Œdipe* and annexes); [179] H6r 'MARIAMNE, / TRAGEDIE; / *Représentée, pour la premiere fois,* / *le 6 Mars 1724.* / *Revue & corrigée par l'Auteur en 1762.* / Hvj'; [180] blank; 181-191 Préface; [192] Acteurs; [between 192 and 193] plate; [193]-265 Mariamne, tragédie; [266]-294 Passages discarded from text with Varus; [295]-466 other texts (*Brutus* and annexes, *La Mort de César* and annexes).

This edition is attributed to Panckoucke. For *Mariamne* it gives the text of w68.

The scene shown in the plate is that depicted in T68 and T70. The plate is without name of artist or engraver, but ressembles very closely in all details of execution the plates of these late 'Richoff' editions.

Bengesco 2140; Trapnell 72P; BnC 152-57.

Paris, Arsenal: Rf 14095 (4).

w75G

La Henriade, divers autres poèmes et toutes les pièces relatives à l'épopée. [Genève: Cramer et Bardin], 1775. 37 [40] vol. 8°.

Volume ii: [*1*] half-title; [*2*] blank; [*3*] title; [*4*] blank; 1-6 Avertissement [general preface, text as in w68]; [7]-151 other texts (*Œdipe* and annexes); [152] blank; [153] K5r '[*all within ornamented border*] [*ornamented capitals*]

MARIAMNE / *TRAGÉDIE* / [rule, 72 mm] / *Représentée pour la première fois le 6. Mars 1724.* / *Revue et corrigée par l'Auteur en 1762.* / [rule, 72 mm]'; [154] blank; 155-161 Préface; [162] Acteurs; [facing p.163] plate; 163-227 Mariamne, tragédie; [228]-250 passages discarded from text with Varus; [251]-403 other texts (*Brutus* and annexes; *La Mort de César* and annexes); 404-405 Table des pièces contenues dans ce volume.

This is the Cramer *encadrée* edition, the last to be revised by Voltaire. For *Mariamne*, it reproduces the text of w68, the only changes being a variant reading introduced at II.301 (and maintained in κ84 and κ85) and an error at V.82.

The plate is a new engraving, left-to-right reversed, of the scene depicted in the plate of w68, and, like its predecessor, is of high artistic merit. The image appears within a frame whose design repeats the motifs of the frame used on the text pages. The same epigraph as in w68 has been placed beneath the plate. The names of the artist and engraver do not appear.

Bengesco 2141; Trapnell 75G; BnC 158-61.

Oxford, Taylor: V1 1775 (2). Paris, BnF: Z 24840.

w75G*

The copy of w75G marked up by Voltaire for the proposed Panckoucke edition of his works (see S. S. B. Taylor, 'The definitive text of Voltaire's works: the Leningrad *encadrée*', *SVEC* 124 (1974) 7-132 (*passim* and in particular p.45). There are two annotations in Voltaire's hand to *Mariamne*: a note on the half-title (p.[153]) quoted in section 5.ii above, and a variant at I.17.

St Petersburg, GpbVM: 3472 C (2).

w75x

Œuvres de M. de Voltaire. [Lyon?], 1775. 40 vol. 8°.

Volume ii: [1] half-title; [2] blank; [3] title; [4] blank; 1-6 Avertissement [general preface, text as in w68]; [7]-151 other texts (*Œdipe* and annexes); [152] blank; [153] K5r '[*all within ornamented border*] [*ornamented capitals*]

MARIAMNE / *TRAGÉDIE* / [*rule, 78 mm*] / *Représentée pour la première fois le 6 Mars 1724.* / *Revue et corrigée par l'Auteur en 1762.* / [*rule, 78 mm*]'; [154] blank; 155-161 Préface; [162] Acteurs; [facing p.163] plate; 163-227 Mariamne, tragédie; [228]-250 passages discarded from text with Varus; [251]-403 other texts (*Brutus* and annexes; *La Mort de César* and annexes); 404-405 Table des pièces contenues dans ce volume.

A close imitation of w75G. The features distinguishing the two editions have been described by J. Vercruysse in 'Les Editions encadrées des Œuvres de Voltaire', *SVEC* 168 (1977), p.1-191. The text of *Mariamne* is identical with w75G, as is the plate.

Bengesco 2141; BnC 162-163.

Paris, BnF: Z 24881.

T76G

Théatre Complet de M. de Voltaire. Genève, 1776. 9 vol.

A reissue of the sheets of w75G, without the plate, under a title apparently produced by the printer of w75X.

London, Queen Mary Westfield: PQ 2076.

T76X

Théatre Complet de monsieur de Voltaire. 1776.

Volume i: [*1*] half-title; [*2*] blank; [*3*] title; [*4*] blank; [1]-7 Avertissement [general preface, text as in w68]; [8]-160 other texts (*Œdipe* and annexes); [161] L1r '*MARIAMNE, / TRAGÉDIE.* / [*rule, 72 mm*] / *Représentée pour la première fois le 6 Mars 1724,* / *Revue & corrigée par l'Auteur en 1762.* / [*rule, 72 mm*] / *Théatre. Tom. I.* L'; [162] blank; [163]-170 Préface and Acteurs; [171]-235 Mariamne, tragédie; [236]-259 Variantes; [260]-538 other texts (*Brutus* and annexes, *La Mort de César* and annexes, *Zaïre* and annexes); [539]-540 Table des pièces contenues dans ce volume.

This edition faithfully copies the w68 text of *Mariamne*. The slight changes made to w68 in w75G are not found in T76X.

Paris, Arsenal: Rf 14096 (1).

78

[*in ornamented capitals*] MARIAMNE, / [*in ornamented italic capitals*]
TRAGEDIE. / EN CINQ ACTES / *ET EN VERS.* / Par Monsieur
DE VOLTAIRE. / [*ornamented rule, 84 mm*] / *NOUVELLE
ÉDITION.* / [*ornamented rule, 84 mm*] / [*woodcut, writing materials
on ornamental shelf, 43 x 31 mm*] / *A PARIS,* / Chez DIDOT, l'aîné,
Imprimeur / & Libraire, Rue Pavée. / [*ornamental rule, 62 mm*] / *M.
DCC. LXXVIII.* /

4°. sig. A-E⁴ F¹; pag. 42 (unnumbered 18, 25, 33); $2 signed, arabic (-A1);
sheet catchwords.

[1] title; [2] Acteurs; [3]-42 Mariamne, tragédie.

This late issue of the Varus version of *Mariamne* is identical with 65, of
which it reproduces not only the readings not found in any other edition,
but also certain errors. Like 65, it thus reproduces the text of w48D as
modified at some points by a 'Richoff' edition (T53, T62 or T64A).

Geneva, ImV: D Hérode 1778/1.

к84

Œuvres complètes de Voltaire. [Kehl] Société littéraire-typographique,
1784-1789. 70 vol. 8°.

Volume i: [1] half-title; [2] blank; [3] title; [4] blank; [i] 'THEATRE. /
Théâtre. Tome I. a'; [ii] blank; [iii]-xij Préface des Rédacteurs de la
nouvelle édition; [xiii]-[xiv] (numbered 'iv') Table des pièces contenues
dans ce volume; [1]-6 Avertissement de l'édition de 1775; [7]-186 other
texts (*Œdipe* and annexes, *Fragments d'Artémire*); [187] M6r
'MARIAMNE, / *TRAGEDIE.* / Représentée, pour la première
fois, / le 6 mars 1724. / *Revue & corrigée par l'auteur en 1762.'*; [188]
blank; [189]-196 Préface de la première édition; [197]-201 Fragment de la
préface de 1730; [202] Personnages; [203]-266 Mariamne, tragédie; [267]-
274 Variantes des premières éditions de Mariamne; [275]-292 Variantes
contenant les changements occasionnés par la substitution du rôle de
Sohème à celui de Varus; [293]-[463] other texts (*Brutus* and annexes;
Eryphile and annexes).

In the two printings of the Kehl text the 'Préface de la première édition' is the shortened version of the preface found in w38 and succeeding editions, but not earlier. The 'Fragment de la préface de 1730' is also misleadingly entitled: it consists of paragraphs 2-13 (lines 18-104) of the original Préface which first appeared in 25P. Under 'Variantes des premières éditions de Mariamne' are found firstly two brief passages from act V of the 25P text which were abandoned in 31 and succeeding editions: these are V.9-12 (the first half of verse 13 is also given, with the reading 'Sur ce trône coupable') and V.228-242, Hérode's final speech in its 25P version. These are followed by the text of the two scenes which survive from M24 (see Appendix A, and section 2.ii above). Pages [275]-292 contain the passages discarded from the Varus version of the play as found in w68 and w75G.

For *Mariamne* K84 and K85 reproduce the text of w75G*, but not absolutely without variation. The error at V.82 is corrected, and several changes are introduced. Some of these are very minor; see critical apparatus at II.265, where the singular *le fils* may simply be an error; and III.225, where *A quel chagrin* replaces *A quels chagrins*. Others are a little more substantial; though bordering in some cases on the pedantic, they may have been prompted by a desire to improve the style or the grammatical or logical consistency of the text. See critical apparatus at I.81 (Sohème version, App. D), where, perhaps for stylistic reasons, *peux* is replaced by *puis*; II.11 (Sohème version, App. D), where the variant, which replaces the words *au défaut du pouvoir* with *où manque le pouvoir*, may also have been dictated by stylistic considerations; II.223, where *ce palais* replaces *mon palais* in a verse spoken by Mariamne (who does not possess her own palace); III.241, where *les siens*, which replaces *les miens*, is more logically and grammatically consistent with a third person singular subject (as MS2 attests, this variant had been in existence since at least 1763); III.302, where it is perhaps more plausible to imagine that Varus's 'escorte secrète' is already in place (rather than still taking up its position) at the time when Mazaël speaks this verse.

The question arises whether these variations from w75G* stem from Voltaire or are due to the hand of another. As is well known, in the months preceding his departure from Ferney for Paris in February 1778, Voltaire undertook a major revision of the *encadré* text in preparation for a new edition of his works which it was initially agreed was to be published by Panckoucke, but which finally appeared as Kehl. In his study of the revisions made by Voltaire for this purpose, S. S. B. Taylor ('The definitive text of Voltaire's works: the Leningrad *encadrée*') lists *Mariamne* as a work completely revised (p.45). Taylor considers that Voltaire completed the revision of all his theatrical works, and argues persuasively that w75G* provides the definitive text for all those works revised by Voltaire before his death. It is therefore tempting to draw the conclusion that the variations introduced into the w75G* text by Kehl must be the work of other persons. These persons can only have been Wagnière, who checked the manuscript revisions and supervised the transcription process described below, or the Kehl editors. Such a conclusion may however be open to question. We know that the revisions which Voltaire had entered onto his set of the *encadrée* (w75G*) were transcribed onto another interleaved set of the same edition supplied by Panckoucke. After Voltaire's death this set was delivered to Panckoucke by Wagnière, and eventually became the basis of the Kehl edition. Professor Taylor allows the possibility that Voltaire may have had the time to check a few of the interleaved transcript volumes before he left for Paris in February 1778, and may have made further minor improvements. Though he considers this possibility to be fairly remote, and adopts the general position that what is not found in the annotated *encadrée* is not authentic Voltaire, he concedes nevertheless that if indeed Voltaire did enter further revisions onto the transcript volumes, this is more likely to have occurred in the theatre volumes than those containing other works.

It is just possible therefore that the variations from the text of w75G* found in k84 and k85 stem from Voltaire himself. None of them are more than small retouches to points of detail, and they represent just the sort of change likely to be made in a hurried skimming of the transcript volume by Voltaire during the hectic days preceding his departure on his last journey to Paris.

Bengesco 2142; BnC 167.

Oxford: VF. Paris, BnF: Rés. p. Z 2209 (1).

K85

Volume i: [*1*] half-title; [*2*] blank; [*3*] title; [*4*] blank; [i]-x Préface des Rédacteurs de la nouvelle édition; [xi] 'THEATRE.'; [xii] blank; [1]-6 Avertissement de l'édition de 1775; [7]-186 other texts (*Œdipe* and annexes, *Fragments d'Artémire*); [187] M6r 'MARIAMNE, / *TRAGEDIE*. / Représentée, pour la première fois, le 6 mars 1724. / *Revue & corrigée par l'auteur en 1762*.'; [188] blank; [189]-196 Préface de la première édition; [197]-201 Fragment de la préface de 1730; [202] Personnages; [203]-266 Mariamne, tragédie; [267]-274 Variantes des premières éditions de Mariamne; [275]-292 Variantes contenant les changements occasionnés par la substitution du rôle de Sohème à celui de Varus; [293]-462 other texts (*Brutus* and annexe, *Eryphile* and annexes): [463]-464 Table des pièces contenues dans ce volume.

The second printing of the Kehl edition introduces three small changes into the text of *Mariamne*. At IV.23 (variant, line 4) 'femme' replaces 'épouse'; at V.13 'Sur ce trône' replaces 'Sous ce trône'. In both cases the reading varied by K85 is not simply that of K84, but of many earlier editions. At V.121, in place of K84 'Hé bien', K85 restores the reading of w75G and earlier editions 'Eh bien'. The last of these changes had already been recorded in the *errata* of K84, which devotes an interesting footnote to explaining the different connotations of 'Hé bien' and 'Eh bien' as used by the Kehl editors (see V.121 in notes).

Bengesco 2142; BnC 4450.

Oxford, Taylor: V1 1785/2 (1).

8. *Translations*

Dutch

Mariamne, treurspel. Gevolgd naar het Fransche van den Heer de Voltaire door Pieter Van Braam. Dordrecht: Van Braam, 1774.

English

A translation of *Mariamne* is included in *The Dramatic Works of Mr de Voltaire. Translated by the Rev. Mr Francklin*, vol.i. London, 1761; re-edited 1769.

Italian

La Marianna, tragedia del Signor de Volter, tradotta in versi italiani dal co. Gasparo Gozzi. Venezia, 1751. Re-edited in Gozzi's *Opere in versi ed in prosa*, vol.iii. Venezia, 1769.

Portuguese

Mariamne: tragedia [...] *traduzida en versos Portuguezes*. Lisboa, 1790.

9. *Principles of this edition*

The base text is 25P, the first edition authorised by Voltaire of the Varus version, and his considered statement about the text of the play in 1725, after the first run of performances. It incorporates all the adjustments, redraftings, and changes of mind that had occurred during the lengthy processes of the writing, production and performance of the play. It is the text approved by Voltaire at the conclusion of a sequence of occasions (readings, rehearsals, performances), each one of which had served to test the play before successively larger audiences. Voltaire then assumed responsibility for this text and had it printed at this own expense.

25P is also the version of the play that enabled Voltaire to reassert his dominance of the theatrical world of Paris in the early 1720s. Its success came at a timely moment for him. After his initial triumph with *Œdipe*, he had seen the failure of his next two plays (*Artémire* and the *Mariamne* of 1724). A third failure would have been a severe, if not fatal, blow to his reputation as a dramatic poet. Furthermore 25P attracted much critical attention, as we have seen. The importance attached to it by commentators can be taken to reflect the place which it held in the literary discourse of its time. To talk about Voltaire's *Mariamne*, after the publication of M25, was to talk about this edition.

Variants are drawn from MS1, 25CH, 25X, 26H, and from the following editions in which Voltaire is known to have participated: 30, 31, W38, W42, W46, W48D, W51, W52, W56, W57G, W57P, W64G, W68, W70G, W70L, W75G and Kehl.

As we have seen, w64G and later editions give the Sohème version of the play, relegating to an appendix the text discarded by Voltaire from the earlier version with Varus. When variants are cited from these appendices, the source is denoted by a small capical v added to the siglum: w64Gv.

Treatment of the base text

I. Punctuation

Intervention has been kept to the minimum. We have retained the use of a colon or semi-colon to mark the end of a subordinate clause introduced by 'si' (or 'tant que, 'quand' or other conjunction) before a main clause. All interventions made have the authority of one or more (and usually most) of 30, 31, w38, w75G, K.

1. The comma
– has been inserted to detach the name or title of the person addressed from the words addressed to him/her at I.311; II.144,148,197; III.106, 153, 225, 278; IV.102, 216; V.160, 166, 235.
– has been inserted at the following points: Préface 34 (after *Ixion*); I.37, 207, 217; II.53; III.235, 289; IV.205, 215; V.176.
– replaces the semi-colons at Préface 71 (after *Histoire*), 101 (after *raisonnable*), 148 (after *sensible*); I.11, 45; III.203; IV.11, 79.
– replaces the colon at II.218.
– replaces the full stops at Préface 164 (after *nuit*); 291 (after *mauvais*); 292 (after *Henri IV*); I.45; II.155, 332; IV.11; V.41, 98.
– has been deleted at Préface 201 (after *Pièce*); II.221; III.141, 232, 282; IV.76, 105, 128; V.111, 131.

2. The full stop
– has been deleted at Préface 19 (after *1724*), 21 (after *1725*).
– has been inserted at V.166.

3. The semi-colon
– replaces the full stop at I.259 and the comma at III.305.
– has been inserted at II.97.

4. The question mark
- has been deleted at II.273.
- replaces the exclamation mark at Préface 137 (after *ouvrages*).

5. The exclamation mark
- has been deleted at V.208.
- replaces a question mark at III.237 and V.3, 151.

II. Proper nouns

The spelling of names of persons and places has been respected, except, in the Préface, for *Hippolite*, and for the correction of *Thesé*, *Britanicus*, *Mithidate*, *Jean-Federic*. In the Préface the Latin proper names *medea ino* and *io* had lower-case initial letters. The dieresis has been added to *Mazaël*.

III. Capitalisation

- Interjections have been given initial capitals at III.168, 171, 237, 291; IV.91, 100, 103, 145, 227; V.159.
- Initial words in sentences have been given capitals at Préface 204 (*Comme*), I.73, 83; IV.17, 83, 86, 161.
- Initial capitals were attributed in the text of the play to: Aïeux, Ancêtres, Armes, Arrêt, Asmonéen, Assassins, Autels, Autorité, Boureaux, Champs, Char, Chefs, Ciel, Cieux, Climats, Concitoyens, Conquérant, Cour, Courtisan, Cytoïen, Diadême, Dieux, Eaux, Echaffaut, Elemens, Empire, Enfans, Ennemie, Epouse, Esclaves, Etat, Exploits, Famille, Favori, Fille, Fils, Frere, Garde, Gouverneur, Grands, Guerre, Hébreu, Héros, Humains, Maison, Maître, Majesté, Mer, Mere, Ministre, Monarque, Morts, Murs, Nations, Ondes, Oracle, Orages, Ordres, Paix, Palais, Parens, Pere, Peuple, Place, Pontifes, Port, Prêteur, Prêtres, Prince, Protecteur, Reine, Remparts, Renommée, Rivale, Rive, Roi, Romain, Sang, Sceptre, Serviteur, Sœur, Soldats, Sources, Souverain, Souveraine, Successeur, Sujets, Terre, Thrône, Tonnerre, Tyran, Univers, Vainqueur, Victoire, Vieillard.
- Initial capitals were attributed in the Préface to: Actes, Acteurs, Action, Arc, Art, Auteur, Avare, Belle-mere, Bois, Bourgeois, Bureau, Captifs, Char, Comédie, Copies, Coursiers, Critique, Dieux, Edition, Epique, Estampes, Famille, Festin, Forêts, Gens,

Gouverneur, Heros, Histoire, Homme, Impression, Imprimeur, Invictaque, Javelots, Juges, Lecteurs, Lecture, Libraire, Ligue, Lions, Loi, Maîtresse, Mars, May, Messieurs, Meurtrier, Ministres, Nation, Nôce, Ours, Ouvrage, Païsans, Peintres, Personnage, Personnes, Piece, Poëme, Poësie, Poëte, Préface, Prêteur, Prince, Princesse, Public, Quay, Recit, Representation, Roi, Rois, Salut, Scene, Spectateur, Sujets, Table, Tableau, Tapisserie, Theâtre, Tracasseries, Tragedie, Univers, Vers, Vieillard.

– Initial capitals were attributed to adjectives denoting nationality: Romain, Asmonéen.

IV. Accents

1. The acute accent

– was not used:
  – within the play, in: Cesar, cheriroit, cherissiez, defenduë, delibere, desarmé, desespoir, desire, desirs, devorans, dexterité, different, differer, elemens, eperdûë, esperance, etenduë, evanoüie, executer, experience, feliciter, genereuses, genereux, generosité, Hebreux, Herode, himenée, imperieux, inalterable, indifferent, inquietude, interêt, Jerusalem, menagé, merité, miserable, misterieux, pene-trez, perir, perisse, persecuter, persecuteurs, persecutez, persevere, posseder, possedez, presence, presens, present, presentée, presen-ter, presentez, pretendez, pretendre, proteger, protegez, regner, regnez, regnoient, repliquez, resolûë, secher, Senat, severe, sterile, succeder, verité
  – and within the Préface in: celebres, decouvrir, desesperé, differens, effraïe (past part.), effrenée, élegance, esperer, Federic, generale, genie, regla, Herode, heros, immoderé, impetueux, interessa, interessant, interesse, interesser, interêt, Iphigenie, Jerusalem, merite, necessaire, necessité, Neron, Pelée, preface, presens, presente, recit, reflexions, regneront, reguliere, Representations, representera, revolta, revolter, serieuses, serieux, sincerité, succe-dant, theâtre, Thebains, Thesé, Thetis, tragedie, Trezene, veritez.
– was used:
  – within the play, in: appésanties, appésantisse, assiégent, éxamine, éxaminez, éxemple, éxil, éxiloient, inéxorable, infléxible, qua-triéme, troisiéme

9. PRINCIPLES OF THIS EDITION

— and within the Préface in: pésanteur, piéce, prés, refléxions, succés.

2. The grave accent
— was not used:
   — within the play, in: acheve, altiere, amene, assiege, austere, barriere, beau-pere, caractere, cede, chere, colere, considere, déja, delibere, enleve, entiere, espere, étrangere, fidele, frere, infidele, levres, mere, misere, modele, pere, persevere, piege, premiere, regne, révere, secrete, severe, sincere, tremblerent, troublerent, zele
   — and within the Préface in: belle-mere, caractere, carriere, celebres, colere, considere, déja, derniere, derriere, entierement, entieres, fidelement, fierement, frere, Grece, grossiere, lumiere, Moliere, pere, Phedre, piece, préfere, premiere, regle, reguliere, scene, sincerement, tres, Trezene.

3. The circumflex accent
— was used:
   — in *vôtre* employed adjectivally (Préface, 163, II.321, III.71, 72, 226, IV.151, V.195).
   — in certain third person singular forms of the pretcrite: *pût* (Préface 20), *fût* (I.38), *eût* (Préface 131, I.138, 270), *fît* (III.79).
   — in the text of the play, in: absoût, ajoûtoit, assûrant, assûré, assûrer, assûrez, avoûe, chûte, croît, crû, diadême, dûssiez, enflâmai, entrevûë, eperdûë, Hâme, imprévûë, lû, plûtôt, Prêteur, prévû, pû, reçû, revôle, soûlevant, soûlevé, soûmettre, soûmis, soûpire, soûpirer, soûtenu, soûtien, toûjours, vôle, vû, vûë
   — and in the Préface in: vûs, ajoûte, aperçûs, chûte, coûtume, entrevûë, eû, Nôce, plûpart, plûtôt, Prêteur, pû, reçûe, reçûës, soûtenir, toûjours, vôtre, vûë.
— was not used:
   — in certain third person singular forms of the imperfect subjunctive: abolit (Préface 1), eut (Préface 54), ressemblat (Préface 65), detestat (Préface 67), plaignit (Préface 67), confondit (I.6)
   — and in ame, couter, disgrace, du (from devoir), grace, idolatrie, oublirai, Théatre.

V. Orthography

The following aspects of orthography have been modified to conform with present day usage:

– Imperfect and conditional endings in *-ois*, *-oit*, *-oient* were used throughout.

– Spellings in *-oi-* were used in: affoiblissent, affoiblissoient, connois, connoissez, connoissois, connoît, connoîtra, connoître, connoîtrez, disparoissez, foible, foibles, foiblesse, foiblesses, François (for Français), méconnoissable, méconnoissant, paroisse (from paraître), paroît, paroître, reconnois, reconnoissance, reconnoître.

– Spellings in *-ï-* were used in: aïant, aïez, croïez, croïois, cytoïen, effraïant, effraïé, essaïer, essuïer, fuïant, fuïez, fuïois, moïens, païsans, renvoïée, revoïez, voïant, voïez, voïois, voïoit.

– Spellings in *-i-* were used in: ennuieux, essuié, himenée, misterieux, stile.

– Spellings in *-y-* were used in: Cytoïen, May, mary, Quay, Roy, yvresse.

– The consonant *t* was not used in syllable endings *-ans*, *-ens*:
  – in the play, in: ardens, chancelans, châtimens, devorans, Elemens, emportemens, Enfans, errans, momens, mouvemens, outrageans, Parens, prenans, presens, puissans, sanglans, sentimens, tourmens, tout-puissans, tremblans
  – and in the Préface in: changemens, combattans, complimens, differens, engagemens, gémissemens, impuissans, mouvemens, sentimens, talens.

– The consonant *d* was not used in the syllable ending *-ens* of certain verbs: deffens, entens-je, j'entreprens, je prétens, tu prétens.

– Initial *sç-* was used in sçavoir and derived forms.

– The forms 'je sçai' (alongside 'je sçais'), je croi, voi-je, je prévoi were used.

– Endings in *-eʒ* were used:
  – in the following nouns: beautez, bontez, côtez, cruautez, extrémitez, succez, veritez, volontez
  – and in the masculine plural forms of adjectives and participles: accablez, agitez, armez, attachez, attirez, baignez, confiez, consacrez, détestez, éclipsez, effacez, égarez, égorgez, empressez, étonnez, fermez, formez, humiliez, interressez, indignez, infortu-

178

nez, irritez, nez [nés], opprimez, passez, penetrez, persecutez, portez, préparez, relevez, reservez, révoltez, sacrez, sacrifiez, semez, troublez.

- Single consonants were used in: amoli, boureaux, couroux, échape, enflâmai, enflamer, falu, falût, flâme, flater, flateur, flateurs, flatois, flatoit, frapée, suplice.
- Double consonants were used in: abbattu, allarme, allarmes, amenne, appellé, deffendez, deffendre, infidelle, interressant, interressée, interressez, Jettez, traittoit, (vous) appellez.
- Old spellings were used in: azile, échauffaut, loix, serains, Thrône.

VI. Various

1. The hyphen
   - was used in: au-delà, aussi-bien, bien-faits, bien-tôt, long-temps, malgré-moi, malgré-vous, par-là, plus-belle, Poëme-Epique, si-tôt, sur-tout, tour-à-tour, très-belles, tres-méchant, yeux-même.
   - was not used in: peut etre, vous même.

2. The apostrophe
   - was used in subject-verb inversions: arriva-t'il, a-t'elle, aura-t'il, faudra-t'il, sera-t'il, souffrira-t'il.
   - was used in quelqu'apparence (Préface 4), entr'eux (II.48).

3. The ampersand was used throughout. *Et* appeared only at beginning of lines and in other circumstances where a capital was required.

4. Titles of works mentioned in the Préface were not italicised.

5. Certain adverbial expressions were written as two words: au tour, par tout, sur tout.

6. *Encor* was used in the Préface, and has been normalised to *encore*. At II.33 and III.81 *encore* has been reduced to *encor*. This brings it into conformity with other editions and achieves the correct syllable count.

7. The dieresis was used in: accüeil, appuïe, avouë, avoüer, avouërai, confonduë, continuë, defenduë, désavouë, désobéïr, desobéïsse, deve-nuë, écüeils, entrevûë, éperdûë, étenduë, eüe, evanoüie, fauteüil, foudroïe, fuïr, füir, füirez, fuïs, füis, füit, haït, imprévûë, joïe, joüée, joüir, nuë, obéïr, obéïs, obéïssance, obéïssez, orgüeil, oüi, perduë,

Poëme, Poësie, Poëte, reconnuë, reçûë, recüeille, rejoüée, rejoüi, renduë, repandüe, resolûë, réünisse, rompuë, soüille, suspenduë, veüille, voïe, vûë.

VII. Errors and misprints

The following errors and misprints have been silently corrected:
– Préface 64: *conservaut* (for *conservant*), 130: *de l'un* (for *de l'une*), 132: *malhonnête* (for *malhonnêtes*), 163: *fonds* (for *fond*), 184: *fond* (for *fonds*), 190: *Qu'elle* (for *Quelle*), 199: *void* (for *voit*), 216: *Mithidate* (for *Mithridate*), 224: *intriguante* (for *intrigante*), 250: *des petits objets* (for *de*), 275: *entieremet* (for *entièrement*)
– Text I.70: *Songons* (for *songeons*), I.176: *quoiqu'il* (for *quoi qu'il*), II.11: *fonds* (for *fond*), II.29: *crainte* (for *contrainte*), II.157: *dégoûtant* (for *dégouttant*), II.193: *vour* (for *vous*), II.298: *reconnuossance* (for *reconnoissance*), III.218: *Deux* (for *Des*), III.287: *charmé* (for *armé*), IV.64: *spectable* (for *spectacle*), IV.87: *espere-tu* (for *espères-tu*), V.27: *quel* (for *quels*), V.72: *vertus* (for *vertu*), V.103: *en secret* deleted, V.170: *leur* (for *leurs*), V.192: *meilleures* (for *meilleurs*)

VIII. Points of grammar

– I.100: The use of the auxiliary *avoir* in the form *auroit tombé* was presumably dictated by metrical considerations.
– I.263: The present participle *prenans*, though used verbally with a direct object, agreed in number and gender with its antecedent.

HÉRODE ET MARIAMNE,

TRAGÉDIE

PRÉFACE

Il serait utile qu'on abolît la coutume que plusieurs personnes ont prise depuis quelques années, de transcrire pendant les représentations, les pièces de théâtre, bonnes ou mauvaises, qui ont quelque apparence de succès.[1] Cette précipitation répand dans le public des copies défectueuses des pièces nouvelles, et expose les auteurs à 5 voir leurs ouvrages imprimés sans leur consentement, et avant qu'ils y aient mis la dernière main. Voilà le cas où je me trouve. Il vient de paraître coup sur coup trois mauvaises éditions[2] de ma tragédie de MARIAMNE, l'une à AMSTERDAM chez CHANGUION, et les deux autres sans nom d'imprimeur. Toutes trois sont pleines de 10 tant de fautes, que mon ouvrage y est entièrement méconnaissable. Ainsi je me vois forcé de donner moi-même une édition de MARIAMNE, où du moins il n'y ait de fautes que les miennes; et cette nécessité où je suis d'imprimer ma tragédie, avant le temps que je m'étais prescrit pour la corriger, servirait d'excuse aux 15 fautes qui sont dans cet ouvrage, si des défauts pouvaient jamais être excusés.

La destinée de cette pièce a été extraordinaire. Elle fut jouée

a-293a   MSI, 25CH, 25X, 26H: [absent]
a   w68, w75G, K: Préface / de la première édition.[3]
1-105   w38, w42-K: [absent]
10   31: les autres
18-104   K: [printed as an appendix under the title Fragment de la Préface de l'Edition de 1730]

[1] La Motte's Inès de Castro had received similar treatment, noted by Voltaire in D244.
[2] These 'mauvaises éditions', along with the general publication history of Hérode et Mariamne, are discussed in the Introduction, section 4.iv.
[3] A misstatement. The Préface does not appear in full in the editions cited (w68, w75G, K). As the apparatus shows, they lack lines 1-105 and 262-93a (though lines 18-104 appear in K, these are printed in an appendix separate from the Préface).

pour la première fois en 1724 au mois de mars, et fut si mal reçue
qu'à peine put-elle être achevée: Elle fut rejouée avec quelques   20
changements en 1725 au mois de mai,[4] et fut reçue alors avec une
extrême indulgence.

J'avoue avec sincérité, qu'elle méritait le mauvais accueil que
lui fit d'abord le public. Et je supplie qu'on me permette d'entrer
sur cela dans un détail, qui peut-être ne sera pas inutile à ceux qui   25
voudront courir la carrière épineuse du théâtre, où j'ai le malheur
de m'être engagé; ils verront les écueils où j'ai échoué. Ce n'est
que par là que je puis leur être utile.

Une des premières règles, est de peindre les héros connus, tels
qu'ils ont été, ou plutôt tels que le public les imagine; car il est bien   30
plus aisé de mener les hommes par les idées qu'ils ont, qu'en
voulant leur en donner de nouvelles.

> Sit Medea ferox invictaque, flebilis Ino.
> Perfidus Ixion, Io vaga, tristis Orestes, etc.[5]

Fondé sur ces principes, et entraîné par la complaisance   35
respectueuse que j'ai toujours eue pour des personnes qui
m'honorent de leur amitié et de leurs conseils, je me résolus de
m'assujetir entièrement à l'idée que les hommes ont depuis
longtemps, de MARIAMNE et d'HÉRODE, et je ne songeai qu'à
les peindre fidèlement d'après le portrait que chacun s'en est fait   40
dans son imagination. Ainsi Hérode parut dans cette pièce, cruel et
politique, tyran de ses sujets, de sa famille, de sa femme, plein
d'amour pour Mariamne; mais plein d'un amour barbare, qui ne lui
inspirait pas le moindre repentir de ses fureurs: je ne donnai à
Mariamne, d'autres sentiments qu'un orgueil imprudent, et qu'une   45

---

19   K [*in appendix*]: 1724, et
20-21   K [*in appendix*]: rejouée en 1725 avec quelques changements, et
29   25A: [*no paragraph indent*]

---

[4] In fact the first performances of M25 were given in April 1725 (see Introduction,
section 4.i).

[5] Horace, *Ars Poetica*, 123-24.

haine inflexible pour son mari. Et enfin, dans la vue de me conformer aux opinions reçues, je ménageai une entrevue entre Hérode et Varus, dans laquelle je fis parler ce préteur avec la hauteur qu'on s'imagine que les Romains affectaient avec les rois. Qu'arriva-t-il de tout cet arrangement? Mariamne intraitable 50 n'intéressa point: Hérode n'étant que criminel, révolta; et son entretien avec Varus le rendit méprisable. J'étais à la première représentation: je m'aperçus dès le moment où parut Hérode, qu'il était impossible que la pièce eût du succès; et je compris que je m'étais égaré en marchant trop timidement dans la route ordinaire. 55

Je sentis qu'il est des occasions où la première règle est de s'écarter des règles prescrites: et que (comme dit monsieur Pascal, sur un sujet plus sérieux)[6] les vérités se succèdent du pour au contre à mesure qu'on a plus de lumières. Il est vrai qu'il faut peindre les héros tels qu'ils ont été; mais il est encore plus vrai qu'il 60 faut adoucir des caractères désagréables; qu'il faut songer au public pour qui l'on écrit, encore plus qu'aux héros que l'on fait paraître; et qu'on doit imiter les peintres habiles, qui embellissent en conservant la ressemblance.

Pour qu'Hérode ressemblât, il était nécessaire qu'il excitât 65 l'indignation: Mais pour plaire il devait émouvoir la pitié. Il fallait que l'on détestât ses crimes, que l'on plaignît sa passion, qu'on aimât ses remords; et que ces mouvements si violents, si subits, si

57 K [in appendix]: (comme le dit
59 25A: de lumière.
64 25A: en observant la

[6] Pascal, *Pensées*: 'Ainsi se vont les opinions succédant du pour au contre, selon qu'on a de lumière' (Brunschvicg 337, Lafuma 90, Le Guern 83). The 'sujet plus sérieux' addressed by Pascal is the alternation between respect and scorn in the attitudes of members of society of increasing intellectual and spiritual insight towards persons of noble birth. R. Pomeau points out the interest of this evidence of Voltaire's early familiarity, dating from several years before the publication of the *Anti-Pascal*, with the writings of the great Jansenist thinker (*La Religion de Voltaire*, 1969, p.97; cf. *Voltaire en son temps*, i.196).

contraires, qui font le caractère d'Hérode, passassent rapidement
tour à tour dans l'âme du spectateur.   70

Si l'on veut suivre l'histoire; Mariamne doit haïr Hérode, et
l'accabler de reproches: mais si on veut que Mariamne intéresse,
ses reproches doivent faire espérer une réconciliation: sa haine ne
doit pas paraître toujours inflexible. Par là le spectateur est
attendri, et l'histoire n'est point entièrement démentie.   75

Enfin je crois que Varus ne doit point du tout voir Hérode; et en
voici les raisons. S'il parle à ce prince avec colère et avec hauteur, il
l'humilie, et il ne faut point avilir un personnage qui doit
intéresser. S'il lui parle avec politesse, ce n'est qu'une scène de
compliments, qui serait d'autant plus froide, qu'elle serait inutile. 80
Que si Hérode répond en justifiant ses cruautés il dément la
douleur et les remords dont il est pénétré en arrivant. S'il avoue à
Varus cette douleur et ce repentir qu'il ne peut en effet cacher à
personne: Alors il n'est plus permis au vertueux Varus de
contribuer à la fuite de Mariamne, pour laquelle il ne doit plus   85
craindre. De plus, Hérode ne peut faire qu'un très méchant
personnage avec l'amant de sa femme; et il ne faut jamais faire
rencontrer ensemble sur la scène des acteurs principaux qui n'ont
rien d'intéressant à se dire.

La mort de Mariamne, qui à la première représentation était   90
empoisonnée et expirait sur le théâtre, acheva de révolter les
spectateurs; soit que le public ne pardonne rien, lorsqu'une fois il
est mécontent, soit qu'en effet il eût raison de condamner cette
invention qui était une faute contre l'histoire, faute qui peut-être
n'était rachetée par aucune beauté.   95

J'aurais pu ne me pas rendre sur ce dernier article. Et j'avoue
que c'est contre mon goût que j'ai mis la mort de Mariamne en
récit, au lieu de la mettre en action: mais je n'ai voulu combattre en
rien le goût du public. C'est pour lui, et non pour moi que j'écris:
Ce sont ses sentiments et non les miens que je dois suivre.   100

Cette docilité raisonnable, ces efforts que j'ai faits pour rendre

77-78   K [*in appendix*]: avec hauteur et avec colère, il

186

intéressant un sujet qui avait paru si ingrat, m'ont tenu lieu du
mérite qui m'a manqué, et ont enfin trouvé grâce devant des juges
prévenus contre la pièce.

Je ne pense pas que ma tragédie mérite son succès, comme elle   105
avait mérité sa chute. Je ne donne même cette édition qu'en
tremblant. Tant d'ouvrages que j'ai vus applaudis au théâtre, et
méprisés à la lecture, me font craindre pour le mien le même sort.
Une ou deux situations, l'art des acteurs, la docilité que j'ai fait
paraître, ont pu m'attirer des suffrages aux représentations: mais il   110
faut un autre mérite pour soutenir le grand jour de l'impression.
C'est peu d'une conduite régulière. Ce serait peu même d'intéresser. Tout ouvrage en vers, quelque beau qu'il soit d'ailleurs,
sera nécessairement ennuyeux, si tous les vers ne sont pas pleins de
force et d'harmonie, si on n'y trouve pas une élégance continue, si   115
la pièce n'a point ce charme inexprimable de la poésie, que le génie
seul peut donner, où l'esprit ne saurait jamais atteindre, et sur
lequel on raisonne si mal, et si inutilement depuis la mort de
monsieur Despreaux.

C'est une erreur bien grossière de s'imaginer que les vers soient   120
la dernière partie d'une pièce de théâtre, et celle qui doit le moins
coûter.[7] M. Racine, c'est-à-dire, l'homme de la terre, qui après
Virgile a le mieux connu l'art des vers, ne pensait pas ainsi. Deux
années entières lui suffirent à peine pour écrire sa PHÈDRE.[8]

106   w38, w42-k: [*Preface begins here*] Je ne donne cette
115-116   25a: d'harmonie, si la pièce

[7] This was the view of the Moderns. As Condorcet was later to write in his *Vie de Voltaire*: 'L'auteur combattit dans la préface l'opinion de La Motte, qui [...] ne trouvait dans les vers d'autre mérite que celui de la difficulté vaincue, et ne voyait dans la poésie qu'une forme de convention, imaginée pour soulager la mémoire, et à laquelle l'habitude seule faisait trouver des charmes' (k85, xcii.17; M.i.198).

[8] According to G. Forestier (ed. of Racine, *Œuvres complètes*, Paris 1999, p.1611), little is known about the time devoted by Racine to the composition of *Phèdre*. Voltaire's assertion appears to be based on the statement of Pradon cited in the next note.

Pradon se vante d'avoir composé la sienne en moins de trois 125
mois.[9] Comme le succès passager des représentations d'une
tragédie ne dépend point du style, mais des acteurs et des
situations, il arriva que les deux *Phèdres* semblèrent d'abord
avoir une égale destinée; mais l'impression régla bientôt le rang
de l'une et de l'autre: Pradon selon la coutume des mauvais 130
auteurs, eut beau faire une préface insolente dans laquelle il traitait
ses critiques de malhonnêtes gens:[10] Sa pièce tant vantée par sa
cabale et par lui, tomba dans le mépris qu'elle mérite, et sans la
Phèdre de monsieur Racine, on ignorerait aujourd'hui que Pradon
en a composé une. 135

Mais d'où vient enfin cette distance si prodigieuse entre ces deux
ouvrages? La conduite en est à peu près la même: Phèdre est
mourante dans l'une et dans l'autre. Thésée est absent dans les
premiers actes: Il passe pour avoir été aux enfers avec Pirrithous:
Hippolyte son fils veut quitter Trézène: il veut fuir Aricie qu'il 140
aime. Il déclare sa passion à Aricie, et reçoit avec horreur celle de
Phèdre, il meurt du même genre de mort, et son gouverneur fait le
récit de sa mort.

Il y a plus. Les personnages des deux pièces se trouvant dans les
mêmes situations, disent presque toujours les mêmes choses: Mais 145

---

140   w70G: Trézène; veut
143-144   w52, w56, w57G, w57P, Sohème texts (w64G, w68, w70G, w70L,
w75G, K): [*no new paragraph*]
145   31-K: presque les

---

[9] At the conclusion of the Preface to *Phèdre et Hippolyte* Pradon had written: 'Au
reste je ne doute point que l'on ne trouve quelques fautes dans cette Pièce, dont les
Vers ne m'ont coûté que trois mois, puisqu'on en trouve bien dans celles qu'on a été
deux ans à travailler et à polir' (*Phèdre et Hippolyte*, ed. O. Classe, University of
Exeter 1987, p.5).

[10] In his Preface Pradon had accused unnamed 'auteurs intéressés' of setting
themselves up 'en Régents du Parnasse ou plutôt en Tyrans', and had described their
efforts to suppress the works of authors of whom they did not approve as falling far
short of 'ce sublime qu'ils tâchent d'attrapper dans leurs Ouvrages' (p.4).

c'est là qu'on distingue le grand homme et le mauvais poète. C'est lorsque Racine et Pradon pensent de même, qu'ils sont les plus différents. En voici un exemple bien sensible, dans la déclaration d'Hippolyte à Aricie. Monsieur Racine fait ainsi parler Hippolyte.

> Mais un soin plus pressant m'occupe et m'embarrasse.   150
> Moi qui contre l'amour fièrement révolté,
> Aux fers de ses captifs ai longtemps insulté;
> Qui des faibles mortels déplorant les naufrages,
> Pensais toujours du bord contempler les orages,
> Asservi maintenant sous la commune loi,   155
> Par quel trouble me vois-je emporté loin de moi?
> Un moment a vaincu mon audace imprudente.
> Cette âme si superbe est enfin dépendante.
> Depuis près de six mois honteux, désespéré,
> Portant partout le trait, dont je suis déchiré,   160
> Contre vous, contre moi, vainement je m'éprouve,
> Présente je vous suis, absente je vous trouve.
> Dans le fond des forêts votre image me suit.
> La lumière du jour, les ombres de la nuit,
> Tout retrace à mes yeux les charmes que j'évite;   165
> Tout vous livre à l'envi le rebelle Hippolyte.
> Moi-même pour tout fruit de mes soins superflus,
> Maintenant je me cherche, et ne me trouve plus.
> Mon arc, mes javelots, mon char, tout m'importune,
> Je ne me souviens plus des leçons de Neptune.   170
> Mes seuls gémissements font retentir les bois,
> Et mes coursiers oisifs ont oublié ma voix. [11]

Voici comment Hippolyte s'exprime dans Pradon.

> Assez et trop longtemps, d'une bouche profane,
> Je méprisai l'amour, et j'adorai Diane;   175

---

147   w56, w57G, Sohème texts: sont le plus

---

[11] Racine, *Phèdre*, II.ii.531-52.

Solitaire, farouche, on me voyait toujours
Chasser dans nos forêts, les lions et les ours.
Mais un soin plus pressant m'occupe et m'embarrasse.
Depuis que je vous vois, j'abandonne la chasse.
Elle fit autrefois mes plaisirs les plus doux,   180
Et quand j'y vais, ce n'est que pour penser à vous.[12]

On ne saurait lire ces deux pièces de comparaison, sans admirer
l'une, et sans rire de l'autre. C'est pourtant dans toutes les deux le
même fonds de sentiments et de pensées. Car quand il s'agit de
faire parler les passions, tous les hommes ont presque les mêmes   185
idées. Mais la façon de les exprimer, distingue l'homme d'esprit
d'avec celui qui n'en a point; l'homme de génie, d'avec celui qui
n'a que de l'esprit, et le poète d'avec celui qui veut l'être.

Pour parvenir à écrire comme M. Racine, il faudrait avoir son
génie, et polir autant que lui ses ouvrages. Quelle défiance ne dois-   190
je donc point avoir, moi qui né avec des talents si faibles, et accablé
par des maladies continuelles, n'ai ni le don de bien imaginer, ni la
liberté de corriger par un travail assidu les défauts de mes
ouvrages. Je sens avec déplaisir toutes les fautes qui sont dans la
contexture de cette pièce, aussi bien que dans la diction. J'en aurais   195
corrigé quelques-unes, si j'avais pu retarder cette édition; mais j'en
aurais laissé encore beaucoup. Dans tous les arts il y a un terme par
delà lequel on ne peut plus avancer. On est reserré dans les bornes
de son talent: on voit la perfection au delà de soi, et on fait des
efforts impuissants pour y atteindre.   200

191   25P, 30: avec talents si
         31-K: avec des talents
197   31-K: aurais encore [w56, w57G, w64G, w68, w70G, w70L, w75G: encor]
laissé beaucoup
198   w57P: peut avancer.

[12] Pradon, *Phèdre et Hippolyte*, I.ii.121-28.

Je ne ferai point une critique détaillée de cette pièce: les lecteurs la feront assez sans moi. Mais je crois qu'il est nécessaire que je parle ici d'une critique générale qu'on a faite sur le choix du sujet de *Mariamne*. Comme le génie des Français est de saisir vivement le côté ridicule des choses les plus sérieuses: on disait que le sujet de   205
Mariamne n'était autre chose qu'*un vieux mari amoureux et brutal, à qui sa femme refuse avec aigreur le devoir conjugal*. Et on ajoutait qu'une querelle de ménage ne pouvait jamais faire une tragédie. [13]
Je supplie qu'on fasse avec moi quelques réflexions sur ce préjugé.

Les pièces tragiques sont fondées ou sur les intérêts de toute une   210
nation, ou sur les intérêts particuliers de quelques princes. De ce premier genre sont l'*Iphigénie en Aulide*, où la Grèce assemblée, demande le sang du fils d'Agamemnon: [14] *les Horaces*, où trois combattants ont entre les mains le sort de Rome: l'*Œdipe*, où le salut des Thébains dépend de la découverte du meurtrier de   215
Laïus. [15] Du second genre sont *Britannicus, Phèdre, Mithridate*, etc.

Dans ces trois dernières tout l'intérêt est renfermé dans la famille du héros de la pièce: Tout roule sur des passions que des

213   25A, W51, W57P, W68, W75G, K: sang de la fille d'Agamemnon
215   25P-W57P: du meurtre de
        W64G-K: du meurtrier de

[13] Voltaire seems here to be addressing himself in particular to the parodists, notably Fuzelier, and above all Dominique and Le Grand, whose comic reduction of the theme of *Mariamne* had trivialised Voltaire's tragic project.

[14] An evident error. The correction is not followed in the early Cramer editions (W56, W57G1, W57G2, W64G), but is generally adopted from W68 on, though surprisingly it is not found in W70G (Cramer) or in W70L (Grasset).

[15] It is surprising that the reading 'du meurtre de Laïus' of the Varus texts survived for so long, as the fact of the murder of Laïus is well known to the population of Thebes at the opening of the Œdipus plays of Sophocles, Corneille and Voltaire himself. What is unknown at the outset, but tragically revealed as the play unfolds, is the identity of his killer: the reading of the Sohème texts given here makes better sense of Voltaire's observation.

bourgeois ressentent comme les princes. Et l'intrigue de ces ouvrages est aussi propre à la comédie, qu'à la tragédie. Otez les noms, *Mithridate n'est qu'un vieillard amoureux d'une jeune fille: Ses deux fils en sont amoureux aussi; et il se sert d'une ruse assez basse pour découvrir celui des deux qui est aimé.* 220

Phèdre est une belle-mère, qui enhardie par une intrigante, fait des propositions à son beau-fils, lequel est occupé ailleurs. 225

Néron est un jeune homme impétueux qui devient amoureux tout d'un coup: qui dans le moment veut se séparer d'avec sa femme, et se cache derrière une tapisserie pour écouter les discours de sa maîtresse. Voilà des sujets que Molière a pu traiter comme Racine. Aussi l'intrigue de l'*Avare* est-elle précisément la même que celle de 230 *Mithridate.* Harpagon et le roi de Pont sont deux vieillards amoureux; l'un et l'autre ont leur fils pour rival; l'un et l'autre se servent du même artifice pour découvrir l'intelligence qui est entre leur fils et leur maîtresse: et les deux pièces finissent par le mariage du jeune homme. 235

Molière et Racine ont également réussi, en traitant ces deux intrigues: l'un a amusé, a réjoui, a fait rire les honnêtes gens; l'autre a attendri, a effrayé, a fait verser des larmes. Molière a joué l'amour ridicule d'un vieil avare: Racine a représenté les faiblesses d'un grand roi, et les a rendues respectables. 240

Que l'on donne une noce à peindre, à Vato, et à le Brun. L'un représentera sous une treille des paysans pleins d'une joie naïve, grossière, et effrénée, autour d'une table rustique, où l'ivresse, l'emportement, la débauche, le rire immodéré régneront. L'autre peindra les noces de Pélée et de Thétis, le festin des dieux, leur joie 245 majestueuse. Et tous deux seront arrivés à la perfection de leur art, par des chemins différents.

225   25A: *occupé d'ailleurs*
227   w56, w57G, Sohème texts: *et qui se*
236   25A: traitant les deux
240   w42, w46: roi, les
245   w48D, w51, w52, w56, w57G, w57P, Sohème texts: Thétis, les festins des

On peut appliquer tous ces exemples à *Mariamne*. La mauvaise humeur d'une femme, l'amour d'un vieux mari, les *tracasseries* d'une belle-sœur, sont de petits objets comiques par eux-mêmes. Mais un roi à qui la terre a donné le nom de grand, éperdument amoureux de la plus belle femme de l'univers, la passion furieuse de ce roi si fameux par ses vertus et par ses crimes: Ses cruautés passées, ses remords présents: ce passage si continuel et si rapide de l'amour à la haine, et de la haine à l'amour: l'ambition de sa sœur, les intrigues de ses ministres; la situation cruelle d'une princesse dont la vertu et la beauté sont célèbres encore dans le monde, qui avait vu son père et son frère livrés à la mort par son mari, et qui pour comble de douleur se voyait aimée du meurtrier de sa famille: Quel champ! quelle carrière pour un autre génie que le mien! Peut-on dire qu'un tel sujet soit indigne de la tragédie![16]

Je souhaite sincèrement que le même auteur, qui va donner une nouvelle tragédie d'*Œdipe*, retouche aussi le sujet de *Mariamne*.[17] Il fera voir au public quelles ressources un génie fécond peut trouver dans ces deux grands sujets: Ce qu'il fera, m'apprendra ce que j'aurais dû faire. Il commencera où je finis. Ses succès me

250 25P, 25A, 30: sont des petits
      K: objets, comiques
254 w57P: passées et ses
261 30: tragédie! / FIN.//
      w46, w48D, w51, w52, w56, w57G, w57P, w64G, w68, w70G, w70L,
w75G, K: tragédie!: C'est là surtout que *selon ce qu'on* [w56, w57G, w64G, w68,
w70G, w70L, w75G: *que l'on*] *peut être, les choses changent de nom.*//
266 w38, w42: faire. Ses

[16] The quotation which ends the Préface from w46 onward is from Molière, *Amphitryon*, Prologue, lines 130-31: 'Et suivant ce qu'on peut être, / Les choses changent de nom.' The form 'que l'on' introduced in place of 'qu'on' in w56 creates metrical irregularity not corrected until K.

[17] The *Œdipe* of La Motte was first given on 18 March 1726. The play was successful and received five further performances in the following fortnight (Lancaster, *French tragedy in the time of Louis XV*, p.93).

seront chers, parce qu'ils seront pour moi des leçons, et parce que
je préfère la perfection de mon art, à ma réputation.

Je profite de l'occasion de cette préface pour avertir que le
Poème de la Ligue que j'ai promis, n'est point celui dont on a   270
plusieurs éditions, et qu'on débite sous mon nom. Sur tout je
désavoue celui qui est imprimé à Amsterdam chez Jean-Frédéric
Bernard en 1724.[18] On y a ajouté beaucoup de pièces, fugitives,
dont la plupart ne sont point de moi. Et le petit nombre de celles
qui m'appartiennent, y est entièrement défiguré.   275

Je suis dans la résolution de satisfaire le plus promptement qu'il
me sera possible, aux engagements que j'ai pris avec le public pour
l'édition de ce poème. J'ai fait graver avec beaucoup de soin des
estampes très belles, sur les desseins de messieurs *de Troye*, *le
Moine* et *Veugle*. Mais la perfection d'un poème demande plus de   280
temps que celle d'un tableau. Toutes les fois que je considère ce
fardeau pénible que je me suis imposé moi-même, je suis effrayé de
sa pesanteur, et je me repens d'avoir osé promettre un poème
épique. Il y a environ quatre-vingt personnes à Paris qui ont
souscrit pour l'édition de cet ouvrage; quelques-uns de ces   285
messieurs ont crié de ce qu'on les faisait attendre. Les Libraires
n'ont eu autre chose à leur répondre que de leur rendre leur argent;
et c'est ce qu'on a fait à bureau ouvert *chez Noël Pissot, libraire, à
la Croix d'Or, quai des Augustins*. A l'égard des gens raisonnables
qui aiment mieux avoir tard un bon ouvrage, que d'en avoir de   290
bonne heure un mauvais, ce que j'ai à leur dire, c'est que lorsque je

273   25A, 31, w38, w42: pièces fugitives,
275   w38, w42: défiguré.//

---

[18] Edition published in fact by Desfontaines at Evreux, Rouen or Troyes. This
edition, and the four other editions of *La Ligue* which had appeared prior to the
publication of *Mariamne*, all here disavowed by Voltaire, are described by O. R.
Taylor, ed., *La Henriade* (*OC*, vol.2, p.236-38). For the publication history of these
editions of 1723 and 1724, see *ibid.*, p.47-55.

ferai imprimer le *Poème de Henri IV*, quelque tard que je le donne, je leur demanderai toujours pardon, de l'avoir donné trop tôt. [19]

Fin.

293a   31: [*absent*]

[19] The significance of Voltaire's statements in this paragraph is discussed by O. R. Taylor (*OC*, vol.2, p.61). Even though a *privilège* for *La Ligue* had been refused, it would seem that at this point Voltaire remained hopeful that a luxurious edition printed in Holland of his epic poem, now revised and expanded as *Le Poème de Henri IV*, could circulate freely and be sold without restriction in France. Hence the reassurances offered here to subscribers.

ACTEURS

VARUS, préteur romain, gouverneur de Syrie.
HÉRODE, roi de la Palestine.
MARIAMNE, femme d'Hérode.
SALOME, sœur d'Hérode.
ALBIN, confident de Varus.   5
MAZAËL, IDAMAS, ministres d'Hérode.

a-10a   Sohème texts:
     ACTEURS [K: PERSONNAGES]
[each name on separate line] HÉRODE, Roi de Palestine. MARIAMNE, femme
d'Hérode. SALOME, sœur d'Hérode. SOHÈME, Prince de la race des Asmonéens.
MAZAËL, IDAMAS, ministres d'Hérode. NARBAS, ancien officier des Rois
Asmonéens. AMMON, confident de Sohème. ELISE, confidente de Mariamne. Un
garde d'Hérode parlant. Suite d'Hérode. Suite de Sohème. Une suivante de
Mariamne, personnage muet. [W64G, W70G, W70L: Une suivante de Mariamne,
muette.]
    La scène est à Jérusalem dans le palais d'Hérode.
  MS1, 25CH, 25X, 26H: β *[with changes to listed order, Hérode and*
Mariamne occupying the first two places]
 2 MS1: Roy de Sirie.
  31-K: de Palestine
 4 W38, W42, W46, W51: SALOME' or SALOMÉ [1]
 6 MS1: MAZAËL, Confidant de Salome.
  25CH: MAZAËL, Juif.

[1] With the exception of W51 (where SALOMÉ appears only in the dramatis
personae, 'Salome' being used at all other points), the editions cited are inconsistent
in their use of these forms not only here but throughout the play. In the body of the
text, the spelling Salome occurs seven times as part of a line (at I.195, II.2, III.3,
III.74, III.135, IV.212 and V.163). At these locations W38 (in most cases) and W51
(in all cases) read 'Salome', the other editions cited (W42, W46) giving 'Salomé'.
The spelling 'Salome' also occurs once in a stage direction (II.116a): W51 reads
'Salome', all other editions cited read 'Salomé'. The *errata* page of W42 notes: 'Dans
toute la tragédie de Mariamne, lisez *Salome* au lieu de *Salomé*'.

NABAL, ancien officier des rois asmonéens.
ELIZE, confidente de Mariamne.
Suite de Varus.
Suite d'Hérode.   10

La scène est à Jérusalem.

---

7   MS1: IDAMAS, Grand de la Cour d'Hérode.
     MS1: NABAL, Confidant de Mariamne.
     25CH: [IDAMAS *absent*] NABAL, Juif.
     25X, 26H: SDAMAS [*error*]
8   26P and succeeding Varus editions: [*insert*] Un garde d'Hérode, parlant. [2]
9-10 25CH:
          PHÉDIME, confidente de Salome.
          GARDES.
10   MS1 [*adds*] Licteurs portant des faisceaux devant Varus. Gardes d'Hérode.
     25X, 26H: [*add*] Suite de Mariamne.
     26P and succeeding Varus editions: [*add*] Une suivante de Mariamne,
     muette. [3]
10a   MS1, 25CH, 25X, 26H: *La Scène est à Jérusalem* [MS1: *à Solyme*; 25CH: *à
     Jérusalem ou Solime*] *dans le Palais d'Hérode.*

[2] Some copies of 25P also give this variant.
[3] Some copies of 25P also give this variant. One copy of M30 reads: 'Une servante
de Mariamne, muette.'

HÉRODE ET MARIAMNE
TRAGÉDIE

ACTE PREMIER[1]

SCÈNE PREMIÈRE

SALOME, MAZAËL

MAZAËL

Oui, cette autorité qu'Hérode vous confie,
Est partout reconnue, et partout affermie.
J'ai volé vers Azor, et repassé soudain,
Des champs de Samarie aux sources du Jourdain.
Madame, il était temps que du moins ma présence,   5
Des Hébreux inquiets confondît l'espérance.
Hérode votre frère à Rome retenu,
Déjà dans ses Etats n'était plus reconnu.
Le peuple pour ses rois toujours plein d'injustices,

a   MSI, 25CH, 25X, 25A, 26H, 26P, 27, 30, 36P: HÉRODE ET MARIAMNE,
    31, W38, W46, W48D, W51, W52, W56, W57G, W57P, W64G, W68, W70G,
W70L, W75G, K: MARIAMNE,
    W42: LA MARIAMNE,
e   MSI, 25CH, 25X, 26H: SALOME ET MAZAËL
2   Sohème texts: Jusques à son retour est du moins affermie
5   25X, 26H: qu'à la fin ma
9   W42, W46: pour ces [W42 errata, W46 errata: ses] rois

[1] Act I was substantially rewritten by Voltaire when he revised the play to
produce the version in which Sohème replaces Varus (M62). The text which the
Sohème version introduces from line 63 to the end of the act is given in Appendix D.
The variants below are from the successive editions of the Varus version. Editions
of the Varus version continued to appear, presumably without Voltaire's authorisation, even after the publication of the Sohème version in 1764.

Hardi dans ses discours, aveugle en ses caprices,   10
Publiait hautement qu'à Rome condamné,
Hérode à l'esclavage était abandonné;
Et que la reine assise au rang de ses ancêtres,
Ferait régner sur nous, le sang de nos grands prêtres.[2]
Je l'avoue à regret, j'ai vu dans tous les lieux[3]   15
Mariamne adorée, et son nom précieux.
Israël[4] aime encore avec idolâtrie,
Le sang de ces héros dont elle tient la vie.
Sa beauté, sa naissance, et surtout ses malheurs,
D'un peuple qui nous hait ont séduit tous les cœurs.   20
Et leurs vœux indiscrets la nommant souveraine,
Semblaient vous annoncer une chute certaine.
J'ai vu par ces faux bruits tout un peuple ébranlé.
Mais, j'ai parlé, madame, et ce peuple a tremblé.
Je leur ai peint Hérode avec plus de puissance,   25
Rentrant dans ses Etats suivi de la vengeance;
Son nom seul a partout répandu la terreur,

12   MSI, 25CH, 25X, 26H: Son maître à
13-14 MSI, 25CH, 25X, 26H:
       Et que César enfin touché de leurs [25X, 26H: ses] misères,
       Replaçait Mariamne au trône de ses pères.
17   W75G*, K84, K85: La Judée aime
18   MSI, 25CH, 25X, 26H: de tant de rois dont
20   MSI, 26H: qui vous hait
22   25CH, 25X, 26H: Semblaient nous annoncer
23   MSI, 25CH, 25X, 26H: tout le peuple
27   25X, 26H: a porté la crainte et la terreur

[2] This couplet, appearing for the first time in 25P, lays stress upon the priestly
ascendancy of Mariamne, in addition to her royal rank.
[3] This line is cited in Nadal's *Observations critiques* (p.29) with the reading *tous ces
lieux* as in 25X and 26H.
[4] The replacement of 'Israël' by 'La Judée' is the sole autograph alteration made
by Voltaire to the text of *Mariamne* in the last revision of his works begun shortly
before he left Ferney for Paris in 1778.

Et les Juifs en silence ont pleuré leur erreur.[5]

SALOME

Vous ne vous trompiez point. Hérode va paraître;
L'indocile Sion va trembler sous son maître.   30
Il enchaîne à jamais la fortune à son char;
Le favori d'Antoine est l'ami de César;[6]
Sa politique habile, égale à son courage,
De sa chute imprévue a réparé l'outrage.
Le sénat le couronne.

MAZAËL

              Eh? que deviendrez-vous,   35
Quand la reine en ces lieux reverra son époux?

29-42 Sohème texts:
    Mazaël, il est vrai qu'Hérode va paraître;
    Et ces peuples et moi, nous aurons tous un maître.
    Ce pouvoir dont à peine on me voyait jouir,
    N'est qu'une ombre qui passe et va s'évanouir.
    Mon frère m'était cher, et son bonheur m'opprime;   5
    Mariamne triomphe, et je suis sa victime.
               MAZAËL
    Ne craignez point un frère.
               SALOME
              Eh? que deviendrons-nous,
    Quand la reine à ses pieds reverra son époux?
    De mon autorité cette fière rivale,
    Auprès d'un roi séduit nous fut toujours fatale: 10
    Son esprit orgueilleux qui n'a jamais plié,
    Conserve encor pour nous la même inimitié.
    Elle nous outragea, je l'ai trop offensée;
    A notre abaissement elle est intéressée.
33 25X, 26H: égalant son
35 25CH, 26H: Et que

[5] Line criticised by Nadal: 'Quelle dureté de vers! Pleurer leur erreur' (*Observations critiques*, p.29).
[6] Cf. M24, 132 : 'J'étais ami d'Antoine, et le suis de César.'

De votre autorité cette fière rivale,
Madame, auprès du roi, vous fut toujours fatale:
Son esprit orgueilleux qui n'a jamais plié,
Conserve encor pour vous la même inimitié.   40
Elle vous outragea, vous l'avez offensée;
A votre abaissement elle est intéressée. [7]
Eh ne craignez-vous plus ces charmes tout-puissants, [8]
Du malheureux Hérode impérieux tyrans!
Depuis près de cinq ans qu'un fatal hyménée,   45
D'Hérode et de la reine unit la destinée,
L'amour prodigieux dont ce prince est épris,
Se nourrit par la haine et croît par le mépris.
Vous avez vu cent fois ce monarque inflexible,
Déposer à ses pieds sa majesté terrible;   50
Et chercher dans ses yeux irrités ou distraits,
Quelques regards plus doux qu'il ne trouvait jamais.
Vous l'avez vu frémir, soupirer et se plaindre,
La flatter, l'irriter, la menacer, la craindre;
Cruel dans son amour, soumis dans ses fureurs,   55

39   MSI: Cet esprit
43   MSI, 25CH, 25X, 26H: Quoi! ne craignez-vous plus ses [25X, 26H: ces]
charmes si [MSI: tout-] puissants
47   MSI, 25CH, 25X, 26H: dont son cœur est
51   MSI: irrités et distraits
     25CH: yeux égarés et distraits
52   MSI: ne trouva jamais
     25X, 26H: n'y trouvait

[7] Lines 35-60, spoken by Mazaël in M25, are transferred to Salome in M62. Is it
possible that Voltaire was mindful of the 1726-1727 observations of J.-J. Bel, who in
the third of his *Lettres* had suggested that he should in this first scene have provided
greater opportunities for Salome to express herself her forebodings and sense of
humiliation, in preference to hearing them described for her by Mazaël? See above
Introduction, section 4.v, p.90-91.
[8] This line and line 47 are quoted in the *Mercure extrait* of M25 with the reading of
MSI, 25CH, 25X, 26H.

Esclave en son palais, héros partout ailleurs.
Que dis-je! en punissant une ingrate famille,
Fumant du sang du père, il adorait la fille:
Le fer encor sanglant et que vous excitiez,
Etait levé sur elle, et tombait à ses pieds.   60
Il est vrai que dans Rome éloigné de sa vue,
Sa chaîne de si loin semblait s'être rompue:
Mais c'en est fait, madame, il rentre en ses Etats,
Il l'aimait, il verra ses dangereux appas:
Ces yeux toujours puissants, toujours sûrs de lui plaire,   65
Reprendront malgré vous leur empire ordinaire.
Et tous ses ennemis bientôt humiliés,
A ses moindres regards seront sacrifiés.
Otons-lui, croyez-moi, l'intérêt de nous nuire. [9]
Songeons à la gagner, n'ayant pu la détruire;   70
Et par de vains respects, par des soins assidus,...

SALOME

Il est d'autres moyens de ne la craindre plus.

59   25X, 26H: Et ce fer tout sanglant et que vous excitiez,
61   Sohème texts: Mais songez que
62   25X, 26H: Sa chaîne pour jamais semblait être rompue;
      Sohème texts: semble s'être
63-312a Sohème texts: [as in Appendix D below]
69   MS1: de vous nuire
70   MS1: Tâchons à
71   25X, 26H: par des vains respects, par des vœux assidus

[9] The *Vérités littéraires* (p.27) accuse Voltaire of taking this line from the *Fables* of La Motte. Presumably the authors have in mind the following line from *Le Chasseur et les Eléphants*: 'Nous t'ôtons seulement l'intérêt de nous nuire' (La Motte, *Fables nouvelles*, Paris 1719, Fable XVIII, p.357). Whether this similarity constitutes a 'petit larçin' as the *Vérités littéraires* allege seems open to question.

MAZAËL

Quel est donc ce dessein? que prétendez-vous dire?

SALOME

Peut-être en ce moment notre ennemie expire.

MAZAËL

D'un coup si dangereux, osez-vous vous charger?   75
Sans que le roi...

SALOME

Le roi consent à me venger.
Zarès est arrivé, Zarès est dans Solime,
Ministre de ma haine, il attend sa victime;
Le lieu, le temps, le bras, tout est choisi par lui, [10]
Il vint hier de Rome, et nous venge aujourd'hui.   80

MAZAËL

Quoi! vous avez enfin gagné cette victoire?

73   MSI: ce moyen?
      25CH: dessein? Et que voulez-vous dire?
75   25CH: De pareils attentats osez-vous
      MSI, 25X, 26H: D'un pareil attentat vous osez-vous charger?
79   25CH: Le lieu, l'ordre, le temps, tout
      MSI, 25X, 26H: Le lieu, l'ordre, le bras
      25CH, 25X: choisi pour lui
80-82   25CH:
                        et me venge aujourd'hui.
      Ce jour doit éclairer sa perte et ma victoire.
                        MAZAËL
      Quoi! malgré
80   MSI, 25X, 26H: et me venge

[10] Cf. *La Mort de César*, III.ii.29-30 (Brutus): 'Et j'avais choisi l'heure, / Le lieu, le bras, l'instant où Rome veut qu'il meure.'

Quoi! malgré son amour, Hérode a pu vous croire?
Il vous la sacrifie! il prend de vous des lois!

SALOME

Je puis encor sur lui bien moins que tu ne crois.
Pour arracher de lui cette lente vengeance,   85
Il m'a fallu choisir le temps de son absence.
Tant qu'Hérode en ces lieux demeurait exposé,
Aux charmes dangereux qui l'ont tyrannisé:
Mazaël, tu m'as vue avec inquiétude,
Traîner de mon destin la triste incertitude.   90
Quand par mille détours assurant mes succès,
De son cœur soupçonneux j'avais trouvé l'accès:
Quand je croyais son âme à moi seule rendue;
Il voyait Mariamne, et j'étais confondue.
Un coup d'œil renversait ma brigue et mes desseins.   95
La reine a vu cent fois mon sort entre ses mains;
Et si sa politique avait avec adresse
D'un époux amoureux ménagé la tendresse;
Cet ordre, cet arrêt prononcé par son roi,
Ce coup que je lui porte aurait[11] tombé sur moi.   100
Mais son farouche orgueil a servi ma vengeance:
J'ai su mettre à profit sa fatale imprudence.
Elle a voulu se perdre, et je n'ai fait enfin

82-105 MSI, 25CH, 25X, 26H:

                    croire?
                SALOME
    Tôt ou tard il falloit que le couroux du roi
    Tombât avec éclat sur la reine ou sur moi.
    Tu te souviens
82   25X, 26H: malgré son devoir
85   25A: Pour pouvoir arracher cette

[11] One copy of 25P (Arsenal GD 11550) has a manuscript note in the margin
substituting 'seroit' for 'auroit'.

Que lui lancer les traits qu'a préparés sa main.
Tu te souviens assez de ce temps plein d'alarmes,   105
Lorsqu'un bruit si funeste à l'espoir de nos armes,
Apprit à l'Orient, étonné de son sort, [12]
Qu'Auguste était vainqueur, et qu'Antoine était mort.
Tu sais comme à ce bruit nos peuples se troublèrent.
De l'Orient vaincu les monarques tremblèrent.   110
Mon frère enveloppé dans ce commun malheur,
Crut perdre sa couronne avec son protecteur.
Il fallut, sans s'armer d'une inutile audace,
Au vainqueur de la terre aller demander grâce.
Rappelle en ton esprit ce jour infortuné;   115
Songe à quel désespoir Hérode abandonné,
Vit son épouse altière abhorrant ses approches, [13]
Détestant ses adieux, l'accablant de reproches,
Redemander encore en ce moment cruel,
Et le sang de son frère, et le sang paternel.   120
Hérode auprès de moi vint déplorer sa peine:
Je saisis cet instant précieux à ma haine:

105 MSI, 25X, 26H: Tu te souviens encor [MSI: β] de ces temps pleins d'alarmes,
112 MSI: perdre la couronne
114 MSI, 25CH, 25X, 25A, 26H: Aux vainqueurs de
115 25CH: en cet instant ce
     25X, 26H: Rappelle à ton
117 25CH: abhorrer
119 MSI: Lui demander encor
     25X, 26H: Redemandant encore
120 25CH: et le bien paternel
121 W46: vient déplorer sa
     MSI, 25CH, 25X, 26H: vint dissiper sa
122 26H: J'ai saisi cet

[12] Cf. Racine, *Britannicus*, IV.ii.1193-94 (Agrippine to Néron): 'On vit Claude, et le people étonné de son sort, / Apprit en même temps votre règne et sa mort.'
[13] The *Vérités littéraires* of Desfontaines and Granet objected (p.24) to this use of the word 'approches': 'Ce terme [...] est trop fort, il aurait fallu s'exprimer avec plus de délicatesse.'

Dans son cœur déchiré je repris mon pouvoir,
J'enflammai son courroux, j'aigris son désespoir,
J'empoisonnai le trait dont il sentait l'atteinte;   125
Tu le vis plein de trouble et d'horreur et de crainte,
Jurer d'exterminer les restes dangereux
D'un sang toujours trop cher aux perfides Hébreux;
Et dès ce même instant sa facile colère,
Déshérita les fils, et condamna la mère.   130
Mais sa fureur encor flattait peu mes souhaits.
L'amour qui la causait en repoussait les traits;
De ce fatal objet telle était la puissance;
Un regard de l'ingrate arrêtait sa vengeance.
Je pressai son départ, il partit. Et depuis   135
Mes lettres chaque jour ont nourri ses ennuis.
Ne voyant plus la reine, il vit mieux son outrage;
Il eut honte en secret de son peu de courage:
De moment en moment ses yeux se sont ouverts,
J'ai levé le bandeau qui les avait couverts: 140
Zarès étudiant le moment favorable,

124   25CH: J'enflammai son courage,
125   MSI, 25X, 26H: il sentit l'atteinte
126-130   MSI, 25CH, 25X, 26H:
        Tu vis l'emportement succéder à ma [MSI: la; 25CH: sa] plainte.
        Souviens-toi qu'il jura [25CH: pensa] d'exterminer enfin
        Les restes odieux du sang asmonéen, [14]
        Et que dès ce moment sa facile colère
        Déshérita le fils en condamnant la mère.   5
134   MSI, 25CH, 25X, 26H: Qu'un regard
        W42, W46: arrêtait la [W42 errata: sa] vengeance
135   25X, 26H: J'ai pressé son
136   MSI: son ennui
137   25CH: Eloigné de la reine
        25X: son ouvrage

[14] Nadal had derided the rhyme used by Voltaire in the earliest version of
Mariamne and found in MSI, 25CH, 25X and 26H (*Observations critiques*, p.28); see
Introduction, section 4.ii, p.68.

A peint à son esprit cette reine implacable,
Son crédit, ses amis, ces Juifs séditieux,
Du sang asmonéen partisans factieux.
J'ai fait plus, j'ai moi-même armé sa jalousie.   145
Il a craint pour sa gloire, il a craint pour sa vie.
Tu sais que dès longtemps en butte aux trahisons,
Son cœur de toutes parts est ouvert aux soupçons.
Il croit ce qu'il redoute, et dans sa défiance
Il confond quelquefois le crime et l'innocence.   150
Enfin j'ai su fixer son courroux incertain,
Il a signé l'arrêt, et j'ai conduit sa main.

MAZAËL

Il n'en faut point douter, ce coup est nécessaire.
Mais avez-vous prévu si ce préteur austère,
Qui, sous les lois d'Auguste, a remis cet Etat,   155
Verrait d'un œil tranquille un pareil attentat?
Varus, vous le savez, est ici votre maître.
En vain le peuple hébreu prompt à vous reconnaître,
Tremble encore sous le poids de ce trône ébranlé:
Votre pouvoir n'est rien si Rome n'a parlé.   160
Avant qu'en ce palais, des mains de Varus même,
Votre frère ait repris l'autorité suprême,
Il ne peut sans blesser l'orgueil du nom romain,
Dans ses Etats encore agir en souverain.
Varus souffrira-t-il que l'on ose à sa vue,   165
Immoler une reine en sa garde reçue?

142 25X, 26H: peint dans son
143 MSI: amis, les Juifs
       25CH, 25X, 26H: amis, ses Juifs
156 25CH: Verra d'un
157 25X, 26H: Vous savez que Varus est ici notre maître.
162 MSI, 25CH, 25A: ait reçu l'autorité
165 25X, 26H: osa sous sa
166 25CH, 25A: reine à sa

Je connais les Romains; leur esprit irrité
Vengera le mépris de leur autorité.
Vous allez sur Hérode attirer la tempête;
Dans leurs superbes mains, la foudre est toujours prête.　170
Ces vainqueurs soupçonneux sont jaloux de leurs droits,
Et surtout leur orgueil aime à punir les rois.

SALOME

Non, non, l'heureux Hérode à César a su plaire;
Varus en est instruit, Varus le considère.
Croyez-moi, ce Romain voudra le ménager;　175
Mais quoi qu'il fasse enfin, songeons à nous venger.
Je touche à ma grandeur, et je crains ma disgrâce.
Demain, dès aujourd'hui, tout peut changer de face.
Qui sait même, qui sait, si passé ce moment,
Je pourrai satisfaire à mon ressentiment!　180
Qui vous a répondu qu'Hérode en sa colère,
D'un esprit si constant jusqu'au bout persévère?
Je connais sa tendresse, il la faut prévenir, [15]
Et ne lui point laisser le temps du repentir.
Qu'après Rome menace, et que Varus foudroie,　185
Leur courroux passager troublera peu ma joie.
Mes plus grands ennemis ne sont pas les Romains.
Mariamne en ces lieux est tout ce que je crains.

178　25CH: D'ailleurs, dès
180　25CH: Je pourrais satisfaire
181　25CH, W52, W56, W57G, W57P, W64GV, W68V, W70LV, W75GV, KV [16]: Qui nous a
182　25CH: esprit inconstant
183　MS1, 25CH, 25X, 26H: sa faiblesse,
　　26H: il faut la prévenir
184　25CH, 25X, 26H: lui pas laisser
　　MS1: ne pas lui laisser

[15] This line is quoted in the *Mercure extrait* of M25 with the reading of 26H.
[16] The sigla W64GV etc. indicate variants in the Sohème texts, see p.174.

Il faut que je périsse, ou que je la prévienne,
Et si je n'ai sa tête, elle obtiendra la mienne. [17]   190
Mais Varus vient à nous; il le faut éviter.
Zarès à mes regards devait se présenter.
Je vais l'attendre, allez, et qu'aux moindres alarmes
Mes soldats [18] en secret puissent prendre les armes.

SCÈNE II

VARUS, ALBIN, MAZAËL, SUITE DE VARUS

VARUS

Salome et Mazaël semblent fuir devant moi.   195
Dans leurs yeux étonnés, je lis leur juste effroi:
Le crime à mes regards doit craindre de paraître.

189-190   MS1, 25CH, 25X, 26H:
    De mes justes terreurs exterminons la cause.
    Qu'on me venge, il suffit, le reste est peu de chose. [19]
191   25CH, 25X, 26H: vient ici; il
192   25CH: devant se
193-194   25X, 26H:
    Je vais l'attendre, allez, sans jeter des alarmes,
    A tous mes délateurs faire prendre les armes.
194   25CH: Nos soldats
196   MS1, 25CH, 25X, 26H: yeux interdits,

---

[17] 25P replaces the call for vengeance in the earlier texts by the suggestion of urgency: Salome must destroy Mariamne if she is not to be destroyed by her.

[18] 25P replaces the reference to 'délateurs' by 'soldats'.

[19] The second line of the variant text of MS1, 25CH, 25X and 26H ('Qu'on me venge') is also found as the second line of a two-line passage quoted in the *Observations critiques* of Nadal (p.6). The first line of the two cited is I.176 (with the substitution of 'on' for 'il'). If Nadal quotes correctly (which cannot be known for certain) this may mean that the arrangement of this section of the play was different at an early stage of its performance history from what has come down to us in the printed texts.

Mazaël, demeurez: mandez à votre maître,
Que ses cruels desseins sont déjà découverts:
Que son ministre infâme est ici dans les fers;   200
Et que Varus peut-être au milieu des supplices,
Eût dû faire expirer ce monstre... et ses complices.
Mais je respecte Hérode assez pour me flatter,
Qu'il connaîtra le piège où on veut l'arrêter,[20]
Qu'un jour il punira les traîtres qui l'abusent,   205
Et vengera sur eux la vertu qu'ils accusent.
Vous, si vous m'en croyez, pour lui, pour son honneur
Calmez de ses chagrins la honteuse fureur;
Ne l'empoisonnez plus de vos lâches maximes:
Songez que les Romains sont les vengeurs des crimes,   210
Que Varus vous connaît, qu'il commande en ces lieux;
Et que sur vos complots il ouvrira les yeux.
Allez, que Mariamne en reine soit servie;
Et respectez ses lois si vous aimez la vie.

MAZAËL

Seigneur...

VARUS

Vous entendez mes ordres absolus,   215
Obéissez, vous dis-je, et ne répliquez plus.

---

198   25X, 26H: Demeurez, Mazaël, mandez
203   25A: je connais Hérode
204   25A: Qu'il sentira le
      MS1, 25CH, 25X, 25A, 26H, 31, W38 and succeeding editions: où l'on
207   MS1: Vous* [*with marginal note*: à Mazaël.]
209   25X, 26H: l'empoisonnez point de
216   MS1: [*with stage direction*] (*Mazaël sort.*)

[20] This line is cited in the *Observations critiques* of Nadal (p.30) with the reading
'où l'on veut' as in MS1, 25CH, 25X, 26H and most other editions.

SCÈNE III

VARUS, ALBIN

VARUS

Ainsi donc sans tes soins, sans ton avis fidèle
Mariamne expirait sous cette main cruelle?

ALBIN

Le retour de Zarès n'était que trop suspect,
Le soin mystérieux d'éviter votre aspect,   220
Son trouble, son effroi fut mon premier indice.

VARUS

Que ne te dois-je point pour un si grand service!
C'est par toi qu'elle vit: c'est par toi que mon cœur
A goûté, cher Albin, ce solide bonheur,
Ce bien si précieux pour un cœur magnanime,   225
D'avoir pu secourir la vertu qu'on opprime.

ALBIN

Je reconnais Varus à ces soins généreux.[21]
Votre bras fut toujours l'appui des malheureux.
Quand de Rome en vos mains vous portiez le tonnerre,
Vous étiez occupé du bonheur de la terre.   230

216a-b   MSI, 25CH, 25X, 26H: [*absent; no new scene*]
216c   MSI, 25CH, 25X, 26H: VARUS *à Albin.*
219   MSI: Ce retour
222   25X, 26H: dois-je pas pour
     MSI, 25CH: pour prix d'un tel service
227   25X, 26H: à ce soin généreux

---

[21] Cf. *La Mort de César*, II.iv.139 (Cassius to Brutus): 'Ah ! je te reconnais à cette noble audace.'

Puissiez-vous seulement écouter en ce jour,
Votre noble pitié plutôt que votre amour.

VARUS

Ah! faut-il donc l'aimer pour prendre sa défense?
Qui n'aurait comme moi chéri son innocence?
Quel cœur indifférent n'irait à son secours? 235
Et qui pour la sauver n'eût prodigué ses jours?

ALBIN

Ainsi l'amour trompeur dont vous sentez la flamme,
Se déguise en vertu pour mieux vaincre votre âme;
Et ce feu malheureux...

VARUS

        Je ne m'en défends pas.
L'infortuné Varus adore ses appas. 240
Je l'aime, il est trop vrai, mon âme toute nue,
Ne craint point, cher Albin, de paraître à ta vue:
Juge si son péril a dû troubler mon cœur![22]
Moi qui borne à jamais mes vœux à son bonheur,
Moi qui rechercherais la mort la plus affreuse, 245
Si ma mort un moment pouvait la rendre heureuse.

ALBIN

Seigneur, que dans ces lieux ce grand cœur est changé!

231-238 MSI, 25CH, 25X, 26H: [absent]
239 MSI, 25CH, 25X, 26H: Mais si d'un feu secret...
243 MSI: a pu troubler
      25CH: a su troubler son cœur
      25X, 26H: Juge donc si sa perte a pu troubler mon cœur,
245 25X, 26H: qui voudrais souffrir la
247 MSI, 25X, 26H: cœur a changé

[22] This line is cited in Nadal's *Observations critiques* (p.29) with the reading 'a su' as in 25CH.

Qu'il venge bien l'amour qu'il avait outragé!
Je ne reconnais plus ce Romain si sévère,
Qui parmi tant d'objets empressés à lui plaire,   250
N'a jamais abaissé ses superbes regards,
Sur ces beautés que Rome enferme en ses remparts.

VARUS

Ne t'en étonne point; tu sais que mon courage
A la seule vertu réserva son hommage.
Dans nos murs corrompus ces coupables beautés,   255
Offraient de vains attraits à mes yeux révoltés.[23]
Je fuyais leurs complots, leurs brigues éternelles,
Leurs amours passagers, leurs vengeances cruelles.
Je voyais leur orgueil accru du déshonneur,
Se montrer triomphant sur leur front sans pudeur;   260
L'altière ambition, l'intérêt, l'artifice,
La folle vanité, le frivole caprice,
Chez les Romains séduits prenant le nom d'amour,
Gouverner Rome entière, et régner tour à tour.[24]

252   25X, 26H: Sur les beautés
254   25CH: vertu resserre son
       25X: vertu réserve son
256   25CH: Offrent de
258   25CH: Leur amour passager,
263   25X, 26H: Chez nos Romains
       MSI, 25CH, 25P, 25A, 30, 31, W38, W42, W46, W48D, W52, W57P: prenans

[23] This line is cited by Nadal (p.26) with the reading 'Offrent' as in 25CH.

[24] Lines 255-64 provoked the ire of Nadal: 'Vous traitez les dames romaines avec une indignité qui n'est pas pardonnable à un Romain' (*Observations critiques*, p.24). The passage was perceived by later commentators to have a topical reference. Such an 'application' is hinted at in the *Mercure de France extrait* of M24, though this aspect was not noted in the critical writings of 1725-1727. But La Harpe saw in it 'la peinture des mœurs de la régence' (*Cours de littérature ancienne et moderne* of M25, ii.205). The marquis de Montmoreau describes it as the 'portrait des dames de Versailles et de Paris sous le nom de celles de la Cour d'Auguste' (D15479).

J'abhorrais, il est vrai, leur indigne conquête,   265
A leur joug odieux je dérobais ma tête;
L'amour dans l'Orient fut enfin mon vainqueur.
De la triste Syrie établi gouverneur,
J'arrivai dans ces lieux, quand le droit de la guerre,
Eut au pouvoir d'Auguste abandonné la terre;   270
Et qu'Hérode à ses pieds au milieu de cent rois,
De son sort incertain vint attendre des lois.
Lieu funeste à mon cœur! malheureuse contrée!
C'est là que Mariamne à mes yeux s'est montrée:
L'univers était plein du bruit de ses malheurs.   275
Son parricide époux faisait couler ses pleurs.
Ce roi si redoutable au reste de l'Asie,
Fameux par ses exploits et par sa jalousie,
Prudent, mais soupçonneux, vaillant, mais inhumain,
Au sang de son beau-père avait trempé sa main.   280
Sur ce trône sanglant il laissait en partage
A la fille des rois la honte et l'esclavage.
Du sort qui la poursuit tu connais la rigueur.
Sa vertu, cher Albin, surpasse son malheur.
Loin de la cour des rois la vérité proscrite,   285
L'aimable vérité sur ses lèvres habite.
Son unique artifice est le soin généreux,
D'assurer des secours aux jours des malheureux.
Son devoir est sa loi, sa tranquille innocence
Pardonne à ses tyrans, méprise sa vengeance,[25]   290

271   25X, 26H: à son trône au
272   25A: Incertain de son sort vint
      MS1, 25CH, 25X, 26H: vint demander des [25X, 26H: les] lois
273   MS1: Lieux funestes à
      25X, 26H: Lieu fatal à
279   25X, 26H: Vaillant, mais soupçonneux, prudent, mais inhumain,
288   MS1, 25CH, 25A: D'assurer du secours
289   25CH: est la loi
290   31, W38, W42 and succeeding editions: à son tyran,

[25] This line is quoted in the *Mercure extrait* of M25 with the reading 'son tyran'.

Et près d'Auguste encore implore mon appui,
Pour ce barbare époux qui l'immole aujourd'hui. [26]
Tant de vertus enfin, de malheurs et de charmes,
Contre ma liberté sont de trop fortes armes.
Je l'aime, cher Albin, mais non d'un fol amour,   295
Que le caprice enfante et détruit en un jour:
Non d'une passion que mon âme troublée
Reçoive avidement par l'espoir aveuglée.
Ce cœur qu'elle a vaincu sans l'avoir amolli,
Par un amour honteux ne s'est point avili.   300
Et plein du noble feu que sa vertu m'inspire,
Je prétends la venger et non pas la séduire. [27]

292   25CH, 25X, 26H: Pour le barbare
293   MS1, 25CH, 25X, 26H: Tant de malheurs enfin, [25X, 26H: Enfin, tant de
malheurs,] de vertus et de charmes,
295   25X, 25P: Albin, non pas d'un
296   w46 errata, w48D, w52 and succeeding editions: et détruise en
        25X, 26H: détruit dans un
297   25X, 26H: Ni d'une
298   31, w38, w42, w46: par l'amour aveuglée
        w48D, w51, w52, w56, w57G, w57P, w64GV, w68V, w70GV, w70LV,
w75GV, KV: par les sens aveuglée
299   25CH: l'avoir avili
300   MS1, 25CH, 25X, 26H: un indigne amour ne
        25CH: point démenti
301   25CH, 25X, 26H: sa beauté m'inspire

[26] Lines 275-92 were admired by La Harpe for their Racinian qualities: 'Rien n'y
ressent la contrainte ni l'effort; l'oreille est toujours flattée; et le langage s'élève au-
dessus de la prose, sans ambition et sans audace' (*Cours de littérature ancienne et
moderne*, ii.205).
[27] This statement by Varus attracted much criticism and ridicule. Nadal objected
strenuously to this line: 'Le mot de *séduire* frise un peu l'obscénité. D'ailleurs, Varus
doit-il se croire assez de mérite pour pouvoir être séducteur?' (*Observations critiques*,
p.30-31).

ALBIN

Mais si le roi, seigneur, a fléchi les Romains,
S'il rentre en ses Etats...

VARUS

     Et c'est ce que je crains.
Hélas! près du sénat je l'ai servi moi-même.   305
Sans doute il a déjà reçu son diadème!
Et cet indigne arrêt que sa bouche a dicté,
Est le premier essai de son autorité.
Ah! son retour ici lui peut être funeste.
Mon pouvoir va finir, mais mon amour me reste.   310
Reine, pour vous défendre on me verra périr.
L'univers doit vous plaindre, et je dois vous servir.

Fin du premier acte.

303 25X, 26H: [*absent*]
304 MS1, 25X, 26H: Ah! c'est
307 25X, 26H: Et ce cruel arrêt de sa bouche dicté
312a 25CH: [*absent*]

ACTE II

SCÈNE PREMIÈRE[1]

SALOME, MAZAËL

SALOME

Enfin vous le voyez, ma haine est confondue.
Mariamne triomphe, et Salome est perdue.
Zarès fut sur les eaux trop longtemps arrêté;
La mer alors tranquille à regret l'a porté.
Mais Hérode en partant pour son nouvel empire,   5
Revole avec les vents vers l'objet qui l'attire.
Et les mers et l'amour, et Varus et le roi,[2]
Le ciel, les éléments, sont armés contre moi.[3]
Fatale ambition que j'ai trop écoutée,
Dans quel abîme affreux m'as-tu précipitée!   10
Je vous l'avais bien dit, que dans le fond du cœur
Le roi se repentait de sa juste rigueur.
De son fatal penchant l'ascendant ordinaire,

1-77 Sohème texts: [*as in Appendix* D *below*]
3   MS1: Zarès s'est trop longtemps sur les eaux arrêté,
     25X, 26H: Zarès s'est sur les eaux trop longtemps arrêté,
7   MS1, 25X, 26H: Et la mer et
8   25CH, 25X, 26H: éléments, tout s'arme contre
11   25X, 26H: Je l'avais bien prévu,
12   MS1, 25CH, 25X, 26H: juste fureur

---

[1] Scene i (lines 1-77) was substantially rewritten by Voltaire for the Sohème version of *Mariamne*. The revised text is given *in extenso* in Appendix D.

[2] In the rhythm of this line there is perhaps a distant echo of Racine, *Iphigénie*, I.i.9 (Arcas to Agamemnon): 'Mais tout dort, et l'armée, et les vents et Neptune.'

[3] This line is cited in Nadal's *Observations critiques* (p.31) with the reading 'tout s'arme' as in 25CH, 25X and 26H.

218

A révoqué l'arrêt dicté dans sa colère.
J'en ai déjà reçu les funestes avis.   15
Et Zarès à son roi renvoyé par mépris,
Ne me laisse en ces lieux qu'une douleur stérile,
Qu'un opprobre éternel, et qu'un crime inutile.
Déjà de ma rivale adorant la faveur,
Le peuple à ma disgrâce insulte avec fureur.   20
Je verrai tout plier sous sa grandeur nouvelle,
Et mes faibles honneurs éclipsés devant elle.
Mais c'est peu que sa gloire irrite mon dépit;
Ma mort va signaler ma chute et son crédit.
Je ne me flatte point: je sais comme en sa place   25
De tous mes ennemis je confondrais l'audace.
Ce n'est qu'en me perdant qu'elle pourra régner;
Et son juste courroux ne doit point m'épargner.
Cependant! ô contrainte! ô comble d'infamie!
Il faut donc qu'à ses yeux ma fierté s'humilie!   30
Je viens avec respect essuyer ses hauteurs,
Et la féliciter sur mes propres malheurs.

MAZAËL

Contre elle encor, madame, il vous reste des armes,
J'ai toujours redouté le pouvoir de ses charmes:
J'ai toujours craint du roi les sentiments secrets.   35
Mais si je m'en rapporte aux avis de Zarès,

18   W52, W56, W57G, W57P, W64GV, W68V, W70GV, W70LV, W75GV, KV: Et le
danger qui suit un éclat inutile.
22   MS1, 25CH, 25X, 26H: honneurs s'éclipser devant
       25A: honneurs éclipser devant
23   MS1, 25CH: Ah! c'est
28   MS1, 25CH, 25X, 26H: Et jamais son courroux ne me doit épargner.
29   25CH, 25A: Cependant! ô disgrâce!
30   MS1, 25X, 26H: Il faudra qu'à
35   25CH: J'ai longtemps craint
36   25X, 26H: aux discours de

La colère d'Hérode autrefois peu durable,
Est enfin devenue une haine implacable.
Il déteste la reine, il a juré sa mort:
Et s'il suspend le coup qui terminait son sort,　　　　40
C'est qu'il veut ménager sa nouvelle puissance:
Et lui-même en ces lieux assurer sa vengeance.
Mais soit qu'enfin son cœur en ce funeste jour,
Soit aigri par la haine, ou fléchi par l'amour,
C'est assez qu'une fois il ait proscrit sa tête.　　　　45
Mariamne aisément grossira la tempête:
La foudre gronde encor: un arrêt si cruel,
Va mettre entre eux, madame, un divorce éternel.
Vous verrez Mariamne à soi-même inhumaine,
Forcer le cœur d'Hérode à ranimer sa haine;　　　　50
Irriter son époux par de nouveaux dédains,
Et vous rendre les traits qui tombent de vos mains.
De sa perte en un mot, reposez-vous sur elle.

SALOME

Non, cette incertitude est pour moi trop cruelle.
Non, c'est par d'autres coups que je veux la frapper:　　　　55
Dans un piège plus sûr, il faut l'envelopper.
Contre mes ennemis mon intérêt m'éclaire.
Si j'ai bien de Varus observé la colère;
Ce transport violent de son cœur agité,
N'est point un simple effet de générosité.　　　　60

37　25X, 26H: du roi autrefois
39　MSI, 25CH, 25X, 26H: Il hait, il craint la
41　25X, 26H: veut affermir sa
45　25X, 26H: il a proscrit
51　MSI, 25CH: Irriter son dépit par ses [MSI: de] nouveaux dédains
　　25X, 26H: son esprit par
55　MSI: je la veux frapper
58　25CH: bien observé de Varus la colère,

La tranquille pitié n'a point ce caractère.
La reine a des appas, Varus a pu lui plaire.
Ce n'est pas que mon cœur injuste en son dépit,
Dispute à sa beauté cet éclat qui la suit:
Que j'envie à ses yeux le pouvoir de leurs armes,   65
Ni ce flatteur encens qu'on prodigue à ses charmes.
Qu'elle goûte à loisir ce dangereux bonheur.
Moi, je veux de mon roi partager la grandeur,
Je veux qu'à mon parti la cour se réunisse,
Que sous mes volontés tout tremble, tout fléchisse;   70
Voilà mes intérêts et mes vœux assidus.
Vous, observez la reine, examinez Varus,
Faites veiller sur eux les regards mercenaires,
De tous ces délateurs aujourd'hui nécessaires,
Qui vendent les secrets de leurs concitoyens,   75
Et dont cent fois les yeux ont éclairé les miens.
Mais, la voici. Pourquoi faut-il que je la voie!

61-62   25X, 26H: [*lines inverted*]
66   MSI: Ni le flatteur
67-72   W52, W56, W57G, W57P, W64GV, W68V, W70GV, W70LV, W75GV, KV:
        Elle peut payer cher ce bonheur dangereux,
        Et soit que de Varus elle écoute les vœux,
        Soit que sa vanité de ce pompeux hommage
        Tire indiscrètement un frivole avantage,
        Il suffit, c'est par là que je peux maintenir   5
        Ce pouvoir qui m'échappe, et qu'il faut retenir.
69   25X, 26H: qu'en mon
70   25CH: sous ma volonté tout
73   W52: sur tout les
        W56, W57G, W64GV, W68V, W70GV, W70LV, W75GV, KV: surtout les
74   MSI: tous les délateurs

SCÈNE II

MARIAMNE, ÉLIZE, SALOME, MAZAËL, NABAL

SALOME

Je viens auprès de vous partager votre joie; [4]
Rome me rend un frère, et vous rend un époux,
Couronné, tout-puissant, et digne enfin de vous.   80
Son amour méprisé, son trop de défiance,
Avait contre vos jours allumé sa vengeance.
Mais ce feu violent s'est bientôt consumé.
L'amour arma son bras, l'amour l'a désarmé.
Ses triomphes passés, ceux qu'il prépare encore,   85
Ce titre heureux de Grand, dont l'univers l'honore,
Les droits du sénat même à ses soins confiés,
Sont autant de présents qu'il va mettre à vos pieds.
Possédez désormais son âme et son empire:
C'est ce qu'à vos vertus mon amitié désire.   90
Et je vais par mes soins serrer l'heureux lien,
Qui doit joindre à jamais votre cœur et le sien.

77b   MSI: MARIAMNE, SALOME, ÉLISE CONFIDANTE DE / MAR-
IAMNE, UNE AUTRE SUIVANTE, MAZAËL
      25CH: MARIAMNE, SALOME
81-84 Sohème texts: [absent]
81   25X, 26H: Son amour outragé de trop de défiance
82   MSI, 25CH: Avait [MSI: Avaient] contre vos jours excité sa vengeance.
83   25CH: violent fut bientôt
86   25CH: Le titre
87   MSI, 25CH, 25X, 26H: même en ses mains confiés
89   25X, 26H: âme, son

[4] Flaubert admired this 'brusque transition [qui] éclaire plus le caractère de
Salome que tout ce qu'elle a dit jusqu'ici. Cela doit être applaudi à la scène'
(Flaubert, *Le Théâtre de Voltaire*, ed. Th. Besterman, *SVEC* 50, 1967, p.17).

MARIAMNE

Je ne prétends de vous, ni n'attends ce service.
Je vous connais, madame, et je vous rends justice.
Je sais par quels complots, je sais par quels détours,   95
Votre haine impuissante a poursuivi mes jours.
Jugeant de moi par vous, vous me craignez peut-être;
Mais vous deviez du moins apprendre à me connaître.
Ne me redoutcz point; je sais également
Dédaigner votre crime, et votre châtiment.   100
J'ai vu tous vos desseins, et je vous les pardonne.
C'est à vos seuls remords que je vous abandonne:
Si toutefois après de si lâches efforts,
Un cœur comme le vôtre écoute des remords. ⁵

SALOME

Je n'ai point mérité cette injuste colère.   105
Ma conduite, mes soins, et l'aveu de mon frère,
Contre tous vos soupçons vont mc justifier.

93   25CH, 25X, 26H: n'attends de service
98   25CH: devriez
      25X, 26H: devez
100   MSI, 25CH: votre haine et
      25X 26H: Mépriser votre haine et votre châtiment,
101   MSI, 25CH, 25X, 26H: J'ai su tous
      25CH: vous le pardonne
104   25CH, 25X, 26H: écoute les remords
      MSI: de remords
105-107 Sohème texts:
      C'est porter un peu loin votre injuste colère.
      Ma conduite, mes soins, et l'aveu de mon frère,
      Peut-être suffiront pour me justifier.
106   25X, 26H: la vue de

⁵ This line is cited in the *Observations critiques* (p.10) with the reading 'les remords' as in 25CH, 25X and 26H.

MARIAMNE

Je vous l'ai déjà dit, je veux tout oublier,
Dans l'état où je suis, c'est assez pour ma gloire:
Je puis vous pardonner, mais je ne puis vous croire.[6]   110

MAZAËL

J'ose ici, grande reine, attester l'Eternel,
Que mes soins à regret...

MARIAMNE

                    Arrêtez, Mazaël.
Vos excuses pour moi sont un nouvel outrage.
Obéissez au roi, voilà votre partage.
A mes tyrans vendu, servez bien leur courroux,   115
Je ne m'abaisse pas à me plaindre de vous.
        (*A Salome*)
Je ne vous retiens point; et vous pouvez, madame,
Aller apprendre au roi les secrets de mon âme.
Dans son cœur aisément vous pouvez ranimer,
Un courroux que mes yeux dédaignent de calmer.   120
De tous vos délateurs armez la calomnie;
J'ai laissé jusqu'ici leur audace impunie:
Et je n'oppose encore à mes vils ennemis,
Qu'une vertu sans tache, et qu'un juste mépris.

115   MS1: vendus servez
      25X, 26H: De vos tyrans vendus,
116a   25A: [*stage direction absent*]
117   25CH: retiens pas;
      MS1, 25X, 26H: retiens plus;
119   MS1, 25CH, 25X, 26H: pouvez rallumer
123   25X, 26H: n'expose encore

[6] According to Nadal, 'la pensée [de ce] vers est un mot de Louis XIII sur le compte d'Anne d'Autriche, et sur ce qu'elle lui envoya dire au sujet de la conspiration de Chalais' (*Observations critiques*, p.31).

MAZAËL

Quel orgueil!

SALOME

Mazaël, on pourra le confondre,   125
Et c'est en me vengeant que je dois lui répondre.

SCÈNE III

MARIAMNE, ÉLIZE, NABAL

ÉLIZE

Ah! madame, à ce point pouvez-vous irriter
Des ennemis ardents à vous persécuter![7]

124a-126   Sohème texts:

SALOME

Ah! c'en est trop, enfin: vous auriez dû peut-être
Ménager un peu plus la sœur de votre maître.
L'orgueil de vos attraits pense tout asservir:
Vous me voyez tout perdre, et croyez tout ravir.
Votre victoire un jour peut vous être fatale.   5
Vous triomphez, – tremblez, imprudente rivale.//

125-126   MSI, 25CH, 25X, 26H: [absent]
125a-126   W46, W48D, W51, W52, W56, W57G, W57P, W64GV, W68V, W70LV,
W75GV, KV:

SALOME

Il aura sa juste récompense,
Viens, c'est à l'artifice à punir l'imprudence.//

126b   Sohème texts: MARIAMNE, ÉLIZE, NARBAS
127-128   MSI, 25CH, 25X, 26H:

Hélas! que faites-vous? Leur haine invétérée [25X, 26H: intéressée]
De votre sang, Madame, est assez altérée.
Vous verrai-je toujours préparant vos malheurs
Donner tant d'avantage à vos persécuteurs?

[7] In lines 125-28, new in 25P, Voltaire tones down Elize's description of the
hostility of Salome and Mazaël towards Mariamne, calling to his aid a line used in

La vengeance d'Hérode un moment suspendue,
Sur votre tête encore, est peut-être étendue.   130
Et loin d'en détourner les redoutables coups,
Vous appelez la mort qui s'éloignait de vous.
Vous n'avez plus ici de bras qui vous appuie.
Ce défenseur heureux de votre illustre vie,
Varus, aux nations qui bornent cet Etat,   135

132   MS1, 25CH, 25X, 26H: s'éloigne de
133   25CH: n'aurez plus
134   25CH: Le défenseur
135-149   Sohème texts:
      Sohème, dont le nom si craint, si respecté,
      Longtemps de vos tyrans contint la cruauté;
      Sohème va partir, nul espoir ne vous reste.
      Auguste à votre époux laisse un pouvoir funeste.
      Qui sait dans quels desseins il revient aujourd'hui?   5
      Tout, jusqu'à son amour, est à craindre de lui;
      Vous le voyez trop bien; sa sombre jalousie
      Au delà du tombeau portait sa frénésie;
      Cet ordre qu'il donna me fait encor trembler.
      Avec vos ennemis daignez dissimuler.   10
      La vertu sans prudence, hélas! est dangereuse.
                    MARIAMNE
      Oui, mon âme, il est vrai, fut trop impérieuse.
      Je n'ai point connu l'art, et j'en avais besoin.
      De mon sort à Sohème abandonnons le soin;
      Qu'il vienne, je l'attends; qu'il règle ma conduite.   15
      Mon projet est hardi, je frémis de la suite.
      Faites venir Sohème.
                           (Elize sort.)
              SCÈNE IV / MARIAMNE, NARBAS
                    MARIAMNE
                  Et vous, mon cher Narbas,
      De mes vœux incertains apaisez les combats.
      Vos vertus,

Artémire, II.ii.31: 'Madame, jusque-là deviez-vous l'irriter?' Mazaël's reaction to the defiant remarks of Mariamne echoes the cry of Racine's Pyrrhus (Andromaque, III.vi.899).

Ira porter bientôt les ordres du sénat. [8]
Hélas! grâce à ses soins, grâce à vos bontés même,
Rome à votre tyran donne un pouvoir suprême:
Il revient plus terrible et plus fier que jamais,
Vous le verrez armé de vos propres bienfaits: 140
Vous dépendrez ici de ce superbe maître, [9]
D'autant plus dangereux qu'il vous aime peut-être;
Et que cet amour même aigri par vos refus...

MARIAMNE

Chère Elize, en ces lieux faites venir Varus.
Je conçois vos raisons; j'en demeure frappée: 145
Mais d'un autre intérêt mon âme est occupée;
Par de plus grands objets mes vœux sont attirés.
Que Varus vienne ici; vous Nabal, demeurez.

136   25X, 26H: Ira bientôt porter les
137-140   MSI, 25CH, 25X, 26H: [absent]
141   25CH, 25X, 26H: dépendez
       MSI, 25CH, 25X, 26H: d'un redoutable maître
143   MSI: par les refus
       25CH: par ses refus
       25X, 26H: par le refus
145   MSI: Je connais vos

[8] This line is cited in the *Observations critiques* (p.13) with the reading 'Ira bientôt porter' as in 25X and 26H.
[9] This line is cited in the *Observations critiques* (p.31) as 'Vous dépendez ici d'un redoutable maître', identical with 25CH, 25X and 26H.

SCÈNE IV

MARIAMNE, NABAL

MARIAMNE

Vos vertus, votre zèle, et votre expérience,
Ont acquis dès longtemps toute ma confiance.   150
Mon cœur vous est connu, vous savez mes desseins,
Et les maux que j'éprouve, et les maux que je crains.
Vous avez vu ma mère au désespoir réduite
Me presser en pleurant d'accompagner sa fuite. [10]
Son esprit agité d'une juste terreur,   155
Croit à tous les moments voir Hérode en fureur,
Encor tout dégouttant du sang de sa famille,
Venir à ses yeux même assassiner sa fille.
Elle veut que mes fils portés entre nos bras,

148a-c   25CH: [*absent; no new scene*] (*à Nabal*)
151   MSI: savez ses desseins
153-154   MSI, 25CH, 25X, 26H:
        Vous voyez en ces lieux ma mère infortunée
        Presser de son départ l'heure déterminée.
155   Sohème texts: esprit accablé d'une
156   MSI: à chaque moment voir
159-164   Sohème texts:
        Elle veut à mes fils menacés du tombeau,
        Donner César pour père, et Rome pour berceau.
        On dit que l'infortune à Rome est protégée;
        Rome est le tribunal où la terre est jugée.
        Je vais me présenter aux rois des souverains.   5
        Je sais qu'il est permis de fuir ses assassins,
159   25CH: entre vos bras
        25X, 26H: entre mes bras

[10] The replacement in 25P of the earlier text of MSI, 25CH, 25X and 26H was perhaps prompted by Nadal's question: 'Peut-on presser une heure déterminée?' (*Observations critiques*, p.32).

S'éloignent avec nous de ces affreux climats.   160
Les vaisseaux des Romains, des bords de la Syrie,
Nous ouvrent sur les eaux les chemins d'Italie.
J'attends tout de Varus, d'Auguste, des Romains.
Je sais qu'il m'est permis de fuir mes assassins,
Que c'est le seul parti que le destin me laisse.   165
Toutefois en secret, soit vertu, soit faiblesse,
Prête à fuir un époux, mon cœur frémit d'effroi,
Et mes pas chancelants s'arrêtent malgré moi.

                          NABAL

Cet effroi généreux n'a rien que je n'admire.
Tout injuste qu'il est, la vertu vous l'inspire.   170
Ce cœur indépendant des outrages du sort,
Craint l'ombre d'une faute, et ne craint point la mort.
Bannissez toutefois ces alarmes secrètes.
Ouvrez les yeux, madame, et voyez où vous êtes.
C'est là que répandu par les mains d'un époux,   175
Le sang de votre père a rejailli sur vous.
Votre frère en ces lieux a vu trancher sa vie.
En vain de son trépas le roi se justifie;
En vain César trompé l'en absout aujourd'hui,
L'Orient révolté n'en accuse que lui.   180
Regardez, consultez les pleurs de votre mère,
L'affront fait à vos fils, le sang de votre père,
La cruauté du roi, la haine de sa sœur,
Et (ce que je ne puis prononcer sans horreur,
Mais dont votre vertu n'est point épouvantée,)   185

160   25X, 26H: avec moi de
162   25CH: Nous couvrent
      25X, 26H: le chemin d'Italie
168a Sohème texts: NARBAS
174   25X, 26H: et songez où
177   25CH: vu finir sa
182   MSI, 25X, 26H: à son fils

La mort en ce jour même à vos yeux présentée. [11]
Enfin si tant de maux ne vous étonnent pas,
Si d'un front assuré vous marchez au trépas:
Du moins de vos enfants embrassez la défense.
Le roi leur a du trône arraché l'espérance,   190
Et vous connaissez trop ces oracles affreux,
Qui depuis si longtemps vous font trembler pour eux.
Le ciel vous a prédit qu'une main étrangère,
Devait un jour unir vos fils à votre père.
Un Arabe implacable a déjà sans pitié,   195
De cet oracle obscur accompli la moitié.
Madame, après l'horreur d'un essai si funeste,
Sa cruauté, sans doute, accomplirait le reste.
Dans ses emportements rien n'est sacré pour lui.
Eh! qui vous répondra que lui-même aujourd'hui,   200
Ne vienne exécuter sa sanglante menace,
Et des Asmonéens anéantir la race?
Il est temps désormais de prévenir ses coups:
Il est temps d'épargner un meurtre à votre époux,

186   MS1, 25CH, 25X, 26H: mort dans ce
      Sohème texts: mort plus d'une fois à
194   MS1, 25X, 26H: Devait unir un jour vos
197   MS1, 25CH, 25X, 25A, 26H: d'un excès si
198   MS1, 25X, 26H: accomplira le
199   MS1: Dans son emportement
200   MS1, 25CH, 25X, 26H: Et qui
201   25CH: n'en vienne

[11] Cf. *Artémire*, IV.iv.17: 'La mort à mes regards s'est déjà présentée.' The variant of M62 ('plus d'une fois') is evidence of Voltaire's efforts in the Sohème version to bring the action of the play closer to the Josephan narrative, in which it will be remembered that Herod had twice left orders for Mariamne's execution should he not return from his meetings with the Romans (see Introduction, section 2.i and 6.i). Though he shows greater fidelity to his source at this point, Nabal's speech seems to imply in line 176 that Mariamne was present at the murder of Hyrcanus II (who was not her father but her grandfather). There is no suggestion in Josephus that this was the case. Cf. V.16.

Et d'éloigner du moins de ces tendres victimes,   205
Le fer de vos tyrans, et l'exemple des crimes.
Nourri dans ce palais près des rois vos aïeux, [12]
Je suis prêt à vous suivre en tout temps, en tous lieux.
Partez, rompez vos fers, allez dans Rome même,
Implorer du sénat la justice suprême,   210
Remettre de vos fils la fortune en sa main,
Et les faire adopter par le peuple romain.
Qu'une vertu si pure aille étonner Auguste. [13]
Si l'on vante à bon droit son règne heureux et juste, [14]
Si la terre avec joie embrasse ses genoux, [15]   215
S'il mérite sa gloire, il fera tout pour vous.

MARIAMNE

Je vois qu'il n'est plus temps que mon cœur délibère;
Je cède à vos conseils, aux larmes de ma mère:
Au danger de mes fils, au sort, dont les rigueurs
Vont m'entraîner, peut-être, en de plus grands malheurs.   220
Retournez chez ma mère, allez; quand la nuit sombre,
Dans ces lieux criminels aura porté son ombre;

---

207   w42, w46: vos ayeuls [w46 errata: ayeux]
210   MSI: l'autorité suprême
       25CH: la volonté suprême
214   MSI, 25CH, 25X, 26H: vante avec droit
221   25X, 26H: mère, et lorsque la
222   25X, 26H: aura jeté son

---

[12] Cf. Racine, *Bajazet*, IV.vii.1423 (Acomat to Osmin): 'Nourri dans le sérail, j'en connais les détours.'

[13] This line prompted a cynical comment from Flaubert: 'Auguste s'étonnait de peu de choses' (Flaubert, *Le Théâtre de Voltaire*, p.19).

[14] This line is cited in the *Observations critiques* (p.32) with the reading 'avec droit' as in MSI, 25CH, 25X and 26H.

[15] 'La terre embrasser les genoux de quelqu'un. Quelle métaphore? Quelle image?' (Nadal, *Observations critiques*, p.32).

Qu'au fond de mon palais, on me vienne avertir. [16]
On le veut, [17] il le faut; je suis prête à partir.

SCÈNE V

MARIAMNE, VARUS, ÉLIZE

VARUS

Je viens m'offrir, madame, à vos ordres suprêmes.   225
Vos volontés, pour moi, sont les lois des dieux mêmes.
Faut-il armer mon bras contre vos ennemis?
Commandez, j'entreprends; parlez et j'obéis.

MARIAMNE

Je vous dois tout, seigneur, et dans mon infortune,
Ma douleur ne craint point de vous être importune,   230
Ni de solliciter par d'inutiles vœux,
Les bontés d'un héros, l'appui des malheureux.

223   K: de ce palais
        MS1, 25CH, 25X, 26H: me fasse avertir,
224   MS1, 25CH, 25X, 26H: Le sort en est jeté;
224a-226   Sohème texts:

SCÈNE V
MARIAMNE, SOHÈME, ÉLIZE
SOHÈME

        Je viens m'offrir, Madame, à votre ordre suprême.
        Vos volontés, pour moi, sont les lois du ciel même.
224a   25CH: *SCÈNE IV*
224b   MS1, 25CH, 25X, 26H: MARIAMNE, VARUS, ALBIN

[16] This line is cited in the *Observations critiques* (p.32) with the reading 'me fasse avertir' as in MS1, 25CH, 25X and 26H.

[17] The removal in 25P of the earlier 'Le sort en est jeté' and the substitution of 'On le veut' perhaps imply that in deciding to flee Mariamne is complying with what others (Nabal, her mother) have suggested rather then obeying the dictates of her own conscience.

Lorsqu'Hérode attendait le trône ou l'esclavage,
J'osai longtemps pour lui briguer votre suffrage.
Malgré ses cruautés, malgré mon désespoir,   235
Malgré mes intérêts, j'ai suivi mon devoir.
J'ai servi mon époux; je le ferais encore.
Souffrez que pour moi-même enfin je vous implore.
Souffrez que je dérobe à d'inhumaines lois,
Les restes malheureux du pur sang de nos rois.   240
J'aurais dû dès longtemps, loin d'un lieu si coupable,
Demander au sénat un asile honorable.
Mais, seigneur, je n'ai pu dans les troubles divers,
Dont vos divisions ont rempli l'univers,
Chercher parmi l'effroi, la guerre et les ravages   245
Un port aux mêmes lieux d'où partaient les orages.
Auguste, au monde entier donne aujourd'hui la paix,
Sur toute la nature il répand ses bienfaits.
Après les longs travaux d'une guerre odieuse,
Ayant vaincu la terre, il veut la rendre heureuse.   250
Du haut du Capitole il juge tous les rois:
Et de ceux qu'on opprime il prend en main les droits.
Qui peut à ses bontés plus justement prétendre,
Que mes faibles enfants que rien ne peut défendre,
Et qu'une mère en pleurs amène auprès de lui,   255
Du bout de l'univers implorer son appui?

233   25CH: trône et l'esclavage
234   Sohème texts: Moi-même des Romains j'ai brigué le suffrage.
238   MSI, 25X, 26H: Souffrez que ma famille aujourd'hui vous implore,
       25CH: Sachez que ma famille aujourd'hui vous implore,
       Sohème texts: Il faut que
239   Sohème texts: Il faut que
244   Sohème texts: Dont la guerre civile a rempli l'univers,
246   MSI: au même lieu d'où
       25CH: au même endroit d'où
248   25X, 26H: il étend ses
250   25CH: Ayant conquis la
253   MSI, 25X, 26H: à sa bonté plus

Loin de ces lieux sanglants que le crime environne,
Je mettrai leur enfance à l'ombre de son trône.
Ses généreuses mains pourront sécher nos pleurs.
Je ne demande point qu'il venge mes malheurs,   260
Que sur mes ennemis son bras s'appesantisse.
C'est assez que mes fils, témoins de sa justice,
Formés par son exemple, et devenus Romains, [18]
Apprennent à régner des maîtres des humains.
Pour conserver les fils, pour consoler la mère,   265
Pour finir tous mes maux, c'est en vous que j'espère.
Je m'adresse à vous seul, à vous, à ce grand cœur,
De la simple vertu, généreux protecteur;
A vous, à qui je dois ce jour que je respire.
Seigneur, éloignez-moi de ce fatal empire.   270
Donnez-moi dans la nuit des guides assurés,

257-264   Sohème texts: [*absent*]
257   MSI: ce lieu sanglant
258   25CH: mettrai mes enfants à
      25X, 26H: à l'abri de
259   MSI, 25CH: Cet appui va tarir la source de mes pleurs.
260   25CH, 25X, 26H: venge nos malheurs
263   25CH: exemple, à devenir Romains
264   MSI, 25CH: du maître des
265   25CH: conserver mes fils
      MSI, 25X, 26H: conserver leurs jours,
      K: conserver le fils
      MSI: consoler leur mère
      25X, 26H: consoler ma mère
267-268   25X 26H:
      Je m'adresse à vous seul, à vous dont le grand cœur,
      De la simple vertu fut toujours protecteur;
271-272   Sohème texts:
      Ma mère, mes enfants, je mets tout en vos mains;
      Enlevez l'innocence au fer des assassins.
271   MSI, 25CH, 25X, 26H: des gardes assurés

[18] This line is cited in the *Observations critiques* (p.33) with the reading 'à devenir Romains' as in 25CH.

Jusques sur vos vaisseaux dans Sidon préparés.
Vous ne répondez rien. Que faut-il que je pense
De ces sombres regards, et de ce long silence?
Je vois que mes malheurs excitent vos refus.   275

VARUS

Non,... je respecte trop vos ordres absolus.
Mes gardes vous suivront jusques dans l'Italie.
Disposez d'eux, de moi, de mon cœur, de ma vie.
Fuyez le roi. Rompez vos nœuds infortunés. [19]
Il est assez puni si vous l'abandonnez.   280
Il ne vous verra plus, grâce à son injustice:
Et je sens qu'il n'est point de si cruel supplice...
Pardonnez-moi ce mot: il m'échappe à regret.
La douleur de vous perdre a trahi mon secret.
Tout mon crime est connu. Mais malgré ma faiblesse,   285
Songez que mon respect égale ma tendresse.
Le malheureux Varus ne veut que vous servir,
Adorer vos vertus, vous venger et mourir.

275a Sohème texts: SOHÈME
276   25CH: Ah! je
279   MSI, 25CH, 25X, 26H: Rompez des nœuds
282   MSI: de plus cruel
      25CH: de plus affreux supplice
285   Sohème texts: J'ai parlé, c'en est fait. Mais
287   MSI, 25CH, 25X, 26H: L'infortuné Varus
      Sohème texts: Sohème en vous aimant ne

[19] This line is cited in the *Observations critiques* (p.14) with the reading 'des nœuds' as in MSI, 25CH, 25X and 26H.

MARIAMNE

Je me flattais, seigneur, et j'avais lieu de croire,
Qu'avec mes intérêts vous chérissiez ma gloire.   290
Et quand le grand Varus a conservé mes jours,
J'ai cru qu'à sa pitié je devais son secours.
Je ne m'attendais pas que vous dussiez vous-même,
Mettre aujourd'hui le comble à ma douleur extrême:
Ni que dans mes périls, il me fallût jamais,   295
Rougir de vos bontés, et craindre vos bienfaits.
Ne pensez pas pourtant, qu'un discours qui m'offense,
Vous ait rien dérobé de ma reconnaissance.
Ma constante amitié respecte encor Varus.
J'oublîrai votre flamme, et non pas vos vertus.   300
Je ne veux voir en vous qu'un héros magnanime,
Qui jusqu'à ce moment mérita mon estime.
Un plus long entretien pourrait vous en priver,
Seigneur; et je vous fuis pour vous la conserver.

290   25CH: vous chercheriez ma
291-294   Sohème texts:
   Quand Sohème en ces lieux a veillé sur mes jours,
   J'ai cru qu'à sa pitié je devais son secours.
   Je ne m'attendais pas qu'une flamme coupable
   Dût ajouter ce comble à l'horreur qui m'accable,
299   Sohème texts: Tout espoir m'est ravi, je ne vous verrai plus.
300   w46: J'oublierai
301   w75G, K: ne peux voir

SCÈNE VI

VARUS, ALBIN

ALBIN

Vous vous troublez, seigneur, et changez de visage.[20]   305

304a-334   Sohème texts: [*no new scene*]

SOHÈME

Arrêtez, et sachez que je l'ai méritée.
Quand votre gloire parle, elle est seule écoutée;
A cette gloire, à vous, soigneux de m'immoler,
Epris de vos vertus, je les sais égaler.
Je ne fuyais que vous, je veux vous fuir encore.   5
Je quittais pour jamais une cour que j'abhorre;
J'y reste, s'il le faut, pour vous désabuser,
Pour vous respecter plus, pour ne plus m'exposer
Au reproche accablant que m'a fait votre bouche.
Votre intérêt, Madame, est le seul qui me touche;   10
J'y sacrifirai tout; mes amis, mes soldats,
Vous conduiront aux bords où s'adressent vos pas.
J'ai dans ces murs encor un reste de puissance.
D'un tyran soupçonneux je crains peu la vengeance;
Et s'il me faut périr des mains de votre époux,   15
Je périrai du moins en combattant pour vous.
Dans mes derniers moments je vous aurai servie,
Et j'aurai préféré votre honneur à ma vie.

MARIAMNE

Il suffit, je vous crois: d'indignes passions
Ne doivent point souiller les nobles actions.   20
Oui, je vous devrai tout; mais moi je vous expose;
Vous courez à la mort, et j'en serai la cause.
Comment puis-je vous suivre? et comment demeurer?
Je n'ai de sentiment que pour vous admirer.

SOHÈME

Venez prendre conseil de votre mère en larmes,   25

[20] Cf. Racine, *Britannicus*, II.iii.527 (Néron to Junie): 'Vous vous troublez, Madame, et changez de visage.' Cf. also *Bérénice*, I.iv.180, and *Mithridate*, III.v.1112.

VARUS

J'ai senti, je l'avoue, ébranler mon courage.
Ami, pardonne au feu, dont je suis consumé,
Ces faiblesses d'un cœur, qui n'avait point aimé.
Je ne connaissais pas tout le poids de ma chaîne.
Je la sens à regret; je la romps avec peine.   310
Avec quelle douceur, avec quelle bonté,
Elle imposait silence à ma témérité!
Sans trouble et sans courroux, sa tranquille sagesse
M'apprenait mon devoir, et plaignait ma faiblesse.
J'adorais, cher Albin, jusques à ses refus.   315
J'ai perdu l'espérance; et je l'aime encor plus.
A quelle épreuve, ô dieux! ma constance est réduite!

ALBIN

Etes-vous résolu de préparer sa fuite?

De votre fermeté plus que de ses alarmes,
Du péril qui vous presse, et non de mon danger;
Avec votre tyran rien n'est à ménager.
Il est roi, je le sais; mais César est son juge:
Tout vous menace ici; Rome est votre refuge;   30
Mais songez que Sohème, en vous offrant ses vœux,
S'il ose être sensible, en est plus vertueux;
Que le sang de nos rois nous unit l'un et l'autre,
Et que le ciel m'a fait un cœur digne du vôtre.
                        MARIAMNE
Je n'en veux point douter: et dans mon désespoir,   35
Je vais consulter Dieu, l'honneur et le devoir.
                        SOHÈME
C'est eux que j'en atteste; ils sont tous trois mes guides;
Ils vous arracheront aux mains des parricides.//
317   MSI, 25CH, 25X, 26H: ô Ciel!
       W42, W46: ô Dieu! [w46 errata: Dieux!]
318   MSI: résolu à préparer

238

VARUS

Quel emploi!

ALBIN

Pourrez-vous respecter ses rigueurs,
Jusques à vous charger du soin de vos malheurs?   320
Quel est votre dessein?

VARUS

Moi, que je l'abandonne?
Que je désobéisse aux lois qu'elle me donne?
Non, non, mon cœur encore est trop digne du sien.
Mariamne a parlé, je n'examine rien.
Que loin de ses tyrans, elle aille auprès d'Auguste,   325
Sa fuite est raisonnable, et ma douleur injuste.
L'amour me parle en vain, je vole à mon devoir.
Je servirai la reine, et même sans la voir.
Elle me laisse, au moins, la douceur éternelle,
D'avoir tout entrepris, d'avoir tout fait pour elle.   330
Je brise ses liens; je lui sauve le jour.
Je fais plus. Je lui veux immoler mon amour,
Et fuyant sa beauté, qui me séduit encore,
Egaler, s'il se peut, sa vertu que j'adore.

Fin du second acte.

---

319   MS1, 25CH, 25X, 26H: Pouvez-vous
320   MS1, 25CH, 25X, 26H: de ses malheurs
321   25CH: Quel est donc votre espoir?
322   MS1: qu'elle m'ordonne

ACTE III

SCÈNE PREMIÈRE

VARUS, NABAL, ALBIN, SUITE DE VARUS

NABAL

Oui, seigneur, en ces lieux l'heureux Hérode arrive.
Les Hébreux pour le voir ont volé sur la rive.
Salome qui craignait de perdre son crédit,
Par ses conseils flatteurs assiège son esprit.
Ses courtisans en foule autour de lui se rendent: 5
Les palmes dans les mains, nos pontifes l'attendent.
Idamas le devance, et député vers vous,

c   25CH: VARUS, NABAL
    25X, 26H: VARUS ET NABAL
    Sohème texts: SOHÈME, NARBAS, AMMON, SUITE
d   Sohème texts: NARBAS
1-4   Sohème texts:
    Le temps est précieux, Seigneur, Hérode arrive;
    Du fleuve de Judée il a revu la rive.
    Salome qui ménage un reste de crédit,
    Déjà par ses conseils assiège son esprit.
1   MSI, 25CH, 25X, 26H: seigneur, dans ces
2   MSI: Vos soldats pour
    25CH: Nos soldats pour
    25X, 26H: Les soldats pour
5   MSI, 25CH, Sohème texts: foule auprès de
6   25X, 26H: palmes à la main les pontifes
7-8   Sohème texts:
    Idamas le devance, et vous le connaissez.
SOHÈME
    Je sais qu'on paya mal ses services passés. [*Sohème remains speaker to line* 12]
7-21   MSI, 25CH, 25X, 26H:
    Cependant Mariamne en son appartement
    Attend de son départ le dangereux moment. [25CH, 25X, 26H: Vos
    secours généreux vont aider sa sortie.]

Il vient au nom d'Hérode embrasser vos genoux.
C'est ce même Idamas, cet Hébreu plein de zèle,
Qui toujours à la reine est demeuré fidèle: 10
Qui sage courtisan d'un roi plein de fureur,
A quelquefois d'Hérode adouci la rigueur:
Bientôt vous l'entendrez. Cependant Mariamne
Au moment de partir s'arrête, se condamne;
Ce grand projet l'étonne, et prête à le tenter,   15
Son austère vertu craint de l'exécuter.
Sa mère est à ses pieds, et le cœur plein d'alarmes,
Lui présente ses fils, la baigne de ses larmes:
La conjure en tremblant de presser son départ:
La reine flotte, hésite, et partira trop tard.   20
C'est vous dont la bonté peut hâter sa sortie,
Vous avez dans vos mains la fortune et la vie [1]
De l'objet le plus rare, et le plus précieux,
Que jamais à la terre aient accordé les cieux.
Protégez, conservez une auguste famille;   25
Sauvez de tant de rois la déplorable fille. [2]
Vos gardes sont-ils prêts? Puis-je enfin l'avertir?

13-28   Sohème texts: [*give these lines to Narbas*]
23   25X, 26H: l'objet le plus pur,
25-26   MSI, 25CH, 25X, 26H:
        Vous êtes son appui, son défenseur, son père,
        Daignez presser l'effet des bontés qu'elle espère.

[1] Cf. Racine, *Bajazet*, III.iv.988 (Bajazet to Atalide about Roxane): 'Elle met dans ma main sa fortune, ses jours.'
[2] The earlier text (lines 25-26) (MSI, 25CH, 25X and 26H) contains an appeal to the compassion of Varus. 25P stresses instead Mariamne's royal lineage.

VARUS

Oui, j'ai tout ordonné; la reine peut partir.

NABAL

Souffrez donc qu'à l'instant un serviteur fidèle,
Se prépare, seigneur, à marcher après elle.   30

VARUS

Allez; sur mes vaisseaux accompagnez ses pas.
Ce séjour odieux ne la méritait pas.
Qu'un dépôt si sacré soit respecté des ondes;
Que le ciel attendri par ses douleurs profondes,
Fasse lever sur elle un soleil plus serein.   35
Et vous, vieillard heureux, qui suivez son destin,
Des serviteurs des rois, sage et parfait modèle,
Votre sort est trop beau; vous vivrez auprès d'elle.

SCÈNE II

VARUS, ALBIN, SUITE DE VARUS

VARUS

Mais déjà le roi vient. Déjà dans ce séjour,

27a   Sohème texts: SOHÈME
28   25CH: ordonné, et vous pouvez partir
28a   Sohème texts: NARBAS
30   25X, 26H: marcher auprès d'elle
30a   Sohème texts: SOHÈME
31   25CH: sur nos vaisseaux
      Sohème texts: Allez, loin de ces lieux je conduirai vos pas.
38   MSI, 25X, 26H: [with stage direction] (Nabal sort.)
38a-c MSI, 25CH, 25X, 26H: [absent; no new scene]
38b   Sohème texts: SOHÈME, AMMON, SUITE DE SOHÈME
38c   Sohème texts: SOHÈME

Le son de la trompette annonce son retour.   40

Quel retour, justes dieux! Que je crains sa présence!

Le cruel peut d'un coup assurer sa vengeance.

Plût au ciel que la reine eût déjà pour jamais,

Abandonné ces lieux consacrés aux forfaits!

Hélas! je ne puis même accompagner sa fuite,   45

Plus je l'adore, (et plus il faut que je l'évite.)

C'est un crime pour moi d'oser suivre ses pas.

Et tout ce que je puis... mais je vois Idamas. [3]

40   MS1: Ce son
41   MS1, 25CH, 25X, 26H: juste Ciel?
43   MS1, 25CH, 25X, 26H: Plût aux Dieux que
44   25CH, 25X, 26H: Abandonné des lieux
45-48 MS1, 25CH, 25X, 26H:
       Hélas! à [MS1: pour] la servir, j'ai trop tardé peut-être.
       Mais quoi! c'est Idamas qu'ici je vois paraître,
       Lui dont on estimait la candeur et la foi,
       Et qui près de César accompagna le [25CH: ce] roi.//
       Sohème texts:
       Oserai-je moi-même accompagner sa fuite,
       Peut être en la servant il faut que je l'évite.
       Est-ce un crime, après tout, de sauver tant d'appas?
       De venger sa vertu?... mais je vois Idamas.//
46   w42 errata: [removes brackets]

[3] The reworking of the earlier editions (MS1, 25CH, 25X and 26H) enabled Voltaire to heighten the dramatic interest of this passage (lines 45-48). The four lines concerning Idamas may have appeared superfluous to Voltaire after he had introduced a more developed description of the character of Idamas in lines 7-13. The inserted text (new in 25P) allows Varus to lament the impossible situation in which he finds himself: it is out of the question for him to seek to be close to the woman whom he loves, a common tragic dilemma. In this context the sentiments expressed by Varus are dramatically appropriate. The passage is enhanced by these changes.

SCÈNE III

VARUS, IDAMAS, ALBIN, SUITE DE VARUS[4]

IDAMAS

Avant que dans ces lieux mon roi vienne lui-même
Recevoir de vos mains le sacré diadème,   50
Et vous soumettre un rang, qu'il doit à vos bontés;
Seigneur, souffrirez-vous?...

VARUS

                    Idamas, arrêtez.
Le roi peut s'épargner ces frivoles hommages,
De l'amitié des grands, importuns témoignages,
D'un peuple curieux trompeur amusement,   55
Qu'on étale avec pompe, et que le cœur dément.
Mais parlez; Rome, enfin, vient de vous rendre un maître,
Hérode est souverain, est-il digne de l'être?
La reine en ce moment, est-elle en sûreté?

48a-53   Sohème texts:
      SCÈNE III / SOHÈME, IDAMAS, AMMON, SUITE
                   SOHÈME
      Ami, j'épargne au Roi de frivoles hommages,
48a   MSI, 25CH, 25X, 26H: *SCÈNE II*
48b   MSI, 25CH, 25X, 26H: VARUS, IDAMAS, ALBIN
49   MSI, 25CH, 25X, 26H: lieux le roi
50   25X, 26H: Recevoir des Romains le
52   MSI: souffririez-vous
58   W42, W46: souverain, il est digne [W46 errata: β]
59-87   Sohème texts:
      Vient-il dans un esprit de fureur ou de paix?
      Craint-on des cruautés? attend-on des bienfaits?
                IDAMAS
      Veuille le juste ciel, formidable au parjure,

---

[4] The 'Suite de Varus' introduced in 25P here and above line 38b may indicate an
intention on Voltaire's part to increase the element of spectacle in the play.

Et le sang innocent sera-t-il respecté?   60

IDAMAS

Veuille le juste ciel, formidable au parjure,
Ouvrir les yeux du roi, qu'aveugle l'imposture.
Mais qui peut pénétrer ses secrets sentiments,
Et de son cœur troublé les soudains mouvements?
Il observe avec nous un silence farouche.   65
Le nom de Mariamne échappe de sa bouche.

Ecarter loin de lui l'erreur et l'imposture.
Salome et Mazaël s'empressent d'écarter   5
Quiconque a le cœur juste et ne sait point flatter.
Ils révèlent, dit-on, des secrets redoutables;
Hérode en a pâli: des cris épouvantables
Sont sortis de sa bouche; et ses yeux en fureur
A tout ce qui l'entoure inspirent la terreur.   10
Vous le savez assez, leur cabale attentive
Tint toujours près de lui la vérité captive.
Ainsi ce conquérant, qui fit trembler les rois,
Ce roi, dont Rome même admira les exploits,
De qui la renommée alarme encor l'Asie,   15
Dans sa propre maison voit sa gloire avilie:
Haï de son épouse, abusé par sa sœur,
Déchiré de soupçons, accablé de douleur,
J'ignore en ce moment le dessein qui l'entraîne.
On le plaint, on murmure, on craint tout pour la Reine; 20
On ne peut pénétrer ses secrets sentiments,
Et de son cœur troublé les soudains mouvements.
Il observe avec nous un silence farouche.
Le nom de Mariamne échappe de sa bouche.
Il menace, il soupire, il donne en frémissant,   25
Quelques ordres secrets, qu'il révoque à l'instant.
D'un sang qu'il détestait, Mariamne est formée;
Il voulut la punir de l'avoir trop aimée.
Je tremble encor pour elle.

SOHÈME
Il suffit, Idamas.

60   25CH: Et ce sang
61   25X, 26H: formidable aux parjures

Il menace, il soupire, il donne en frémissant,
Quelques ordres secrets, qu'il révoque à l'instant.
D'un sang qu'il détestait, Mariamne est formée;
Il la hait d'autant plus qu'il l'avait trop aimée.   70
Le perfide Zarès par votre ordre arrêté,
Et par votre ordre enfin remis en liberté,
Artisan de la fraude, et de la calomnie,
De Salome, avec soin, servira la furie.
Mazaël en secret leur prête son secours.   75
Le soupçonneux Hérode écoute leurs discours;
Ils l'assiègent sans cesse; et leur haine attentive
Tient toujours loin de lui la vérité captive.
Ainsi ce conquérant, qui fit trembler les rois,
Ce roi, dont Rome même admira les exploits,   80
De qui la renommée alarme encor l'Asie,
Dans sa propre maison voit sa gloire avilie:
Haï de son épouse, abusé par sa sœur,
Déchiré de soupçons, accablé de douleur,
J'ignore en ce moment le dessein qui l'entraîne.[5]   85
Mais je le plains, seigneur, et crains tout pour la reine;

67   25CH: donne ainsi flottant
69   MSI: Du sang
75   MSI, 25CH, 25X, 26H: secret lui prête
76   MSI, 25CH, 25X, 26H: écoute ses discours
77   25X, 26H: leur âme attentive
80   MSI, 25CH, 25X, 26H: admirait les
82   MSI: gloire ternie
85-87a   MSI, 25CH, 25X, 26H:
          Je n'ai pu découvrir le sujet qui l'amène.
          Mais je le plains, Seigneur, et je crains pour la Reine.
          Un moment peut la perdre.
                    VARUS

[5] We can perhaps detect in this line an echo of the musicality of Oreste's
uncertainties in Racine's *Andromaque* (I.i.25): 'Hélas! qui peut savoir le destin qui
m'amène'.

Daignez la protéger. [6]

VARUS

Il suffit, Idamas.
La reine est en danger; Albin, suivez mes pas,
Venez; c'est à moi seul de sauver l'innocence.

IDAMAS

Seigneur, ainsi, du roi vous fuirez la présence?   90

VARUS

Je sais qu'en ce palais je dois le recevoir,
Le sénat me l'ordonne, et tel est mon devoir:
Mais un autre intérêt, un autre soin m'anime;
Et mon premier devoir est d'empêcher le crime.

(*Il sort.*)

---

88 Sohème texts: danger; Ammon, suivez
89a-90a   25X, 26H: [*absent*]
90-93   Sohème texts:
Seigneur, ainsi du Roi vous fuirez la présence?
Vous de qui la vertu, le rang, l'autorité,
Imposeraient silence à la perversité?
SOHÈME
Un intérêt plus grand, un autre soin m'anime:
90   MS1, 25CH: fuyez
94a   MS1, 25CII, 25X, 26H: [*stage direction absent*]

[6] Voltaire's reworking in M62 of this speech by Idamas (lines 61-87) shows interesting detail. The first six lines are new (from 'Salome et Mazaël' to 'inspirent la terreur'). Voltaire then re-uses two groups of lines from 25P, firstly lines 77-86, and then lines 63-70, which he presents in reversed sequence from the original speech, and into which he introduces a small number of changes. He abandons lines 71-76 from 25P, with their reference to Zarès, the bearer of Hérode's unconditional order for the death of Mariamne, an essential element in the plot of M25 which Voltaire eliminates in the M62 revision.

IDAMAS

Quels orages nouveaux! quel trouble je prévoi!   95
Puissant Dieu des Hébreux, changez le cœur du roi.

SCÈNE IV

HÉRODE, MAZAËL, IDAMAS, SUITE D'HÉRODE

HÉRODE

Eh quoi! Varus aussi semble éviter ma vue!
Quelle horreur devant moi s'est partout répandue![7]
Ciel! ne puis-je inspirer que la haine, ou l'effroi?[8]
Tous les cœurs des humains sont-ils fermés pour moi?[9]   100
En horreur à la reine, à mon peuple, à moi-même,
A regret sur mon front je vois le diadème.[10]
Hérode en arrivant, recueille avec terreur,

95   25CH: Quel orage nouveau!
      25X, 26H: quels troubles j'aperçoi!
96a   MS1, 25CH, 25X, 26H: *SCÈNE III*
96b   25CH: HÉRODE, MAZAËL, &c.
      W51, W57P: SUITE DE VARUS
97   Sohème texts: quoi! Sohème aussi
      MS2: quoi! <Varus> ↑Soheme+ aussi
98   25X, 26H: moi est
99   MS1: haine et l'effroi
      25CH, 25X, 26H: l'horreur et l'effroi

---

[7] Cf. Racine, *Phèdre*, III.v.953-54 (Thésée on his return to Trézène): 'Que vois-je? quelle horreur dans ces lieux répandue / Fait fuir devant mes yeux ma famille éperdue?'

[8] This line is cited in Nadal's *Observations critiques* (p.33) with the reading 'que l'horreur et l'effroi' as in 25CH, 25X and 26H. Nadal objected to Voltaire's use of the word 'horreur' three times in what he declared to be three lines (in fact four). Nadal's criticism may have prompted Voltaire to replace 'l'horreur' by 'la haine' in this line.

[9] Cf. *Artémire*, IV.v.29: 'Et pour moi tous les cœurs sont fermés désormais'.

[10] Cf. *Artémire*, III.iv.88: 'S'il est las sur mon front de voir le diadème'.

Les chagrins dévorants qu'a semés sa fureur.
Ah Dieu!

MAZAËL

Daignez calmer ces injustes alarmes. 105

HÉRODE

Malheureux, qu'ai-je fait?

MAZAËL

Quoi! vous versez des larmes?
Vous, ce roi fortuné, si sage en ses desseins,
Vous, la terreur du Parthe, et l'ami des Romains?
Songez, seigneur, songez, à ces noms pleins de gloire,
Que vous donnaient jadis Antoine et la victoire. 110
Songez que près d'Auguste, appelé par son choix,
Vous marchiez, distingué de la foule des rois.[11]
Revoyez à vos lois Jérusalem rendue,
Jadis par vous conquise, et par vous défendue
Reprenant aujourd'hui sa première splendeur, 115
Et contemplant son prince, au faîte du bonheur.
Jamais roi plus heureux dans la paix, dans la guerre...

---

105   MSI, 25CH, 25X, 26H: Ah Dieux!
110   25CH, 25X, 25A, 26H: donna jadis
113   25X, 26H: Vous voyez à
115   25CH: Recouvrant aujourd'hui
116   W40, W42, W46, W48D, W51, W52, W56, W57G, W57P, Sohème texts: En
[W42 errata: Et] contemplant
117   MSI, 25CH, 25X, 26H: Jamais aucun destin [25X: aucuns destins], dans la
paix

---

[11] Lines 111-12: cf. M24, 123-24: 'Et bientôt dans sa cour appelé par son choix, /
Je marchai distingué dans la foule des rois'. Cf. Racine, *Bérénice*, III.i.673-74 (Titus
to Antiochus): 'Vous avais-je sans choix / Confondu jusqu'ici dans la foule des
rois?' Cf. also *Britannicus*, II.ii.451-52.

HÉRODE

Non, il n'est plus pour moi de bonheur sur la terre.
Le destin m'a frappé de ses plus rudes coups;
Et pour comble d'horreurs, je les mérite tous.   120

IDAMAS

Seigneur, m'est-il permis de parler sans contrainte?[12]
Ce trône auguste et saint qu'environne la crainte,
Serait mieux affermi s'il l'était par l'amour.
En faisant des heureux, un roi l'est à son tour,[13]
A d'éternels chagrins votre âme abandonnée,   125
Pourrait tarir d'un mot leur source empoisonnée.
Seigneur, ne souffrez plus que d'indignes discours,
Osent troubler la paix, et l'honneur de vos jours;
Ni que de vils flatteurs écartent de leur maître,
Des cœurs infortunés qui vous cherchaient peut-être.[14]   130
Bientôt de vos vertus, tout Israël charmé...

HÉRODE

Eh! croyez-vous encor que je puisse être aimé?

MAZAËL

Seigneur, à vos desseins Zarès toujours fidèle,

---

119   MS1: Ce destin
120   MS1, 25CH, 25X, 25A, 26H, Sohème texts: d'horreur,
120a-132   MS1, 25CH, 25X, 26H: [absent]
131   W70L: tout le peuple charmé
133-144   Sohème texts: [absent; no scene change]

---

[12] Cf. M24, 198 : 'Seigneur, m'est-il permis de parler à mon roi?'
[13] In a letter to Damilaville in 1763 Voltaire declined a suggestion that this line
should be submitted for inscription on a statue of Louis XV created for the city of
Reims by Pigalle: 'Je conviens que ce vers [...] figurerait très bien au bas de la statue
de Louis 15, mais je ne saurais me résoudre ni à me citer ni à me piller' (D11426).
[14] Lines 129-30: cf. M24, 77-78: 'C'est lui qui, le premier, écarta de son maître /
Des cœurs infortunés qui vous cherchaient peut-être.'

Renvoyé près de vous, et plein du même zèle,
De la part de Salome attend pour vous parler.   135

HÉRODE

Quoi! tous deux sans relâche, ils veulent m'accabler!
Que jamais devant moi ce monstre ne paraisse.
Je l'ai trop écouté... Sortez tous; qu'on me laisse.
Ciel! qui pourra calmer un trouble si cruel?...
Demeurez Idamas, demeurez Mazaël.   140

SCÈNE V

HÉRODE, MAZAËL, IDAMAS

HÉRODE

Eh bien! voilà ce roi si fier et si terrible,
Ce roi dont on craignait le courage inflexible;
Qui sut vaincre et régner: qui sut briser ses fers;
Et dont la politique étonna l'univers.
Qu'Hérode est aujourd'hui différent de lui-même!   145

MAZAËL

Tout adore à l'envi votre grandeur suprême.

---

134 w40, w46, w48d, w52, w56, w57g, w57p, w64gv, w68v, w70lv,
w75gv, kv: d'un même
135 25x, 26h: attend à vous
137 25x, 26h: jamais à mes yeux ce
140 msi, 25ch, 25x, 26h: Ne m'abandonnez pas,
     25x, 26h: [with stage direction] (*sa suite étant sortie*)
140a-c 25x, 26h: [absent; no new scene]
140a msi, 25ch, w46: *SCÈNE IV*
140b msi, 25ch: HÉRODE, MAZAËL
143 msi: régner et sut
146 msi, 25ch, 25x, 26h: Tout admire à

IDAMAS

Un seul cœur vous résiste, et l'on peut le gagner.

HÉRODE

Non, je suis un barbare, indigne de régner.

IDAMAS

Votre douleur est juste, et si pour Mariamne...

HÉRODE

Et c'est ce nom fatal, hélas! qui me condamne;   150
C'est ce nom qui reproche à mon cœur agité,
L'excès de ma faiblesse, et de ma cruauté.

MAZAËL

Seigneur, votre clémence augmente encor sa haine.
Elle fuit votre vue.

HÉRODE

Ah! j'ai cherché la sienne. [15]

MAZAËL

Qui, vous, seigneur?

HÉRODE

Eh quoi! mes transports furieux,   155
Ces pleurs, que mes remords arrachent de mes yeux,

147   MS1, 25CH, 25X, 26H: [*give this line to Mazaël*] Un seul cœur se [MS1: s'y]
refuse, et s'il faut le gagner...
149   MS1, 25CH, 25X, 26H: [*give this line to Mazaël*] Quoi! Seigneur, se peut-il
que déjà Mariamne...
150   MS1: fatal qui déjà me
153   MS2 [<β>], Sohème texts: Elle sera toujours inflexible en sa haine.
154   25X, 26H: Et j'ai

[15] Hérode's words in this line had appeared in M24, 150.

Ce changement soudain, cette douleur mortelle,
Tout ne te dit-il pas que je viens d'auprès d'elle?
Toujours troublé, toujours plein de haine et d'amour,
J'ai trompé, pour la voir, une importune cour.   160
Quelle entrevue! ô cieux! quels combats! quel supplice!
Dans ses yeux indignés, j'ai lu mon injustice.
Ses regards inquiets n'osaient tomber sur moi;
Et tout, jusqu'à mes pleurs, augmentait son effroi.

MAZAËL

Seigneur, vous le voyez, sa haine envenimée,   165
Jamais par vos bontés ne sera désarmée.
Vos respects dangereux nourrissent sa fierté.

HÉRODE

Elle me hait! ah Dieu! je l'ai trop mérité. [16]
Je lui pardonne, hélas! dans le sort qui l'accable,
De haïr à ce point un époux si coupable. [17]   170

MAZAËL

Vous, coupable? eh! seigneur, pouvez-vous oublier
Ce que la reine a fait, pour vous justifier?

158   25X, 26H: d'avec elle
161   25CH: ô Dieux! quels combats! quels supplices!
      MS1, 25X, 26H: ô Ciel!
      MS1: quel combat!
162   25CH, 25X, 26H: j'ai vu mon
166   MS1, 25CH: ne peut être calmée
169   25CH: dans l'excès qui
      MS2: qui m'accable
171   25CH: coupable? Ah! Seigneur
      25X, 26H: coupable? Seigneur
      MS1: pouviez-vous
172   25X, 26H: Ce qu'elle-même a

[16] Lines 163-68 had appeared in M24, 173-78, except that Mazaël's first line (165) had been: 'Sans doute elle vous hait, sa haine envenimée.'
[17] Lines 169-70 had appeared in M24, 183-84.

Ses mépris outrageants, sa superbe colère,
Ses desseins contre vous, les complots de son père?
Le sang qui la forma, fut un sang ennemi.   175
Le dangereux Hircan vous eût toujours trahi:
Et des Asmonéens la brigue était si forte,
Que sans un coup d'état vous n'auriez pu...

              HÉRODE

                              N'importe.
Hircan était son père; il fallait l'épargner.
Mais je n'écoutai rien que la soif de régner.   180
Ma politique affreuse a perdu sa famille.
J'ai fait périr le père; et j'ai proscrit la fille:
J'ai voulu la haïr; j'ai trop su l'opprimer.
Le ciel pour m'en punir, me condamne à l'aimer.
Mes rigueurs, ses chagrins, la perte de son père,   185

174   25X, 26H: vous, le meurtre de
176   MS1: Ce dangereux
180   MS1, 25CH, 25X, 25A, 26H: n'écoutais rien
183   25CH: j'ai voulu l'opprimer
      25X, 26H: trop pu l'opprimer
184-185   MS2, 30, 31-K:

                                        l'aimer.
              IDAMAS
      Seigneur, daignez m'en croire; une juste tendresse
      Devient une vertu, loin d'être une faiblesse:
      Digne de tant de biens que le ciel vous a faits,
      Mettez votre amour même au rang de ses [MS2: vos] bienfaits.   5
              HÉRODE
      Hircan, mânes sacrés, fureurs que je déteste!
              IDAMAS
      Perdez-en pour jamais le souvenir funeste.
              MAZAËL
      Puisse la Reine aussi l'oublier comme vous.
              HÉRODE
      O père infortuné! plus malheureux époux!
      Tant d'horreurs, tant de sang, le meurtre de son père,   10
184   MS1, 25CH, 25X, 26H: me punir

Les maux que je lui fais me la rendent plus chère. [18]
Si son cœur,... si sa foi,... mais c'est trop différer.
Idamas, en un mot, je veux tout réparer.
Va la trouver; dis-lui que mon âme asservie,
Met à ses pieds mon trône, et ma gloire et ma vie. [19]　　190
Je veux dans ses enfants choisir un successeur.
Des maux qu'elle a soufferts, elle accuse ma sœur: [20]
C'en est assez. Ma sœur, aujourd'hui renvoyée,
A ce cher intérêt sera sacrifiée.
Je laisse à Mariamne un pouvoir absolu.　　195

MAZAËL

Quoi! seigneur, vous voulez...

HÉRODE

　　　　　　　　Oui, je l'ai résolu. [21]
Oui, mon cœur désormais la voit, la considère,
Comme un présent des cieux, qu'il faut que je révère.
Que ne peut point sur moi l'amour qui m'a vaincu!
A Mariamne, enfin, je devrai ma vertu.　　200
Il le faut avouer: on m'a vu dans l'Asie,
Régner avec éclat, mais avec barbarie.

187　MS1, 25CH, 25X, 26H: Si sa foi, si son cœur... mais
188　MS1, 25CH, 25X, 26H: Mazaël, en
198　MS1, 25CH: des Dieux,
201　25X: Il te faut
　　26H: Il faut te l'avouer

---

[18] Lines 184-86: cf. M24, 222-24: 'Le ciel pour m'en punir me condamne à l'aimer. / Les chagrins, sa prison, la perte de son père, / Les maux que je lui fais me la rendent plus chère.'

[19] Apart from the first word in 188, which had been 'Mariamne', lines 188-90 had appeared in M24, 226-28.

[20] This line had appeared in M24, 229.

[21] Lines 193-96 had appeared in M24, 23-34, with 'A ces chers intérêts' in line 194.

Craint, respecté du peuple, admiré, mais haï;[22]
J'ai des adorateurs, et n'ai pas un ami.
Ma sœur, que trop longtemps mon cœur a daigné croire,   205
Ma sœur n'aima jamais ma véritable gloire.
Plus cruelle que moi dans ses sanglants projets,
Sa main faisait couler le sang de mes sujets,
Les accablait du poids de mon sceptre terrible:
Tandis qu'à leurs douleurs Mariamne sensible,   210
S'occupant de leur peine, et s'oubliant pour eux,
Portait à son époux les pleurs des malheureux.
C'en est fait. Je prétends, plus juste et moins sévère,
Par le bonheur public, essayer de lui plaire.
Sion va respirer sous un règne plus doux.   215
Mariamne a changé le cœur de son époux.
Mes mains loin de mon trône écartant les alarmes,
Des peuples opprimés vont essuyer les larmes.[23]
Je veux sur mes sujets régner en citoyen,
Et gagner tous les cœurs pour mériter le sien.   220

208   25CH: main a fait couler
210   MS1, MS2: leur douleur
        25X, 26H: Tandis que Mariamne à leur douleur sensible
211   MS1: S'occupait de leur peine, intercédant pour eux,
        25CH: S'occupant de leur peine, intercédant pour eux
        25X, 26H: S'occupait de leurs peines, intercédait pour eux,
215-218   MS2: [*Lekain adds these lines later, in smaller writing. Later again, they
are crossed out in red.*]
215   MS1: Si on va
        Sohème texts: L'Etat va
217   MS1: Mes mains, dessus mon trône écoutant les alarmes,
        25X, 26H: trône éloignant les

[22] Lines 201-203: cf. M24, 33-35: 'On vous a vu longtemps respecté dans l'Asie, /
Régner avec éclat, mais avec barbarie. / Craint de tous vos sujets, admiré mais haï'.
[23] Lekain did not include these lines (215-18) in the original of his transcript of the
role of Hérode (MS2), but added them later, in smaller writing, between lines 214
and 219. Later again they were crossed out in red. These facts may betray the actor's
successive hesitations with regard to this passage, suggesting that he first excluded
it, then inserted it, and finally omitted it from his performances of the role.

Va la trouver, te dis-je; et surtout, à sa vue,
Peins bien le repentir de mon âme éperdue.
Dis-lui que mes remords égalent ma fureur.
Va, cours, vole, et reviens. Que vois-je! C'est ma sœur. [24]
   (*à Mazaël*)
Sortez... Termine, ô ciel, les chagrins de ma vie.   225

SCÈNE VI

HÉRODE, SALOME

SALOME

Hé bien? vous avez vu votre chère ennemie?
Avez-vous essuyé des outrages nouveaux?

224-227 MSI, 25CII, 25X, 26II:
> Va, cours, vole, et reviens. Que vois-je, c'est ma sœur.
> *SCÈNE V* / HÉRODE, SALOME
> SALOME
> Eh bien! avez vous vu cette reine si fière?
> A-t-elle avec bonté reçu votre prière?
> Avez-vous essuyé des [M25X M26H: quelqu'] outrages nouveaux?

225 Sohème texts: Sortez... A quels chagrins [K: A quel chagrin] ma vie est condamnée!

MS2: <β> Sortez. A quels chagrins ma Vie est condamnée

225a W46: *SCÈNE V*

225a-228 MS2 (pasted in), Sohème texts:
> *SCÈNE V* / HÉRODE, SALOME
> SALOME
> Je les partage tous: mais je suis étonnée
> Que la Reine et Sohème évitant votre aspect,
> Montrent si peu de zèle, et si peu de respect.
> HÉRODE
> L'un m'offense, il est vrai, – mais l'autre est [MS2: vrai: l'autre était] excusable;

[24] Lines 221-24 had appeared in M24, 235-38, with 'Juste ciel' in place of 'Que vois-je?' in line 224. Line 224 is close to bathos when set alongside Corneille, *Le Cid*, I.iv.290 (Don Diègue to Don Rodrigue): 'Va, cours, vole et nous venge.'

HÉRODE

Madame, il n'est plus temps d'appesantir mes maux.
Je cherche à les finir. Ma rigueur implacable,
En me rendant plus craint, m'a fait plus misérable.   230
Assez et trop longtemps sur ma triste maison,
La vengeance et la haine ont versé leur poison.
De la reine et de vous, les discordes cruelles,
Seraient de mes tourments les sources éternelles.
Ma sœur, pour mon repos, pour vous, pour toutes deux,   235
Eloignez-vous; partez; fuyez ces tristes lieux;
Il le faut.

SALOME

Ciel, qu'entends-je? ah! fatale ennemie!

HÉRODE

Un roi vous le commande, un frère vous en prie.
Que puisse désormais ce frère malheureux,
N'avoir point à donner d'ordre plus rigoureux,   240

N'en parlons plus.
SALOME
           Sohème à vos yeux condamnable,   5
A toujours de la Reine allumé le courroux.
HÉRODE
Ah! trop d'horreurs enfin se répandent sur nous;
229 MS1: finir. Mariamne implacable
230 25X, 26H: [absent]
231-232 26H: [lines inverted]
234 25X, 26H: tourments des sources
236 MS1, 25X, 26H: Eloignez-vous, partez, quittez ces tristes lieux;
     25CH: De grâce éloignez-vous, partez, quittez ces lieux;
     Sohème texts: Séparons-nous, quittez ce palais malheureux;
     MS2: <β> ↑Separons nous quittés ce palais malheureux
239 MS1: Ah! puisse
240 25X, 26H: d'ordres plus

N'avoir plus sur les miens de vengeances à prendre,
De soupçons à former, ni de sang à répandre.
Ne persécutez plus mes jours trop agités.
Murmurez; plaignez-vous, plaignez-moi: mais partez.

SALOME

Moi, seigneur, je n'ai point de plaintes à vous faire.   245
Vous croyez mon exil, et juste et nécessaire;
A vos moindres désirs instruite à consentir,
Lorsque vous commandez, je ne sais qu'obéir.
Vous ne me verrez point, sensible à mon injure,
Attester devant vous le sang et la nature.   250
Sa voix trop rarement se fait entendre aux rois,
Et près des passions le sang n'a point de droits.
Je ne vous vante plus cette amitié sincère,
Dont le zèle aujourd'hui commence à vous déplaire.
Je rappelle encor moins mes services passés.   255
Je vois trop qu'un regard les a tous effacés.
Mais avez-vous pensé que Mariamne oublie,
Qu'Hérode en ce jour même attenta sur sa vie?
Vous, qu'elle craint toujours, ne la craignez-vous plus?
Ses vœux, ses sentiments, vous sont-ils inconnus?   260

---

241 25CH: plus désormais de
     MS2: plus sur les <miens> ⁺siens⁺ de
     K: les siens de
242 25CH: former, et de
243 MS1, 25CH, 25X, 26H: mes [MS1: des] sens trop
245 MS1, 25X, 26H: Non, Seigneur, je n'ai plus [MS1: point] de
     25CH: Mon Seigneur,
250 25CH: le rang et
252 25CH: Auprès des
     MS1, 25CH, 25X, 26H: n'a plus de
255 25CH: moins les services
258 MS1: Qu'Hérode ce jour même attente sur
     25X, 26H: attentât sur
     MS2⁺, Sohème texts: Cet ordre d'un époux donné contre sa vie?

Qui préviendra jamais, par des avis utiles,
De son cœur outragé les vengeances faciles?
Quels yeux intéressés à veiller sur vos jours,
Pourront de ses complots démêler les détours?
Son courroux aura-t-il quelque frein qui l'arrête?   265
Et pensez-vous enfin, que lorsque votre tête
Sera par vos soins même exposée à ses coups,
L'amour qui vous séduit, lui parlera pour vous?
Quoi donc! tant de mépris, cette horreur inhumaine...

HÉRODE

Ah! laissez-moi douter un moment de sa haine.   270
Laissez-moi me flatter de regagner son cœur.
Ne me détrompez point, respectez mon erreur.
Je veux croire, et je crois que votre haine altière,
Entre la reine et moi mettait une barrière;
Que vous seule excitiez son courroux endurci,   275
Et que sans vous, enfin, j'eusse été moins haï.

261   25CH: Qui pourra désarmer par
265   25CH, 26H: quelque soin qui
269-271   25CH:
           Et croyez-vous devoir ce triomphe à sa haine?
           Quoi! donc tant de mépris, cette horreur inhumaine?
                          HÉRODE
           Laissez-moi
269   25X, 26H: cette haine inhumaine
274   25CH: mettait
       25X, 26H: moi a mis une
275   25CH: [*absent*]
       MS1, 25X, 26H: seule aigrissez son
       MS2: seule aigrissiez son
       W48D, W51, W52, W56, W57G, W57P, Sohème texts: Que par vos cruautés
son cœur s'est endurci,
276   25X, 26H: je serais moins
       25CH: moins trahi

260

SALOME

Si vous pouviez savoir, si vous pouviez comprendre
A quel point...

HÉRODE

Non, ma sœur, je ne veux rien entendre.
Mariamne, à son gré peut menacer mes jours:
Ils me sont odieux; qu'elle en tranche le cours.   280
Je périrai du moins d'une main qui m'est chère.

SALOME

Ah! c'est trop l'épargner, vous tromper et me taire.
Je m'expose à me perdre, et cherche à vous servir;
Et je vais vous parler, dussiez-vous m'en punir.
Epoux infortuné! qu'un vil amour surmonte,   285
Connaissez Mariamne, et voyez votre honte.
C'est peu des fiers dédains dont son cœur est armé,
C'est peu de vous haïr;... un autre en est aimé.

HÉRODE

Un autre en est aimé! Pouvez-vous bien, barbare,
Soupçonner devant moi la vertu la plus rare?   290
Que dis-je? ah, malheureux! je sens qu'au fond du cœur

281   25X, 26II: périrais
290   25X, 26H: vertu si rare
291-292   MS2, 30, 31-K:
  Ma sœur, c'est donc ainsi que vous m'assassinez?
  Laissez-vous pour adieux ces traits empoisonnés?
  Ces flambeaux de discorde, et la honte et la rage,
  Qui de mon cœur jaloux sont l'horrible partage?
  Mariamne... mais non, je ne veux rien savoir,   5
  Vos conseils sur mon âme ont eu trop de pouvoir;
  Je vous ai longtemps crue, et les cieux m'en punissent;
  Mon sort était d'aimer des cœurs qui me haïssent;
  Oui, c'est moi seul ici que vous persécutez.

Je n'écoute que trop ce soupçon plein d'horreur.
Un autre en est aimé! Nommez-moi donc, cruelle,
Le sang que doit verser ma vengeance nouvelle.
Poursuivez votre ouvrage. Achevez mon malheur.   295

SALOME

Vous le voulez...

HÉRODE

Parlez, je l'ordonne.

SALOME
Hé bien donc, loin de vous...
HÉRODE
                    Non, Madame, arrêtez...   10
293   MS2, Sohème texts: aimé! Montrez-moi
296   MS2, 30, 31-K:
       Puisque vous le voulez...
                    HÉRODE
                    Frappe, voilà mon cœur.
       Dis-moi qui m'a trahi; mais quoi qu'il en puisse être,
       Songe que cette main t'en punira peut-être:
       Oui, je te punirai de m'ôter mon [MS2: cette] erreur.
       Parle, à ce prix...
                    SALOME
                    N'importe.
                    HÉRODE
                    Eh bien...
                    SALOME
                                        C'est   5

262

SCÈNE VII

HÉRODE, SALOME, MAZAËL

MAZAËL

Ah! seigneur,
Venez, ne souffrez pas que ce crime s'achève:
Votre épouse vous fuit; et Varus vous l'enlève.

HÉRODE

Mariamne! Varus! où suis-je? justes cieux!

MAZAËL

Varus et ses soldats sont sortis de ces lieux.　　　　300
Il prépare à l'instant cette indigne retraite;
Il place auprès des murs une escorte secrète.
Mariamne l'attend pour sortir du palais;

296b-c　25X, 26H: [absent; no new scene]
296b　MS1, 25CH, Sohème texts: SCÈNE VI
296c　MS1: HÉRODE, SALOME, UN HÉBREUX
296d　MS1: L HÉBREUX
　　　　25X, 26H: [with stage direction] (Mazaël arrive.)
298　Sohème texts: et Sohème vous
　　　　MS2: <Varus> ↑Soheme
299　25X: Mariamne et Varus, où
　　　　Sohème texts: Mariamne! Sohème! où
　　　　MS1, 25CH, 25X, 26H: justes Dieux!
　　　　MS2: <Varus> ↑Soheme
299a　MS1: L'HÉBREUX
300-301　Sohème texts:
　　　　Sa mère, ses enfants quittaient déjà ces lieux.
　　　　Sohème a préparé cette indigne retraite;
300　MS1, 25CH, 25X, 26H: et les [MS1: ses] Romains sont
302　25CH: des mers une
　　　　MS1, 25X, 26H: place autour des
　　　　K: Il a près de ces murs

Et vous allez, seigneur, la perdre pour jamais.[25]

HÉRODE

Ah! le charme est rompu; le jour, enfin, m'éclaire.   305
Venez; à son courroux, connaissez votre frère.
Surprenons l'infidèle: et vous allez juger,
S'il est encor Hérode, et s'il sait se venger.

Fin du troisième acte.

304   MS1, 25CH: allez enfin la
306   25CH: Venez à son courroux connaître votre frère.

[25] MS1, which gives lines 300-304 to 'un Hébreux' who has no other role in the play, attests an alternative solution to the difficulty which arose for Voltaire, in the first run version of M25, from the use of Mazaël twice over, in the concluding scenes of both acts III and IV, to bring the news which precipitates Hérode's violent change of feeling. The similarity in the endings of these two acts had been criticised by Nadal and others. Voltaire's response in 25P was to introduce variation by creating the role of Le Garde as the messenger of bad news at the end of act IV (see Introduction, section 4.iv). But MS1 suggests that he may have experimented also with the converse solution of bringing in the alternative voice at the conclusion of act III.

ACTE IV

SCÈNE PREMIÈRE

SALOME, MAZAËL

MAZAËL

Jamais, je l'avouerai, plus heureuse apparence,
N'a d'un mensonge adroit soutenu la prudence:
Ma bouche auprès d'Hérode avec dextérité,
Confondait l'artifice avec la vérité.
Mais lorsque sans retour Mariamne est perdue,   5
Quand la faveur d'Hérode à vos vœux est rendue,
Dans ces sombres chagrins, qui peut donc vous plonger?
Madame; en se vengeant, le roi va vous venger.
Sa fureur est au comble: et moi-même je n'ose
Regarder sans effroi les malheurs que je cause.   10
Vous avez vu tantôt ce spectacle inhumain,
Ces esclaves tremblants, égorgés de sa main,
Près de leurs corps sanglants, la reine évanouie,
Le roi, le bras levé, prêt à trancher sa vie,
Ses fils baignés de pleurs, embrassant ses genoux,   15
Et présentant leur tête au-devant de ses coups.

1-4 Sohème texts (w64G, w68, w70G, w70L, w75G, K): [*absent*]
1   MS1, 25X, 26H: heureuse espérance
5   Sohème texts: Quoi! lorsque
6   MS1, 25CH, 25X, 26H: Que la
     MS1, 25X: vos yeux est
8   MS1: L'esprit du Roi ne peut pour la Reine changer.
     25X, 26H: Madame? En vous vengeant le roi veut se venger.
9   25X: La fureur
16   W40, W42, W46, W48D, W51, W52, W57P: En présentant
     MS1: leurs têtes

Que vouliez-vous de plus? que craignez-vous encore?

SALOME

Je crains le roi; je crains ces charmes qu'il adore,
Ce bras prompt à punir, prompt à se désarmer,
Cette colère, enfin, facile à s'enflammer;   20
Mais qui toujours douteuse, et toujours aveuglée,
En ces transports soudains s'est peut-être exhalée.
Mazaël, mon triomphe est encore incertain.
J'ai deux fois en un jour vu changer mon destin;
Deux fois j'ai vu l'amour succéder à la haine;   25
Et nous sommes perdus, s'il voit encor la reine.

17   MSI, 25CH, 25X, 26H: Que voulez-vous
18   MSI, 25CH, 25X, 26H: crains les charmes
19   25X, 26H: Son bras
22   MSI, 25CH, 25X, 26H: Dans ses transports
      25CH: peut-être exaltée
23-24 Sohème texts:
      Quel fruit me revient-il de ses emportements?
      Sohème a-t-il pour moi de plus doux sentiments?
      Il me hait encor plus; et mon malheureux frère,
      Forcé de se venger d'une épouse [K85: femme] adultère,
      Semble me reprocher sa honte et son malheur.   5
      Il voudrait pardonner dans le fond de son cœur:
      Il gémit en secret de perdre ce qu'il aime;
      Il voudrait, s'il se peut, ne punir que moi-même.
      Mon funeste triomphe est encor incertain. [W70L: Il est faible et tyran; son
      cœur est incertain.]
      J'ai   10
24   MSI, 25CH: fois dans un
25   MSI, 25CH, 25X, 26H: J'ai déjà vu
      25CH: Tout est à redouter du penchant qui l'entraîne,

SCÈNE II

HÉRODE, SALOME, MAZAËL, GARDES

MAZAËL

Il vient: de quels ennuis son front paraît chargé!

26b   MS1, 25CH, 25X, 26H: HÉRODE, SALOME, MAZAËL

27   MS1, 25CII, 25X, 26H: [*last line of scene i*; 25CH: *gives this line to Salome*]
      25X: paraît changé

27-28   30, 31, other Varus texts:
      Il vient: de quelle horreur il paraît agité!
               SALOME
      Seigneur, votre vengeance est-elle en sûreté?
               MAZAËL
      Me préserve le ciel que ma voix téméraire,
      D'un Roi clément et sage irritant la colère,
      Ose se faire entendre entre la Reine et lui.   5
      Mais, Seigneur, contre vous, Varus est son appui.
      Non, ne vous vengez point, mais sauvez votre vie,
      Prévenez de Varus l'indiscrète furie:
      Ce superbe préteur, ardent à tout tenter,
      Se fait une vertu de vous persécuter.   10
      W64GV,[1] W68V, W70GV, W70LV, W75CV, KV [*lines 7 10 only*]

27-31   MS2, Sohème texts:
      Il vient: de quelle horreur il paraît agité!
               SALOME
      Seigneur, votre vengeance est-elle en sûreté?
               MAZAËL
      Me préserve le ciel que ma voix téméraire,
      D'un Roi clément et sage irritant la colère,
      Ose se faire entendre, entre la Reine et lui!   5
      Mais, Seigneur, contre vous Sohème est son appui.
      Non, ne vous vengez point: mais veillez sur vous-même.
      Redoutez ses complots et la main de Sohème.
               HÉRODE
      Ah! je ne le crains point.

[1] The sigla w64Gv etc. indicate printed variants in the Sohème texts.

SALOME

Eh bien, seigneur, enfin, n'êtes-vous pas vengé?

HÉRODE

Ah! ma sœur, à quel point ma flamme était trahie!
Venez contre une ingrate animer ma furie.   30
De ma douleur mortelle, ayez quelque pitié.
Mon cœur n'attend plus rien que de votre amitié.
Hélas! plein d'une erreur, trop fatale, et trop chère,
Je vous sacrifiais au seul soin de lui plaire;
Je vous comptais déjà parmi mes ennemis.   35
Je punissais sur vous sa haine et ses mépris.
Ah! j'atteste à vos yeux ma tendresse outragée,
Qu'avant la fin du jour vous en serez vengée.
Je veux, surtout, je veux, dans ma juste fureur,

MAZAËL

Seigneur, n'en doutez pas.
De l'adultère au meurtre il n'est souvent qu'un pas.   10

HÉRODE

Que dites-vous?

MAZAËL

Sohème incapable de feindre,
Fut de vos ennemis toujours le plus à craindre.
Ceux dont il s'assura le coupable secours,
Ont parlé hautement d'attenter à vos jours.

HÉRODE

Mariamne me hait, c'est là son plus grand crime.   15
Ma sœur, vous approuvez la fureur qui m'anime:
Vous voyez mes chagrins, vous en avez pitié.

30 MSI: contre l'ingrate
    25CH, 25X, 26H: ingrate exciter ma
33 25CH: d'une horreur,
34 25CH: au bonheur de
36 25CH, 25A: et son mépris

268

La punir du pouvoir qu'elle avait sur mon cœur.[2]   40
Hélas! jamais ce cœur ne brûla que pour elle.
J'aimai, je détestai, j'adorai l'infidèle.
Et toi, Varus, et toi, faudra-t-il que ma main,
Respecte ici ton crime et le sang d'un Romain?
Non, je te punirai dans un autre toi-même.   45
Tu verras cet objet, qui m'abhorre, et qui t'aime,
Cet objet à mon cœur jadis si précieux,
Dans l'horreur des tourments expirant à tes yeux.
Que sur toi, s'il se peut, tout son sang rejaillisse.
Tu l'aimes, il suffit, sa mort est ton supplice.   50
Mais... croyez-vous qu'Auguste approuve ma rigueur?

40   25X: qu'elle aurait sur
42   25CH: J'aimai, j'idolâtrai, j'adorai
       25X, 26H: J'aimais et je déteste à présent l'infidèle,
43 45 MS2 <β>, Sohème texts:
       Et toi, Sohème, et toi, ne crois pas m'échapper,
       Avant le coup mortel dont je dois te frapper.
       Va, je
46   25X, 26H: qui t'adore et
48   25X, 26H: expirante
49   Sohème texts: toi, sous mes coups, tout
       MS2: <s'il se peut> ⌐sous mes coups⌐
50-59 Sohème texts:
                           supplice.
                    MAZAËL
       Ménagez, croyez-moi, des moments précieux;
51-59 MS1, 25CH, 25X, 26H:
       Allez de ma vengeance ordonner [MS1: ordonnons] les apprêts.
                    SALOME
       Je n'envisage ici que vos seuls intérêts,
       Seigneur, votre vengeance est nécessaire et juste,
       Et vous aurez l'aveu des Romains et d'Auguste.
                    MAZAËL
       Ménagez cependant [25X, 26H: Cependant ménagez] ces instants [MS1:
       moments] précieux,

[2] Cf. Roxane's words in Racine, *Bajazet*, IV.iv.1243-46: 'Je saurai bien toujours
trouver le moment / De punir, s'il le faut, la rivale et l'amant: / Dans ma juste
fureur observant le perfide, / Je saurai le surprendre avec son Atalide.'

SALOME

Il la conseillerait. N'en doutez point, seigneur.
Auguste a des autels où le Romain l'adore;
Mais de ses ennemis le sang y fume encore.
Auguste à tous les rois a pris soin d'enseigner,   55
Comme il faut qu'on les craigne, et comme il faut régner. [3]
Imitez son exemple, assurez votre vie,
Tout condamne la reine, et tout vous justifie.

MAZAËL

Ménagez cependant des moments précieux: [4]
Et tandis que Varus est absent de ces lieux,   60
Que par lui, loin des murs, sa garde est disposée,
Saisissez, achevez une vengeance aisée.

SALOME

Mais, surtout, aux Hébreux, cachez votre douleur.
D'un spectacle funeste épargnez-vous l'horreur.
Loin de ces tristes lieux, témoins de votre outrage,   65

60   Sohème texts: que Sohème est
61   Sohème texts: est dispersée
63   Sohème texts: Mais au peuple, surtout, cachez
64   MSI, 25CH, 25X, 25A, 26H: spectacle odieux épargnez-vous [25X: épargnez-moi] l'honneur
65   25X, 26H: témoin de
       MSI: de cet outrage

[3] Lines 55-56: cf. M24, 59-60: 'Rome, dont vous voulez que je suive l'exemple, / Aux rois, qu'elle gouverne, a pris soin d'enseigner, / Comme il faut qu'on la craigne et comme il faut régner.' The change of pronoun from 'la' (M24) to 'les' (M25) alters considerably the meaning of these lines, from lessons in the fear of Rome given to client kings (M24) to lessons in the fear of their rulers to be given by those kings to their subjects (M25).
[4] Cf. *Artémire*, II.ii.56: 'Croyez-moi, ménageons ces instants.'

Fuyez de tant d'objets la douloureuse image.
Venez, seigneur, venez au fond de mon palais,
A vos esprits troublés, daignez rendre la paix.

HÉRODE

Non, ma sœur, laissez-moi la voir et la confondre.
Je veux l'entendre ici, la forcer à répondre: 70
Jouir du désespoir de son cœur accablé,

---

66   MS2, Sohème texts: d'affronts la
67-68   W52, W56, W57G, W57P, W64GV, W68V, W70GV, W70LV, W75GV, KV:
    Ne montrez qu'à des yeux éclairés et discrets
    Un cœur encor perce de ces indignes traits.
67-69   MS2, Sohème texts:

                         image.
              HÉRODE
    Je vois quel est son crime, et quel fut son projet.
    Je vois pour qui Sohème ainsi vous outrageait.
              SALOME
    Laissez mes intérêts; songez à votre offense.
              HÉRODE
    Elle avait jusqu'ici vécu dans l'innocence;   5
    Je ne lui reprochais que ses emportements,
    Cette audace opposée à tous mes sentiments,
    Ses mépris pour ma race, et ses altiers murmures.
    Du sang asmonéen j'essuyai trop d'injures.
    Mais a-t-elle en effet voulu mon déshonneur?   10
              SALOME
    Ecartez cette idee: oubliez-la, Seigneur,
    Calmez-vous.
              HÉRODE
          Non, je veux la voir et la confondre.
70   25X, 26H: forcer de répondre
71-72   MS2, W48D, W51, W52, W56, W57G, W57P, Sohème texts:
    Qu'elle tremble en voyant l'appareil du trépas;
    Qu'elle demande grâce, et ne l'obtienne pas.
71   25X, 26H: du vain espoir de

Et qu'au moins elle meure, après avoir tremblé. [5]

SALOME

Quoi! seigneur, vous voulez vous montrer à sa vue?

HÉRODE

Ah! ne redoutez rien. Sa perte est résolue.
Vainement l'infidèle espère en mon amour. 75
Mon cœur à la clémence est fermé sans retour.
Loin de craindre ces yeux, qui m'avaient trop su plaire,
Je sens que sa présence aigrira ma colère.
Gardes, que dans ces lieux on la fasse venir.
Je ne veux que la voir, l'entendre, et la punir. 80
Ma sœur, pour un moment, souffrez que je respire.
Qu'on appelle la reine. Et vous, qu'on se retire.

---

73   MS1, 25CH, 25X, 26H: vous offrir à
74   MS1: Sa mort est
75   25CH: Vainement elle espère en arrêter le cours,
76   25CH: fermé pour toujours
77   MS1, 25CH, 25X, 26H: craindre ses yeux
      MS1: m'avaient su trop plaire
81   MS1, 25CH, 25X, 26H: sœur, en un
82   MS1: [with stage direction] (Ils se retirent.)

---

[5] Lines 69-72: cf. Racine, *Bajazet*, IV.vi.1360-64 (Roxane to Acomat): 'Laissez-moi le plaisir de confondre l'ingrat. / Je veux voir son désordre, et jouir de sa honte. / Je perdrais ma vengeance en la rendant si prompte.'

SCÈNE III[6]

HÉRODE seul.

HÉRODE

Tu veux la voir, Hérode! à quoi te résous-tu?[7]
Conçois-tu les desseins de ton cœur éperdu?
Quoi? son crime à tes yeux n'est-il pas manifeste?   85
N'es-tu pas outragé? que t'importe le reste?
Quel fruit espères-tu de ce triste entretien?
Ton cœur peut-il douter des sentiments du sien?
Hélas! tu sais assez combien elle t'abhorre.
Tu prétends te venger! Pourquoi vit-elle encore?   90
Tu veux la voir! ah! lâche, indigne de régner,
Va soupirer près d'elle, et cours lui pardonner...
Va voir cette beauté, si longtemps adorée...
Non, elle périra; non, sa mort est jurée.
Vous serez répandu, sang de mes ennemis,   95

---

83   25X, 26H: Tu la veux voir
84   MSI, 25CH, 25X, 26H: Connais-tu les desseins [25CH: le dessein]
87   MSI, 25CH, 25X, 26H: Quel prix espères-tu
90   MSI: venger! D'où vient vit-elle
94   25CH: périra, et sa

---

[6] Although there are similar scenes in both Hardy (IV.2) and Tristan (IV.1), Hérode's description of his conflicting emotions in this monologue was probably derived from a passage in Josephus which recounts Herod's inner turmoil after being received with contemptuous hostility by Mariamne on his return from Octavian: 'Son extrême amour pour elle lui rendait ce mépris insupportable. Mais en même temps sa colère se trouvait tellement combattue par son affection, qu'il passait de la haine à l'amour, et de l'amour à la haine. Ainsi flottant entre ces deux passions il ne savait quel parti prendre' (*Histoire des Juifs*, xv.xi.576; *Jewish Antiquities*, xv, para.211).

[7] Cf. Roxane's speech in Racine's *Bajazet* expressing similar hesitations whether to punish or forgive (V.ii.1461-68).

Sang des Asmonéens, dans ses veines transmis,
Sang, qui me haïssez, et que mon cœur déteste.
Mais la voici. Grand Dieu! quel spectacle funeste!

SCÈNE IV [8]

MARIAMNE, HÉRODE, ÉLIZE, GARDES

ÉLIZE

Reprenez vos esprits, madame, c'est le roi. [9]

MARIAMNE

Où suis-je? où vais-je? ô Dieu! je me meurs... je le vois. [10]   100

---

96   MS1, 25X, 26H: Asmonéens, en scs
98   MS1: Grands Dieux!
98b   MS1: HÉRODE, MARIAMNE, ELISE, UNE SUIVANTE
      25CH: HÉRODE, MARIAMNE, PHÉDIME
      25X, 26H: HÉRODE, MARIAMNE, ÉLIZE
98c   25CH: PHÉDIME
100   MS1, 25CH, 25X, 26H: vais-je? Ah Dieux! je

---

[8] The movement of this and the following scenes may have its source in Josephus's account of a failed attempt at reconciliation after Herod's return from his interview with Antony. Salome accuses Mariamne of adultery, and this angers Herod against her. But when Mariamne convinces him of her innocence, Herod begs forgiveness. Mariamne then reveals her knowledge of his secret order for her death; Herod concludes at once that this proves her adultery, and anger sweeps over him once more (*Histoire des Juifs*, xv.iv.563-64; *Jewish Antiquities*, xv, para.81-87).

[9] Scene iv attracted much praise. To the testimonies noted in the Introduction we may add La Harpe's opinion concerning 'cette éloquente scène': 'c'est la seule où il y ait du mouvement et de l'effet'. La Harpe goes on however to deplore 'la faiblesse trop évidente des motifs qui font revenir Hérode de l'attendrissement à la fureur' (*Cours de Littérature ancienne et moderne*, ii.204).

[10] This line had been used in *Artémire*, IV.iv.7.

ACTE IV, SCÈNE IV

HÉRODE

D'où vient qu'à son aspect mes entrailles frémissent? [11]

MARIAMNE

Elize, soutiens-moi, mes forces s'affaiblissent.

ÉLIZE

Avançons.

MARIAMNE

Quel tourment!

HÉRODE

Que lui dirai-je? ô cieux!

MARIAMNE

Pourquoi m'ordonnez-vous de paraître à vos yeux?
Voulez-vous de vos mains m'ôter ce faible reste   105
D'une vie, à tous deux également funeste?
Vous le pouvez; frappez, le coup m'en sera doux:
Et c'est l'unique bien, que je tiendrai de vous. [12]

HÉRODE

Oui, je me vengerai, vous serez satisfaite.

101   MS1, MS2, 25CH, 25X, 26H: vient qu'en la voyant [MS2: <qu'en la
voyant> ↑β] mes
102   25CH: Phédime, soutiens-moi
102a 25CH: PHÉDIME
103   25X, 26H: [first hemistich absent]
      25CH, 25A: Quels tourments! Que lui dirai-je? ô Dieux! [line 103b absent]
      25X: dirai-je? Ah Cieux!
104   25X, 26H: paraître en ces lieux

[11] This line is cited in the Observations critiques (p.33) with the reading 'qu'en la
voyant' as in MS1, 25CH, 25X and 26H.
[12] Cf. Artémire, I.ii.173: 'Et c'est l'unique bien que j'ai reçu de lui.'

Mais parlez; défendez votre indigne retraite.   110
Pourquoi, lorsque mon cœur, si longtemps offensé,
Indulgent pour vous seule, oubliait le passé:
Lorsque vous partagiez mon empire et ma gloire,
Pourquoi prépariez-vous cette fuite si noire?
Quel dessein! quelle haine a pu vous posséder?   115

MARIAMNE

Ah! seigneur, est-ce à vous à me le demander?
Je ne veux point vous faire un reproche inutile.
Mais si loin de ces lieux j'ai cherché quelque asile,
Si Mariamne, enfin, pour la première fois,
Du pouvoir d'un époux méconnaissant les droits,   120
A voulu se soustraire à son obéissance;
Songez à tous ces rois, dont je tiens la naissance,
A mes périls présents, à mes malheurs passés, [13]
Et condamnez ma fuite après, si vous l'osez.

HÉRODE

Quoi! lorsqu'avec un traître un fol amour vous lie;   125
Quand Varus...

110 MS2: défendez cette indigne
111 MS2: longtemps abusé
113 25CH: vous partagez mon
114 25CH: prépariez-vous une fuite
115 25CH: [absent]
116 MS1, 25CH: vous de me
117 MS1: faire de reproche
120 25CH: époux méconnaissait les
121 25CH: J'ai voulu me soustraire
125 MS1, 25CH, 25X, 26H: lorsque pour un traître
126 MS2, Sohème texts: Quand Sohème
       25X, 26H: Arrêtez; c'est assez de

[13] Cf. *Artémire*, IV.iv.103: 'Ni mes périls presents, ni mes malheurs passés.'

MARIAMNE

Arrêtez; il suffit de ma vie.
D'un si cruel affront cessez de me couvrir.
Laissez-moi chez les morts descendre sans rougir.
N'oubliez pas du moins, qu'attachés l'un à l'autre,
L'hymen, qui nous unit, joint mon honneur au vôtre.[14]   130
Voilà mon cœur. Frappez. Mais en portant vos coups,
Respectez Mariamne, et même son époux.

HÉRODE

Perfide! il vous sied bien de prononcer encore
Ce nom qui vous condamne et qui me déshonore!
Vos coupables dédains vous accusent assez;   135
Et je crois tout de vous, si vous me haïssez.

MARIAMNE

Quand vous me condamnez, quand ma mort est certaine,
Que vous importe, hélas! ma tendresse, ou ma haine?
Et quel droit désormais avez-vous sur mon cœur,[15]
Vous qui l'avez rempli d'amertume et d'horreur;   140
Vous, qui depuis cinq ans insultez à mes larmes,
Qui marquez sans pitié mes jours par mes alarmes:
Vous, de tous mes parents destructeur odieux;
Vous, teint du sang d'un père, expirant à mes yeux?
Cruel! ah! si du moins votre fureur jalouse,   145
N'eût jamais attenté qu'aux jours de votre épouse;
Les cieux me sont témoins, que mon cœur tout à vous

139   25CH, 25X, 26H: droit avez-vous à présent sur
       MSI: Et quels droits avez-vous à prendre sur

[14] Lines 127-30: cf. *Artémire*, IV.iv.61-64: 'Mais l'hymen dont le nœud nous unit l'un à l'autre, / Tout malheureux qu'il est, joint mon honneur au vôtre: / Pourquoi d'un tel affront voulez-vous nous couvrir? / Laissez-moi chez les morts descendre sans rougir.'

[15] Cf. *Artémire*, V.iv.75: 'Et quel droit, en effet, aviez-vous sur mon cœur?'

Vous chérirait encore, en mourant par vos coups:
Mais qu'au moins mon trépas calme votre furie.
N'étendez point mes maux au delà de ma vie: 150
Prenez soin de mes fils, respectez votre sang;
Ne les punissez pas d'être nés dans mon flanc:
Hérode, ayez pour eux des entrailles de père.
Peut-être un jour, hélas! vous connaîtrez leur mère.
Vous plaindrez, mais trop tard, ce cœur infortuné,   155
Que seul dans l'univers, vous avez soupçonné;
Ce cœur qui n'a point su, trop superbe, peut-être,
Déguiser ses douleurs, et ménager un maître:
Mais qui jusqu'au tombeau conserva sa vertu,
Et qui vous eût aimé, si vous l'aviez voulu.   160

HÉRODE

Qu'ai-je entendu? quel charme, et quel pouvoir suprême,
Commande à ma colère, et m'arrache à moi-même?
Mariamne...

MARIAMNE

Cruel!

HÉRODE

... O faiblesse! ô fureur!

158   25CH: Déguiser sa douleur,
159   25CH: tombeau couronna sa
161   25CH: Qu'entends-je, ô Ciel! quel charme,
162-170   MSI, 25CH, 25X, 26H:
      Commande à ma fureur [25X: à mes fureurs], et m'arrache à moi-même?
      Mariamne, il est temps de calmer votre effroi,
      Puisque vous m'avez vu, vous triomphez de moi.
      Vous n'avez plus besoin d'excuse et de défense.
      L'amour que j'ai pour vous, vous tient lieu d'innocence.   5
      Je n'examine point un mystère odieux.
      Je veux tout oublier, je veux fermer les yeux.
      En vain j'avais dicté la sentence mortelle,
      Vivez, régnez sur moi, fussiez-vous criminelle.

MARIAMNE

De l'état où je suis voyez du moins l'horreur,
Otez-moi par pitié cette odieuse vie.   165

HÉRODE

Ah! la mienne à la vôtre est pour jamais unie.
C'en est fait: je me rends; bannissez votre effroi.
Puisque vous m'avez vu, vous triomphez de moi.
Vous n'avez plus besoin d'excuse et de défense,
Ma tendresse pour vous, vous tient lieu d'innocence. [16]   170
En est-ce assez, ô ciel! en est-ce assez, amour?
C'est moi qui vous implore, et qui tremble à mon tour.
Serez-vous aujourd'hui la seule inexorable?
Quand j'ai tout pardonné, serai-je encor coupable?
Mariamne, cessons de nous persécuter.   175
Nos cœurs ne sont-ils faits que pour se détester?
Nous faudra-t-il toujours redouter l'un et l'autre?
Finissons à la fois ma douleur et la vôtre [17]
Commençons sur nous-même à régner en ce jour.
Rendez-moi votre main, rendez-moi votre amour.   180

MARIAMNE

Vous demandez ma main! Juste ciel que j'implore,
Vous savez de quel sang la sienne fume encore.

---

171   MS1: ciel! en est-ce assez, d'amour?

[16] The new lines (163-70) in 25P retain from the earlier version the notion of
Hérode's surrender to Mariamne: overwhelmed by love, he is willing to lay aside all
suspicion. At the same time they introduce Mariamne's plea to Hérode to bring her
suffering to an end by putting her to death. Line 170 is cited in the *Observations
critiques* (p.35) with the reading 'L'amour que j'ai pour vous' as found in MS1, 25CH,
25X and 26H.
[17] Cf. Racine, *Bajazet*, III.iv.1005-1006 (Bajazet to Roxane): 'Madame, finissons
et mon trouble et le vôtre. / Ne nous affligeons point vainement l'un et l'autre.'

HÉRODE

Eh bien, j'ai fait périr et ton père et mon roi.
J'ai répandu son sang pour régner avec toi.
Ta haine en est le prix, ta haine est légitime: 185
Je n'en murmure point, je connais tout mon crime.
Que dis-je? son trépas, l'affront fait à tes fils,
Sont les moindres forfaits que mon cœur ait commis.
Hérode a jusqu'à toi porté sa barbarie;
Durant quelques moments je t'ai même haïe: 190
J'ai fait plus, ma fureur a pu te soupçonner;
Et l'effort des vertus est de me pardonner.
D'un trait si généreux, ton cœur seul est capable.
Plus Hérode à tes yeux doit paraître coupable,
Plus ta grandeur éclate à respecter en moi,   195
Ces nœuds infortunés qui m'unissent à toi.[18]
Tu vois où je m'emporte, et quelle est ma faiblesse.
Garde-toi d'abuser du trouble qui me presse.
Cher et cruel objet d'amour et de fureur,
Si du moins la pitié peut entrer dans ton cœur,   200
Calme l'affreux désordre où mon âme s'égare.
Tu détournes les yeux... Mariamne...

MARIAMNE

                                        Ah! barbare,
Un juste repentir produit-il vos transports?

183   25CH: et ton roi
184   25X, 26H: répandu ton sang
188   MSI, 25CH, 25X, 26H: cœur a commis
192   MSI: Mais l'effort
203   MSI, 25CH: produit-il tes transports

[18] Cf. *Artémire*, I.ii.161: 'Aux nœuds infortunés qui l'unissent à moi.'

Et pourrai-je en effet, compter sur vos remords? [19]

HÉRODE

Oui, tu peux tout sur moi, si j'amollis ta haine.   205
Hélas! ma cruauté, ma fureur inhumaine,
C'est toi qui dans mon cœur as su la rallumer.
Tu m'as rendu barbare, en cessant de m'aimer.
Si mon crime est affreux; que le remords l'efface.
Je te jure...

SCÈNE V

HÉRODE, MARIAMNE, ÉLIZE, UN GARDE

LE GARDE

Seigneur, Varus est dans la place.   210

204   MS1: pourrais-je
       MS1, 25CH: sur tes remords
205   MS1: tout de moi
206   MS1, 25CH, 25X, 26H: ma vengeance inhumaine
       MS2: <vengeance> †β
209   MS1: que mon remord l'efface
       MS2, 31-K: Que ton crime et le mien soient noyés dans mes larmes;
210b   MS1, 25CH, 25X, 26H: HÉRODE, MARIAMNE, MAZAËL
210c   MS1, 25CH, 25X, 26H: MAZAËL
210c-219   MS2, 31-K:
          LE GARDE [W42, W46: absent]
             Seigneur, tout le peuple est en armes.
       Dans le sang des bourreaux il vient de renverser
       L'échafaud que Salome a déjà fait dresser.
       Au peuple, à vos soldats, Varus commande [Sohème texts: Sohème parle;
       MS2: <Varus commande> Soheme parle] en maître:

---

[19] Lines 203-204 are cited in the *Observations critiques* (p.21) with the readings 'tes transports' and 'tes remords' found in MS1 and 25CH. Nadal's commentary alludes specifically to the *tutoiement* which Mariamne adopts in these lines, showing that the *attendrissement* of both characters has now reached its highest point.

Dans le sang des bourreaux il a fait renverser
L'échafaud que Salome a déjà fait dresser. [20]
A nos chefs étonnés, Varus commande en maître:
Il marche vers ces lieux, il vient, il va paraître.

HÉRODE

Quoi! dans le moment même où je suis à vos pieds,   215
Vous avez pu, perfide?...

MARIAMNE

                    Ah! seigneur, vous croiriez?...

HÉRODE

Qu'on la garde, soldats, qu'on l'ôte de ma vue.
(*On emmène Mariamne.*)
Vous: rassemblez ma garde en ces lieux répandue.

Il marche vers ces lieux, il vient, il va paraître.   5
HÉRODE
Quoi! dans le moment même où je suis à vos pieds,
Vous auriez pu, perfide?...
MARIAMNE
Ah! Seigneur, vous croiriez?...
HÉRODE
Tu veux ma mort! eh bien, je vais remplir ta haine.
Mais au moins dans ma tombe il faut que je t'entraîne,
Et [31, w38: En] qu'unis malgré toi... Qu'on la garde, soldats.//   10
213   MSI, 25CH, 25X, 26H: A vos chefs
217a   MSI: (*Elle sort.*)
      25CH, 25X, 26H: [*stage direction absent*]

---

[20] Lines 210d-212 are cited in the *Observations critiques* (p.21), where they are given to Mazäel, as in MSI, 25CH, 25X and 26H. Nadal's commentary alludes specifically to the role of Mazaël '[qui] vient encore troubler ce raccommodement et renfoncer au cœur d'Hérode un retour de tendresse et d'équité qui venait de s'exalter à la satisfaction de tout le monde'. See Introduction, section 4.iv, for the reasons which led Voltaire to introduce a new character to speak these lines.

Je ne connais plus Rome, et je vais de ce pas...

SCÈNE VI

HÉRODE, SALOME, GARDES

SALOME

Ah! mon frère, aux Hébreux ne vous présentez pas.   220
Le peuple soulevé demande votre vie. [21]
Le nom de Mariamne excite leur furie.
De vos mains, de ces lieux, ils viennent l'arracher.

HÉRODE

Allons. Ils me verront, et je cours les chercher.
Mais quoi! laisser ici la coupable impunie?   225

219   MS1, 25CH, 25X, 26H: plus rien,
219b   MS1, 25CH, 25X, 26H: HÉRODE, SALOME
       31-K: HÉRODE, MARIAMNE, SALOME, MAZAËL, ÉLIZE,
GARDES
220   W70L: Mon frère, aux citoyens ne
221   MS1, 25CH, 25X, 26H: peuple révolté demande
223   MS1, 25CH: De ces lieux, de nos mains,
       25X, 26H: Dans ces lieux de nos mains
224-225 MS2, 31-K:
       Allons, ils me verront, et je cours les chercher.
       De l'horreur où je suis tu répondras, cruelle.
       Ne l'abandonnez pas; ma sœur, veillez sur elle.
                    MARIAMNE
       Je ne crains point la mort, mais j'atteste les cieux.
                    MAZAËL
       Eh, Seigneur, les Romains [Sohème texts: Seigneur, vos ennemis]
       sont déjà sous vos yeux.   5
                    HÉRODE
       Courons... Mais quoi! laisser la coupable impunie!
224   25X, 26H: je vais les

[21] This line is cited in the *Observations critiques* (p.25) with the variant reading 'Le peuple révolté' as in MS1, 25CH, 25X and 26H.

Ah! je veux dans son sang laver sa perfidie.
Je veux,... j'ordonne... hélas! dans mon funeste sort,
Je ne puis rien résoudre, et vais chercher la mort.

Fin du quatrième acte.

ACTE V

SCÈNE PREMIÈRE

MARIAMNE, ÉLIZE

MARIAMNE

Eloignez-vous, soldats; daignez laisser du moins,
Votre reine, un moment, respirer sans témoins.
(*Les gardes se retirent au coin du théâtre.*)
Voilà donc, juste Dieu, quelle est ma destinée!
La splendeur de mon sang, la pourpre où je suis née,
Enfin ce qui semblait promettre à mes beaux jours,   5
D'un bonheur assuré, l'inaltérable cours;
Tout cela n'a donc fait que verser sur ma vie,
Le funeste poison, dont elle fut remplie.
Mes yeux n'ont jamais vu le jour qu'avec douleur.
L'instant où je naquis, commença mon malheur.   10
Mon berceau fut couvert du sang de ma patrie.
J'ai vu du peuple saint, la gloire anéantie.

c   MSI: MARIAMNE, SES GARDES
25CH: MARIAMNE *seule.*
25X, 26H: MARIAMNE, SUITE, GARDES
31-K: MARIAMNE, ÉLIZE, GARDES
1   MSI: Eloignez-vous de moi, daignez
2-3   MSI: [*adds*] *SCENE SECONDE* / MARIAMNE, ELIZE / MARIAMNE
2a   MSI, 25X, 26H: (*Les Gardes sortent.*)
3   MSI: justes Dieux,
9-12   31-K:
         O naissance! ô jeunesse! Et toi, triste beauté,
         Dont l'éclat dangereux enfla ma vanité,
         Flatteuse illusion dont je fus occupée,
         Vaine ombre de bonheur, que vous m'avez trompée!
9   25X, 26H: vu ce jour

285

Sous ce trône coupable, un éternel ennui,[1]
M'a creusé le tombeau, que l'on m'ouvre aujourd'hui.
Dans les profondes eaux j'ai vu périr mon frère,   15
Mon époux à mes yeux a massacré mon père:[2]
Par ce cruel époux, condamnée à périr,
Ma vertu me restait. On ose la flétrir.
Grand Dieu! dont les rigueurs éprouvent l'innocence,
Je ne demande point ton aide ou ta vengeance.   20
J'appris de mes aïeux, que je sais imiter,
A voir la mort sans crainte, et sans la mériter.
Je t'offre tout mon sang. Défends au moins ma gloire.
Commande à mes tyrans d'épargner ma mémoire.
Que le mensonge impur n'ose plus m'outrager.   25
Honorer la vertu, c'est assez la venger.
Mais quel tumulte affreux! quels cris! quelles alarmes!
Ce palais retentit du bruit confus des armes.
Hélas! j'en suis la cause, et l'on périt pour moi.
On enfonce la porte. Ah! qu'est-ce que je vois?   30

13   MS1, 25CH, 25X, 26H, K85: Sur ce
15   W48D-K: Dans les eaux du Jourdain j'ai
19   MS1, 25CH: dont la rigueur éprouve
20   MS1, 25CH, 25X, 26H: aide et ta
22   MS1: sans craindre,
25   25CH: Qu'un mensonge odieux n'ose plus l'outrager.
      MS1, 25X, 26H: [*with stage direction*] (*On entend un grand bruit.*)
26   25X, 26H: [*absent*]
      31, W38, W42: Que mon pays m'honore, au lieu de me venger. [W42 errata:
restores base text, 'suivant la bonne édition d'Amsterdam']
27   25X, 26H: affreux! quel bruit, quelles
28   MS1, 25X, 26H: bruit affreux des
30   MS1: L'on

---

[1] This line is quoted in the *Mercure extrait* of M25 with the variant reading of MS1,
25CH, 25X and 26H.
[2] This line is used in *Artémire*, I.i.73. See also II.186n.

SCÈNE II

MARIAMNE, VARUS, ÉLIZE, ALBIN,
SOLDATS D'HÉRODE, SOLDATS DE VARUS

VARUS

Fuyez, vils ennemis qui gardez votre reine;
Hébreux, disparaissez. Romains, qu'on les enchaîne.
(*Les gardes et soldats d'Hérode s'en vont.*)
Venez, reine, venez; secondez nos efforts. [3]
Suivez mes pas. Marchons dans la foule des morts.
A vos persécuteurs vous n'êtes plus livrée.   35
Ils n'ont pu de ces lieux me défendre l'entrée.
Dans son perfide sang Mazaël est plongé;
Et du moins à demi, mon bras vous a vengé. [4]

30a MSI: *SCÈNE TROISIÈME*
30b-c MSI: MARIAMNE, VARUS ET SA SUITE
        Sohème texts (and *passim* scene ii): SOHÈME [*in place of* VARUS]
AMMON [*in place of* ALBIN]
        25CH: MARIAMNE, VARUS
        25X, 26H: VARUS, MARIAMNE
32 Sohème texts: Lâches, disparaissez. Soldats,
32a MSI, 25CH, 25X, 26H: [*stage direction absent*]
        w38-K: *et les soldats*
33 MSI, 25CH, 25X, 26H: venez seconder [25CH: secondez] mes efforts
36 MSI, 25CH, 25X, 26H: me disputer l'entrée

[3] This line is cited in Nadal's *Observations critiques* (p.34) with the reading 'mes efforts' as in MSI, 25CH, 25X and 26H.
[4] Voltaire was taken to task by Nadal for failing to make the past participle *vengé* agree in gender with the preceding object pronoun *vous* designating Mariamne: 'M. de V... a-t-il oublié que Varus parle à Mariamne, et qu'il faut dire mon bras vous a vengée' (*Observations critiques*, p.34); see also La Harpe: 'La grammaire exige qu'en parlant à une femme, on dise mon bras vous a vengée. C'est une règle sans exception, et ces sortes de fautes sont sans excuses, parce qu'il n'y a ici ni licence poétique, ni hardiesse de style, ni aucune des raisons qui autorisent quelquefois à sacrifier la grammaire à la poésie. Voltaire a commis plusieurs fois cette meme faute' (*Cours de littérature ancienne et moderne*, ii.212).

D'un instant précieux saisissez l'avantage.
Mettez ce front auguste à l'abri de l'orage.   40
Avançons.

MARIAMNE

Non, seigneur; il ne m'est plus permis
D'accepter vos bontés contre mes ennemis,
Après l'affront cruel, et la tache trop noire,
Dont les soupçons d'Hérode ont offensé ma gloire;
Je les mériterais, si je pouvais souffrir,   45
Cet appui dangereux que vous venez m'offrir.
Je crains votre secours, et non sa barbarie.
Il est honteux pour moi de vous devoir la vie;
L'honneur m'en fait un crime. Il le faut expier,
Et j'attends le trépas pour me justifier.[5]   50

VARUS

Que faites-vous, hélas! malheureuse princesse!
Un moment peut vous perdre. On combat. Le temps presse.
Craignez encor Hérode, armé du désespoir.

MARIAMNE

Je ne crains que la honte, et je sais mon devoir.

---

39   25X, 26H: L'instant est précieux, saisissez l'avantage,
40   MSI, 25CH, 25X, 26H: à couvert de
41   MSI, 25CH, 25X, 26H: Avancez
     Sohème texts: Non, Sohème;
44   25CH: ont attaqué ma
47   25CH: secours, je crains sa
54   25CH: crains point la mort, et
     MSI, 25CH, 25X, 26H: je fais mon

---

[5] Cf. Corneille, *Cinna*, IV.v.1388 (Emilie to Maxime): 'Viens mourir avec moi pour te justifier.' Nadal claims that line 50 is 'une mauvaise copie' of this line.

VARUS

Quoi! faudra-t-il toujours que Varus vous offense?   55
Je vais donc, malgré vous, servir votre vengeance.
Je cours à ce tyran, qu'en vain vous respectez,
Je revole au combat, et mon bras...

MARIAMNE

                    Arrêtez.
Je déteste un triomphe, à mes yeux si coupable.
Seigneur, le sang d'Hérode est pour moi respectable.   60
C'est lui de qui les droits...

VARUS

                    L'ingrat les a perdus.

MARIAMNE

Par les nœuds les plus saints...

VARUS

                    Tous vos nœuds sont rompus.

MARIAMNE

Le devoir nous unit.

VARUS

                    Le crime vous sépare. [6]

54a-55   Sohème texts:

SOHÈME
    Faut-il qu'en vous servant, toujours je vous offense?
56   25x, 26h: donc de ce pas servir

---

[6] Lines 61-63: cf. *Artémire*, III.i.21-23: 'ARTÉMIRE / Les droits qu'il a sur moi... /
PHILOTAS / Tous ses droits sont perdus. / ARTÉMIRE / Je suis soumise à lui. /
PHILOTAS / Non, vous ne l'êtes plus. / ARTÉMIRE / Les dieux nous ont unis. /
PHILOTAS / Son crime vous dégage.'

N'arrêtez plus mes pas. Vengez-vous d'un barbare.
Sauvez tant de vertus...

MARIAMNE

Vous les déshonorez. 65

VARUS

Il va trancher vos jours.

MARIAMNE

Les siens me sont sacrés.[7]

VARUS

Il a souillé sa main du sang de votre père.

MARIAMNE

Je sais ce qu'il a fait, et ce que je dois faire.
De sa fureur ici j'attends les derniers traits,
Et ne prends point de lui l'exemple des forfaits. 70

VARUS

O courage! ô constance! ô cœur inébranlable!
Dieux! que tant de vertu rend Hérode coupable!
Plus vous me commandez de ne point vous servir,
Et plus je vous promets de vous désobéir.
Votre honneur s'en offense, et le mien me l'ordonne. 75
Il n'est rien qui m'arrête. Il n'est rien qui m'étonne.

64   MS1: N'arrêtez pas mes
72   MS1, 25X, 26H: vertus font Hérode
      25P, other Varus editions from 25CH except W57G1: vertus rend
      W57G1, Sohème texts: β
73   MS1, 25CH: Plus vous me demandez de ne vous plus servir,
      25X, 26H: ne vous point servir

[7] Cf. *Artémire*, I.i.165: 'Il peut trancher mes jours, les siens me sont sacrés.'

Et je cours réparer, en cherchant votre époux,
Ce temps que j'ai perdu sans combattre pour vous.

MARIAMNE

Seigneur...

SCÈNE III

MARIAMNE, ÉLIZE, GARDES

MARIAMNE

Mais il m'échappe; il ne veut point m'entendre.
Ciel! ô ciel! épargnez le sang qu'on va répandre;   80
Epargnez mes sujets; épuisez tout sur moi.
Sauvez le roi lui-même.

SCÈNE IV

MARIAMNE, ÉLIZE, NABAL, GARDES

MARIAMNE

Ah! Nabal, est-ce toi?
Qu'as-tu fait de mes fils? et que devient ma mère?

78   MS1, 25CH, 25X, 26H: Le temps
79   MS1, 25H, 26H: veut plus m'entendre
79a-c MS1, 25CH, 25X, 26H: [absent; no new scene]
80   MS1, 25CH, 25X, 26H: Hélas! Ciel, épargnez
      MS1: qu'on veut répandre
82   W75G: Suivez le
      25X, 26H: O Nabal
      Sohème texts: Ah! Narbas,
82a   25CH, 25X, 26H: SCÈNE III
82b   MS1, 25CH, 25X, 26H: MARIAMNE, NABAL
      25P (some copies), 30 (most copies): [add on a separate line] UNE
SUIVANTE
      Sohème texts passim scene iv: NARBAS [in place of NABAL]

NABAL

Le roi n'a point sur eux étendu sa colère.
Unique, et triste objet de ses transports jaloux,   85
Dans ces extrémités ne craignez que pour vous.
Le seul nom de Varus augmente sa furie.
Si Varus est vaincu, c'est fait de votre vie.
Déjà même, déjà le barbare Zarès
A marché vers ces lieux, chargé d'ordres secrets.   90
Osez paraître, osez vous secourir vous-même.
Jetez-vous dans les bras d'un peuple qui vous aime.
Faites voir Mariamne à ce peuple abattu.
Vos regards lui rendront son antique vertu.
Appelons à grands cris nos Hébreux et nos prêtres.   95
Tout Juda défendra le pur sang de ses maîtres.
Madame, avec courage, il faut vaincre, ou périr.
Daignez...

MARIAMNE

        Le vrai courage est de savoir souffrir,
Non d'aller exciter une foule rebelle,
A lever sur son prince une main criminelle.   100
Je rougirais de moi, si craignant mon malheur,
Quelques vœux pour sa mort avaient surpris mon cœur,

85   MSI, 25CH, 25X, 26H: Triste et fatal objet
86   MSI, 25X, 26H: Dans cette extrémité ne
87   MSI, 25CH, 25X, 26H: Varus excite sa
     Sohème texts: de Sohème augmente
88   Sohème texts: Si Sohème est
89   MSI, 25CH, 25X, 26H: le perfide Zarès
95-96   W70L:
          Appelons à grands cris nos peuples et nos prêtres;
          Ils protégeront tous le pur sang de leurs maîtres.
95   25X, 26H: à grand bruit nos
99   25X, 26H: une troupe rebelle
102 MSI, 25CH, 25X, 26H: avaient séduit mon

Si j'avais un moment souhaité ma vengeance,
Et fondé sur sa perte un reste d'espérance.
Nabal, en ce moment, le ciel met dans mon sein   105
Un désespoir plus noble, un plus digne dessein.
Le roi qui me soupçonne, enfin, va me connaître.
Au milieu du combat on me verra paraître.
De Varus et du roi j'arrêterai les coups,
Je remettrai ma tête aux mains de mon époux.   110
Je fuyais ce matin sa vengeance cruelle;
Ses crimes m'exilaient; son danger me rappelle.
Ma gloire me l'ordonne; et prompte à l'écouter,
Je vais sauver au roi le jour qu'il veut m'ôter.[8]

103   25P (most copies): moment en secret souhaité
105   MS1, 25CH, 25X, 26H: ciel verse en mon
109   Bohème texts: De Bohème et
112   MS1: Si ses cris m'exilaient,
      25CH: m'évitaient,
114-119 MS2, 31-K:
                                        m'ôter.
                         NABAL
      Hélas! où courez-vous! dans quel désordre extrême?....
                       MARIAMNE
      Je suis perdue, hélas! c'est Hérode lui-même.
                        SCÈNE V
      HÉRODE, MARIAMNE, ÉLIZE, NABAL, IDAMAS, GARDES
                        HÉRODE
      Ils se sont vus! Ah Dieu... perfide, tu mourras.
                       MARIAMNE
      Pour la dernière fois, Seigneur, ne souffrez pas...   5
                        HÉRODE
      Sortez... Vous, qu'on la suive.
                         NABAL
                         O justice éternelle![9]
114   MS1: [with stage direction] (Elle sort.)

[8] Cf. *Artémire*, II.i.27: 'Et lui conserverai le jour qu'il veut m'ôter.'
[9] MS2 gives this variant and the variant for lines 122-127 on a slip pasted over the base text (legible beneath).

SCÈNE V

ÉLIZE, NABAL

NABAL

O Dieu! qui l'inspirez, ô justice éternelle!   115
Défendez l'innocence, et combattez pour elle.
Elize, sur ses pas, courrons chercher le roi.

ÉLIZE

Ciel! Hérode revient; je l'entends; je le vois.

SCÈNE VI

HÉRODE, IDAMAS, GARDES

HÉRODE

Que je n'entende plus le nom de l'infidèle
C'est un crime envers moi d'oser me parler d'elle.   120

114a-b   MS1, 25CH, 25X, 26H: [*absent; no new scene*]
114b-c   Sohème texts: NARBAS [*in place of* NABAL]
115   MS1: O Dieux!
          25X, 26H: Ah! Dieu!
117-118   MS1, 25CH, 25X, 26H: [*absent*]
118a-b   MS1: *SCÈNE CINQUIÈME* / HÉRODE, IDAMAS, SUITE
D'HÉRODE
          25CH: *SCÈNE IV* / HÉRODE, IDAMARE
          25X, 26H: *SCÈNE IV* / HÉRODE, IDAMAS, SUITE
119-120   25CH: [*absent*]
          MS1, 25X, 26H:
          Que je n'entende plus parler de l'infidèle,
          C'est un crime envers moi que de me parler d'elle.
120   MS2, Sohème texts: [*absent*]

Eh bien, [10] braves soldats, n'ai-je plus d'ennemis?

IDAMAS

Les Romains sont défaits; les Hébreux sont soumis:
Varus, percé de coups, vous cède la victoire.
Ce jour vous a comblé d'une éternelle gloire.
Mais le sang de Varus, répandu par vos mains,   125
Peut attirer sur vous le courroux des Romains.
Songez-y bien, seigneur, et qu'une telle offense...

HÉRODE

De la coupable, enfin, je vais prendre vengeance.
Je perds l'indigne objet que je n'ai pu gagner,
Et de ce seul moment je commence à régner.   130
J'étais trop aveuglé; ma fatale tendresse

121   K: Hé [K84 errata, K85: Eh] bien
122-127   MS2, Sohème texts:
      Seigneur, ils sont défaits; les Hébreux sont [W70L: votre peuple est] soumis:
      Sohème tout sanglant vous laisse [MS2: cède] la victoire.
      Ce jour vous a comblé d'une nouvelle gloire.
                    HÉRODE
      Quelle gloire!
                  IDAMAS
              Elle est triste; et tant de sang versé,
      Seigneur, doit satisfaire à votre honneur blessé.
      Sohème a de la reine attesté l'innocence.
129   MS1, 25CH, 25X, 26H: objet qui m'avait su charmer
130   25X, 26H: Et dès ce

[10] In an Avertissement which first appears in K85 and which introduces 'Eclaircissements, additions et corrections' to their edition, the Kehl editors explain their reasons for reversing the change from 'Eh bien' to 'Hé bien' made in K84 and restoring in K85 the former reading found in all other editions: 'L'interjection *Eh*, qui ne doit commencer par un *h* que lorsqu'elle est appellative ou quand elle exprime le rire, (et alors l'*h* est aspiré) doit toujours commencer par un *e* lorsqu'elle marque la surprise et l'admiration; cette différence est essentielle, surtout en poésie, à cause des hiatus. Le lecteur attentive y suppléera aisément. Il lira partout *Eh quoi! Eh oui!*' (K85, in-8, lxx.429-30).

Etait ma seule tache, et ma seule faiblesse.
Laissons mourir l'ingrate; oublions ses attraits;
Que son nom dans ces lieux s'efface pour jamais;
Que dans mon cœur, surtout, sa mémoire périsse.   135
Enfin tout est-il prêt pour ce juste supplice?

IDAMAS

Oui, Seigneur.

HÉRODE

                    Quoi! sitôt on a pu m'obéir?
Infortuné monarque! elle va donc périr?
Tout est prêt, Idamas?

IDAMAS

                    Vos gardes l'ont saisie,
Votre vengeance, hélas! sera trop bien servie.   140

HÉRODE

Elle a voulu sa perte; elle a su m'y forcer,
Que l'on me venge. Allons, il n'y faut plus penser.
Hélas! j'aurais voulu vivre et mourir pour elle!
A quoi m'as-tu réduit, épouse criminelle?

134   25X, 26H: nom de ces
135   25CH: Que de mon
136   MS1, 25CH, 25X, 26H: Eh bien! tout
137   25X, 26H: sitôt l'on
138   MS1, 25CH, 25X, 26H: donc mourir
140   MS1: sera bientôt servie
      25CH, 25X, 26H: trop tôt servie
144   25X, 26H: me réduis-tu,

SCÈNE DERNIÈRE[11]

HÉRODE, IDAMAS, NABAL

HÉRODE

Nabal, où courez-vous? Juste ciel! vous pleurez?   145
De crainte, en le voyant, mes sens sont pénétrés.

NABAL

Seigneur...

HÉRODE

Ah! malheureux, que venez-vous me dire?

NABAL

Ma voix en vous parlant, sur mes lèvres expire.

HÉRODE

Mariamne...

NABAL

O douleur! ô regrets superflus!

144a-b MS1: *SCÈNE SIXIÈME* /HÉRODE, NABAL, LES ACTEURS DE
L'AUTRE SCÈNE
      25X, 26H: *SCÈNE V* / HÉRODE, IDAMAS, NABAL, SUITE
144b 25P (some copies), 30 (most copies): [*add on a separate line*: GARDES]
      Sohème texts *passim* this scene: NARBAS [*in place of* NABAL]
146 25X, 26H: en vous voyant

[11] Voltaire's account of the death of Mariamne and Hérode's remorse follows
Josephus closely: 'Sans faire paraître la moindre crainte ni seulement changer de
couleur, elle témoigna jusques à la mort la même générosité qu'elle avait fait paraître
durant tout le cours de sa vie. [...] [Hérode] crut que Dieu lui redemandait son sang.
On l'entendait à toute heure prononcer le nom de Mariamne: il faisait des plaintes
indignes de la majesté d'un roi' (*Histoire des Juifs*, xv.xi.578-79; *Jewish Antiquities*,
xv, para.236).

HÉRODE

Quoi! c'en est fait?

NABAL

Seigneur, Mariamne n'est plus.   150

HÉRODE

Elle n'est plus? grand Dieu!

NABAL

                    Je dois à sa mémoire,
A sa vertu trahie, à vous, à votre gloire,
De vous montrer le bien que vous avez perdu,
Et le prix de ce sang par vos mains répandu.
Non, seigneur, non, son cœur n'était point infidèle.   155
Hélas! lorsque Varus a combattu pour elle,
Votre épouse à mes yeux détestant son secours,
Volait pour vous défendre au péril de ses jours.

HÉRODE

Qu'entends-je? ah malheureux! ah désespoir extrême!
Nabal, que m'as-tu dit?

149b-150   25X, 26H:

HÉRODE
Quoi, Nabal! c'en est fait?
NABAL
Mariamne n'est plus.
        MS1: [*absent*]
151   MS1, 25CH, 25X, 26H: grands Dieux!
154   MS1: De son sang
156   Sohème texts: lorsque Sohème a
        MS2: <Varus> Sohême
157   25X, 26H: Votre épouse, Seigneur, détestant
158   25CH, 25X, 26H: aux dépens de

298

NABAL

C'est dans ce moment même,   160
Où son cœur se faisait ce généreux effort,
Que vos ordres cruels l'ont conduite à la mort.
Salome avait pressé l'instant de son supplice.

HÉRODE

O monstre, qu'à regret épargna ma justice![12]
Monstre, quels châtiments sont pour toi réservés!   165
Que ton sang, que le mien... Ah! Nabal, achevez.
Achevez mon trépas par ce récit funeste.

NABAL

Comment pourrai-je hélas! vous apprendre le reste?
Vos gardes de ces lieux ont osé l'arracher.
Elle a suivi leurs pas, sans vous rien reprocher,   170
Sans affecter d'orgueil, et sans montrer de crainte.
La douce majesté sur son front était peinte.
La modeste innocence, et l'aimable pudeur,
Régnaient dans ses beaux yeux, ainsi que dans son cœur.
Son malheur ajoutait à l'éclat de ses charmes.   175
Nos prêtres, nos Hébreux dans les cris, dans les larmes,
Conjuraient vos soldats, levaient les mains vers eux,
Et demandaient la mort avec des cris affreux.

160   MSI: dans le moment
164   MSI: regret épargnait ma
       25X, 26H: regret épargne ma
165   25CH: toi préservés
166-167   MSI:

                                        achevez,
              Dût causer mon trépas, un récit si funeste.
166   MSI, 25CH, 25X, 26H: Que mon sang, que le tien...
176   MSI: Hébreux par des cris, par des larmes

[12] Cf. Racine, *Phèdre*, IV.i.1045 (Thésée to Hippolyte): 'Monstre, qu'a trop longtemps épargné le tonnerre.'

Hélas! de tous côtés, dans ce désordre extrême,
En pleurant Mariamne, on vous plaignait vous-même.   180
L'on disait hautement qu'un arrêt si cruel
Accablerait vos jours d'un remords éternel.

HÉRODE

Grand Dieu! que chaque mot me porte un coup terrible!

NABAL

Aux larmes des Hébreux Mariamne sensible,
Consolait tout ce peuple, en marchant au trépas.   185
Enfin vers l'échafaud on a conduit ses pas.
C'est là qu'en soulevant ses mains appesanties, [13]
Du poids affreux des fers indignement flétries,
'Cruel a-t-elle dit, et malheureux époux!
Mariamne, en mourant, ne pleure que sur vous.   190
Puissiez-vous par ma mort finir vos injustices!
Vivez, régnez heureux sous de meilleurs auspices;
Voyez d'un œil plus doux mes peuples et mes fils;
Aimez-les: je mourrai trop contente à ce prix.'
En achevant ces mots, votre épouse innocente   195
Tend au fer des bourreaux cette tête charmante,

180   MS1, 25CH, 25X, 26H: vous pleurait vous-même
181   MS1, 25CH, 25X, 26H, W56, W57G, Sohème texts: On
183   MS1, 25CH: Grands Dieux!
187   25CH, 25X, 26H: que soulevant
189   25P, 30: dit, malheureux
       MS1, 25CH, 25X, 26H: dit, mais malheureux
       31-K: dit, et malheureux
190   MS1: Mariamne en pleurant,
       25CH, 25X, 26H: que pour vous
192   25X, 26H: Régnez, vivez heureux
196   W57P: aux fers des

[13] This line is cited in the *Observations critiques* (p.22) with the variant reading
'que soulevant' as in 25CH, 25X and 26H.

Dont la terre admirait les modestes appas.
Seigneur, j'ai vu lever le parricide bras;
J'ai vu tomber...

HÉRODE

Tu meurs, et je respire encore?
Mânes sacrés, chère ombre, épouse que j'adore,   200
Reste pâle et sanglant de l'objet le plus beau,
Je te suivrai du moins dans la nuit du tombeau. 14
Quoi! vous me retenez? Quoi! citoyens perfides,
Vous arrachez ce fer à mes mains parricides.
Ma chère Mariamne, arme-toi, punis-moi,   205
Viens déchirer ce cœur, qui brûle encor pour toi.
Je me meurs.
    (*Il tombe dans un fauteuil.*)

NABAL

De ses sens, il a perdu l'usage:
Il succombe à ses maux.

HÉRODE

Quel funeste nuage
S'est répandu soudain sur mes esprits troublés!

---

197   MSI: les célestes appas
202   MSI, 25CH, 25X, 26H: Je vous suivrai
       MSI: [*with stage direction*] (*Il veut se poignarder.*)
       25X, 26H: [*with stage direction*] (*Il veut se percer. On lui ôte son épée.*)
       MS2: [*with stage direction*] (*Il tire son épée et on luy arrache.*)
207a   MSI, 25CH, 25X, 26H: [*stage direction absent*]
209   25CH: sur mon esprit troublé

---

14 Cf. Voltaire, *Œdipe*, V.ii.22 (Icare about Polybe): 'Dans la nuit du tombeau les ans l'ont fait descendre.' Cf. also Racine, *Iphigénie*, II.i.525 (Eriphile): 'Dans la nuit du tombeau j'enfermerai ma honte'.

D'un sombre et noir chagrin mes sens sont accablés.   210
D'où vient qu'on m'abandonne au trouble qui me gêne?
Je ne vois point ma sœur, je ne vois point la reine.
Vous pleurez, vous n'osez vous approcher de moi!
Triste Jérusalem, tu fuis devant ton roi?
Qu'ai-je donc fait? Pourquoi suis-je en horreur au monde?   215
Qui me délivrera de ma douleur profonde?
Par qui ce long tourment sera-t-il adouci?
Qu'on cherche Mariamne, et qu'on l'amène ici.

NABAL

Mariamne, seigneur?

HÉRODE

        Oui: je sens que sa vue,
Va rendre un calme heureux à mon âme éperdue.   220
Toujours devant ses yeux que j'aime et que je crains,
Mon cœur est moins troublé; mes jours sont plus sereins.
Déjà même à son nom mes douleurs s'affaiblissent.
Déjà de mon chagrin les ombres s'éclaircissent.
Qu'elle vienne.

NABAL

Seigneur...

HÉRODE

Je veux la voir.

210   25CH: chagrin mon cœur est accablé
       MSI, 25X, 26H: sont pénétrés
211   MSI, 25CH, 25X, 26H: au transport qui
212   MSI: Je ne vois plus ma sœur, je ne vois plus la Reine,
222   MSI: mes yeux sont
225   25CH:
       Qu'elle vienne, Nabal, je la veux voir.
               NABAL
                   Hélas!
       25X, 26H: Je la veux voir.

NABAL

Hélas!   225
Avez-vous pu, seigneur, oublier son trépas!

HÉRODE

Cruel! que dites-vous?

NABAL

La douleur le transporte:
Il ne se connaît plus.

HÉRODE

Quoi! Mariamne est morte?
Infidèles Hébreux, vous ne la vengez pas!
Cieux qui la possédez, tonnez sur ces ingrats.   230

---

227   25X, 26H: Nabal, que
229-242a   MSI, 25CH, 25X, 26H:

        Ah! funeste raison, pour quoi m'éclaires-tu?
        Jour triste, jour affreux, pourquoi m'es-tu rendu?
        Quoi! Mariamne est morte, et j'en suis l'homicide!
        Punissez, déchirez ce monstre parricide,
        Armez-vous contre moi, sujets qui la perdez,   5
        Tonnez, écrasez-moi, cieux qui la possédez.
                        Fin.

            31-K:
        Ah! funeste raison, pour quoi m'éclaires-tu?
        Jour triste, jour affreux, pourquoi m'es-tu rendu?
        Lieux teints de ce beau sang que l'on vient de répandre,
        Murs que j'ai relevés, palais, tombez en cendre:
        Cachez sous les débris de vos superbes tours,   5
        La place où Mariamne a vu trancher ses jours.
        Quoi! Mariamne est morte, et j'en suis l'homicide!
        Punissez, déchirez ce monstre parricide,
        Armez-vous contre moi, sujets qui la perdez,
        Tonnez, écrasez-moi, cieux qui la possédez.   10
                Fin du cinquième et dernier acte.

Lieux teints de ce beau sang[15] que l'on vient de répandre,
Murs que j'ai relevés, palais, tombez en cendre:
Cachez sous les débris de vos superbes tours,
La place où Mariamne a vu trancher ses jours.
Temple, que pour jamais tes voûtes se renversent.   235
Que d'Israël détruit, les enfants se dispersent.
Que sans temple et sans rois, errants, persécutés,
Fugitifs en tous lieux, et partout détestés,
Sur leurs fronts égarés, portant dans leur misère,
Des vengeances de Dieu, l'effrayant caractère;   240
Ce peuple aux nations transmette avec terreur,
Et l'horreur de mon nom, et la honte du leur.[16]

Fin.

---

[15] Cf. Voltaire, *Œdipe*, V.iv.169 (Œdipe): 'Ces murs sont teints de sang'.
[16] Hérode's final speech is quoted in the *Mercure* extrait of M25 in the text of MS1, 25CH, 25X and 26H.

APPENDIX A

The surviving fragments of the Mariamne of 1724

These fragments are discussed in the Introduction, section 3.ii. The text is taken from the *Mercure de France*, March 1768, p.55-65. It has been collated with MS3 and K. The lines carried forward from M24 into M25 are indicated in the notes. In some cases they were given to a character other than Hérode or Varus, and this sometimes required changes in the pronouns used. The *Mercure* introduces the text with the following note: 'On sera sans doute charmé de trouver ici les scènes suivantes de la tragédie de Mariamne qui ne sont dans aucune édition des œuvres de M. Voltaire, et qui n'ont jamais été imprimées, à l'exception de quelques vers de la quatrième scène.'

ACTE III

SCÈNE III

VARUS, HÉRODE, MAZAËL, SUITE

HÉRODE

Avant que sur mon front je mette la couronne
Que m'ôta la fortune, et que César me donne,
Je viens en rendre hommage au héros dont la voix
De Rome en ma faveur a fait pencher le choix.
De vos lettres, Seigneur, les heureux témoignages   5
D'*Auguste* et du Sénat m'ont gagné les suffrages;
Et pour premier tribut j'apporte à vos genoux
Un sceptre que ma main n'eût point porté sans vous;
Je vous dois encor plus: vos soins, votre présence
De mon peuple indocile ont dompté l'insolence.   10
Vos succès m'ont appris l'art de le gouverner;

Et m'instruire était plus que de me couronner.
Sur vos derniers bienfaits excusez mon silence,
Je sais ce qu'en ces lieux a fait votre prudence;
Et trop plein de mon trouble et de mon repentir,   15
Je ne puis à vos yeux que me taire et souffrir.

VARUS

Puisqu'aux yeux du Sénat vous avez trouvé grâce,
Sur le trône aujourd'hui reprenez votre place;
Régnez, César le veut: je remets en vos mains
L'autorité qu'aux rois permettent les Romains.   20
J'ose espérer de vous qu'un règne heureux et juste
Justifiera mes soins et les bienfaits d'*Auguste*;
Je ne me flatte pas de savoir enseigner
A des rois tels que vous, le grand art de régner.
On vous a vu longtemps, dans la paix, dans la guerre,   25
En donner des leçons au reste de la terre:
Votre gloire en un mot ne peut aller plus loin;
Mais il est des vertus dont vous avez besoin.
Voici le temps surtout, que sur ce qui vous touche,
L'austère vérité doit passer par ma bouche;   30
D'autant plus qu'entouré de flatteurs assidus,
Puisque vous êtes roi, vous ne l'entendrez plus.
On vous a vu longtemps respecté dans l'Asie,
Régner avec éclat, mais avec barbarie.
Craint de tous vos sujets, admiré mais haï, [1]   35
Et par vos flatteurs même à regret obéi.
Jaloux d'une grandeur avec peine achetée,
Du sang de vos parents vous l'avez cimentée.
Je ne dis rien de plus; mais vous devez songer
Qu'il est des attentats que *César* peut venger;   40
Qu'il n'a point en vos mains mis son pouvoir suprême
Pour régner en tyran sur un peuple qu'il aime,
Et que du haut du trône, un prince en ses états

22   K84, K85: les bontés d'Auguste

[1] Lines 33-35: cf. M25, III.201-203.

Est comptable aux Romains du moindre de ses pas:
Croyez-moi, la Judée est lasse de supplices;   45
Vous en fûtes l'effroi, soyez-en les délices.
Vous connaissez le peuple, on le change en un jour,
Il prodigue aisément sa haine et son amour.
Si la rigueur l'aigrit, la clémence l'attire;
Enfin souvenez-vous, en reprenant l'empire,   50
Que Rome à l'esclavage a pu vous destiner,
Et du moins apprenez de Rome à pardonner.

HÉRODE

Oui, Seigneur, il est vrai que les destins sévères
M'ont souvent arraché des rigueurs nécessaires;
Souvent, vous le savez, l'intérêt des états   55
Dédaigne la justice et veut des attentats;
Rome, que l'Univers avec frayeur contemple,
Rome, dont vous voulez que je suive l'exemple,
Aux rois, qu'elle gouverne, a pris soin d'enseigner,
Comme il faut qu'on la craigne et comme il faut régner. [2]   60
De ses proscriptions nous gardons la mémoire;
César même, César, au comble de la gloire,
N'eût point vu l'Univers à ses pieds prosterné,
Si sa bonté facile eût toujours pardonné.
Ce peuple de rivaux, d'ennemis et de traîtres   65
Ne pouvait...

VARUS

                Arrêtez, et respectez vos maîtres!
Ne leur reprochez point ce qu'ils ont réparé,
Et du sceptre aujourd'hui par leurs mains honoré,
Sans rechercher en eux cet exemple funeste,
Imitez leurs vertus, oubliez tout le reste;   70
Sur votre trône assis ne vous souvenez plus
Que des biens que sur vous leurs mains ont répandus.
Gouvernez en bon roi; si vous voulez leur plaire,

---

[2] Lines 59-60: cf. M25, IV.55-56.

Commencez par chasser ce flatteur mercenaire,[3]
Qui du masque imposant d'une feinte bonté   75
Cache un cœur ténébreux par le crime infecté.
C'est lui qui, le premier, écarta de son maître
Des cœurs infortunés qui vous cherchaient peut-être;[4]
Le pouvoir odieux dont il est revêtu
A fait fuir devant vous la timide vertu.   80
Il marche accompagné de délateurs perfides,
Qui, des tristes Hébreux inquisiteurs avides,
Par cent rapports honteux, par cent détours abjects
Trafiquent avec lui du sang de vos sujets.
Cessez, n'honorez plus leurs bouches criminelles   85
D'un prix que vous devez à des sujets fidèles;
De tous ces délateurs le secours tant vanté
Fait la honte du trône et non la sûreté.
Pour *Salome*, Seigneur, vous devez la connoître,
Et si vous aimez tant à gouverner en maître,   90
Confiez à des cœurs plus fidèles pour vous,
Ce pouvoir souverain dont vous êtes jaloux:
Après cela, Seigneur, je n'ai rien à vous dire,
Reprenez désormais les rênes de l'empire,
De Tyr à Samarie allez donner la loi,   95
Je vous parle en Romain, songez à vivre en roi.

SCÈNE IV

HÉRODE, MAZAËL

MAZAËL

Vous avez entendu ce superbe langage,
Seigneur; souffrirez-vous qu'un Préteur vous outrage,
Et que dans votre cœur il ose impunément?...

---

[3] The allusion is presumably to Mazaël.
[4] Lines 77-78: cf. M25, III.129-30.

HÉRODE *à sa suite.*

Sortez, et qu'en ces lieux on nous laisse un moment.   100
Tu vois ce qu'il m'en coûte, et sans doute on peut croire,
Que le joug des Romains offense assez ma gloire.
Mais je règne à ce prix: leur orgueil fastueux
Se plaît à voir des rois s'abaisser devant eux.
Leurs dédaigneuses mains jamais ne nous couronnent   105
Que pour mieux avilir les sceptres qu'ils nous donnent;
Pour avoir des sujets qu'ils nomment souverains,
Et sur des fronts sacrés signaler leurs dédains.
Il m'a fallu dans Rome avec ignominie
Oublier cet éclat tant vanté dans l'Asie: 110
Tel qu'un vil courtisan dans la foule jeté,
J'allais des affranchis caresser la fierté;
J'attendais leurs moments, je briguais leurs suffrages;
Tandis qu'accoutumés à de pareils hommages,
Au milieu de vingt rois à leur cour assidus,   115
A peine ils remarquaient un monarque de plus.
Je vis *César* enfin; je sus que son courage
Méprisait tous ces rois qui briguaient l'esclavage.
Je changeai ma conduite: une noble fierté
De mon rang avec lui soutint la dignité: 120
Je fus grand sans audace, et soumis sans bassesse;
César m'en estima, j'en acquis sa tendresse,
Et bientôt dans sa cour appelé par son choix,
Je marchai distingué dans la foule des rois. [5]
Ainsi, selon les temps, il faut qu'avec souplesse   125
Mon courage docile ou s'élève ou s'abaisse;
Je sais dissimuler, me venger et souffrir,
Tantôt parler en maître et tantôt obéir;
Ainsi j'ai subjugué Solime et l'Idumée,
Ainsi j'ai fléchi Rome à ma perte animée,   130
Et toujours enchaînant la fortune à mon char,

124   K84, K85: distingué dans la foule

[5] Lines 123-24: cf. M25, III.111-12.

J'étais ami d'*Antoine* et le suis de *César*. [6]
Heureux après avoir, avec tant d'artifice,
Des destins ennemis corrigé l'injustice,
Quand je reviens en maître à l'Hébreu consterné   135
Montrer encor le front que Rome a couronné!
Heureux si de mon cœur la faiblesse immortelle
Ne mêlait à ma gloire une honte éternelle.
Si mon fatal penchant n'aveuglait pas mes yeux,
Si *Mariamne* enfin n'était point en ces lieux.   140

MAZAËL

Quoi! Seigneur, se peut-il que votre ame abusée
De ce feu malheureux soit encore embrasée?

HÉRODE

Que me demandes-tu? Ma main, ma faible main
A signé son arrêt et l'a changé soudain.
Je cherche à la punir, je m'empresse à l'absoudre;   145
Je lance en même instant et je retiens la foudre.
Je mêle, malgré moi, son nom dans mes discours,
Et tu peux demander si je l'aime toujours?

MAZAËL

Seigneur, a-t-elle au moins cherché votre présence?

HÉRODE

Non... j'ai cherché la sienne.

MAZAËL

                    Eh quoi! son arrogance... [7]   150
A-t-elle en son palais dédaigné de vous voir?

---

[6] Lines 105-32: this 'portrait de la conduite que les Romains tenaient à l'égard des rois' is quoted in the *Anecdotes dramatiques* of J.-M.-B. Clément (1775), i.522-23. Line 132: cf. M25, I.32.
[7] Cf. M25, III.154.

HÉRODE

Mazaël, je l'ai vue, et c'est mon désespoir.
Honteux, plein de regret de ma rigueur cruelle,
Interdit et tremblant j'ai paru devant elle.
Ses regards, il est vrai, n'étaient point enflammés   155
Du courroux dont souvent je les ai vus armés.

Ces cris désespérés, ces mouvements d'horreur
Dont il fallut longtemps essuyer la fureur,
Quand par un coup d'état, peut-être trop sévère,
J'eus fait assassiner et son père et son frère.   160
De ses propres périls son cœur moins agité
M'a surpris aujourd'hui par sa tranquillité.
Ses beaux yeux, dont l'éclat n'eut jamais tant de charmes,
S'efforçaient devant moi de me cacher leurs larmes.
J'admirais en secret sa modeste douleur;   165
Qu'en cet etat, ô ciel, elle a touché mon cœur!
Combien je détestais ma fureur homicide!
Je ne le cèle point, plein d'un zèle timide,
Sans rougir, à ses pieds je me suis prosterné,
J'adorais cet objet que j'avais condamné.   170
Hélas! mon désespoir la fatiguait encore,
Elle se détournait d'un époux qu'elle abhorre;
Ses regards inquiets n'osaient tomber sur moi,
Et tout, jusqu'à mes pleurs, augmentait son effroi.

MAZAËL

Sans doute elle vous hait, sa haine envenimée   175
Jamais par vos bontés ne sera désarmée.
Vos respects dangereux nourrissent sa fierté.

HÉRODE

Elle me hait!... Ah dieu! je l'ai trop mérité.[8]
Je n'en murmure point; ma jalouse furie
A de malheurs sans nombre empoisonné sa vie.   180
J'ai, dans le sein d'un père, enfoncé le couteau;

[8] Lines 173-78: cf. M25, III.163-68.

Je suis son ennemi, son tyran, son bourreau:
Je lui pardonne, hélas, dans le sort qui l'accable,
De haïr à ce point un époux si coupable. [9]

MAZAËL

Etouffez les remords dont vous êtes pressé,   185
Le sang de ses parents fut justement versé;
Les rois sont affranchis de ces règles austères
Que le devoir inspire aux âmes ordinaires.

HÉRODE

Mariamne me hait! cependant autrefois,
Quand ce fatal hymen te rangea sous mes loix,   190
O reine, s'il se peut que ton cœur s'en souvienne,
Ta tendresse en ce temps fut égale à la mienne.
Au milieu des périls son généreux amour
Aux murs de Massada me conserva le jour.
Mazaël, se peut-il que d'une ardeur si sainte,   195
La flamme sans retour soit pour jamais éteinte?
Le cœur de *Mariamne* est-il fermé pour moi?

MAZAËL

Seigneur, m'est-il permis de parler à mon roi? [10]

HÉRODE

Ne me déguise rien, parle, que faut-il faire?
Comment puis-je adoucir sa trop juste colère?   200
Par quel charme, à quel prix puis-je enfin l'apaiser?

MAZAËL

Pour la fléchir, seigneur, il faut la mépriser.
Des superbes beautés tel est le caractère.
Sa rigueur se nourrit de l'orgueil de vous plaire,

202   K84, K85: il la faut mépriser

[9] Lines 183-84: cf. M25, III.169-70.
[10] Cf. M25, III.121.

Sa main qui vous enchaîne, et que vous caressez,   205
Appesantit le joug sous qui vous gémissez.
Osez humilier son imprudente audace,
Forcez cette âme altière à vous demander grâce;
Par un juste dédain songez à l'accabler,
Et que devant son maître elle apprenne à trembler.   210
Quoi donc? ignorez-vous tout ce que l'on publie?
Cet *Hérode*, dit-on, si vanté dans l'Asie,
Si grand dans ses exploits, si grand dans ses desseins,
Qui sut dompter l'Arabe et fléchir les Romains,
Aux pieds de son épouse, esclave sur son trône,   215
Reçoit d'elle, en tremblant, les ordres qu'il nous donne.

HÉRODE

Malheureux! à mon cœur cesse de retracer
Ce que de tout mon sang je voudrais effacer.
Ne me parle jamais de ces temps déplorables;
Mes rigueurs n'ont été que trop impitoyables.   220
Je n'ai que trop bien mis mes soins à l'opprimer;
Le ciel pour m'en punir me condamne à l'aimer.
Les chagrins, sa prison, la perte de son père,
Les maux que je lui fais me la rendent plus chère. [11]
Enfin c'est trop vous craindre et trop vous déchirer,   225
Mariamne, en un mot, je veux tout réparer.
Va la trouver, dis-lui que mon âme asservie
Met à ses pieds mon sceptre, et ma gloire et ma vie. [12]
Des maux qu'elle a soufferts elle accuse ma sœur; [13]
Je sais qu'elle a pour elle une invincible horreur: 230
C'en est assez, ma sœur, aujourd'hui renvoyée,
A ses chers intérêts sera sacrifiée.
Je laisse à *Mariamne* un pouvoir absolu...

MAZAËL

Quoi! Seigneur, vous voulez...

---

[11] Lines 222-24: cf. M25, III.184-86.
[12] Lines 226-28: cf. M25, III.188-90.
[13] Cf. M25, III.192.

HÉRODE

Oui, je l'ai résolu.[14]
Va la trouver, te dis-je, et surtout à sa vue   235
Peins bien le repentir de mon âme éperdue;
Dis-lui que mes remords égalent ma fureur.
Va, cours, vole et reviens... Juste ciel, c'est ma sœur![15]

[14] Lines 231-34: cf. M25, III.193-96.
[15] Lines 235-38: cf. M25, III.221-24.

APPENDIX B

The extrait of the 1724 Mariamne printed in the Mercure [1]

EXTRAIT DE MARIAMNE

Le 6 mars, premier lundi du Carême, les Comédiens français donnèrent la première représentation de *Mariamne*, tragédie de M. de Voltaire. Cette pièce était attendue du public avec tant de patience, que toutes les loges étaient retenues depuis longtemps, et c'est sans doute ce grand empressement qui a fait exiger le double du prix ordinaire, sans en $_5$ excepter le parterre même. On prêta beaucoup d'attention pendant les trois premiers actes, et dans une partie du quatrième; mais le reste de la pièce ne fut pas exempt de ces tumultes si ordinaires depuis quelques années. Le cinquième acte fut le plus maltraité; quelques mauvais plaisants, ou mal-intentionnés, ayant crié *la reine boit*, dans le temps $_{10}$ que Mariamne s'empoisonnait, on ne fut plus en état de rien entendre, et voilà à quoi sont exposés les meilleurs ouvrages. Comme l'auteur, piqué d'un accueil si peu attendu, et peut-être si injuste, a retiré sa pièce, nous n'en pouvons donner qu'un extrait, tel qu'une représentation unique nous le peut permettre; nous demandons grâce pour quelques transposi- $_{15}$ tions de scènes, et quelques changements de nom, etc.

ACTEURS

Hérode, roi de Judée. *Le sieur le Baron.*
Mariamne, femme d'Hérode. *La D^{lle} le Couvreur.*

---

[1] *Mercure de France*, March 1724, p.529-39.

Salome, sœur d'Hérode. *La D^{lle} Duclos.*
Varus, gouverneur de Judée pour les Romains. *Le sieur Dufrêne.* 20
Mazaël, confident de Salome. *Le sieur le Grand, le pere.*
Nabal, confident de Mariamne. *Le sieur Fontenay.*
D'autres acteurs suivants d'Hérode, de Mariamne et de Varus.

La scène est à Jérusalem.

ACTE I

La premiere scène se passe entre Salome et Mazaël; ce dernier, dont le
caractère a paru assez équivoque, et qu'on peut appeler un méchant 25
homme, qui par faiblesse a quelquefois des remords, et une espèce de
retour au bien, applaudit à la nouvelle que lui apprend Salome, elle lui dit
que bientôt elle ne craindra plus Mariamne, parce qu'Hérode a envoyé de
Rome l'arrêt de sa mort qui doit être executé au moment qu'elle lui en
parle. 30

SCÈNE II

VARUS, MAZAËL, UN CONFIDENT DE VARUS

Varus arrête Mazaël qui veut suivre Salome, que son arrivée vient de
chasser. Il lui dit qu'il a découvert l'attentat comploté contre les jours de
Mariamne, qu'il en a garanti cette reine infortunée, qu'il en a puni les
auteurs, et qu'Hérode même pourrait bien éprouver l'indignation des
Romains, pour avoir donné un ordre si barbare à leur insu, et contre leur 35
volonté.

SCÈNE III

VARUS ET SON CONFIDENT

Le confident de Varus loue ce gouverneur du soin qu'il a pris de protéger
l'innocente opprimée, Varus lui fait connaître que sa seule générosité
l'aurait pu porter à une action si digne d'un Romain; mais que l'amour l'a

rendu encore plus ardent à sauver une reine qu'il adore. Le confident est 40
surpris qu'un cœur qui avait toujours fait profession d'une insensibilité à
l'épreuve de toutes les beautés de la Cour d'Auguste, se soit rendu aux
charmes d'une Juive. Varus lui répond que Mariamne est encore plus
recommandable par sa vertu que par sa beauté, toute grande qu'elle est,
d'où il prend occasion de faire un tableau de la cour d'Auguste, et surtout 45
des dames romaines. On ne croit pas qu'il y ait aucune application à faire,
mais le public a souvent plus de malignité que l'auteur. Passons au
second acte.

ACTE II

La première scène commence encore par Salome, et son confident; lequel
toujours complaisant, félicite Salome sur le retour d'Hérode, qui doit 50
arriver le même jour. Il lui fait entrevoir que ce mari jaloux achèvera son
ouvrage, malgré tous les obstacles que Varus pourrait y apporter.
Salome pense tout autrement, elle craint que Mariamne d'un seul
regard ne reprenne tout le pouvoir qu'elle avait autrefois sur lui; ce
qui la confirme dans sa crainte, c'est que l'arrêt de mort tracé de la main 55
d'Hérode contre Mariamne, a été révoqué de la même main, et presque
dans le même jour. Elle conclut qu'il faut absolument se défaire de
Mariamne avant l'arrivée d'Hérode, ou du moins empêcher ce prince de
la voir. Mazaël soupçonne Varus d'aimer Mariamne, Salome se livre à ce
soupçon; sur lequel elle fonde la perte de son ennemie. 60

SCÈNE II

MARIAMNE, SALOME, MAZAËL, NABAL ET QUELQUES
SUIVANTES DE MARIAMNE

Salome fait compliment à Mariamne sur le retour de son époux.
Mariamne lui répond fièrement qu'elle ne prend point le change sur
les sentiments qu'elle a pour elle, et qu'elle est très-persuadée de sa haine
secrète: Salome se retire assez mécontente. Mariamne ordonne qu'on
cherche Varus, et reste seule avec Nabal. Mariamne après avoir permis à 65
Nabal de s'asseoir, consulte ce sage et fidèle sujet sur sa situation

317

présente. Les fureurs éternelles d'Hérode, et surtout le dernier ordre qu'il a envoyé de Rome pour la faire périr, l'alarment encore plus pour ses chers enfants que pour elle-même. Elle lui dit qu'elle a formé le dessein de ne pas attendre Hérode, et de partir pour Rome avant son 70 arrivée, par le secours des vaisseaux de Varus. Nabal approuve sa résolution, et l'invite à l'exécuter sans aucun délai.

SCÈNE III

Mariamne après avoir remercié Varus de la générosité avec laquelle il l'a garantie d'une mort certaine, le prie d'achever son ouvrage, et de lui prêter un de ses vaisseaux pour aller à Rome. Le silence que Varus garde 75 à une proposition si peu attendue, confond Mariamne; elle lui en demande la raison. Varus lui fait entendre son amour, par la peine que son absence lui va coûter. Cette déclaration a paru très fine, et très neuve. Mariamne témoigne de la colère à Varus, mais ne pouvant lui refuser son estime, elle ne laisse pas d'accepter le secours qu'elle vient de lui 80 demander. Cette scène est remplie de sentiments très-nobles, et très-délicats de part et d'autre, et tous les connaisseurs en sont convenus. Mariamne quitte Varus de peur qu'il ne lui échappe quelques mouvements qui la rendent indigne de son estime.

SCÈNE IV

Varus se confirme dans la résolution de rendre à Mariamne tous les 85 services qu'elle doit attendre du plus parfait amour qui fut jamais.

ACTE III

Dans la première scène Nabal presse Varus de tenir parole à Mariamne. Varus lui répond que ses ordres sont donnés, et que ses vaisseaux sont prêts.

SCÈNE II

VARUS ET SON CONFIDENT

Varus fait entendre que l'amour le plus parfait est celui qui s'attache à la   90
vertu, et qu'il aimera toujours Mariamne sans espérance.

SCÈNE III

HÉRODE, VARUS, SUITE D'HÉRODE ET DE VARUS, MAZAËL

Varus prêt à couronner Hérode, conformément aux ordres qu'il a reçus
de Rome, lui fait des leçons de régner, dont ce roi s'offense. Hérode lui
répond à peu près sur le même ton; mais Varus lui coupe la parole en
maître, et lui dit de respecter les Romains, par qui seuls il remonte sur le   95
trône. Il lui conseille sur tout d'éloigner de sa cour Salome et Mazaël.

SCÈNE IV

HÉRODE ET MAZAËL

Hérode a beaucoup de peine à digérer les durs reproches que Varus vient
de lui faire; cependant par politique il se détermine à éloigner Mazaël et
Salome contre qui Varus s'est déclaré ouvertement. Salome vient,
Mazaël se retire. Salome demande à Hérode d'où vient que Mariamne   100
n'est pas auprès de son époux et de son roi. Hérode lui répond en
soupirant, que cette superbe reine n'a pas encore daigné paraître à ses
yeux. Salome n'oublie rien pour l'irriter contre elle; mais Hérode bien
loin de recevoir les impressions qu'elle tâche de lui donner, la prie de
vouloir bien s'exiler de sa cour, pour ne pas donner de nouveaux sujets   105
de mécontentement à Mariamne. Salome lui répond qu'il est bien
aveugle de sacrifier une sœur qui le chérit à une épouse qui en aime
un[2] autre que lui. Dans la scène suivante Mazaël vient annoncer à
Hérode que Mariamne lui est enlevée par Varus; Hérode frappé de cette

---

[2] The *Extrait* reads *une*. An obvious error.

nouvelle ne respire plus que vengeance. Il demande pardon à Salome, et   110
sort pour aller courir après le ravisseur de Mariamne.

ACTE IV

Salome et son confident commencent encore cet acte. Salome triomphe
de la disgrâce de sa rivale, qui vient d'être arrêtée et ramenée à Jérusalem
par ceux qui ont couru après ses ravisseurs. Mazaël lui dit avec une
espèce de repentir que Mariamne est innocente, et qu'il s'en est éclairci   115
par lui-même, s'étant tenu caché pendant qu'elle parlait à ses femmes. Ce
caractère a paru à tous les spectateurs éclairés, ménagé exprès, pour en
venir à un aveu que Mazaël devait faire à la fin de la pièce en faveur de
Mariamne.

SCÈNE II

HÉRODE, SALOME, MAZAËL

Hérode furieux, et tout sanglant encore du meurtre de toutes les femmes   120
qu'il a cru complices du crime de Mariamne, demande pardon à Salome
de l'avoir voulu sacrifier à une ingrate, et à une infidèle épouse. Salome
fait tout ce qu'elle peut pour l'empêcher de revoir Mariamne; mais il veut
lui parler, dit-il, pour avoir le plaisir de la confondre et de la braver.
Mariamne vient, tout le monde se retire.   125

SCÈNE III

HÉRODE, MARIAMNE

Cette scène a paru très-belle. Mariamne se justifie avec une hauteur dont
Hérode est confondu. Il la prie d'oublier le passé, et de répondre à ses
bontés; elle lui dit qu'elle ne trahira jamais le devoir d'une épouse envers
son époux, mais qu'elle n'aimera jamais le meurtrier de ses frères et de
son père même. Ce dernier aveu, peut-être trop sincère, fait rentrer   130
Hérode dans sa première fureur, Mariamne se retire, et Hérode s'affermit
dans le dessein de la faire mourir.

Le tumulte nous ayant empêché d'entendre le cinquième acte, nous n'en dirons qu'un mot. Mariamne récite des stances qui conviennent à la situation d'une personne qui attend la mort. Varus qui n'a point paru 135 depuis le milieu du troisième acte, vient prier Mariamne de le suivre, escortée de ses Romains. Mariamne refuse le secours d'un homme qu'elle est soupçonnée et accusée d'aimer; Varus ne pouvant rien obtenir la quitte, résolu de périr ou de la sauver. Mariamne reste seule; on vient lui apporter le poison qu'Hérode, ou Salome lui ont fait préparer. Elle boit 140 dans la coupe empoisonnée; Hérode vient, instruit de son innocence par Mazaël mourant, il veut sauver Mariamne; mais la trouvant expirante, il se livre à ses remords. On a déjà annoncé dans une des scènes de ce cinquième acte que Varus a été défait, et peut-être tué, en voulant secourir Mariamne. 145

APPENDIX C

The Avertissement of w38

The Avertissement, first printed in w38, is found in the following subsequent editions: w40, w41c, w41r, w42, w43, w46, w48d, w50, w51, t53, oc56, t62, t64a, t64g, w64r, t68, t70. It is not found after w51 in editions published under Voltaire's supervision, or in which he is thought to have participated.

The base text is w38. In line 1 we have corrected the date of first performance (erroneously given as 1723), in line 10 we have altered 'fit pour Mariamne d'un autre genre de mort' to 'fit mourir Mariamne d'un autre genre de mort', the reading of w48d, w50, w51.

AVERTISSEMENT

La Mariamne fut jouée en 1724 pour la première fois. Baron, qu'on a surnommé l'Æsopus des Français, joua le rôle d'Hérode; mais il était trop vieux pour soutenir ce caractère violent. Adrienne le Couvreur, la meilleure comédienne qui ait jamais été, représenta Mariamne. L'auteur faisait mourir cette princesse par le poison, et on le lui donnait sur le théâtre. C'était vers le temps des rois que la pièce fut jouée, un petit-maître dans le parterre, voyant donner la coupe empoisonnée à Mariamne, s'avisa de crier *la Reine boit*. Tous les Français se mirent à rire, et la pièce ne fut point achevée. On la redonna l'année suivante. On fit mourir Mariamne d'un autre genre de mort. La pièce eut 40 représentations.

Le Sr. Rousseau, qui commençait à être un peu jaloux de l'auteur, fit alors une Mariamne d'après l'ancienne pièce de Tristan; il l'envoya aux

vc

5

vc

10

1-2 w48d: Baron surnommé
12-13 w41r, w64r: fit périr Mariamne

comédiens qui n'ont jamais pu la jouer, et au libraire Didot qui n'a jamais
pu la vendre. Ce fut-là l'origine de la longue querelle entre notre auteur   15
et Rousseau. [1]

---

[1] The following handwritten note is appended to the printed text in two copies of
w38 (Brussels, Br FS 227 A(2) and Paris, BnF, Rés. Z Bengesco 468(2)), and one
copy of w40 (Paris, Arsenal 8° B 34045(2)): 'Cela n'est pas vrai, l'origine de la
querelle est une pièce de vers infâme que Rousseau fit contre M. le maréchal de
Noailles. Je sais qu'il a fait une Mariamne, mais je ne l'ai jamais lue. Voltaire.' This
note is apparently in Voltaire's own hand in Br FS 227 A(2), (vol.ii, p.124): see
J. Vercruysse, *Inventaire raisonné des manuscrits voltairiens de la Bibliothèque Royale
Albert Ier* (Turnhout 1983).

APPENDIX D

The Sohème version of Mariamne

The Sohème version of *Mariamne* (discussed in the Introduction, section 6) appears in w64G, w68, w70G, w70L, w71, 72P, 72X, w72P, w72X, w75G, w75X, T76G, T76X, K84, K85. Voltaire's rewriting of Act I, beginning at line 63, and of Act II scene i, is here reproduced in the text of w75G.

SALOME

Croyez-moi, son retour en resserre les nœuds,
Et ses trompeurs appas sont toujours dangereux.

MAZAËL

Oui, mais cette âme altière à soi-même inhumaine,
Toujours de son époux a recherché la haine.
Elle l'irritera par de nouveaux dédains,   5
Et vous rendra les traits qui tombent de vos mains.
La paix n'habite point entre deux caractères,
Que le ciel a formés l'un à l'autre contraires.
Hérode en tous les temps sombre, chagrin, jaloux,
Contre son amour même aura besoin de vous.   10

SALOME

Mariamne l'emporte, et je suis confondue.

MAZAËL

Au trône d'Ascalon vous êtes attendue;
Une retraite illustre, une nouvelle cour,
Un hymen préparé par les mains de l'amour,
Vous mettront aisément à l'abri des tempêtes,   15
Qui pourraient dans Solime éclater sur nos têtes.

Sohème est d'Ascalon paisible Souverain,
Reconnu, protégé par le peuple Romain,
Indépendant d'Hérode, et cher à sa province;
Il sait penser en sage, et gouverner en prince.   20
Je n'aperçois pour vous que des destins meilleurs;
Vous gouvernez Hérode, ou vous régnez ailleurs.

SALOME

Ah! connais mon malheur et mon ignominie:
Mariamne en tout temps empoisonne ma vie;
Elle m'enlève tout, rang, dignités, crédit,   25
Et pour elle, en un mot, Sohème me trahit.

MAZAËL

Lui! qui pour cet hymen attendait votre frère?
Lui dont l'esprit rigide, et la sagesse austère,
Parut tant mépriser ces folles passions,
De nos vains courtisans vaines illusions?   30
Au roi son allié ferait-il cette offense?

SALOME

Croyez qu'avec la reine il est d'intelligence.

MAZAËL

Le sang et l'amitié les unissent tous deux;
Mais je n'ai jamais vu...

SALOME

                    Vous n'avez pas mes yeux;
Sur mon malheur nouveau je suis trop éclairée: 35
De ce trompeur hymen la pompe différée,
Les froideurs de Sohème, et ses discours glacés,
M'ont expliqué ma honte, et m'ont instruite assez.

MAZAËL

Vous pensez en effet qu'une femme sévère,
Qui pleure encor ici son ayeul et son frère,   40

Et dont l'esprit hautain (qu'aigrissent ses malheurs)
Se nourrit d'amertume, et vit dans les douleurs,
Recherche imprudemment le funeste avantage,
D'enlever un amant qui sous vos loix s'engage?
L'amour est-il connu de son superbe cœur? 45

SALOME

Elle l'inspire, au moins, et c'est là mon malheur.

MAZAËL

Ne vous trompez-vous point? Cette âme impérieuse,
Par excès de fierté semble être vertueuse;
A vivre sans reproche elle a mis son orgueil.

SALOME

Cet orgueil si vanté trouve enfin son écueil. 50
Que m'importe, après tout, que son âme hardie
De mon parjure amant flatte la perfidie,
Ou qu'exerçant sur lui son dédaigneux pouvoir,
Elle ait fait mes tourments, sans même le vouloir?
Qu'elle chérisse, ou non, le bien qu'elle m'enlève, 55
Je le perds, il suffit; sa fierté s'en élève;
Ma honte fait sa gloire; elle a dans mes douleurs
Le plaisir insultant de jouir de mes pleurs.
Enfin, c'est trop languir dans cette indigne gêne;
Je veux voir à quel point on mérite ma haine. 60
Sohème vient: allez: mon sort va s'éclaircir.

SCÈNE II

SALOME, SOHÈME, AMMON

SALOME

Approchez; votre cœur n'est point né pour trahir,
Et le mien n'est pas fait pour souffrir qu'on l'abuse.
Le roi revient enfin, vous n'avez plus d'excuse.
Ne consultez ici que vos seuls intérêts, 65

Et ne me cachez plus vos sentiments secrets.
Parlez; je ne crains point l'aveu d'une inconstance,
Dont je mépriserais la vaine et faible offense.
Je ne sais point descendre à des transports jaloux,
Ni rougir d'un affront dont la honte est pour vous.   70

SOHÈME

Il faut donc m'expliquer, il faut donc vous apprendre
Ce que votre fierté ne craindra point d'entendre.
J'ai beaucoup, je l'avoue, à me plaindre du roi;
Il a voulu, Madame, étendre jusqu'à moi
Le pouvoir que César lui laisse en Palestine;   75
En m'accordant sa sœur il cherchait ma ruine.
Au rang de ses vassaux il osait me compter.
J'ai soutenu mes droits, il n'a pu l'emporter.
J'ai trouvé comme lui des amis près d'Auguste:
Je ne crains point Hérode, et l'Empereur est juste.   80
Mais je ne peux souffrir (je le dis hautement)
L'alliance d'un roi dont je suis mécontent.
D'ailleurs, vous connaissez cette cour orageuse.
Sa famille avec lui fut toujours malheureuse;
De tout ce qui l'approche il craint des trahisons   85
Son cœur de toutes parts est ouvert aux soupçons [1]
Au frère de la reine il en coûta la vie;
De plus d'un attentat cette mort fut suivie.
Mariamne a vécu, dans ce triste séjour,
Entre la barbarie, et les transports d'amour.   90
Tantôt sous le couteau, tantôt idolâtrée,
Toujours baignant de pleurs une couche abhorrée,
Craignant et son époux, et de vils délateurs,
De leur malheureux roi lâches adulateurs.

74-75   W70L:
        Il a voulu, Madame, abuser contre moi
        Du pouvoir
81   K: ne puis souffrir

[1] This line had been used in M25, I.148.

SALOME

Vous parlez beaucoup d'elle.[2]

SOHÈME

Ignorez-vous, Princesse,   95
Que son sang est le mien, que son sort m'intéresse?

SALOME

Je ne l'ignore pas.

SOHÈME

Apprenez encor plus:
J'ai craint longtemps pour elle, et je ne tremble plus.
Hérode chérira le sang qui la fit naître,
Il l'a promis, du moins, à l'Empereur son maître.   100
Pour moi, loin d'une cour, objet de mon courroux,
J'abandonne Solime, et votre frère et vous;
Je pars: ne pensez pas qu'une nouvelle chaîne
Me dérobe à la vôtre, et loin de vous m'entraîne.
Je renonce à la fois à ce Prince, à sa cour,   105
A tout engagement, et surtout à l'amour.
Epargnez le reproche à mon esprit sincère,
Quand je ne m'en fais point, nul n'a droit de m'en faire.

SALOME

Non, n'attendez de moi ni courroux, ni dépit;
J'en savais beaucoup plus que vous n'en avez dit.   110
Cette cour, il est vrai, Seigneur, a vu des crimes;
Il en est quelquefois où des cœurs magnanimes
Par le malheur des temps se laissent emporter,
Que la vertu répare, et qu'il faut respecter.
Il en est de plus bas, et de qui la faiblesse   115
Se pare arrogamment du nom de la sagesse.
Vous m'entendez peut-être? En vain vous déguisez,
Pour qui je suis trahie, et qui vous séduisez.

[2] Salome's rejoinder was admired by Flaubert, who saw in it '[une] réponse qui peut faire un grand effet au théâtre' (*Le Théâtre de Voltaire*, p.17).

Votre fausse vertu ne m'a jamais trompée;
De votre changement mon âme est peu frappée; 120
Mais si de ce palais, qui vous semble odieux,
Les orages passés ont indigné vos yeux,
Craignez d'en exciter qui vous suivraient peut-être
Jusqu'aux faibles Etats dont vous êtes le maître.

(*Elle sort.*)

SCÈNE III

SOHÈME, AMMON

SOHÈME

Où tendait ce discours? que veut-elle? et pourquoi 125
Pense-t-elle en mon cœur pénétrer mieux que moi?
Qui? moi, que je soupire! et que pour Mariamne
Mon austère amitié ne soit qu'un feu profane!
Aux faiblesses d'amour moi j'irais me livrer,
Lorsque de tant d'attraits je cours me séparer! 130

AMMON

Salome est outragée, il faut tout craindre d'elle.
La jalousie éclaire, et l'amour se décelle.

SOHÈME

Non, d'un coupable amour je n'ai point les erreurs;
La secte dont je suis forme en nous d'autres mœurs.
Ces durs Esséniens, stoïques de Judée, 135
Ont eu de la morale une plus noble idée.
Nos maîtres, les Romains, vainqueurs des nations,
Commandent à la terre, et nous aux passions.
Je n'ai point, grâce au ciel, à rougir de moi-même.
Le sang unit de près Mariamne et Sohème. 140
Je la voyais gémir sous un affreux pouvoir;
J'ai voulu la servir; j'ai rempli mon devoir.

329

AMMON

Je connais votre cœur et juste, et magnanime;
Il se plaît à venger la vertu qu'on opprime.
Puissiez-vous écouter, dans cette affreuse cour,   145
Votre noble pitié plutôt que votre amour.

SOHÈME

Ah! faut-il donc l'aimer pour prendre sa défense?
Qui n'aurait comme moi chéri son innocence?
Quel cœur indifférent n'irait à son secours?
Et qui pour la sauver n'eût prodigué ses jours?[3]   150
Ami, mon cœur est pur, et tu connais mon zèle.
Je n'habitais ces lieux que pour veiller sur elle,
Quand Hérode partit, incertain de son sort,
Quand il chercha dans Rome ou le sceptre ou la mort.
Plein de sa passion, forcenée et jalouse,   155
Il tremblait qu'après lui sa malheureuse épouse,
Du trône descendue, esclave des Romains,
Ne fût abandonnée à de moins dignes mains.
Il voulut qu'une tombe à tous deux préparée
Enfermât avec lui cette épouse adorée.   160
Phérore fut chargé du ministère affreux
D'immoler cet objet de ses horribles feux.
Phérore m'instruisit de ces ordres coupables.
J'ai veillé sur des jours si chers, si déplorables,
Toujours armé, toujours prompt à la protéger,   165
Et surtout à ses yeux dérobant son danger;
J'ai voulu la servir sans lui causer d'alarmes;
Ses malheurs me touchaient encor plus que ses charmes.
L'amour ne règne point sur mon cœur agité;
Il ne m'a point vaincu, c'est moi qui l'ai dompté;   170
Et plein du noble feu que sa vertu m'inspire,
J'ai voulu la venger, et non pas la séduire.[4]
Enfin l'heureux Hérode a fléchi les Romains:

---

[3] Lines 146-50 had been used in M25, I.232-36.

[4] Lines 301-302 of Act I of M25 reappear here, with a change of main verb and tense.

Le sceptre de Judée est remis en ses mains.
Il revient triomphant sur ce sanglant théâtre;   175
Il revole à l'objet dont il est idolâtre,
Qu'il opprima souvent, qu'il adora toujours.
Leurs désastres communs ont terminé leur cours;
Un nouveau jour va luire à cette cour affreuse;
Je n'ai plus qu'à partir – Mariamne est heureuse.   180
Je ne la verrai plus – mais à d'autres attraits,
Mon cœur, mon triste cœur est fermé pour jamais.
Tout hymen à mes yeux est horrible et funeste;
Qui connaît Mariamne, abhorre tout le reste.
La retraite a pour moi des charmes assez grands;   185
J'y vivrai vertueux, loin des yeux des tyrans:
Préférant mon partage au plus beau diadême,
Maître de ma fortune, et maître de moi-même.

SCÈNE IV

SOHÈME, ÉLISE, AMMON

ÉLISE

La mère de la reine en proie à ses douleurs,
Vous conjure, Sohème, au nom de tant de pleurs,   190
De vous rendre près d'elle, et d'y calmer la crainte,
Dont pour sa fille encor elle a reçu l'atteinte.

SOHÈME

Quelle horreur jetez-vous dans mon cœur étonné?

ÉLISE

Elle a su l'ordre affreux qu'Hérode avait donné.
Par les soins de Salome elle en est informée.   195

SOHÈME

Ainsi cette ennemie au trouble accoutumée,

Par des troubles nouveaux pense encor maintenir
Le pouvoir emprunté qu'elle veut retenir!
Quelle odieuse cour! et combien d'artifices!
On ne marche en ces lieux que sur des précipices.   200
Hélas! Alexandra, par des coups inouïs,
Vit périr autrefois son époux et son fils.
Mariamne lui reste, elle tremble pour elle;
La crainte est bien permise à l'amour maternelle.
Elise, je vous suis, je marche sur vos pas –.   205
– Grand Dieu, qui prenez soin de ces tristes climats,
De Mariamne encor écartez cet orage;
Conservez, protégez votre plus digne ouvrage!

Fin du premier acte.

ACTE II

SCÈNE PREMIÈRE

SALOME, MAZAËL

MAZAËL

Ce nouveau coup porté, ce terrible mystère,
Dont vous faites instruire et la fille, et la mère,
Ce secret révélé, cet ordre si cruel,
Est désormais le sceau d'un divorce éternel.
Le roi ne croira point que pour votre ennemie,   5
Sa confiance en vous soit en effet trahie;
Il n'aura plus que vous dans ses perplexités,
Pour adoucir les traits par vous-même portés;
Vous seule aurez fait naître et le calme et l'orage.
Divisez pour régner; c'est là votre partage.   10

SALOME

Que sert la politique au défaut du pouvoir?

197   K: Par ces troubles
11   K: politique où manque le pouvoir

Tous mes soins m'ont trahi, tout fait mon désespoir.
Le roi m'écrit: il veut, par sa lettre fatale,
Que sa sœur se rabaisse aux pieds de sa rivale.
J'espérais de Sohème un noble et sûr appui,   15
Hérode était le mien; tout me manque aujourd'hui.
Je vois crouler sur moi le fatal édifice,
Que mes mains élevaient avec tant d'artifice.
Je vois qu'il est des temps où tout l'effort humain
Tombe sous la fortune, et se débat en vain,   20
Où la prudence échoue, où l'art nuit à soi-même;
Et je sens ce pouvoir invincible et suprême,
Qui se joue à son gré, dans nos climats voisins,
De leurs sables mouvants comme de nos destins.

MAZAËL

Obéissez au roi, cédez à la tempête;   25
Sous ses coups passagers il faut courber la tête.
Le temps peut tout changer.

SALOME

             Trop vains soulagements!
Malheureux qui n'attend son bonheur que du temps!
Sur l'avenir trompeur tu veux que je m'appuie,
Et tu vois cependant les affronts que j'essuie.   30

MAZAËL

Sohème part au moins; votre juste courroux
Ne craint plus Mariamne, et n'en est plus jaloux.

SALOME

Sa conduite, il est vrai, paraît inconcevable;
Mais m'en trahit-il moins? en est-il moins coupable?
Suis-je moins outragée? Ai-je moins d'ennemis,   35
Et d'envieux secrets, et de lâches amis?
Il faut que je combatte, et ma chute prochaine,
Et cet affront secret, et la publique haine.
Déjà de Mariamne adorant la faveur,

333

Le peuple à ma disgrâce insulte avec fureur.   40
Je verrai tout plier sous sa grandeur nouvelle,
Et mes faibles honneurs éclipsés devant elle.
Mais c'est peu que sa gloire irrite mon dépit;
Ma mort va signaler ma chute et son crédit.
Je ne me flatte point: je sais comme en sa place   45
De tous mes ennemis je confondrais l'audace.
Ce n'est qu'en me perdant qu'elle pourra régner;
Et son juste courroux ne doit point m'épargner.
Cependant! ô contrainte! ô comble d'infamie!
Il faut donc qu'à ses yeux ma fierté s'humilie!   50
Je viens avec respect essuyer ses hauteurs,
Et la féliciter sur mes propres malheurs. [5]

MAZAËL

Elle vient en ces lieux.

SALOME

Faut-il que je la voie!

---

[5] Lines 39-52 had been used in M25, II.19-32.

APPENDIX E

LETTRE DE Mr TIRIOT
À M^r L'ABBÉ NADAL

This pamphlet, published in Paris in 1725 (Bengesco 1549, BnC 3656), was printed in four pages on a backed up single sheet, 22cm x 16.5cm. As the woodcut placed at the top of the first page is identical with that found at several points in 25P, we may surmise that the document was produced by the presses of Louis Sevestre. Four copies are held at the BnF: 8° Yf. Pièce 265, Rés. Z Bengesco 991, Rés. Z Beuchot 1793 and 1794. According to Bengesco, the pamphlet entered Voltaire's collective works in the Lefèvre and Deterville edition of 1818 (vol.xxxi). It is included by Besterman in Voltaire's correspondence and related documents (D226).

For Nadal and his failed tragedy *Mariamne* see Introduction, section 3.iv and v. The letter reproduced below contains Voltaire's riposte, written under the name of Thiriot, to remarks in the Préface to Nadal's *Mariamne* concerning the disruption which had brought down his play. Nadal refers to the general belief that this had been due to a 'cabale' organised by Voltaire. Claiming to be convinced himself that Voltaire was incapable of such dishonourable tactics, he attributes the responsibility for the 'cabale' to a close friend of Voltaire, unnamed but evidently Thiriot, upon whom he heaps abundant disparagement. The ironic quotation of a line from Racine makes it clear however that the casting of the blame upon Thiriot is a mere pretence, and that Nadal's real target is Voltaire, whom he regards as the prime organiser of the affair. In addition Voltaire could well have considered himself the target of an implicit jibe in a sentence where Nadal claims that his own play follows history faithfully, without replacing 'des événements consacrés' by 'les égarements d'une imagination séduite par la nouveauté des idées'.

Lettre de Mr Tiriot à M^r l'abbé Nadal

Tout le monde admire, M. l'Abbé, la grandeur de votre courage, qui ne peut être ébranlé par les injustes sifflets, dont la cabale du public vous opprime depuis quarante ans.[1] Pour châtier ce public séditieux, vous avez en même temps fait jouer votre *Mariamne*, et fait débiter votre *Livre des Vestales*;[2] et pour dernier trait vous faites imprimer votre tragédie.   5

Je viens de lire la préface de cet inimitable ouvrage; vous y dites beaucoup de bien de vous, et beaucoup de mal de M. de Voltaire et de moi. Je suis charmé de voir en vous tant d'équité et de modestie, et c'est ce qui m'engage à vous écrire avec confiance et avec sincérité.

Vous accusez M. de Voltaire d'avoir fait tomber votre tragédie par   10
une *brigue horrible et scandaleuse*.[3] Tout le monde est de votre avis, Monsieur; personne n'ignore que M. de Voltaire a séduit l'esprit de tout Paris pour vous faire bafouer à la première représentation, et pour empêcher le public de revenir à la seconde. C'est par ses menées et par ses intrigues qu'on entend dire si *scandaleusement* que vous êtes le plus   15
mauvais versificateur du siècle, et le plus ennuyeux écrivain. C'est lui qui a fait berner vos *Vestales*, vos *Machabées*, votre *Saül* et votre *Hérode*:[4] il faut avouer que M. de Voltaire est un bien méchant homme, et que vous avez raison de le comparer à Néron, comme vous faites si à propos dans votre belle préface.[5]   20

Quelques personnes pourraient peut-être vous dire que la ressource des mauvais poètes, M. l'Abbé, a toujours été de se plaindre de la cabale; que Pradon votre devancier accusait M. Racine d'avoir fait tomber sa *Phèdre*, et que de Brie à qui on prétend que vous ressemblez en tout si parfaitement,   25

---

[1] In fact only twenty years: Nadal's first play, *Saül*, was produced in 1705.

[2] *Histoire des Vestales, avec un traité du luxe des dames romaines* (1725).

[3] In his Préface Nadal refers to 'l'horrible et scandaleuse cabale qui s'est élevée contre moi'.

[4] For the dates of Nadal's dramatic works see Introduction, section 3.iv, n.96.

[5] In his feigned praise of Voltaire's character Nadal had quoted from Racine Britannicus's sarcastic question to Néron: 'Est-ce ainsi que Néron sait disputer un cœur?' (*Britannicus* III.viii.1082).

> Pour disculper ses œuvres insipides,
> En accusait et le froid et le chaud. [6]

On pourrait ajouter que personne ne peut avoir assez d'autorité pour empêcher le public de prendre du plaisir à une tragédie, et qu'il n'y a que l'auteur qui puisse avoir ce crédit; mais vous vous donnerez bien de   30
garde d'écouter tous ces mauvais discours.

On dit même que ce n'est pas d'aujourd'hui que vous faites imprimer des préfaces pleines d'injures à la tête de tragédies sifflées. Quelques curieux se souviennent qu'il y a deux ans, vous imputâtes à M. de la Motte et à ses amis la chute d'un certain *Antiochus*, [7] et que vous accusâtes   35
Mademoiselle le Couvreur, qui représentait votre premier rôle, d'avoir mal joué une fois en sa vie, de peur que vous ne fussiez applaudi une fois en la vôtre.

Il est vrai pourtant, et j'en suis témoin, qu'à la première représentation de votre *Mariamne* il y avait une cabale dans le parterre, elle était composée   40
de plusieurs personnes de distinction de vos amis, qui pour 20 sols par tête étaient venus vous applaudir. L'un d'eux même présentait publiquement des billets gratis à tout le monde; mais quelques-uns de ces partisans ennuyés malheureusement de votre pièce, rendirent publiquement l'argent en disant: Nous aimons mieux payer et siffler comme les autres.   45

Je vous épargne mille petits détails de cette espèce, et je me hâte de répondre aux choses obligeantes que vous avez imprimées sur mon compte.

Vous dites que je suis intimement attaché à M. de Voltaire, et c'est à cela que je me suis reconnu. Oui, Monsieur, je lui suis tendrement   50
dévoué par estime, par amitié, et par reconnaissance. [8]

---

[6] Adapted from J.-B. Rousseau's epigram on the minor author De Brie (*Œuvres*, Paris 1820, ii.307).

[7] The original title of Nadal's *Les Machabées*. Moland (xxii.44n) points out that though in his preface to this play Nadal had denounced 'l'animosité effrénée des partisans de La Motte', he had not made reference to Mlle Lecouvreur.

[8] Voltaire is responding in this and the following three paragraphs to Nadal's unflattering portrait of Thiriot: 'Je ne puis à la vérité ne pas soupçonner un homme qui lui [sc. à Voltaire] est intimement attaché [...] C'est une espèce de facteur de bel esprit et de littérature; dépositaire de toutes les conceptions de cet auteur, il en est devenu l'organe ; il récite ses pieces partout, et affecte jusqu'aux inflexions de sa voix, il les porte dans toutes les ruelles, et va montrant, pour ainsi dire, sous le manteau le génie de M. Voltaire [...] Il rapporte au logis les avis et les observations du dehors.'

Vous dites que je récite ses vers souvent;[9] c'est la différence, M. l'Abbé, qui doit être entre les amis de M. de Voltaire et les vôtres, si vous en avez.

Vous m'appelez facteur de bel esprit: je n'ai rien du bel esprit, je vous jure; je n'écris en prose que dans les occasions pressantes, et jamais en vers, car on sait que je ne suis pas poète non plus que vous, mon cher abbé.

Vous me reprochez de rapporter à M. de Voltaire les avis du public. J'avoue que je lui apprends avec sincérité les critiques que j'entends faire de ses ouvrages, parce que je sais qu'il aime à se corriger, et qu'il ne répond jamais aux mauvaises satires que par le silence, comme vous l'éprouvez heureusement, et aux bonnes critiques, que par une grande docilité.

Je crois donc lui rendre un vrai service, en ne lui celant rien de ce qu'on dit de ses productions. Je suis persuadé que c'est ainsi qu'il en faut user avec tous les auteurs raisonnables; et je veux bien même faire ici par charité pour vous ce que je fais souvent par estime et par amitié pour lui.

Je ne vous cacherai donc rien de tout ce que j'entendais dire de vous, lorsqu'on jouait votre *Mariamne*. Tout le monde y reconnut votre style, et quelques mauvais plaisants qui se ressouvenaient que vous étiez l'auteur des *Machabées*, d'*Hérode* et de *Saül*, disaient que vous aviez mis l'ancien Testament en vers burlesques; ce qui est *véritablement horrible et scandaleux*.

Il y en avait qui ayant aperçu les gens que vous aviez apostés pour vous applaudir, et les archers que vous aviez mis en sentinelle dans le parterre, où ils étaient forcés d'entendre vos vers, disaient:

> Pauvre Nadal, à quoi bon tant de peine
> Tu serais bien sifflé sans tout cela:[10]

d'autres citaient les *Satires* de M. Rousseau, dans lesquels vous tenez si dignement la place de l'abbé Pic.[11]

---

[9] Besterman observes (D226n) that in their comic opera *Les Noces de la folie* (1725) Fuzelier, Le Sage and Orneval, included a character 'Monsieur Prône-Vers' based on Thiriot.

[10] Adapted from an epigram of J.-B. Rousseau (ii.6).

[11] The abbé Picque, author of a *Naissance de Vénus* with music by Colasse, and satirised by Rousseau (ii.317).

Enfin, Monsieur, il n'y avait ni grand ni petit qui ne vous accablât de ridicule; et moi qui suis naturellement bon, je sentais une vraie peine de voir un vieux prêtre si indignement vilipendé par la multitude. J'en ai encore de la compassion pour vous, malgré les injures que vous me dites, et même malgré vos ouvrages; et je vous assure que je suis du meilleur de mon cœur tout à vous, TIRIOT. [12]

85

A Paris ce 20 Mars 1725.

---

[12] On Voltaire's spelling of this name see Pomeau, *Voltaire en son temps*, i.916, n.42. Thiriot himself always spelled his name with an *h*. Its absence here supports the accepted view that he was not the author of the pamphlet.

WORKS CITED

Apologie de Monsieur de Voltaire adressée à lui-même (n.p.n.d).

[Bachaumont, Louis Petit de], *Mémoires secrets pour servir à l'histoire de la République des Lettres en France depuis [1762]* (London 1780-1789).

Bailly, Jacques, *Théâtres et œuvres mêlées* (Paris, Nyon, 1768).

Bengesco, Georges, *Voltaire: Bibliographie de ses Œuvres* (Paris 1882-1890).

Besterman, Th., *Voltaire* (Oxford 1976).

Bibliothèque de Voltaire: catalogue des livres (Moscow 1961).

Carmody, F., *Le Répertoire de l'opéra comique en vaudevilles de 1708 à 1764* (Berkeley, Calif. 1933).

Carriat, Amédée, *Bibliographie des œuvres de Tristan L'Hermite* [Limoges 1955].

Cioranescu, Alexandre, *Bibliographie de la littérature française du XVIIIe siècle*, 3 vols (Paris 1969).

Clément, J.-M.-B. and Joseph de La Porte, *Anecdotes dramatiques contenant [...] toutes les pièces de théâtre [...] jusqu'en 1775*, 3 vols (Paris, Duchesne, 1775).

Collé, Charles, *Journal historique ou mémoires critiques et littéraires* (Paris 1809).

Conlon, P. M., *Voltaire's literary career*, *SVEC* 14 (1961).

Corpus des notes marginales de Voltaire, vols i-v (Berlin 1979-1994).

Desboulmiers, Jean Auguste Jullien, *Histoire du théâtre italien* (Paris 1769).

Desfontaines, Pierre-François Guyot, and François Granet, *Vérités littéraires sur la tragédie d'Hérode et de Mariamne adressées à M. de Voltaire* (Paris 1725).

Desmolets, Pierre-Nicolas (ed.), *Continuation des mémoires de littérature et d'histoire de Mr. de Salengre* (Paris, Simart, 1726-1727).

– *Nouvelles littéraires curieuses et intéressantes* (Paris 1723-1724).

Desnoiresterres, G., *Voltaire et la société au XVIIIe siècle. La Jeunesse de Voltaire*, 2nd edn (Paris 1871).

Dominique (Pierre-François Biancolelli), and Marc Antoine Le Grand, *Le Mauvais Ménage, parodie, représentée sur le théâtre de l'Hôtel de Bourgogne par les Comédiens italiens ordinaires du Roi* (Paris, Flahaut, 1725).

Donvez, Jacques, *De quoi vivait Voltaire?* (Paris 1949).

Duvernet, T. I., *La Vie de Voltaire* (Geneva 1786).

Favart, C.-S., *Mémoires et correspondance littéraires dramatiques et anecdotiques* (Paris 1808).

Feniger, H., 'Voltaire et le théâtre anglais', *Orbis Litterarum* 7 (Copenhagen 1949).

Fenton, Elijah, *Mariamne. A Tragedy. Acted at the Theatre Royal in Lincoln's Inn Fields* (London 1723).

Flaubert, Gustave, *Le Théâtre de Voltaire*, ed. Th. Besterman, *SVEC* 50 (1967).

[Fuzelier, Louis], *Les Quatre Mariamnes, opéra comique représenté pour la première fois le jeudi premier mars mil sept cens vingt-cinq, à la suite de l'Audience du Temps et de Pierrot Perrette* (Paris, François Flahaut, 1725).

– *Les Vacances du théâtre, opéra comique représenté à la Foire Saint-Germain* (Paris, G. Cavelier and N. Pissot, 1724).

Grannis, V. B., *Dramatic parody in eighteenth-century France* (New York 1931).

Grimm, Friedrich Melchior, *Correspondance littéraire*, ed. M. Tourneux (Paris 1877-1882).

Gunny, Ahmad, *Voltaire and English literature: a study of English literary influences on Voltaire*, *SVEC* 177 (1979).

Hardy, Alexandre, *Mariamne*, ed. Alan Howe (Exeter 1989).

Hartley, K. H., 'The sources of Voltaire's *Mariamne*', *AUMLA* 21 (1964).

Josephus, Flavius, *Histoire de la Guerre des Juifs contre les Romains* [...]. *Traduit du grec par M. Arnauld d'Andilly*, 2 vols (Paris 1668).

– *Histoire des Juifs écrite par Flavius Joseph sous le titre de Antiquités Judaïques. Traduite sur l'original grec revu sur divers manuscrits par M. Arnauld d'Andilly*, 3 vols (Paris 1667).

Lagrave, Henri, *Le Théâtre et le public à Paris de 1715 à 1750* (Paris 1992).

La Harpe, Jean François de, *Cours de littérature ancienne et moderne*, vol.ii (Paris 1840).

La Motte, Antoine Houdar de, *Fables nouvelles* (Paris 1719).

Lancaster, Henry C., *The Comédie-Française 1701-1774: plays, actors, spectators, finances, Transactions of the American Philosophical Society* 41 (Philadelphia 1951).

– *French tragedy in the time of Louis XV and Voltaire 1715-1774* (Baltimore 1950; New York 1977).

Lecouvreur, Adrienne, *Lettres*, ed. Georges Monval (Paris 1892).

Lekain, Henri Louis, *Mémoires* (Paris 1825).

Lion, Henri, *Les Tragédies et les théories dramatiques de Voltaire* (Paris 1895).

Luchet, Jean-Pierre-Louis de, *Histoire littéraire de Monsieur de Voltaire* (Cassel 1780).

Marais, Matthieu, *Journal et mémoires* [...] *sur la régence et sur le règne de Louis XV, 1715-1737*, ed. M. F. A. de Lescure (Paris 1863-1868).

Nadal, abbé Augustin, *Mariamne, tragédie* (Paris, Veuve Ribou, 1725).

– *Observations critiques sur la tragédie d'Hérode et Mariamne de M. de V**** (Paris 1725).

Olivier, Jean-Jacques, *Les Comédiens français dans les cours d'Allemagne au XVIII* siècle (Paris 1903).

– *Henri-Louis Lekain de la Comédie-Française* (Paris 1907).

– *Voltaire et les Comédiens interprètes de son théâtre* (Paris 1900).

Origny, Antoine d', *Annales du théâtre italien, depuis son origine jusqu'à ce jour* (Paris 1788).

Palissot, Ch., *Le Génie de Voltaire apprécié dans tous ses ouvrages* (Paris 1806).

Parfaict frères, *Mémoires pour servir à l'histoire des spectacles de la Foire* (Paris 1743).

Pascal, Blaise, *Pensées*, ed. Ph. Sellier (Paris 1999).

Piron, Alexis, *Œuvres complètes, publiées par M. Rigoley de Juvigny* (Paris, Lambert, 1776).

Pomeau, René, *La Religion de Voltaire* (Paris 1969).

– (ed.), *Voltaire en son temps*, 2nd edn, 2 vols (Oxford 1995).

Pope, Alexander, *Correspondence*, ed. G. Sherburn (Oxford 1956).

Pradon, Jacques, *Phèdre et Hippolyte*, ed. O. Classe (Exeter 1987).

Quintessence des nouvelles historiques, politiques, critiques, morales et galantes (La Haye 1725).

Racine, Jean, *Œuvres complètes*, ed. G. Forestier (Paris 1999).

Rousseau, Jean-Baptiste, *Œuvres choisies* [...] *suivies de sa correspondance avec l'abbé d'Olivet* (Paris, Didot l'aîné, 1818).

Sgard, Jean (ed.), *Dictionnaire des journalistes*, 2nd edn (Oxford 1999).

– *Dictionnaire des journaux, 1600-1789* (Paris and Oxford 1991).

Taylor, S. S. B., 'The definitive text of Voltaire's works: the Leningrad *encadrée*', in *SVEC* 124 (1974).

Thiébault, Dieudonné, *Mes souvenirs de vingt ans de séjour à Berlin*, 2nd edn (Paris 1805).

Trapnell, William H., 'Survey and analysis of Voltaire's collective editions, 1728-1789', *SVEC* 77 (1970).

Tristan L'Hermite, *La Mariane, tragédie*, ed. Jacques Madeleine (Paris 1917).

Valency, Maurice Jacques, *The Tragedies of Herod and Mariamne* (New York 1940).

Vercruysse, Jeroom, 'Les éditions encadrées des œuvres de Voltaire', *SVEC* 168 (1977).

– *Inventaire raisonné des manuscrits voltairiens de la Bibliothèque Royale Albert Ier* (Turnhout 1983).

– *Les Voltairiens*, 2e série, *Voltaire jugé par les siens 1719-1749*, vol.ii (1724-1732) (New York 1983).

Verèb, Pascale, *Alexis Piron, poète (1689-1773) ou la difficile condition d'auteur sous Louis XV*, *SVEC* 349 (1997).

Voltaire, *An essay on epic poetry*, ed. David Williams, in *OC*, vol.3B (Oxford 1996).

– *Artémire*, ed. D. Jory, in *OC*, vol.1A (Oxford 2000).

– *Commentaires sur Corneille*, ed. David Williams, *OC*, vol.53-55 (Oxford 1974).

– *Correspondance (1726-1729)*, ed. Lucien Foulet (Paris 1913).

– *Correspondence and related documents*. Definitive edition by Theodore Besterman (Geneva, later Banbury, then Oxford, 1968-1977).

– *Essai sur les mœurs*, ed. R. Pomeau (Paris 1963).

– *La Henriade*, ed. O. R. Taylor, *OC*, vol.2 (Oxford 1970).

– *Lettres philosophiques*, ed. G. Lanson and A.-M. Rousseau (Paris 1964).

– *Mérope*, ed. Jack Vrooman and Janet Godden, in *OC*, vol.17 (Oxford 1991).

– *Œdipe*, ed. David Jory, in *OC*, vol.1A (Oxford 2001).

– *Œuvres complètes*, ed. Louis Moland (Paris 1877-1885).

Wirz, Charles, 'L'Institut et Musée Voltaire en 1981', *Genava*, n.s. 30 (1982), p.187-89.

INDEX

Actium, battle of, 14n
Agamemnon, 161, 191
Agnès de Chaillot, 59
Alexandra, mother of Mariamne, 13
Amsterdam, 99, 101, 131-62 *passim*, 183, 194
Anecdotes dramatiques (Clément and La Porte), 30, 58n, 61n, 310n
Antigonus, nephew of Hyrcanus II, 13
Antipater, father of Herod the Great, 12
Antony, Mark, 12, 13, 14, 274n
Apologie de Monsieur de Voltaire adressée à lui-même, 25, 49, 82
Argenson, Antoine René de Voyer, *see* Paulmy
Argenson, Marc-Pierre, comte d', lieutenant-général de police, 4
Argental, Charles-Augustin Feriol, comte d', 10, 34n, 35n, 93n, 94n, 95n, 105, 106, 107, 108, 118, 119
Argental, Jeanne Grâce Bose Du Bouchet, comtesse d', 105, 106, 107, 108, 118
Aristobulus III, brother of Mariamne, 13, 14n
Arkstée and Merkus, printers, 146
Armand, François, actor, 72n
Arnauld d'Andilly, Robert, 11, 12n, 14n, 17, 18, 21, 110n
Asmonean/Asmoneans, 12, 13
Augustus, 65; *see also* Octavian
Avignon, 159

Bachaumont, Louis Petit de, *see Mémoires secrets*
Baculard d'Arnaud, François Thomas Marie de, 97

Bailly, Jacques, 62; *Momus, censeur des théâtres*, 62-63
Baron (Michel Boyron), actor, 4, 5n, 28, 31, 46n
Barrois, Marie Jacques, 145
Basel, 142
Bastille, prison, 2, 91n
Bayreuth, 96
Beauregard, Salenne de, 2, 7
Bel, Jean-Jacques, 85n, 88-91, 202n
Bernard, Jean Frédéric, 84, 88, 194
Bernières, Marguerite-Madeleine Du Moutier, marquise de, 2, 5, 7, 56, 71, 72n, 74, 75, 76, 82n
Bernigeroth, engraver, 148, 151
Bernis, cardinal François Joachim de Pierres de, 104, 105
Besterman, Th., 2, 3, 4n, 5n, 10n, 33, 34n, 63n, 64n, 77n, 335
Bibliothèque française ou histoire littéraire de la France, 8n, 49, 64n, 84, 88, 89, 90, 91n
Bicêtre, prison, 83n
Bolingbroke, Henry St John, first viscount, 3, 9, 23
Bouhier, président Jean, 46, 53, 78
Bourbon, Louis Henri, duc de, 70
Bousquet, Marc-Michel, 145
Brandmüller, Jean Louis, 142
Brèvedent (friend of Cideville), 76
Bruel, 2
Brussels, 63

Cailleau, André Charles, 104
Calas family, 104-105
Cambiague, Isaac, 77
Carmody, F., 42n

345